7/11

3000 800064 88434
St. Louis Community College

**Meramec Library**
**St. Louis Community College**
**11333 Big Bend Blvd.**
**Kirkwood, MO 63122-5799**
**314-984-7797**

WITHDRAWN

D0926634

R. Smith

# DESIGN FOR A VULNERABLE PLANET

AUSTIN

ROGER FULLINGTON SERIES IN ARCHITECTURE

# DESIGN FOR A VULNERABLE PLANET

## FREDERICK STEINER

University of Texas Press
Austin

*Publication of this book was made possible in part by support from Roger Fullington and a challenge grant from the National Endowment for the Humanities.*

Copyright © 2011 by the University of Texas Press
All rights reserved
Printed in the United States of America
First edition, 2011

Requests for permission to reproduce material from this work
should be sent to:
    Permissions
    University of Texas Press
    P.O. Box 7819
    Austin, TX 78713-7819
    www.utexas.edu/utpress/about/bpermission.html

♾ The paper used in this book meets the minimum requirements
of ANSI/NISO Z39.48-1992 (R1997) (Permanence of Paper).

LIBRARY OF CONGRESS CATALOGING-IN-PUBLICATION DATA
Steiner, Frederick R.
Design for a vulnerable planet / Frederick Steiner. — 1st ed.
    p.    cm. — (Roger Fullington series in architecture)
Includes bibliographical references and index.
ISBN 978-0-292-72385-6 (cloth : alk. paper)
1. Architecture — Environmental aspects. I. Title.
NA2542.35.S83  2011
720'.47—dc22                        2010047371

TO MY UNIVERSITY OF TEXAS COLLEAGUES
WHO MAKE EACH DAY IN AUSTIN AN INSPIRATION

# CONTENTS

PREFACE  ix

ACKNOWLEDGMENTS  xiii

INTRODUCTION: Interdisciplinary Design and the Fate of Our Planet  1


**I. LIVING URBAN ENVIRONMENTS**  7

1. Architecture and the Wealth of Regions  9

2. Sustaining Design: The Solar Decathlon Competitions  21

3. Twenty-First-Century Architecture  31

4. Architecture Has Left the Building: The Sustainable Sites Initiative  39

5. Making Territory: The Potential of Landscape Urbanism  51


**II. LESSONS FROM PAUL CRET, IAN MCHARG, AND GEORGE MITCHELL**  65

6. City Limits: Pioneer Plans in Austin  67

7. The Woodlands: The Ecological Design of a New City  77


**III. EMERGING URBANISM IN TEXAS**  87

8. The Trinity River Corridor: Another Emerald Necklace or an Emerald Choker?  89

9. Making Limoncello from Lemons: The Blanton Museum of Art Plaza Design  99

10. True Urbanism: The Design of Performance Park in the Dallas Arts District  107

11. Legacies  115

**IV. NEW REGIONALISM IN TEXAS AND BEYOND**  125

   12. The Green Heart of Texas  127

   13. Envision Central Texas  135

   14. The Texas Triangle Megaregion  147

   15. New Regionalism  161


**V. LEARNING FROM ABROAD**  169

   16. Environmental Readings: The Italian Design Tradition  171

   17. Autumn Moon: Design and Planning in China  179


**VI. LEARNING FROM DISASTER**  217

   18. In Search of a Fitting Tribute: The Flight 93 National Memorial  219

   19. Resilient Foundations: Planning for the Gulf Coast after Hurricane Katrina  229


**VII. CONCLUSION**  243

   20. The Sedimentation of Our Minds: Prospects for New Design Thinking  245

   NOTES  259

   BIBLIOGRAPHY  269

   INDEX  275

# PREFACE

Since 2001, I have served as dean at a leading school of architecture and, as a result, engaged in the front line of creating the next generation of architects, planners, landscape architects, interior designers, architectural historians, urban designers, and historic preservationists.

During that time, sustainability and environmentally conscious design have migrated from the fringe to the mainstream. Following the lead of other nations, we Americans are finally becoming more serious about sustainable development—that is, economic progress that meets all our needs without leaving future generations with fewer resources—a way of living from nature's income rather than mining its capital accounts. Meanwhile, 9/11, the 2005 Asian tsunami, the 2010 earthquake in Haiti, and Hurricane Katrina provide graphic displays of the vulnerability of our species. As a result, we witness growing interest in "re" topics like restoration, resilience, and regeneration as important concepts for design and planning.

Another "re" word, reflection, offers a method to probe these ideas. Reflective practice presents a useful, logical framework to advance the design and planning disciplines. One undertakes a project and then contemplates its meaning, successes and failures, and lessons learned. Reflections are personal, as is this book. As a result, some personal information helps set the stage. I am an accidental academic, entering landscape planning through practice. At the beginning of my teaching life in 1977, I soon realized that the university presented an opportunity to work on projects of my own choosing, thus enabling me to become an academic practitioner.

My academic journey began in the Pacific Northwest, where I moved after receiving a Master of Regional Planning from Ian McHarg's landscape architecture department at the University of Pennsylvania. In Washington State and Idaho, I became involved in projects relating to farmland protection, soil conservation, and growth management at all levels of government. When I returned to Philadelphia to pursue a Ph.D., the National Park Service provided the opportunity to work on a pioneering heritage conservation plan for the Blackstone River corridor between Providence, Rhode Island, and Worcester, Massachusetts. Our plan advanced the "greenline" approach involving local-state-federal government partnerships with private and nonprofit organizations. Our efforts led to the restoration of the river corridor and contributed to the renaissance of Providence. I witnessed the power of the federal government to stimulate local and state conservation through incentives and an inspirational regional vision for the future.

While on the University of Colorado faculty, I focused on growth management at the city and county levels. Later, Arizona State University opened wide-ranging possibilities for me, including projects at the watershed scale, explorations into sustainability, work in Mexico, and opportunities to design landfill sites and botanical gardens. I also helped launch one of the first National Science Foundation Long-Term Ecological Research studies devoted to an urban region. The work in Arizona, Colorado, and Mexico involved large, complex landscapes. I was able to apply principles from landscape ecology to illustrate the value of concepts like corridor, matrix, and node to balance preservation and development interests.

Extended visits to The Netherlands, Italy, and China introduced me to how other cultures design and plan. I lived in The Netherlands as a Fulbright research scholar, in Italy as a Rome Prize fellow, and in China as a visiting professor. These experiences abroad led to friendships and collaborations that enabled me to better understand how architecture and city planning are practiced in other nations. In addition, my work in Europe and Asia revealed a common concern within many societies about the future of the built and natural environments. Throughout this time, I wrote and published about these adventures, including my early experiences in new community planning that inspired me to pursue this line of work in the first place.

In this book, I reflect on changes in the field and future directions of design and planning practice and education. I have been influenced by my first ten years as dean of the School of Architecture at the University of Texas at Austin, where I became something beyond my wildest expectations, a Texan. The second largest state in size and population, Texas is becoming something beyond its wildest expectations, too. In spite of its cowboy ethos, Texas is an urban state where whites compose less than half the population. Its size contributes to its diversity: El Paso is geographically closer to San Diego than to Houston. Although Fort Worth and Dallas occupy the same metropolitan region, their cultures contrast and sometimes clash. While their state grows, Texans, like many other Americans, have been slow to embrace planning and have imported their skylines with architects from New York, Chicago, and Los Angeles.

Living in a big, politically conservative state, I sometimes reflect upon my time in The Netherlands, a tiny, progressive nation. The Dutch culture thrives through planning at all levels and a strong, homegrown design tradition with many international ties. They have about as many terms for planning as the Inuit have for snow. In addition to being successful in agriculture in a small, largely human-made landscape, the Dutch are capable capitalists who enjoy a high standard of living. They are also not satisfied with the status quo and are currently remaking their coastlines and river corridors to adapt to climate change.

The perception of my job as a dean varies from the vantage of the various constituencies I serve. My faculty colleagues often seem to view me as an ATM machine. Although my president and provost expect academic leadership, they also expect me to raise large amounts of money. Each week, someone from the public creates an idea that would make the perfect student studio project (for free). The alumni want their alma mater to be a top school (and many would like their children to follow in their footsteps). The students would like to have bright, reasonably entertaining teachers, whose classes begin after 10 a.m.

I see my role as managing all of the above, plus my job provides the opportunity to be an agent of change. I believe the design and planning disciplines in my School should play a more prominent position in our culture. To fulfill this promise, these programs need to pursue a more ecologically and socially responsible path. Design should involve more than aesthetic and technical concerns and recognize deeper cultural purposes. This is a change for most programs, including mine at the University of Texas. I helped facilitate this change in Austin and beyond. But change is a tricky and sometimes very slow phenomenon. It cannot be forced. Some ideas I advocated and pursued worked out better than others. Some remain unresolved.

My tenure as dean has coincided with several design and planning endeavors in Texas, around the nation, and in China and Italy. I believe that we have much to learn from these and other cultures that endure and are adaptable to change. China and Italy, in particular, constantly color my views of change and continuity. Both cultures are ancient yet modern, even beyond modern, or whatever we are calling postmodern these days. Authentic perhaps. Family, history, regionalism, and food play important stabilizing forces in both nations. Especially China is well known for its current, dizzyingly rapid change and, as a result, I give particular attention to my time there.

Reflective practice is a form of learning. I have learned much from looking at past experience and taking stock. My hope is that others might learn from these reflections and find my journey interesting.

Toward the end of this book, I criticize some aspects of the New Urbanist movement. Actually, I find many tenets of this movement to be good common sense, offering considerable value to regional planning and urban design. In fact, my work with Envision Central Texas, a nonprofit organization dedicated to developing a growth plan for the region and described in Chapter 13, is largely an outgrowth of the work of New Urbanists Peter Calthorpe and John Fregonese.

As I was completing this manuscript, I found myself on a panel with leading New Urbanism spokesmen Calthorpe and Andres Duany at the Congress for the New Urbanism (CNU) annual meeting in Austin. We discussed regional planning. Duany stated that all state growth management programs were dismal failures, especially that of his home state of Florida. Calthorpe disagreed and pointed to the success of Washington's Growth Management Act.

I had helped then State Senator (later Washington Supreme Court Justice) Phil Talmadge draft early versions of that act. The initial versions focused on farmland preservation. Although the bill evolved beyond our original proposal, a key provision that I had suggested remained. In order to mute opposition from rural interests, I recommended that plans only be required for urban

counties and cities above a certain population size. Rural counties below that threshold could prepare growth management plans if they wanted, but were not obliged to do so. This flexibility worked both to get the legislation passed and to advance planning in Washington State.

I prefer flexibility over rigid solutions. Some New Urbanists advocate a process that results in a predetermined formal solution. This bothers me.

Back to the Austin CNU panel, Duany declared that there are only three regional planning models. The first is the urban growth boundary. He noted this model is exemplified by Portland, Oregon's growth boundary but was pioneered by the greenbelt planning in England. The second, a rural boundary model, Duany attributed to Benton McKaye's ideas for a metropolitan system of protected lands. Jack Ahern of the University of Massachusetts-Amherst noted that this system was "conceived and configured to control urban expansion." McKaye's concepts clearly grew from Frederick Law Olmsted Sr. and Charles Eliot's earlier plans for metropolitan Boston, including their Emerald Necklace park system. Duany stated that the rural boundary model involves drawing lines around natural resources or historic resources that need to be preserved. Calthorpe's transit-oriented development model was Duany's third example. Through Calthorpe's approach, new, dense development is concentrated in nodes around transit stops.

As Duany eloquently presented black-and-white diagrams of these three models, I realized he was missing a fourth, one more difficult to diagram and one that is the focus of my regionalism and, as a result, the theoretical foundation for this book. If we start with process rather than with form, we conclude with different forms from those generated only from purely formal design. My goal is to illustrate such an approach through historical and personal examples.

The first process I suggest is what we can learn from natural phenomena, what Anne Spirn has called the deep structure and the deep context of the place. Ecological understanding suggests ways to arrange large infrastructure more efficiently and economically. We can also design green infrastructure to take advantage of the ecological services that nature can provide, from clean water to healthy plants. Ecological planning enables us to understand natural and social interactions at various scales, from our own home and workplace to the regional level and beyond.

On our panel, Duany noted a preference for the rural boundary model because development can be pushed away from preservation corridors. He also said the rural model can be more defensible because protection areas are defined by tangible elements such as streams or mountains. Much of my work has involved drawing such lines for preservation. I continue to believe we should avoid development in floodplains and preserve prime farmland. However, I suggest we go further and integrate nature into our everyday lives.

Second, I believe in democracy and as a result suggest we need to engage in the messy political process. In doing so, planners and designers should use precedents, looking at what has worked in other settings to suggest options for the situation at hand. We should also use our own creativity, as well as that of local residents, to derive other possibilities for the future.

What diagram would result? One that might appear chaotic at first. Actually, a colorful animation may be more appropriate than a black-and-white diagram. The animation would illustrate change and various scenarios for the future. The network would be more multicolored than the figure-ground representations presented by Duany. However, one might see the verdant organic corridors suggested like those drawn by Olmsted, Eliot, and McKaye; Calthorpe's transit-oriented developments may be present, too, as might growth boundaries around selected jurisdictions. Look closer and we might even find neighborhoods that would warm the hearts of New Urbanists. However, although my neighborhoods would include neat houses with front porches, there would also be room for homes with more jarring shapes by the likes of Zaha Hadid (but energy-efficient, of course, with sidewalks and easy access to transit).

A challenge for regionalism is to encourage policy makers and average citizens (and even architects and planners) to think regionally. The theory is that if we can learn to think regionally then we can apply that view to planning and design on many scales. Landscapes are visual combinations of natural and social processes. As a result, the design of landscapes represents one outcome of this fourth model for regionalism. At a finer grain, the design of buildings and urban spaces can be informed by this new regionalism.

# ACKNOWLEDGMENTS

This book evolved from several independent papers and projects since 2001. These undertakings were often collaborative endeavors and, as a result, I incurred many debts. Chapter 1, "Architecture and the Wealth of Regions," was originally published in *Platform*, a periodical of the University of Texas at Austin School of Architecture, and I am grateful to editor Pamela Peters for her ongoing contributions to our School's publications. The paper was inspired by my University of Texas colleagues Michael Benedikt and Steven Moore.

I appreciate the many students, faculty, and staff who have contributed to our three Solar Decathlon houses, the focus of Chapter 2, "Sustaining Design." In particular, Michael Garrison, Samantha Randall, Russell Krepart, Pliny Fisk, Elizabeth Alford, Marjie French, Kris Vetter, Julie Hooper, and Jeff Evelyn have provided invaluable leadership and support.

The Sustainable Sites Initiative, discussed in Chapter 4, resulted from a partnership involving the Lady Bird Johnson Wildflower Center, the American Society of Landscape Architects, and the U.S. Botanic Garden. I would like to express my most sincere appreciation of the hard work undertaken by the staff and more than fifty experts from a range of disciplines who have contributed to the development of the Sustainable Sites Initiative. The leadership of Susan Rieff, Nancy Somerville, and Holly Shimizu was essential to foster this partnership. Steve Windhager, Heather Venhaus, Danielle Pieranunzi, Ray Mims, and Elizabeth Guthrie did much of the heavy lifting for the project. Intellectual leadership came from Deb Guenther, José Almiñana, Deon Glaser, Jean Schwab, Richard Dolesh, Valerie Vartanian, Karen Nikolai, Karen Kabbes, Mike Clar, Susan Day, James Urban, and Meg Calkins. Many others contributed through committee and review activities. Nancy Solomon, the editor of the Urban Land Institute's *Urban Land Green* magazine, invited me to write an article, and I was helped greatly with that effort by Steve Windhager, Heather Venhaus, and Amy Crossette.

Chapter 5, "Making Territory," was originally written for Dean Almy and Michael Benedikt for an issue of the University of Texas School of Architecture journal *CENTER*, devoted to Landscape Urbanism. I rewrote the article for a 2008 Urban and Landscape Perspectives conference in Sardinia, organized by Professor Giovanni Maciocco, dean of the Faculty of Architecture at the University of Sassari. I further refined my ideas about Landscape Urbanism in an article for the architecture journal *Log*. I especially appreciate managing editor Gavin Keeney's prodding to express what I really think about Landscape Urbanism.

Chapter 3, "Twenty-First Century Architecture," evolved from an article I wrote for *Tribeza*, an

Austin arts magazine. *Oz* editor Joshua Bender of Kansas State University asked me to write an earlier version of what became Chapter 6, "City Limits." Chapter 7, "The Woodlands," originally appeared in the Rice Design Alliance's *Cite*. Chapter 8, "The Trinity River Corridor: Another Emerald Necklace or an Emerald Choker?" was first written for *Texas Architect* at the request of editor Stephen Sharpe. I thank editors of these four publications for their invitations and guidance.

My modest contributions to the Dallas Center for the Performing Arts, the focus of Chapter 10, helped me appreciate the selfless generosity of Deedie Rose and Howard Rachofsky, who truly know how to make limoncello from lemons. Both are my heroes because of their many contributions to art, architecture, landscape architecture, and city planning.

Lady Bird Johnson is clearly the inspiration for Chapter 11, which focuses on the Wildflower Center. It was an honor to have worked with her and other members of the Johnson family. I have also enjoyed my work with the Center's directors Bob Breunig and Susan Rieff, as well as with the Board of Directors, the Advisory Council, and the staff. As the Wildflower Center became part of the University of Texas, the ancillary benefit for me was gaining a friend in the College of Natural Sciences, Dean Mary Ann Rankin.

I wrote an earlier version of Chapter 12, "The Green Heart of Texas," with Kent Butler. I added and updated material from a co-authored paper with Stuart Glasoe, Bill Budd, and Jerry Young, originally published in *Landscape and Urban Planning* in 1990.

My work with Envision Central Texas, detailed in Chapter 13, involves considerable collaboration. I appreciate the invitation of Neal Kocurek and Lowell Lebermann to become involved in the first place. Beverly Silas, Sally Campbell, Diane Miller, Robin Rather, Jim Walker, Bill McLellan, Judge Ronnie McDonald, Judge H. T. Wright, Jim Skaggs, Cid Galindo, Travis Froehlich, Jay Hailey, and many others contributed to this worthwhile experience.

Chapter 14 explores the Texas Triangle work, which grew out of Bob Yaro's efforts with the Regional Plan Association, the Lincoln Institute, and the University of Pennsylvania. I appreciate my ongoing collaboration with Bob, as well as with Armando Carbonell, Petra Todrovich, Kent Butler, Ming Zhang, Talia McCray, and Sara Hammerschmidt.

My work with the Texas Triangle led to collaborations with others involved in megaregions and national-scale planning. These efforts, known as America 2050, are discussed in Chapter 15. The white paper Bob Yaro and I wrote subsequently was adapted as an article in *Landscape Architecture*, portions of which were adapted for this chapter.

Perhaps the most meaningful collaboration I have ever experienced was being a part of the Flight 93 National Memorial Team. I learned much from Jason Kentner, Karen Lewis, and Lynn Miller. We benefited from the involvement of three graduate students: Scott Biehle, Jennifer Gelber, and Megan Taylor, as well as my daughter Halina Steiner. I appreciate Bill Thompson for urging me to write about this experience.

"Autumn Moon: Design and Planning in China" resulted from Laurie Olin asking me to become part of his Tsinghua team. I appreciate that transforming invitation, as well as the faculty, students, and staff I met in Beijing, in particular Yang Rui, Wu Liangyong, Ron Henderson, Hu Jie, Dang Anrong, Liu Hailong, Zhuang Youbo, Que Zhenqing, and He Rui. Bill Thompson asked me to focus some of that rich experience in an article about the Olympic Forest Park for *Landscape Architecture*. Ron Henderson, Hu Jie, Alan Ward, and Wu Yixia made helpful suggestions for that article.

"Resilient Foundations" also derived from a Bob Yaro request. I learned much from Bob, as well as from the advisory group that we invited to help map the Gulf Coast from Pensacola, Florida, to Galveston, Texas. Barbara Faga and Jim Sipes of AECOM contributed much to this effort, as did Petra Todorovich of the Regional Plan Association. Genie Birch of the University of Pennsylvania urged us to write about our mapping project for a conference and a book that she organized about planning lessons we should learn from Katrina. This work provided an initial base for our exhibition at the Venice Biennale. Wilfried Wang created the opportunity for this involvement, which included several faculty members and students, especially Barbara Hoidn, Nichole Wiedemann, Jason Sowell, Larry Doll, and Kevin Alter. Nichole encouraged me to continue to write about ecology and Katrina for a subsequent conference she had organized with Jason.

Although based on these various previous works, I rewrote and reorganized the material for this book. Deedie Rose, Raquel Elizondo, Danilo Palazzo, Laurie Olin, Mirka Beneš, Michael Benedikt, Ming Zhang, Yang Rui, Michael Garrison, Ron Henderson, Chris Marcin, and Anita Ahmadi generously read the manuscript (or parts of it) and offered numerous helpful suggestions. Mack White and Anita Ahmadi typed and retyped the manuscript. Sara Hammerschmidt and Pamela Peters provided invaluable support in helping to compile the illustrations and secure permissions for their use.

Genie Birch and Tom Fisher, who reviewed the manuscript for the University of Texas Press, did much to help me focus my thinking and to fine-tune the writing, as did Heather Boyer, my long-time Island Press editor. I am especially grateful to the University of Texas Press team who transformed my manuscript into a book, in particular Joanna Hitchcock, Jim Burr, Victoria Davis, Ellen McKie, and Sally Furgeson. Last, special thanks to my family—Anna, Halina, and Andrew—whose enduring support made this work possible.

## INTRODUCTION

### INTERDISCIPLINARY

### DESIGN AND THE FATE

### OF OUR PLANET

The planet is in peril. The Earth will go on with or without us. But we know enough about how human actions are impacting the planet to change the role we play.

Designers conceive the future. Therefore, design can help us address this planetary emergency. Designs involve plans to guide deliberate actions. Oberlin environmental philosopher David Orr suggests that designers need to learn to make five key contributions: to use nature as the standard, to power the world on current sunlight, to eliminate waste, to pay the full cost of development, and to build prosperity on a durable basis. These contributions derive from looking closer at the world around us, understanding nature better in the process, then applying that knowledge to use the power of the sun and to see waste as a resource. By understanding the full costs—economic, social, and environmental—of development, we can design a brighter future.

Although designers and planners and their educators must think about integrating sustainability at every scale, the regional scale provides a good starting point for thinking about change. Through understanding the landscapes of the regions in which they work, architects and planners can critically consider cultural and ecological processes at the broad scale that can be employed locally.

This book explores how we can make the necessary changes through planning and design. The book contains seven parts. Part I establishes the foundations for a more ecological approach to planning and design. Ecology includes human and natural, urban and wild environments. The second part explores precedents for human ecological planning and design provided by the architect Paul Cret, the landscape architect Ian McHarg, and the developer George P. Mitchell. I discuss emerging Texas urbanism in Part III. This exploration is extended to broader considerations of regionalism in the fourth part, which also expands beyond the Lone Star State. In Part V, I reflect on lessons from abroad, most specifically from Italy and China. The sixth part is dedicated to learning from disaster; the final part to reflection and prospects for the future.

Part I contains five chapters that build the case for new regionalism. In Chapter 1, I look at three essential needs for integrating ecology into architecture and planning: thinking comprehensively, making places matter, and designing with time. I advocate a new approach to architecture. Such an approach is necessary because of the pressing issues we face and the failures of Modernism and Postmodernism. Modernism moved architecture, art, and design away from history and context toward free expression and abstraction. In architecture, the resulting emphasis on geometric form divorced buildings from their surroundings, creating autonomous structures floating in the landscape. Practitioners of Postmodernism, with borrowed images from the past, designed buildings and spaces with little regard for the contemporary city.

In the second chapter, I focus on the University of Texas at Austin's efforts to advance sustainable design. In addition to establishing a Center for Sustainable Development and a Master of Science in Sustainable Design, our School of Architecture has participated in three Solar Decathlon competitions organized by the U.S. Department of Energy. These hands-on competitions involve architecture and engineering students designing and building solar-powered houses, then displaying them on the National Mall in Washington, D.C.

From these first two chapters, ideas for twenty-first-century architecture, the focus of Chapter 3, begin to emerge. Five elements are suggested as important considerations for architecture: the location of a site, energy efficiency, water conservation, building materials, and beauty. I use examples to explore each of these elements.

Landscape design and planning at all scales will benefit from the Sustainable Sites Initiative, led by the Lady Bird Johnson Wildflower Center, the American Society of Landscape Architects, and the U.S. Botanic Garden. Chapter 4 reviews how this initiative adds to standards for buildings developed and promoted by the U.S. Green Building Council.

In Chapter 5, I close Part I with an argument in support of the emerging multidisciplinary field of Landscape Urbanism. Seven key concepts contribute to Landscape Urbanism: the constant change of the places where we live, the connective power of technology, the distinctiveness of certain places and regions, the ability of some cities to foster the creative class, the repetition of patterns across scale, the blurring of disciplinary boundaries, and the resiliency of human settlements.

Part II includes two chapters about projects that pioneered alternative paths for design and planning in Texas. If these precedents had been followed more widely, a very different Texas would

exist today. The projects offer lessons for the future of Texas and beyond. In Chapter 6, I discuss the design for the University of Texas campus and the Lake Austin drainage area. In both cases, the principal designers and planners—Paul Cret and Ian McHarg—adapted their work to the specific characteristics of the site and the drainage area and significantly improved the quality of the built environment.

The campus and the drainage area are both located in the Austin metropolitan region. In Chapter 7, we shift to the Houston region, where I review the planning and design of The Woodlands. I analyze this community's environmental, economic, and social successes and shortcomings. The leadership of its developer, George Mitchell, and its ecological planner, Ian McHarg, is central to The Woodlands' story. Its design, like the Lake Austin plan, was undertaken in the 1970s, an important period in American history when public policy focused on environmental concerns and turned to the environmental design arts for solutions. We need to build on the lessons learned from those pioneering efforts.

Emerging urbanism in Texas is the focus of Part III, which includes four chapters. Texas helps to make the case for a new regionally based approach to design and planning. The state possesses strong regional traditions and identities, and its large cities also have distinct, diverse identities. Indeed, the very word "Texas" sparks strong reactions. Texas iconography has been successfully appropriated by sports teams and musicians. However, except for the extensive use of Lone Stars on highway overpass bridges, regional identities have not been successfully incorporated widely into Texas architecture and city planning. Examples of promising beginnings follow.

In Chapter 8, we move to another Texas metropolis. Dallas and Fort Worth differ strikingly from Austin and Houston. In fact, even though the region is known as "The Metroplex," these two neighboring cities are quite different from each other. In fact, all the rapidly growing cities in Texas vary and are competitive with each other, which makes the state an interesting urban laboratory for design and planning.

Designers frequently must make the most from less-than-ideal circumstances. The ninth chapter describes the work of a leading landscape architect on the University of Texas at Austin campus. Peter Walker entered the design of the Blanton Museum of Art after a prominent Swiss architecture firm left the project amidst controversy over the building design. He not only completed the design of the plaza between the two buildings but also presented a broader vision for the campus, inspired, in part, by Cret's earlier plan. Walker's design has been embraced by the university's leadership. In this case, a landscape architect salvaged a project where architecture had faltered.

In Chapter 10, design and planning are explored through the Dallas Arts District. This project is transforming a major section of the city's downtown and provides significant new venues for the performance arts. Its planning also illustrates the challenges in designing urban landscapes. The two major new facilities in the district were designed by prominent architecture "stars," a continuation of the Texas tradition of importing brand-name outsiders to design significant buildings. Although the two star architects certainly produced dramatic buildings for the Dallas Arts District, the design of associated outside spaces faced serious challenges, as it failed to respond to its social and environmental context.

Chapter 11 focuses on the Lady Bird Johnson Wildflower Center. Mrs. Johnson contributed much to Central Texas and the nation. As first lady, she championed environmental quality and helped create the foundation for many of the federal environmental laws of the 1960s and 1970s. Back in Austin, she established the Lady Bird Johnson Wildflower Center. She advocated native plants as an indicator of regional environmental health. In founding the Wildflower Center, Mrs. Johnson also insisted on the use of state-of-the-art green building technologies for its structures. She directed the architects to site the buildings as if "God had placed them there."

Part IV focuses on regionalism and includes four chapters. In Chapters 12 and 13, I return to the regional scale and Central Texas. I describe in more detail the ecology and human ecology of this green heart of Texas and reflect on an innovative regional visioning effort called Envision Central Texas. I have been deeply involved in this organization and offer my perspective from that participation.

In Chapter 14, I explore the relatively new concept of megaregions or conglomerations of metropolitan areas. The focus is on the Texas Triangle, one of the eleven fastest growing megaregions in the nation. With Houston and San Antonio forming the base and the Dallas-Fort Worth Metroplex at its apex, the Texas Triangle offers a new way to approach planning. In addition to practical applications, four theories for megaregions are presented: descriptive, analytical, normative, and procedural.

Buildings and landscapes should respond to their regions. As the Sustainable Sites Initiative is a national effort to advance the way we design landscapes, America 2050 seeks to strengthen the role of regions in national planning. Chapter 15 reviews the leadership of the Regional Plan Association, the Rockefeller Foundation, and others in the America 2050 effort.

In Part V, we move from the United States to Italy and China, countries with deep histories in regionalism, architecture, and urbanism. Both countries face challenges similar to those in Texas (and the United States) when it comes to incorporating regional thinking into architecture and planning. For example, in rapidly growing China, leaders are well known for seeking international "star architects" to design new landmarks, with mixed results.

In many Italian universities, large numbers of students pursue architectural studies. At Milan Polytechnic, for instance, around a fourth (9,800) of its 37,000 students were architecture and planning majors in 2008, with another 4,200 industrial design students.

"What do they all do?" Americans ask.

"What do all your business majors do?" Italians respond.

Italian architecture education provides the basis for making fashion, film, automobiles, fur-

1. The planet is becoming more urban, which is especially evident in China. City of Wuhan from Yellow Crane Tower, looking down the Yangtze River. Photograph by Ming Zhang.

2. As military technology rendered city walls obsolete, many European cities tore down the fortifications and replaced them with parks. Lucca, Italy, retained its walls and built a park on the ramparts. Photograph by Frederick Steiner.

niture, and a multitude of products we use every day. Knowledge of architecture and urbanism are considered fundamental for being a well-educated Italian. Architecture and urbanism are regarded as much as humanities as professions.

Urban planning has ancient heritages in China and Italy but, as professions and academic disciplines, they are more recent (Figure 1). In Italy,

planning emerged in the early twentieth century (Figure 2). Although Benito Mussolini played a strong role in Italian planning during the 1930s, the field also had more democratic influences. In 1942, Italy approved one of the most advanced planning laws in all Europe. Unfortunately, it remained unimplemented for years. During the reconstruction following the Second World War and the economic boom period, the law was only partially enacted. In the 1970s, the national planning system acted as a framework for the urban laws approved by the Italian regions. Most recently, some regions enhanced their urban laws to give more power to single cities and to reduce bureaucracy. Academia, and hence the urban plan-

ning theory literature, was influenced mainly by France (because of the similar cultural heritage, except for the centralistic tendency). In China, the field came into being just after the Second World War. Mao Zedong and the Communist Party loom large over Chinese planning. However, Chinese urban-level planning has more diverse and com-

**3.** Garden at Rockefeller Foundation Bellagio Center, Lago di Como, Italy. Photograph by Frederick Steiner.

**4.** Garden of Cultivation, Suzhou, China. Photograph by Frederick Steiner.

plex strains. Architects, trained in prewar America and Europe, influenced planning discussions and ideas somewhat, even during Mao's reign. Since the 1990s, Chinese planning has opened to even wider influences.

Garden design also has ancient lineages in both Italy and China (Figures 3 and 4). Landscape architecture is a more recent development and is capturing considerable interest. I have been present at the academic birth of landscape architecture in both nations. In both cases, I played a small role as more of an observer than a participant. In my own nation, I participate in shaping landscape architecture more directly as well as architecture, planning, interior design, historic preservation, architectural history, urban design, and sustainable design. This list gets long. As a result, I have used design as an umbrella term in the title of this book. In the pages that follow, I attempt to give all the fields in my School their due consideration, but I admit my direct involvement is greater in some than in others.

I focus on the villas and gardens in and around Rome in Chapter 16. These places reveal much about Italian design ideas and the origins of Italian views concerning the environment. Italian architecture and urbanism have had enduring influences on the western tradition of city building.

From Italy, we travel to Beijing in Chapter 17, where I served as visiting professor in the new landscape architecture program at Tsinghua University. In addition to discussing my teaching activities, I review my impressions of Beijing: its rapid growth, ancient culture, environmental challenges, and architecture and urban traditions. In particular, I describe the physical planning activities for the 2008 Olympics. The resulting Olympic Forest Park provides vast new open space and recreational areas for the citizens of Beijing.

Part VI focuses on disaster and what we can learn from our resilience in the face of hardship. One challenge is how to remember the victims of terrorism. Chapter 18 is devoted to the design of the memorial for United Flight 93. I was part of a finalist team for the memorial. We sought to create a memorial that would recall the valor of the passengers and crew of Flight 93, as well as restore a Pennsylvania landscape ravished by years of strip mining.

The post-Katrina Gulf Coast region exemplifies the need for better planning. In Chapter 19, I explore the concept of resilience in the context of an exhibit prepared for the 10th International Architecture Exhibition of the Venice Biennale, the major global venue for new architectural explorations. The 10th Architecture Biennale was devoted to the future of large city-regions around the world. Resilience involves the ability of communities to bounce back from disaster. As New Orleans and the Gulf Coast illustrate, the future of city-regions rests between vulnerability and sustainability. Resilience is necessary to move away from risk toward restoration on to resurrection and regeneration.

In the final chapter, I reflect on architecture and planning in Texas and our nation. I suggest some directions for architecture, planning, landscape architecture, and interior design. I conclude with four positive steps for healing our planet and saving humanity. First, we should acknowledge the relationship between health and the built environment. Second, we need to build green. Third, we should stop sprawling and do a better job restoring and conserving the built environment. Fourth, we need to think regionally.

Design and planning both offer hope and help distinguish us as a species. In his insightful *The World Without Us*, Alan Weisman notes how we advanced as a species as we learned the skill to plan. Planning requires both "memory and foresight." As we inhabited temperate regions, we learned to store food in times of plenty for the winter. These are times that call on us to remember how we have built successful environments in the past, as well as to have the foresight to construct more sustainable environments in the future.

# LIVING
# URBAN
# ENVIRONMENTS

Regions possess strong cores and fuzzy edges. The Miami Valley, where I grew up, is defined by geological, hydrological, and cultural phenomena including Wisconsin glaciations, rivers flowing south to the Ohio, and Native Americans who gave the place its name. Nowadays, suburban Dayton merges with suburban Cincinnati along Interstate 75. For many years, sports teams and media coverage have overlapped.

Hydrological forces have also sculpted the region where I now live. Here, groundwater complements surface water in creating a regional identity. Another defining force in that identity is Austin, which is simultaneously situated in the heart of Texas and at odds culturally and politically with much of the rest of the state.

In the next five chapters, I explore how new thinking about the regions where we live can shape architecture and planning. Designs and plans better suited to their place will certainly be more sustainable than conventional approaches. New regionalism should also yield designs and plans that are more resilient to unexpected change and, ultimately, possess a greater capacity for regeneration.

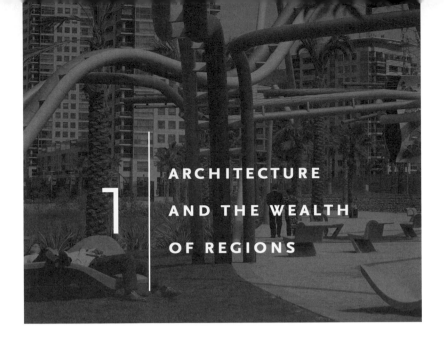

# ARCHITECTURE AND THE WEALTH OF REGIONS

1

In the Modern era, architects turned their backs on the natural and cultural characteristics of specific places. They advocated an International Style to be applied universally, regardless of local climate or soil. Central heating and air conditioning enabled the spread of glass boxes everywhere. Modern architects also declared that we should ignore architectural history. Ludwig Mies van der Rohe defined Modernism as "a revolution against the architecture of the past."

In reaction, Postmodern architects suggested we relearn history. However, their work appeared quaint and out-of-touch with contemporary times. The New Urbanists, who originally called themselves "neo-traditionalists," also advocated we learn from design and planning history. However, they went further in their appreciation of vernacular building traditions and regional environmental processes. Still, New Urbanist communities can appear to be romantic throwbacks to an era that never really happened.

Regionalism is important for design and planning because it provides a scale for reading natural processes. For example, regional climate, or mesoclimate, forms a bridge between many microclimates and more continental megaclimates. Likewise, watersheds and larger drainage basins are formed by clear hydrologic boundaries. Understanding climate and water flows at a regional scale enables us to design more appropriate, more sustainable buildings, parks, and communities.

Ancient cultures valued regions. Specific climate and terrain set the stage for all that followed, from the crops that could be grown to social relationships. Such conditions are evident in Italy and China, where cuisines and building styles vary from region to region. Even today, regional phenomena are reflected in the walls of the Hebei province of China and the ancient streets of the Lazio region of Italy. Stone from both regions divides space and provides surfaces to walk. Regional phenomena guided architecture and urbanism for generations of Chinese and Italians.

Modern design and planning drifted away from regionalism. Refrigeration, air conditioning, central heating, television, radio, computers, automobiles, and cell phones—all the technology of the past century—enable us to separate ourselves from nature for most of each day. We construct walls between ourselves and the outdoors in climate-controlled bubbles.

Our current condition requires that we reconnect with the nature of our regions instead of designing spaces under the old ethos of "conquering nature" and isolating humans from their natural environments. We need to look back at what our society has collectively learned about our environments in order to move ahead.

## NATURAL, SOCIAL, AND KNOWLEDGE CAPITAL

The Roman Marcus Vitruvius Pollio wrote the first guide to architecture and dedicated *On Architecture* to his emperor, Augustus. A good architect, according to Vitruvius, is not a narrow professional but an intellectual of wide-ranging abilities. For example, Vitruvius included medicine in his extensive list of subjects of which an architect should "have some knowledge." An architect should understand medicine, "in its relation to the regions of the earth (which the Greeks call *climata*)" in order to answer questions regarding the healthiness and unhealthiness of sites. A knowledge of the atmosphere and the water supply of localities is essential, "[f]or apart from these considerations, no dwelling can be regarded as healthy."[1]

Vitruvius devoted much of his writing to site-specific, or landscape, considerations. As one classicist observes, "Vitruvius' conception of architecture is . . . wide, at times almost approaching what we define as urban studies."[2] Vitruvius made detailed pronouncements for planning new urban developments. The very first consideration must be salubrity:

*First, the choice of the most healthy site. Now this will be high and free from clouds and hoar frost, with an aspect neither hot nor cold but temperate. Besides, in this way a marshy neighborhood shall be avoided. For when the morning breezes come with the rising sun to a town, and clouds rising from these shall be conjoined, and with their blast, shall sprinkle on the bodies of the inhabitants the poisoned breaths of marsh animals, they will make the site pestilential.*[3]

In addition to his directions for using an understanding of nature to design houses and plan cities, Vitruvius provided considerable advice for building civic structures and spaces. The Romans constructed many new communities, a good number of which continue to prosper today throughout Europe, the Middle East, and North Africa. Twenty centuries after Vitruvius, in their detailed study of architectural education for the Carnegie Foundation, Ernest Boyer and Lee Mitgang urge architects to shift their focus from designing objects to "building community."[4] Such a change requires careful consideration of what constitutes "community" and what is the relationship of communities to their physical and biological regions.

In his book, *Bowling Alone*, Harvard political scientist Robert Putnam argues that social capital is critical for civic well-being.[5] He maintains that community associations—bowling together—are necessary for people to thrive. Community activities appear to flourish or to wane depending upon their regional context. Harkening back to Lewis Mumford's use of regionalism, several contemporary architects and planners—including Peter Calthorpe, William Fulton, Gary Hack, and Roger Simmonds—advocate the notion of the "regional city" or the "city-region."[6] Healthy city-regions fit their natural environments and foster civil interactions. Healthy building and landscape designs, in turn, fit their city-regions and deepen human interactions (Figure 1.1).

For example, Calthorpe and Fulton contend that "the Regional City must be viewed as a cohesive unit—economically, ecologically, and socially—made up of coherent neighborhoods and communities, all of which play a vital role in creating the metropolitan region as a whole."[7]

Because I fly so much for work, I especially avoid airplanes during the holidays. As a result, I drive from Austin to Dayton, Ohio, to visit my family at Christmas. The landscapes across this mid-American transect offer variety and possibility. The built environment is beyond dull; it is ugly and predictable. The Interstate interchanges in Texas, Arkansas, Tennessee, Kentucky, and Ohio, or alternatively through Georgia, Alabama, Mississippi, and Louisiana, wound nature and culture. These assaults on our senses blend together with the same hotels, gas stations, fast food chains, and mega-churches. The edge-city malls combine the same shops. The skylines of Dallas, Little Rock, Memphis, Nashville, Louisville, and Cincinnati may be taller or shorter, but all look pretty similar. Even redeveloped urban areas are hard

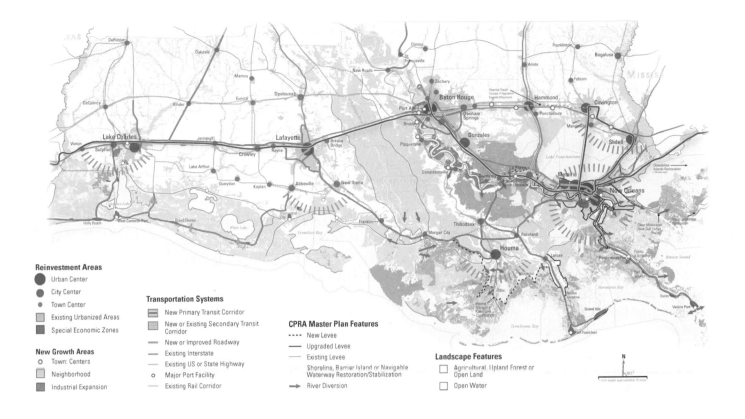

**Reinvestment Areas**

- ● Urban Center
- ● City Center
- ● Town Center
- ▢ Existing Urbanized Areas
- ▢ Special Economic Zones

**New Growth Areas**

- ○ Town: Centers
- ▢ Neighborhood
- ▢ Industrial Expansion

**Transportation Systems**

- ▭ New Primary Transit Corridor
- ▭ New or Existing Secondary Transit Corridor
- — New or Improved Roadway
- — Existing Interstate
- — Existing US or State Highway
- ○ Major Port Facility
- ---- Existing Rail Corridor

**CPRA Master Plan Features**

- ---- New Levee
- — Upgraded Levee
- — Existing Levee
- Shoreline, Barrier Island or Navigable Waterway Restoration/Stabilization
- ➔ River Diversion

**Landscape Features**

- ▢ Agricultural, Upland Forest or Open Land
- ▢ Open Water

N

1.1. Regional Plan Map, Louisiana Speaks (2006–2007). Courtesy of Calthorpe Associates.

to distinguish from one another. Sixth Street in Austin, Beale Street in Memphis, and Broadway in Nashville feature the same types of shops and musicians. Across this heartland of sweetened ice tea and deep fried everything, one searches long for an NPR station among those dominated by Jesus, Rush, and country; one yearns for a decent salad.

Off the Interstate, there are wonderful exceptions: the courthouse squares in Texas, the Clinton Library, the Bourbon Trail, downtown Covington across the Ohio River from Cincinnati, and Chattanooga's transformed riverfront. Authenticity and good design distinguish these places. One of the multiple tragedies swirling around New Orleans is the loss of a truly original place (its predictable skyline aside). The design of Austin's airport offers an alternative to civic leaders seeking to set their city apart from others. The airport features a live music stage and permits only local businesses to operate. One cannot find a Starbucks, but there is Austin Java. There is no McDonald's, but there are opportunities to savor Central Texas barbeque.

What if a similar approach was applied across the mid-American transect from Texas to Ohio? Across other regions as well? Might we reconceive downtown Louisville and its peripheries based on its regional context? McDonald's has adapted its design for Paris and Amsterdam. Why not have different designs for McDonald's in Little Rock and Dayton? Designs constructed with the stones, wood, and/or bricks from the region and surrounded with native plants?

University of Texas Professor Steven Moore, a leading sustainability theorist, links regionalism to place-making. He concludes "it is politically desirable and ecologically prudent to reproduce regionalism as a practice relevant to contemporary conditions."[8] Moore builds on Kenneth Frampton's advocacy of Critical Regionalism. According to Frampton:

*The fundamental strategy of Critical Regionalism is to mediate the impact of universal civilisation with elements derived indirectly from the peculiarities of a particular place.*

*. . . Critical Regionalism depends upon maintaining a high level of critical self-consciousness. It may find its governing inspiration in such things as the range and quality of local light, or in a tectonic derived from a peculiar structural mode, or in the topography of a given site.[9]*

Regional understanding is important for architects and landscape architects to design specific buildings and sites much the way medical doctors need to understand human anatomy in order to treat an individual patient. Such a design practice would involve the critical understanding of the region as well as the shaping of its futures. The future can be shaped by a series of individual smaller projects as well as grand gestures (as discussed in Chapter 5).

For a dozen years, I lived in a region that its residents call "The Valley of the Sun." The nickname reveals this region's principal natural attributes. Water, now mostly captured by dams in the mountains to the north and east, is relatively plentiful (even more so if properly used and conserved). The Salt, Verde, and Gila Rivers flowing from the mountains deposited fertile soils in the broad valleys. Sunshine attracts winter visitors, tourists, and retirees. Taken together, sunny winter weather and a flat alluvial plain give the

Greater Phoenix region a rich natural and social capital. Understanding that capital forms the essential bedrock for the practice envisioned by Moore.

Regionalism is an attractive concept because we can identify the place we inhabit as something specific, but regional boundaries are fuzzier. A city, on the other hand, has legal limits. So a city-region or a regional city possesses an identity but contains bounded entities.

Music helps provide an identity for Austin and the Central Texas region. The self-proclaimed "Live Music Capital of the World," music contributes to Austin's reputation as a cool place to live and to work. This reputation is important for the region's economic prosperity as it attracts the creative class. Beyond music, Austin's identity is closely associated with the environmental features of the region, including its many natural springs, the rolling wooded Hill Country, and the rich deep soils of the Blackland Prairie.

Arizona State University (ASU) president and science policy guru Michael Crow observes that city-regions in the future will be either "knowledge importers" or "knowledge exporters." Innovation and creativity are necessary for city-regions to maintain their competitive edge in the global economy. For the past century, research univer-

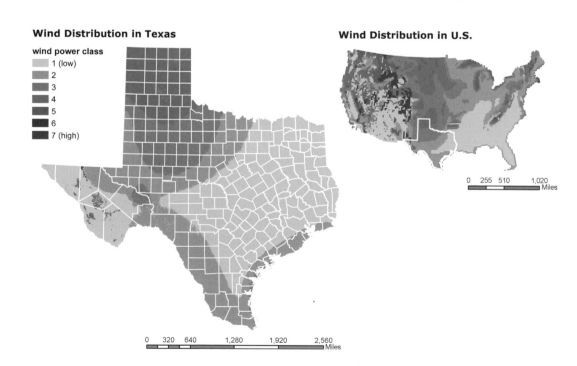

**Wind Distribution in Texas**

wind power class
- 1 (low)
- 2
- 3
- 4
- 5
- 6
- 7 (high)

0 320 640 1,280 1,920 2,560 Miles

**Wind Distribution in U.S.**

0 255 510 1,020 Miles

**1.2** Geographic Information System technology can be used to combine mapped data to reveal opportunities and constraints for human settlement, such as this map of areas of Texas suitable for wind power. Map by Jenna Kamholz.

sities have been the most fertile seed bank of knowledge production. Observers of the new economy argue that city-regions will not be able to prosper economically in the future without at least one major research university.

But what kinds of knowledge? We are becoming connected to a global web of information that has opened new ways of understanding. Jack Dangermond, founder and CEO of the Geographic Information System (GIS) software company ESRI, likens this network to our central nervous system (Figure 1.2). With real-time satellite imagery, the World Wide Web, global positioning systems, palm pilots, and other electronic and digital technologies, we can sense and identify regional conditions in much the same way our bodies sense and identify their surroundings through the central nervous system. But where is the brain of Dangermond's system?

We need to rethink traditional ways of looking at the world. What is the place of architecture in this more complex, this more chaotic, worldview?

These expanded forms of capital—natural, social, and knowledge—roughly correspond to the three "e"s advocated by proponents of sustainable development: environment, equity, and economy. My former Arizona State dean, the architect John Meunier, advocated a fourth "e" in sustainability: esthetics.[10] (The secondary spelling is used to keep it parallel with the other three "e"s.) By integrating esthetics into the sustainability discussion, architects and other designers may be more explicitly drawn into the sustainable development discussion. Designers are visual people who need esthetic stimuli. Often green concerns have been advanced at the expense of esthetic concerns. If such esthetics are viewed as integral and central to sustainable development, rather than peripheral, then designers would become more engaged. Designers need little convincing.

For example, Barbara Faga of the landscape architecture and planning firm EDAW (now AECOM) asked me in 1998 to provide advice on sustainability for the new Parc Diagonal Mar in Barcelona. At the time, sustainability was a relatively unknown concept and still emerging issue. The late Catalàn architect Enric Miralles and the

American landscape architects from EDAW led the design team for the Houston-based, global development company Hines. At first, Miralles was skeptical. During our discussions, he remarked, "Good design is sustainable." As we worked through an analysis of the Parc Diagonal Mar using sustainability criteria, it became clear that he and EDAW had already considered many of the factors. In fact, Miralles had proposed the consideration of several elements on my list but had been prevented from incorporating them into his design by city officials. He quickly saw that our analysis could be used for leverage to advance his design ideas. Rather than limit design innovation, our sustainability analysis opened new political possibilities.

Good design forms part of the cultural capital of Barcelona and the Catalàn region. From the work of Antonio Gaudí through the 1992 Olympics to Parc Diagonal Mar, Barcelona abounds with architecture and landscapes that provide visual manifestations of its distinct urbane culture (Figure 1.3). This cultural capital may lie at the heart of a region's wealth. Cultural capital can be viewed as the nexus of other forms of capital. Our culture reflects how we regard our environments, others, and learning.

Are there American equivalents to the kind of effect that Gaudí had on the Barcelona region, an influence that has been carried on by contemporary architects like Miralles? Frederick Law Olmsted's New York City and Brooklyn masterpieces—Central Park and Prospect Park—certainly informed the more recent designs of the Battery Park City Esplanade and Bryant Park. As Olmsted worked in other regions, he exhibited considerable understanding of the natural and social capitals of those places. Take, for example, his campus plan for Stanford University, which employs his appreciation of northern California. The Mediterranean-inspired campus layout differs significantly from his picturesque eastern parks.

Olmsted's final three major projects reinforce this point and also exhibit his collaborative acumen. Building on previous park work in Boston, Olmsted designed the Emerald Necklace with Charles Eliot in the 1890s. They used the region's

1.3 Parc Diagonal Mar, Barcelona. Design by EMBT Architects and EDAW (now AECOM). © 2003 AECOM. Photograph by Dixi Carillo.

drainage system to create a park and open space network that also provided flood management and water quality benefits. Olmsted's work on the Biltmore Estate in Asheville, North Carolina, for George W. Vanderbilt contains both highly formal and innovative ecological designs. At Biltmore, Olmsted collaborated with the young conservationist Gifford Pinchot among others. Pinchot and Olmsted applied concepts for "multiple use and sustained yield" that are the precursors of today's interest in sustainability. For the World's Columbian Exposition of 1893 in Chicago, architect Daniel Burnham brought in Olmsted, along with many of the leading artists and architects of the era (Figure 1.4). The multidisciplinary team provided the groundwork for the City Beautiful Movement that transformed urban life for the better in many American cities in the early twentieth century.

Frank Lloyd Wright presents another American example of a designer who understood, and influenced the change of, regions. The horizontality of his houses echoed the flatness of the Midwest prairie landscape. His Prairie Style left a considerable imprint on the upper Midwest region. Many architects followed Wright's lead with single-story,

1.4 Court of Honor, World's Columbian Exposition of 1893, Chicago. Source: Official Guide Book, 1893.

horizontal houses as did landscape architects like Jens Jensen and Alfred Caldwell, who advocated and advanced the use of native prairie plants. Indeed, metropolitan Chicago may be viewed as a confluence of four important strains in American design and planning during the turn of and early twentieth century: the Prairie Style of Wright (and, in a related vein, Jensen and Caldwell), the skyscrapers of Louis Sullivan and many others, the City Beautiful Movement of Burnham and Olmsted and their followers, and the urban ecology of the Chicago School sociologists (Figure 1.5).

Like Olmsted's achievements, Wright's great work adapted to its context but also transformed it. Neither the Guggenheim Museum nor the Marin County Civic Center could be confused with a Prairie House. The former matches the energy of its urban setting, the latter fits into its suburban hills. As Wright took up winter residency in Arizona, his work exhibited great sensitivity to the desert, as is exemplified by one of his masterworks—Taliesin West. Wright's influence reverberates through generations of Arizona architects as diverse as Paolo Soleri, Will Bruder, and Rick Joy, each of whom has developed Wright's ideas about "organic architecture" in his own way. "Organic architecture" seeks to achieve harmony between people and the natural world, so it quite obviously responds to the ecology of the place. A beauty of Wright's work is how it adds value to its location.

Olmsted and Wright practiced a form of Critical Regionalism long before Kenneth Frampton advocated the term, as the Stanford campus and the Robie House help illustrate. Yet, Frampton is right on target, in my view, with his advocacy. As Moore explains Critical Regionalism, this term means "that architecture should evoke meaning and thought rather than emotion and excitement—that architecture should evoke critical consideration of cultural and ecological origins of construction practices."[11] Meaning and thought may also evoke emotion and excitement, but such responses would be grounded in the deep structure, the deep context of the region, rather than in fashions or trends.[12]

Such grounding can help inform the designer on the use of materials and the appropriate siting of buildings. Building materials from the region link the built environment to the natural environment. The material use can be more sustainable both for the environment and for the local economy. The careful siting of buildings can help reduce energy use and, in the process, limit greenhouse gas production.

1.5 The Coonley House, Riverside, Illinois. Design by Frank Lloyd Wright. Photograph by Dean Eastman.

## RETHINKING ARCHITECTURAL AND PLANNING EDUCATION

What are the implications of this view of city-regions and their wealth for architectural and planning education? Three essential needs emerge.

### THINK COMPREHENSIVELY AND BROADLY

First, if one sphere of knowledge is privileged at the expense of others, then the result is deleterious and not sustainable. For example, if a building design favors esthetics and ignores concerns about its environmental or social context or the economics of the project, it will sooner or later fail. My own discipline, planning, tended to ignore the esthetic principles of good community design for much of the second half of the twentieth century. One does not need to look far to see the negative consequences of this oversight. Fortunately, the architects of the Congress for the New Urbanism helped redirect planners back to the art of community design.[13]

As these architects assert:

*Put simply, the New Urbanism sees physical design—regional design, urban design, architecture, landscape design, and environmental design [and presumably interior design, product design, and graphic design]—as critical to the future of our communities. . . . The belief is that design can play a critical role in resolving problems that government programs and money alone cannot.*[14]

Design can help accomplish this aspiration through creativity. Instead of predetermined, fixed solutions, designers explore new ways to invent the future. Although New Urbanism redirected planning back to physical form, it has fallen short in creating truly "new" models for urbanism.

New Urbanists advocate the centrality of design in community and regional issues. They provide a stinging criticism of the planning profession for abandoning design as a policy and

implementation tool. "Town planning," Andres Duany and his colleagues write, "until 1930 considered a humanistic discipline based on history, aesthetics, and culture, became a technical profession based upon numbers. As a result, the American city was reduced into simplistic categories and quantities of sprawl. Because these tenets still hold sway, sprawl continues largely unchecked."[15]

Blaming planners for sprawl seems a bit excessive. Still, the argument that a humanistic understanding has value for community building is sound. However, numbers are not necessarily simplistic. They represent values. Often, quantifying things can be helpful as we plan and design places. A comprehensive view suggests that we evolve beyond either/or arguments, that we may have humanities with numbers.

To be comprehensive, we need to heed the advice of Vitruvius and think broadly again. If an architect is a wide-ranging intellectual, then architecture should reflect a broad understanding of other fields. Such understanding certainly should encompass those fields closest to architecture, arguably landscape architecture and city planning.

Conversely, landscape architects and planners can gain much by seeking to understand architecture, rather than by leaving building design solely to architects. As reading Vitruvius reminds us, architecture has a more ancient history than related fields. That history, as well as the theories architects have promulgated for designing interior and exterior spaces and for planning cities and regions, set the stage for those of us in sibling fields.

Such comprehensive, strategic thinking should be grounded in theory. The design and planning disciplines could benefit from a few more good theories. Landscape architecture is a discipline that illustrates the adage that there is nothing as practical as a good theory. Two theories have catapulted landscape architecture into greater prominence. In the mid-nineteenth century, Olmsted advocated the use of public parks to address the ills of urbanization brought on by the Industrial Revolution. A century later, Ian McHarg urged us to "design with nature," publishing his immensely

**1.6** Lower Don Lands proposal, Toronto, Canada: a hybridized river and river marsh—carefully structured with a full range of armored to porous surfaces—give rise to a new habitat for fish and wildlife and to a new type of green city. Design by StossLU. © StossLU.

influential book with the same title. McHarg's theory highlights the integration of the biophysical setting, ecology, planning, design, and execution of projects that reflect an understanding of people and nature.

These two theories—that public parks have social benefits and that design should be derived from environmental understanding—sustained landscape architecture for two centuries. Like jazz, landscape architecture originated as a particularly American art form. Landscape plays a central role in American culture that is akin to the city in Italian culture. A newer theory than McHarg's shows signs of emerging by combining concerns about urban welfare with ecologically based design. New urban ecology-based theories promise to address a range of pressing issues, from environmental justice to the reclamation of postindustrial, marginalized sites. Such theories are beginning to yield new forms of Landscape Urbanism, like those generated by West 8 Urban Design & Landscape Architecture in The Netherlands, as well as the New York landscape architecture firm, Field Operations, and the Boston design and planning studio, StossLU, in the United States (Figure 1.6). Fresh urban theory is moving landscape architecture closer to emerging ideas about the structure of cities in architecture and planning as well as to new theories in urban ecology being put forth by biologists and geographers.

Theory fuels the academic engine. In the sciences, theories are tested through experimentation. In the design fields, they are explored in studios and through reflection upon projects. Ecological design and urban ecology extend outside the bounds of the traditional sciences and arts. This suggests, to advance these new theories, science education needs to learn from the creativity of studios, while designers could benefit from more fact-based education.

With Modernism, design education turned its back on history. Postmodernism embraced history, but its design applications (including some that are New Urbanist) incorporate past elements too literally and romantically. We must learn from precedent without becoming prisoners of the past. By thinking broadly, we can design several solutions based on local and regional considerations rather than looking in on a single, predetermined course of action.

## MAKE PLACES MATTER

A second implication for architectural and planning education within this city-region perspective is perhaps the most obvious but one often overlooked by our own culture: place matters. Places exist as a result of the meanings we assign to them through experience, memory, or aspiration.

Such meanings create a sense of place, which is also informed by the physical attributes of the locale. We continually shape and re-shape places in response to changing social and environmental conditions. In return, places shape us.

To remain competitive in the global economy, city-regions must offer compelling places for people to live. Architects can, and should, contribute to creating such urban places. My former College of Architecture and Environmental Design at ASU provides a nice model in this regard. Beginning in the late 1960s, then architecture dean Jim Elmore began advocating for converting the abandoned, dry Salt River bed into a linear greenway through the metropolitan region (Figure 1.7). Generations of ASU architecture, planning, and landscape architecture faculty and students followed Dean Elmore's vision, and components of the Rio Salado project are now realized in Phoenix and Tempe. Water now again occurs in the once-dry riverbed of Tempe, which enhances recreational and economic development opportunities. More recently, former dean John Meunier encouraged faculty and students to become engaged in the

pressing issues affecting the region, especially through design and planning charrettes. ASU's influence on the design and planning of the northern, rapidly urbanizing 20 percent of the City of Phoenix is especially evident.[16] As a result of collaboration between ASU faculty and city staff, large portions of the north area have been set aside as desert preserves. Most of the university's sustainability programs and projects are now wrapped into the Global Institute of Sustainability established by ASU President Michael Crow.

As the global population continues to grow and to become more urban, place-making possibilities expand. At the beginning of the twentieth century, two billion people inhabited the planet. The Earth currently has more than 6.8 billion inhabitants. The United Nations projects the world's population to plateau at 9.4 billion by the year 2050 and then slowly rise to 10.4 billion by 2100.[17] After death rates are considered, this translates into some 12.6 billion additional new individuals appearing on the planet over the next century.[18] Half of the world's population now lives in cities, and the number of these urban inhabit-

**1.7** Rio Salado, Phoenix. River restored after years of abuse by gravel mining and dumps. Design by Ten Eyck Landscape Architects. Photograph by Bill Timmerman.

**1.8** From President Juscelino Kubitschek de Oliveira mausoleum, Brasília, Brazil. Brasília was planned by Lúcio Costa, with main buildings by Oscar Niemeyer, inaugurated in 1960. Photograph by Frederick Steiner.

ants is expected to double by 2030.[19] We live in the first urban century. By 2050, two-thirds of the people in the world will be living in urban regions. Our challenge is to design healthy, sustainable, and safe city-regions for those who will be joining us on the planet.

To make place matter, designers and planners must become ecologically literate. Certainly, this was the foundation of McHarg's argument that we should "design with nature." Architect Grant Hildebrand contends that such design is fundamental to our species. He writes that "some characteristics of our surroundings, natural and artificial, may bear to some of our innate survival-supportive behaviors."[20] In his exploration of architecture's biological roots, George Hersey concludes, "we build and inhabit giant plants, animals, or body parts."[21] Stephen Kellert and others call such an approach "biophilic design," which emphasizes "the necessity of maintaining, enhancing, and restoring the beneficial experience of nature in the built environment."[22]

### DESIGN WITH TIME

Third, we need to consider time more seriously. ASU Vice President for Research Jonathan Fink asked me to lead the preparation of a plan for the next one hundred years for the Phoenix region. A century was a relatively short time for a geologist like Dr. Fink, who gave me Stewart Brand's *The*

*Clock of the Long Now*[23] to read. No one had ever asked me to think a century ahead until Dr. Fink's request, and Greater Phoenix 2100, as we named the project, indeed gave me the opportunity to ponder "time and responsibility" (the subtitle of Brand's book).

The British architectural theorist Jeremy Till argues "that time, and not space, should be seen as the primary context in which architecture should be conceived."[24] Till's thesis could certainly be extended to landscape architecture and planning, and probably interior design. Arguably, how time is addressed distinguishes the education of architects from that of planners and landscape architects, who must deal with time in their work as parks and communities are conceived for change. Certainly, time already falls in the providence of historic preservation.

In 2009, I visited Brazil for the first time. I found Brasilia both amazing and disheartening. One wonders what would have been the consequences if the designers of the new city—the urban planner Lúcio Costa, the architect Oscar Niemeyer, and the landscape architect Roberto Burle Marx—would have given time equal attention as space (Figure 1.8). As it is, Brasilia's spaces are frozen in a time that, although impressive in scale and ambition, creates an anachronism. Still, Brasilia is only fifty years old, and time will indeed tell.

This is probably my bias, but I find Niemeyer's works in collaboration with Marx stronger than his projects without the innovative landscape architect. Marx constructed living elements from Brazil in Niemeyer's geometric spaces. However, Marx's more impressive works are those without all the concrete, such as his home just outside Barra (Rio de Janeiro's fastest growing suburb), where he painted with plants (Figure 1.9). The concrete of Brazilian Modernism implies that time is frozen, which is not possible with plants that, by their nature, grow through time.

Marx clearly understood the regions where he worked. He adjusted his designs to respond to regional conditions. Regions provide a scale where the consequences of time become evident.

**1.9** Sítio Roberto Burle Marx, Barra de Guaratiba, Brazil. Photograph by Frederick Steiner.

## PROSPECTUS

As architects, designers, and planners, we are often faced with apparently conflicting goals. Do we remain absolute or compromise? Can we sustain nature, meet the demands of the marketplace, serve social justice, and create beauty, all at the same time? "Only, I suspect," John Meunier has observed, "with the exercise of great talent, wit, hard work, and intellectual flexibility." He further notes, and I concur, that a great university is the right place to prepare individuals for that daunting challenge.

Architecture and planning programs at our great universities need to adapt in order to lead in this first urban century. A starting point would be to require ecological literacy for all architecture, planning, and landscape architecture students. Such literacy would include an understanding of climate, geology, hydrology, and biology (as Vitruvius suggested long ago), as well as exposure to the humanities and the ability to measure certain phenomena. Literacy would help us understand the patterns that surround us, the patterns that emerge from many interacting processes. This would enable our graduates to better connect their work to built and natural environments. We should also teach students how to learn from precedent and how to become reflective practitioners.

One of the principal lessons of design is that we do not know the end when we begin. It is a process of discovery. We explore many options through design. We start with a challenge; we take that challenge into the studio, where we test concepts. Our concepts do not come out of thin air but are informed from our experience and our knowledge. The more we explore, the more we expand that experience and that knowledge.

We face many challenges in our built environments. In this first urban century, the future of the city poses a significant challenge. We should embrace this challenge and explore new concepts for designing and planning our cities with creativity and with knowledge.

The artifacts of design provide physical shape to cultural identity. An improved environment can provide the context for positive interactions among people. The more we know about and care for our surroundings, and the more we interact with and care about other people on that account, the greater is the potential for knowledge to thrive. Such knowledge is capital. Only with such capital can a civilization—a culture—be created for a city-region that is worthy of the grandeur of its natural surroundings.

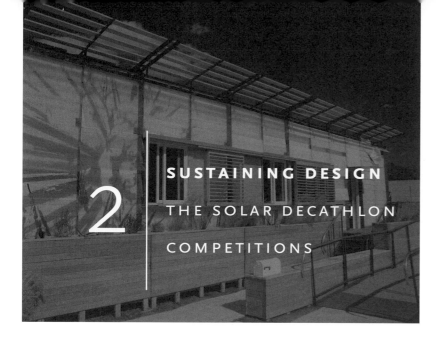

## 2

### SUSTAINING DESIGN
### THE SOLAR DECATHLON
### COMPETITIONS

To enable our students to think comprehensively and to empower place-making, my colleagues and I have taken several actions in Austin to advance sustainability in design and planning education. For instance, we created the Center for Sustainable Development in 2002 as a multidisciplinary effort led by the architecture, planning, and historic preservation programs at the University of Texas at Austin (UT-Austin) School of Architecture. Since a landscape architecture degree did not exist, we created a new master's degree. We renamed the "design with climate" master's program, which had been established in 1972. The renamed Master of Science in Sustainable Design complements concentrations in sustainable design that were available to architecture, planning, and historic preservation majors. The sustainable design program with landscape architecture forged strong ties across campus with geography, natural science, engineering, and public affairs. Adapting former ASU dean John Meunier's fourth "e," we added esthetics to the traditional three "e"s—equity, environment, and economics—to help define our new center and degrees.[1]

The four "e"s suggest strengthening interdisciplinary education. We need to find better ways for social scientists to communicate with natural scientists and for both to communicate with economists. The design disciplines can play a mediating and communicative role among the scientists. To do so, architects can build on traditional strengths in physics and climatology; landscape architects with their strengths in ecology, soil science, and hydrology; and planners in social science and economics. Beyond the sciences, the skills of other professions—most notably law and engineering, as well as the humanities—must be engaged in a truly interdisciplinary approach to sustainability education.

The basic concept of sustainability is that we leave the planet a better place than we found it. This concept forms the very heart of the design and planning disciplines: We seek to build a better world. From its Latin roots "*sub*" and "*tenere*," to sustain means "to uphold" or "to keep."[2] Sustainable development can be traced back to the innovative American forester Gifford Pinchot, who pioneered an approach to managing natural resources based on "multiple use and sustained yield." The concept gained much broader attention after the Brundtland Commission of the United Nations issued its well-known 1987 report, *Our Common Future*. The Brundtland report noted that the present generation should consider the consequences of their actions on future generations and defined sustainable development as "development that meets the needs of the present generation without compromising the ability of future generations to meet their own needs."[3]

Critics argue that sustainable development goes too far or does not go far enough. Sustainable development seeks to balance the three "e"s of environment, economics, and equity. Laissez-faire economic determinists argue that the market will create development with the greatest good. More environmentally inclined scholars argue that we must go beyond sustaining the planet—that is, maintaining what is—and create new organic forms of human settlement. For example, the late landscape architect and architect John Lyle of Cal Poly Pomona advocated a regenerative approach to planning and design.[4]

Still, we need to begin by sustaining what we have. The design and planning of the built environment has much to contribute to that goal. As noted by Philip R. Berke, "There is a growing consensus in scientific and technical evidence that greening urban form has significant effects on advancing sustainable development."[5]

Deep interest in and knowledge about sustainable development exists in the UT-Austin School of Architecture. Professor Michael Garrison, who helped establish our School's innovative design with climate program in the 1970s and contributed to Austin's pioneering green building program, led our first Solar Decathlon effort.[6] He, Pliny Fisk, and a student team designed and built an environmentally and energy-savvy house. Our team joined finalists from thirteen other schools of architecture and engineering on the National Mall in Washington, D.C., in fall 2002. The Yoda of green design, Fisk and I share a common background at the University of Pennsylvania, but he had a checkered past with the UT-Austin School of Architecture because he had been on the faculty during the 1970s, then left to start an independent center in Austin. I was an admirer who was looking forward to working with Pliny, who has the temperament of a scruffy academic. (At our first meeting, the week after I became dean, he presented me with a bill for $150,000 for past services rendered. Not an auspicious beginning.)

Our energetic, gangling associate dean for undergraduate programs, David Heymann, had already designed and built a house using some

sustainable technologies for George W. Bush and Laura Bush near Crawford, Texas. This bold design would have received broad national acclaim had not 9/11 created greater concerns for presidential security, a relatively minor casualty in the larger tragedy of the 2001 terrorist attacks. Sadly, President Bush did not follow the standard he established for his own house and advocate sustainable design for the nation—a more significant casualty, which cannot be blamed on foreign terrorists.

Through the spring of 2002, a group of students and recent graduates continued to work with Michael Garrison and Pliny Fisk on our first Solar Decathlon house. The project required that I seek out support not only to build the house, but also to transport it to Washington, D.C. Several alumni and businesses made generous contributions to the effort.

Sustainable, or green, design, such as that of the Solar Decathlon entry, was a focus of our broader efforts to build the Center for Sustainable Development. Our alumni embraced and encouraged this endeavor. For example, one day I had lunch at the studio of TeamHaas Architects. Alumnus Stan Haas had recently designed an inventive combination elementary school/community center using sustainable design principles. The St. John Community Center/J. J. Pickle Elementary School in a neglected East Austin neighborhood received a sustainability grant from the Texas Energy Conservation Office to incorporate green building features such as a rain collection system and a site design orientation to maximize solar lighting and heating (Figure 2.1). The facility, located in one of the city's first African-American communities, also includes a public library, a public gym, a police substation, and a senior center. As a result, the social equity dimensions of sustainability are addressed along with environmental features.

The combination school and neighborhood center required both considerable intergovernmental cooperation and active community engagement in the planning and design process. The J. J. Pickle Elementary School makes generous use of natural daylight, as schools did before air conditioning and central heating sealed us off

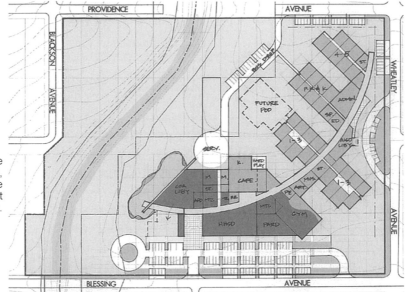

The schoolrooms bend with the bow, allowing ideal exposure to the North and South for all of the classrooms.

This orientation was desirable for the Public Library as well, so it is pulled away from the rest of the building mass as if it were the tip of the bow.

Parking for visitors and teachers alike is concentrated along Blessing Avenue, leaving the school's main entry on Wheatley Avenue to the East free of obvious conflicts with drop-off traffic and school bus queuing.

The school's wings, called "pods" in Austin school parlance, are separated by courtyards planted with trees to shade southern exposures, and possibly to serve as gardens for the schoolchildren.

A pedestrian bridge will tie the center and school to the existing park across Buttermilk Creek.

A fire lane and turning circle to the West of the gymnasium has been appropriated as a hardscape play space with basketball goals, and direct access to the gym.

**2.1** Site design for solar orientation of the St. John Community Center/J. J. Pickle Elementary School, Austin. Design by TeamHaas (now Nelson Partners). Courtesy of Stan Haas.

from the outdoors. The project includes rainwater harvesting and employs natural and native materials. The school district and the City of Austin expect overall energy costs will be reduced by 25 percent compared to similar projects, which will result in a $4.5 million savings to the taxpayers over a twenty-five-year period. Perhaps most significantly, schoolchildren, teachers, and local residents enjoy visiting a beautiful facility to learn, to recreate, and to congregate.

Our lunch coincided with a visit by Jim Hartzfield of Interface. The CEO of Interface, Ray Anderson, had reoriented the carpet manufacturing business around sustainability. Hartzfield made a presentation to the TeamHaas staff and me about sustainable development. He reiterated Anderson's seven corporate strategies to pursue sustainability:

- eliminate waste
- eliminate harmful emissions
- use renewable energy
- create closed-loop processes
- minimize moving people and material
- integrate sustainability into the corporate culture
- pioneer new business models for sustainability

Interface's corporate strategies, like those of its rival Shaw Industries, exert growing influence on both architecture and interior design practice. Clients began expecting materials from carpets to paint to be environmentally responsible. As firms led by alumni, such as Stan Haas, became more involved in green design, their support and encouragement for programs like the Solar Decathlon increased.

Our students designed a house for the Department of Energy Solar Decathlon in early 2002 and built it over the summer at Pliny Fisk's Center for Maximum Potential Building Systems (CMPBS) compound in East Austin. In September, the 800-square-foot (74.32-m²) house was deconstructed, loaded on four flatbed trucks, and shipped across the nation to Washington, D.C. The students reconstructed it on the National Mall in five days.

Our team received considerable attention from the other thirteen finalist teams because the UT-Austin students constructed their house as a set of parts (to sit more lightly on the land), rather than taking the prefabricated approach used by other university teams. They worked without a crane, which had originally been a National Park Service requirement for decathlon construction on the Mall. Our group was busy on site in Washington late into the night and thus was highly visible and accessible for interviews.

Michael Garrison noted how moving it was to be building the house on September 22, the fall equinox, a little more than a year after the 9/11 terrorist attacks, and on the same night Congress stayed in late session debating the invasion of Iraq. As the sun set in line with the Washington Monument, the full moon rose over the lighted Capitol dome and illuminated the night as Garrison and Fisk worked with the student team to realize their creation.

Our team's approach was initially greeted with some skepticism because other groups appeared to be finishing more quickly. But by the time I arrived on September 27, the UT-Austin students were almost done, while other teams struggled to make the deadline. At the last minute, the team determined the house needed some plants, so

they bought several hanging flowers from Home Depot, and Fisk presented the bill to me. Our Home Depot plants were among the few landscape elements evident in the Solar Village on the National Mall in this first decathlon.

The next morning, the Design and Livability jury (which included 2002 Pritzker Laureate Glenn Murcutt; University of Washington professor and green design pioneer Steve Badanes, a founding member of the design-build practice known as "Jersey Devil"; and Ed Mazria, a leading architect in the energy conservation potentials of buildings, of New Mexico) inspected the house. The jurors liked our house and conducted a constructive feedback session with six of our students. (About twenty-five students contributed to the project, but only six could participate in the design review.) The UT-Austin team received third place for Design and Livability. Among other features, the team's concept of transportability intrigued the judges. Many mechanical systems fit in an Airstream trailer, which was integral to our team's overall design.

The competition includes ten categories: design and livability, design presentation and simulation, graphics and communication, the comfort zone, refrigeration, hot water, energy balance, lighting, home business, and getting around. After the scores were totaled for the ten contests, the University of Colorado team emerged as the overall winner and the University of Virginia as the runner-up. The Colorado team had done an especially good job integrating the engineering and architectural concerns of the competition. More than one hundred thousand people visited the first U.S. Department of Energy Solar Decathlon. John D. Quale, the faculty advisor for the Virginia entry, made the following observation about the initial competition: "In this day and age of deepening cynicism about the role of government in society, it is incredible to me that such an extraordinary group of people can survive and even thrive while working for a vast government bureaucracy. It gives me hope that government really can have a positive impact."[7]

Considerable collegiality existed among the teams and with the competition organizers, including that "vast government bureaucracy." The event occurred in the heart of the nation's capital and provided a positive example of the potential of sustainable design. The first Solar Decathlon presented an important learning and outreach effort for all participants, especially the students, but also for their faculty advisors. In our case, Garrison, Fisk (and his CMPBS colleagues), and even those of us who watched on the sidelines learned in the way that teachers often learn from their students. We cheered on the home team, helped to raise funds, and assisted with various bureaucratic approvals.

As soon as the first competition ended, we began planning for the second. Our 2005 Solar Decathlon entry was named "SNAP House" (Super Nifty Action Package). Mayor Will Wynn proclaimed Tuesday, September 6, 2005, "Solar D Day" in the City of Austin. We held a ribbon-cutting celebration at the Solar Decathlon SNAP House in East Austin to recognize the mayor's proclamation, as well as the efforts of our students and their faculty advisors, including Michael Garrison, Samantha (Sam) Randall, and Elizabeth Alford.

Like the 2002 Solar Decathlon entry, the 2005 SNAP House involved a modular design intended to minimize the environmental impact, but instead of thousands of parts to be assembled, the SNAP House was built in four chunks that are snapped together to reduce on-site construction time (Figure 2.2). The student team used programmatic modules for the kitchen, bath, bed, and office areas to maximize livability and adaptability of the small 800-square-foot (74-m²) dwelling.

In addition to our ongoing Solar Decathlon projects, our faculty engaged in several other initiatives under the banner of our Center for Sustainable Development. A grant from the Henry Luce Foundation supported fellowships for graduate students in sustainable design. Building on our M.S. in Sustainable Design, we created a portfolio program (like a graduate minor) in sustainability for master's and doctoral candidates in eight academic units across campus.

Along with helping students, the Luce grant enabled us to retain visiting professor Sergio Palleroni, who engaged our students in design-build projects for the poor in Sonora, Mexico, and East Austin. Palleroni and Steven Moore's work was featured in an episode of the 2006 PBS documentary series *design e²*, narrated by Brad Pitt.

At the same time, Liz Mueller, of the School of

**2.2** Congressman Lamar Smith visits students at the University of Texas at Austin's solar-powered SNAP House during the first day of the Solar Decathlon at the National Mall in Washington, D.C., Friday, October 7, 2005. Photograph by Stefano Paltera/Solar Decathlon.

Architecture's Community and Regional Planning Program, received a grant from the Rockefeller Foundation to assess the effectiveness of affordable housing programs in Texas. She published detailed report cards on city housing programs in Texas, generally indicating deficiencies in providing affordable housing for poor people. As a result, in addition to advancing green building design, activities of the Center for Sustainable Development focused on equity concerns as exemplified by the work supported by the Rockefeller grant.

In the 2005 Solar Decathlon, our team placed fifth out of a field of eighteen finalists selected by the Department of Energy. The solar houses came from colleges and universities from around the country, as well as Spain, Canada, and Puerto Rico. The Decathlon took place during intense and prolonged rain, limiting the "solar" in the competition. Again, the University of Colorado team emerged as the victor, repeating their strong integration of engineering and architecture. The second-place team from Cornell University made nice advances in the consideration of landscape, planting a lush garden fed by water from the house's roof. In fact, although still mostly on the margins, landscape architecture had advanced beyond our Home Depot plants in 2002 with a couple of green roofs and rain-fed gardens like Cornell's.

Again, we began planning for the next Solar Decathlon immediately after completing the 2005 contest. In both 2005 and 2007, our team won the BP Solar Award, which came with $80,000

worth of solar collectors. With the event's growing success, the Department of Energy decided to increase its base funding from $10,000 to $100,000 per team for up to twenty universities in 2007. This prompted more interest and increased the competition to be selected for the Solar Decathlon on the National Mall. Sam Randall and Michael Garrison submitted a successful grant to the Department of Energy, and we continued our fund-raising.

The members of the 2007 team took a different approach from those of their predecessors. The 2002 and 2005 teams designed kits-of-parts, which had minimal site impacts, but involved building the structure in Austin, deconstructing it, rebuilding it with considerable on-site labor in Washington, then deconstructing it again, and rebuilding the house once again in Austin. The University of Michigan team had taken a similar approach in 2005 with disastrous results: when the heavy rains came, the Michigan students had not completed the roof.

In contrast, the University of Colorado team, which had won the overall first prize in 2002 and 2005, built their house in Boulder, then shipped it intact to Washington. Other top-placing teams used a similar approach. Our faculty and students had resisted designing a "trailer," but adopted this approach for the 2007 Solar Decathlon.

Our team also followed the Colorado example and worked much closer with faculty and students from the College of Engineering. An architectural engineering faculty member remained engaged throughout the process, as did several engineer-

**2.3** Open floor plan of the BLOOMhouse. Drawing by Crystal Bryant Coppinger.

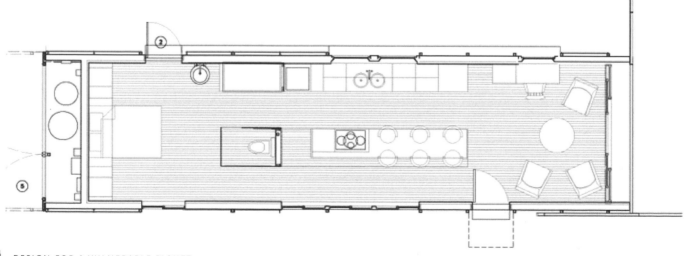

**2.4** University of Texas at Austin team members Liz Jackson, left, Gerby Marks, center, and Christie Zangrilli get ready to host their solar village neighbors on October 15 at the 2007 Solar Decathlon at the National Mall in Washington, D.C. Teams host dinner parties to get to know one another and to fulfill a requirement in the appliances portion of the competition. Photograph by Kaye Evans-Lutterodt/Solar Decathlon.

ing students. A graphic design student contributed much to our team identity. Landscape architects were involved, too, but more on the margins than in the core of the effort.

Indeed, the lack of landscape design was evident throughout the field of competitors. "For all the dramatic solar technologies, contemporary architecture, and engineering applications showcased in the competition, resource-saving landscape design was largely absent," Seth Wilberding observed in *Landscape Architecture* magazine, adding that "relatively few teams took full advantage of the opportunity to demonstrate landscape as an integral and viable component of energy-saving residential design."[8]

As our team built the 2007 house in an abandoned hangar at the former Mueller Airport, Pliny Fisk, now at Texas A&M University, led a rival team, using a kit-of-parts approach. Our students dubbed their 530-square-foot (49.24-m²), one-bedroom entry "BLOOMhouse," symbolizing a home that blossoms new ideas. Through its design, they sought to demonstrate the adaptable and dynamic nature of both the house itself, as well as solar power more generally. The students based their design on five "principles of life: community, adaptability, harvest, endurance, and delight."

BLOOMhouse was designed as a prototype that could be expanded to 1,540 square feet (143.07 m²) with three bedrooms and two baths with a $175,000 sales price (Figure 2.3).

The 2007 design used a new type of building envelope. A steel "moment" frame was used, instead of sheer walls, for structural stability. The moment frame allows the interior to be completely open to make small interior spaces appear larger. This structure enhances the possibilities for daylighting, cross-ventilation, and easy indoor/outdoor relationships (Figure 2.4). The design incorporated photovoltaic panels in a butterfly shape on the roof. The building envelope was made with airtight, 6-inch (15.2 cm) Structurally Insulated Panels (SIPS) with an R-24 insulation valve to reduce heating and cooling costs.[9] The insulation-sandwiched SIPS are aluminum-skinned for the walls and roof and wood-skinned for the floors. Applied to the outside of the SIP is a graphic printed on material donated by 3M. The skin shingles are polycarbonate sheets (made by Polygal and Gallina), which were cut to fit between each of the moment frames of the house. The 3M material skin permitted the students to design striking visual images on the building skins. Our team also received the donation of a solar-heated

hot tub, which was used to discharge excess heat from the solar system and to be enjoyed during the autumn nights in Washington.

On Friday, September 28, our Solar Decathlon BLOOMhouse slid off the flatbed truck that would take it to Washington. Fortunately, the accident occurred near the hangar on the Mueller Airport site where the BLOOMhouse had been constructed. Also fortunately, beyond a few sore fingers, there were no serious injuries. The community of students with their faculty advisor Russell Krepart pulled the house back on the truck. They were aided by film workers from the nearby Austin Film Studio. Krepart reported later in the day that the truck and a second one carrying parts for the BLOOMhouse had successfully departed (Figure 2.5).[10]

I arrived in Washington on a sunny Saturday afternoon as the competition was coming to an end. Large crowds of people continued to queue up to visit the twenty solar houses. After meeting our faculty and students, I stopped by several other entries. At this point, the results were already known. Our team finished construction before the others and started in first place. For most of the competition, the Longhorn team scored between third and seventh. On the last day, our team fumbled on one of the events and fell to tenth place. The buzz on the Mall that afternoon (and the preceding days) was about the German team from the Technische Universität Darmstadt. In the spacious kitchen of the BLOOMhouse, Sam Randall noted that every time the Darmstadt team won an event, and they won or placed high in many events, the rumored amount of how much the house cost jumped another $1 million, eventually reaching $10 million.

That evening, the student leader of the Darmstadt team set the record straight: "Our house *only* cost $1.5 million." In addition, they had shipped the house and around fifty students and faculty from Germany. With food and lodging, the Germans' expenses probably ran another $250,000. We had spent a total of $410,000 on ours, a respectable amount. Clearly, the Germans (as well as the team from Spain) spent more on their projects than any of their American

counterparts in the event sponsored by the U.S. Department of Energy. Indicating their support for alternative forms of energy, Spain hosted a Solar Decathlon Europe in 2010, the year after the fourth U.S. event, in Madrid.

On Sunday evening in September 2007, most of the houses had been taken apart and loaded on trucks for their journeys home. I stopped by the BLOOMhouse, then walked across the path to the De Stijl–patterned University of Cincinnati entry. The students asked me if I was connected to Texas or Cincinnati. I answered, "Both," explaining that I was a Cincinnati alumnus. They wondered if the Texas team was in deficit. "No," I responded, reflecting on the final $16,000 I had recently reimbursed for yet another unexpected expense. The Cincinnati team noted that they were thousands of dollars in the red.

As I said my farewells to the Cincinnatians and walked back to the hotel, I wondered if it was all worth it. On the positive side, the competition provides a worthwhile learning opportunity for the students and great visibility for the participants. It introduces the possibilities of solar energy to a broad constituency. On the other hand, the research advances are minimal, and the costs high. I frequently ponder if the money we raise might not be better spent for housing for our less affluent neighbors than on ephemeral competition. In fact, we have shifted our design-build activities in the School away from the Solar Decathlon and toward our Alley Flat Initiative in east Austin. Through this initiative, we are building homes in one of the city's poorest neighborhoods. Also, a few of the School's strongest designers remain critical of the aesthetic values of our entries. Although such criticism often smacks of a visual-only value of esthetics, the appearance of our entries has emphasized function over beauty.

The Darmstadt house was a technical tour de force and elegant architecture (Figure 2.6). The well-crafted skin of oak shutters kept the house cool during the day and opened to create a box that glowed at night. The Germans were capable of advancing bold design and sound technical

2.5 The University of Texas at Austin BLOOMhouse. Photograph by Jeff Kubina.

2.6 Technische Universität Darmstadt 2007 Solar Decathlon house. Photograph by Jim Tetro/Solar Decathlon.

**2.7** BLOOMhouse at McDonald Observatory, Fort Davis, Texas. Photograph by Michael Garrison.

qualities with the generous support of governments and businesses at all levels.

The Solar Decathlon helps advance interdisciplinary education in Europe and North America. At the University of Texas, for example, we developed closer relationships with the College of Engineering as a result of the competition. Architecture faculty increasingly collaborate with engineering faculty on research projects, and we created two new faculty positions, one each in engineering and architecture, to further this cooperation. We also initiated some collaboration between architecture faculty and colleagues in graphic design, interior design, and, to a lesser extent, landscape architecture. Solar Decathlon teams with more mature landscape architecture programs, like Penn State, have advanced this relationship more than we have thus far. Overall, however, the Solar Decathlon advances interdisciplinary education, which is necessary to further learning about sustainable design.

The competition contributes to our growing understanding of solar energy. For instance, the BLOOMhouse now resides at the McDonald Observatory near Ft. Davis, Texas (Figure 2.7). It houses observatory staff and helps power scientific experiments. In the future, the Observatory's visitor center will display information about the BLOOMhouse, solar energy, and zero-net energy housing.

# 3 TWENTY-FIRST-CENTURY ARCHITECTURE

s I sat below the giant live oaks in my Austin, Texas, backyard, reading *The Perfect House*, Witold Rybczynski's insightful book about architect Andrea Palladio,[1] a mosquito bit my forearm. The bite and the muggy early September weather reminded me of my childhood in southern Ohio. I grew up where small rivers navigate among the moraines created by Wisconsin glaciers. Ohio pioneers built their settlements with nature in mind. Our house had a large front porch and a screened-in room in the rear. A mature hard maple shaded the front yard and separated the house from the sidewalk and the street. A pitched roof directed melting snow into gutters, then down to the ground. After a flooding season or two, the early Ohioans avoided building shops and houses in river lowlands, choosing instead the slopes of small hills, the wealthy somewhat higher up.

Between Ohio and Austin, I lived in the desert city of Phoenix. New settlement in the Sonoran Desert is made possible by air conditioning, refrigeration, and an efficient water collection and distribution system. I never felt natural living there, though others do. The Tohono O'odham people still do, their ancestors having adapted to the desert long before electricity.

Reading about Palladio, I ponder the future of architecture. Twentieth-century technology allowed us to settle places like southern Arizona, southern California, and much of Texas in great numbers. Around the planet, we produced an architecture of boxes, some glass and transparent, others opaque and windowless. We created cities disconnected from nature; cities kept alive by networks of wires and pipes and roads. Where nature recycles all of the "wastes" naturally produced, these contemporary cities are waste factories. Indeed, the very concept of waste is a recent urban invention, emerging with the Industrial Revolution in the nineteenth century. For instance, human excreta, once considered a raw material, became sewage as concern for hygiene in growing cities increased.[2]

Terrorism, AIDS, global warming, biological and nuclear weapons, population pressures, desertification, erosion, mad cow disease, suburban sprawl, diminished farmland and fishery habitats, the decline in biodiversity: We face an uncertain, even dangerous, future. Increasingly, the wires, the pipes, and the roads resemble the life-support systems of patients in hospital recovery wards. Within this mix of issues, buildings and the built environment contribute much to current challenges.

Buildings produce around 46 percent of the greenhouse gases in the United States and consume about 50 percent of the energy used in the nation. Meanwhile, because of population growth, we will need to produce many more build-

3.1 Fredericks or White House, Jamberoo, New South Wales, Australia. Design by Glenn Murcutt. Photograph by Max Dupain, April 1983.

ings. By 2030, half the buildings will have been constructed between 2000 and then.[3] Beyond buildings, we will also need twice as many roads, parks, water and sewer lines, and other infrastructure. The implications for architecture, planning, landscape architecture, historic preservation, and interior design should be clear.

Beyond the building, elements like paving, especially black asphalt for roads and parking lots, result in several problems. For instance, dark surfaces absorb much more heat than light surfaces, which reflect sunlight. As a result, dark surfaces, such as those consisting of black asphalt, contribute to urban heat islands. In addition, hard surfaces increase surface runoff after storms and decrease water infiltration. Flooding and groundwater recharge problems result. Meanwhile, the more we pave, the more wildlife habitat and prime farmland we lose. Green roofs, colored concrete pavement, rubberized asphalt, absorbent paving materials, smaller parking lots and roads, and more trees would do much to improve urban microclimates, enhancing comfort and livability.

We need an architecture for these times, a broadly defined architecture that helps us

3.2 View from Scottsdale Road in Arizona of a reused shopping center from the Flip a Strip Competition, sponsored by the Scottsdale Museum of Contemporary Arts. Design by AEDS Ammar Eloueini with Smoothcore Architects.

address many of the issues we have created and now face. More comprehensive architecture would help us restore the health of our planet through the design of regenerative buildings and communities.

What do I mean by regenerative? A design that begins with sustainability in mind but goes even further to create living, self-organizing networks of structures: organic, living machines.

At least five elements should be addressed in comprehensive, twenty-first-century architecture: the location of the site, energy efficiency, water conservation, building materials, and beauty.

## REUSE EXISTING SITES

From Vitruvius through Palladio, from Frank Lloyd Wright to Glenn Murcutt, architects have been concerned with identifying the ideal site or, at least, making the most out of challenged ones (Figure 3.1). For example, Murcutt's Fredericks House in Jamberoo, New South Wales, consists of two parallel pavilions designed in the landscape to allow natural light to permeate the living areas. Ideal sites involve healthy and safe locations with good solar orientation and drainage. By now, nearly all of the best sites have been taken. A first rule for this new architecture would be: do not build on prime farmland or valuable habitats or vulnerable floodplains or any other environmentally sensitive area. After ruling out such areas, little of the so-called green-field sites would remain.

So where do we build? We should restore places that have already been built upon. Reusing built land requires changing how we analyze sites (Figure 3.2). We need to explore if soils have been contaminated. If so, what are the reasonable prospects for their restoration? We need to study the footprints of those who have preceded us. This involves understanding the history and context of the site. We should seek out places accessible by transit, which is especially important for young people, the disabled, and the elderly. Pedestrian and bicycle connectivity are important considerations as well.

## DESIGN WITH RENEWABLE SOURCES

At one time, site analysis considered maximizing the potential for natural heating and cooling. Central heating and air conditioning systems forced the art of such analyses to the sidelines. A second rule for a new architecture then would be: design with renewable sources. The twentieth-century city was built by mining the compost of the distant past. Most of the world's energy comes from coal, natural gas, and oil, that is, fuels made from fossils, which are not renewable. Additional energy is

**3.3** Five thousand wind turbines stretch out over the Tehachapi hills in California. Wind power represents only about 3 percent of installed electricity-generating capacity. The U.S. wind industry grew by 45 percent in 2007. Wind generators require no water for steam or cooling, no outside fuel for operation, and produce no greenhouse gases. Photograph by Alex MacLean.

derived from nuclear power, which produces hazardous waste that persists for generations. The United States and China possess considerable coal resources, but coal presents significant social and environmental challenges when mined and burned. Persian Gulf nations possess two-thirds of the world's known oil supplies, which has exacerbated international tensions and conflicts.

By contrast, geothermal, hydroelectric, solar, and wind sources are renewable (Figure 3.3). Twenty-first-century design would require an understanding of climate and hydrology. Obviously, weather and water flows vary from place to place, so region- and landscape-specific knowledge will be vital.

## DESIGN TO COLLECT WATER AND REDUCE RUNOFF

Such understanding is also crucial to ensure sustainable supplies of clean drinking water. The design of buildings and communities has considerable impact on the hydrologic cycle. The more impervious surfaces we create, the less water infiltrates the ground, recharging valuable aquifers. As more water runs across the surface, more soil erosion results, and more pollutants are carried from our driveways and lawns into streams and rivers. Increased runoff also contributes to flooding as more water enters rivers and streams, and more quickly than it would naturally.

A third rule of new architecture, therefore, would be: conserve water. We can design buildings and communities to capture water and reduce runoff. Imagine individual buildings, each with its own water-harvesting device, surrounded by native plants that reduce the need for irrigation (Figure 3.4). Imagine streets and parking lots constructed of permeable surfaces recharging aquifers and reducing heating effects of black asphalt.

## KNOW THE ENVIRONMENTAL COSTS

Materials, like asphalt, come from somewhere in the earth and return to someplace else after they

are used. The environment is a source and a sink. Look around. Where does that carpet come from? What materials were used to create it? When you tire of its look and tear it up, where will it go? Keep looking around at the walls and the ceilings. Go outside and look at the roofs and the foundations (Figure 3.5).

Architecture involves the assembly of stuff. How we put it together has long-term consequences for our health and for the quality of our lives. Our fourth rule then becomes: know both the source of the materials used to construct designs, as well as the environmental costs of transforming them from raw material states into a finished product. In addition, plan for the next use of the building materials: can they be recycled

**3.4** Rainwater capture system, Lady Bird Johnson Wildflower Center, Austin. Design by Overland Partners. Photograph by Bruce Leander.

**3.5** A view of the American Society of Landscape Architects headquarters green roof from an adjacent building, Washington, D.C. Design by Michael Van Valkenburgh Associates and Conservation Design Forum. Courtesy of the American Society of Landscape Architects.

or biodegraded back to the earth? Local materials can be efficient while reinforcing the indigenous character of the region.

## ADVANCE BEAUTY

And what about beauty? Attempts to create green buildings and sustainable designs have yielded too little of it. Many early buildings produced by green architects appear like post-hippie structures, habitable granola bars, which may be good for us, but leave us wanting. Since the late twentieth century, a handful of inventive green architects have emerged who marry environmentalism and aesthetics: Glenn Murcutt from Australia, Will Bruder and Rick Joy from Arizona, Philadelphia's Andropogon Associates, Ken Yeang of Kuala Lumpur, Brian MacKay-Lyons in Nova Scotia, and several young Dutch, Scandinavian, Swiss, and German architects. But still, a compelling environmental aesthetic remains just beyond our reach.

The creation of such an aesthetic presents an important architectural challenge and a creativity opportunity. Our final rule then should be: advance beauty. We have much to learn from nature's design. Nature has been in the business of design much longer than we humans, who are, after all, but one product of nature's design.

## FROM PRINCIPLES TO ACTION

Architects need to foster new approaches to building design for the twenty-first century. Schools, libraries, and other public buildings offer a good starting point.

Several years ago, I found myself in a Dallas hotel on a Sunday morning watching "Meet the Press." Laura Bush and Caroline Kennedy were the featured guests. Ms. Kennedy observed, "When you go to some of the schools that were built maybe one hundred years or ninety years ago and you see kind of these cathedrals to education and the immigrant dream of coming here and what people can become, I think that is what we really want to get back to." Mrs. Bush, a librarian

and former public school teacher, added: "Education has to be the most important thing. I remember reading an article once about John Updike, who said in his little town, the school, the high school, was the prettiest building. It was the best architecture. And it made him think that everyone in the city thought that the children and their education was most important, because that building, that school building, was the best-looking building in the city."

Indeed, both public schools and libraries are cathedrals to education. And our public libraries are one area where we hold a competitive edge over our Chinese brethren.

I have visited China five times in the past five years. The Chinese are famously commited to grand architecture, as was showcased in the 2008 Olympics. At the neighborhood level, when walking around Beijing, it is evident that significant investments are being made in their schools. The shock and outrage following the May 2008 earthquake in Sichuan Province especially focused on faulty school construction. Already, Chinese officials have made progress to reform school design and construction.

However, we have something the Chinese do not.

A free flow of information.

By making information accessible to all, our public libraries are *beacons* of enlightenment. For without knowledge, democracy is unattainable.

I grew up in Dayton, Ohio, an active manufacturing city where lots of things were built, including cash registers, batteries, tires, refrigerators, and various automobile and airplane parts—many of which are now constructed in China—and I remember fondly our cathedral to education, the Dayton Public Library.

Two American cities, Phoenix and Seattle, stand out for their recent leadership in library design. These two cities took very different approaches. Phoenix selected Will Bruder, an up-and-coming local architect, sculptor, and Rome Prize winner who had studied with the ecological idealist and urban visionary, Paolo Soleri. The result was brilliant. Completed in 1995, the

Phoenix Central Library pioneered green building technology into its design (Figure 3.6). It is a lovely building that has become a civic landmark. Architect Bruder also brought the library in under budget.

In contrast, Seattle hired international superstar Rem Koolhaas and his firm, the Office for Metropolitan Architecture (OMA). As in Phoenix, though, the result was a stunning, popular success. Like the Phoenix Central Library, the Seattle Central Library has become an important civic icon. Opened in 2004, more than 2 million individuals visited the new library in the first year. In 2007, the building was voted number 108 on the American Institute of Architects' list of America's 150 favorite structures. The list also includes Battle Hall on the University of Texas at Austin campus—the original university library on cam-

pus and now home to the Architecture and Planning library.

However, to me, the big Seattle story is not so much its Central Library, but rather its incredible branch libraries (Figure 3.7). Seattle passed a $196.4 million bond measure called "Libraries for All" and made a system-wide commitment to high quality library design.

I serve on many design awards juries, and the Seattle branch libraries have received an incredible number of awards. Although Seattle chose a superstar for its main library, they took a similar approach to that of Phoenix for the branches, selecting important regional talent. They have both produced real gems.

The William J. Clinton Presidential Library in Little Rock (Figure 3.8) and the Pyramid Arena in Memphis both possess unusual shapes in their

**3.6** Phoenix Central Library south elevation with solar tracking operable horizontal louvers. Design by Will Bruder and DWL. Photograph by Bill Timmerman.

**3.7** Seattle Public Library, Ballard Branch. Design by Bohlin Cywinski Jackson. Photograph by Nic Lehoux.

**3.8** William J. Clinton Presidential Library and Museum, Little Rock, Arkansas. Design by Polshek and Partners (buildings) and Hargreaves Associates (park). Photograph by John Gollings and Hargreaves Associates. Courtesy of Hargreaves Associates.

waterfront settings. One is a successful design, the other not. As a result, they offer lessons for design in this first urban century. The clumsy, stainless steel–clad pyramid was imported from another time and place. The structure is surrounded by highway ramps and forms a barrier

to the Mississippi River. Originally used for basketball, the 32-story arena remained vacant for several years. By contrast, architect James Polshek drew on local and regional references for the presidential library, which cantilevers toward the

Arkansas River, forming "a bridge to the twenty-first century." The library achieved a Leadership in Energy and Environmental Design (LEED) Platinum rating from the U.S. Green Building Council (USGBC).

The Clinton Library is surrounded by a park, which, like the building, is designed to conserve water and energy. Designed by Hargreaves Associates, the 27-acre (11-ha) waterfront park transformed one derelict area into a campus-like setting for the library. Hargreaves performed similar waterfront restorations in Louisville and Chattanooga.

The Clinton Library and Park illustrate the imaginative reuse of an existing site, as well as the wise use of energy, water, and materials. The library and park are also works of beauty. Their success results, in part, from the reintroduction of nature into Little Rock. The library and park offer a new way of looking at nature, a word with ancient roots. Nature is derived from the Latin word *natura*, which is a translation from the Greek *physis*. The library and park help connect people to the natural course of things. Considerable evidence suggests that humans need connections to nature, especially in urban areas.

# 4

## ARCHITECTURE HAS
## LEFT THE BUILDING
### THE SUSTAINABLE
### SITES INITIATIVE

In September 2005, a site sustainability summit commenced in the basement meeting room at the Lady Bird Johnson Wildflower Center. I welcomed the forty-five invited participants—including landscape architects, architects, ecologists, planners, engineers, experts in sustainable materials, and park professionals—to the two-day event on behalf of the Wildflower Center, the co-organizer with the American Society of Landscape Architects (ASLA). The goal of the two organizations was to set in motion the development of an evaluation tool. The purpose of the tool would be to measure the sustainable attribute of a site beyond what was currently measured within the certification process for the U.S. Green Building Council's (USGBC) Leadership in Energy and Environmental Design (LEED) program. Although the LEED program has significantly advanced green building—and awards credit for some site-related strategies, such as planting native species and conserving water— the summit's organizers believed more could be accomplished in regard to the land itself (Figure 4.1). The participants at the summit reached the same conclusion and advocated the development of a national sustainability metric for landscapes. This metric would be designed as a stand-alone tool, as well as one that could subsequently be incorporated into the LEED certification process pending approval by the USGBC.

Austin was the right place, and it was the right time to start this initiative. In November 2002, the USGBC held its first international conference in Austin. The organizers expected two thousand registrants. More than forty-one hundred attended from sixteen different countries. Since the inaugural Austin meeting, the annual USGBC Greenbuild International Conferences have grown exponentially to reach an attendance of more than twenty-seven thousand at the 2009 meeting in Phoenix.

### GETTING STARTED

In order to produce a LEED or LEED-like product for sites, it is useful to understand the evolution of the USGBC, which had been initiated in 1994 by the Natural Resources Defense Council (NRDC). NRDC senior scientist Robert Watson, a protégé of Amory Lovins and Hunter Lovins of the Rocky Mountain Institute, organized and chaired a steering committee, which consisted of diverse organizations (nonprofits, government agencies, developers, and product manufacturers), as well as several disciplines (architecture, engineering, and business). This broad approach contributes to the success of both the LEED program and the USGBC.

The LEED certification process was first released in 2000 as a standard for new building

construction. It offers four levels of certification—certified, silver, gold, and platinum—depending on how many credits a project accrues from within six categories: sustainable sites, water efficiency, energy and atmosphere, materials and resources, indoor air quality, and innovations and the design process (Figure 4.2). The LEED program also involves an accreditation program "to develop and encourage green building expertise across the entire building industry."[1]

From its early focus on new building construction, the LEED program has expanded to address major renovation projects, green buildings that existed before LEED, commercial interiors, homes, neighborhoods, campuses, schools, and retail spaces. The LEED for Neighborhood Development (ND) Program provides a good model for the Sustainable Sites Initiative because of the collaboration among the USGBC, the NRDC, and the Congress for the New Urbanism. This rating system "integrates the principles of smart growth, urbanism, and green building into the first national standard for neighborhood design."[2]

As a result of the 2005 meeting, and using the LEED-ND Program as a model, ASLA formed a partnership with the Lady Bird Johnson Wildflower Center and the U.S. Botanic Garden to launch the

**4.1** Field of bluebonnets at the Lady Bird Johnson Wildflower Center, Austin. Photograph by Bruce Leander.

**4.2** The Visionaire, a thirty-three-story residential condominium building in Battery Park City, Lower Manhattan, featuring a high-efficiency fresh air supply and exhaust system, centrally filtered water, an in-building wastewater treatment system that resupplies toilets and central air-conditioning makeup water, and rainwater harvested on the pesticide-free roof gardens. Design by Rafael Pelli. The Visionaire received a LEED Platinum rating from the U.S. Green Building Council. Photograph by Pelli Clarke Pelli. Courtesy of Pelli Clarke Pelli.

Sustainable Sites Initiative in August 2006. In addition to these leading partners, the Sustainable Sites Initiative includes organizations such as the USGBC, U.S. Environmental Protection Agency, National Recreation and Parks Association, Nature Conservancy, National Association of County and City Health Officials, American Society of Civil Engineers' Environmental and Water Resources Institute, and Center for Sustainable Development of the University of Texas at Austin. The Initiative involved more than fifty subject matter experts in soils, vegetation, hydrology, materials, and human health and well-being from around the country from disciplines such as landscape architecture, urban planning, botany, ecology, engineering, horticulture, soil science, and forestry. This dynamic group of experts was drawn from governmental agencies, universities, and private design and engineering firms that have been on the front lines in trying to improve sites sustainability across the United States.

### THE SCOPE OF THE TASK

The Product Development Committee (PDC) was formed as the steering committee to guide the process and to create regionally sensitive design, implementation, and maintenance standards for sustainable sites. The Initiative aims to apply sustainability principles to any site, with or without buildings, that will be protected, developed, or redeveloped for public or private purposes. We defined the site as the entire project area that is experiencing development and management. Sustainable Sites focuses on the landscape attributes of the site and the integration of the buildings and landscape. A roof could be considered, for example, as well as a yard and a parking lot built for a residence or an office building (Figures 4.3 and 4.4). In addition, the Initiative would add relevance to sites—such as parks, cemeteries, and botanic gardens—without significant buildings, which are not currently covered by the existing LEED standards. The principles of Sustainable Sites will also apply to integrated building-landscape projects like college campuses, urban plazas, and business parks.

4.3 Parking lot at Morris Arboretum, University of Pennsylvania. Top: during rain. Bottom: on dry day. Design by Andropogon Associates, Ltd. Courtesy of Andropogon Associates, Ltd.

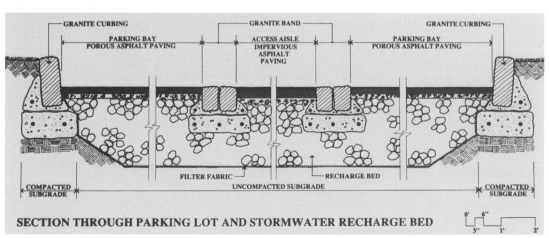

4.4 Section through Morris Arboretum parking lot and stormwater recharge bed. Courtesy of Andropogon Associates, Ltd.

**TABLE 4.1** GOALS FOR THE SUSTAINABLE SITES INITIATIVE

1. Establish a standard for sustainable site-related planning, design, construction, operations, and maintenance practices with clearly defined, measurable benchmarks for attaining sustainability.
   a. Establish quantitative metrics to link sustainable site practices with ecosystem services, such as climate change, biodiversity, clean air and water.
   b. Test performance benchmarks to define and measure the desired relationships between natural and built systems.
2. Link research and practice so that knowledge gained strengthens and supports both. Develop and advance best practices with the intent of accelerating change in the marketplace and gaining broad public acceptance.
3. Transform the market by encouraging adoption of sustainability standards through incentives.
   a. Integrate sustainable sites into existing tools that improve sustainability in buildings and landscapes.
   b. Explore future options for developing a certified stand-alone site rating system.
   c. Promote awareness of best practices and sustainability standards and their relevance in the marketplace.
   d. Identify and quantify cost savings associated with specific best practices used in lieu of conventional practices.
   e. Assess and quantify the value of ecosystem services preserved or gained through use of landscapes and sustainable site practices.
4. Drive decision-making in landscape-related issues by incorporating economics, the environment, and human well-being.

Source: *Preliminary Report of the Practice Guidelines and Metrics*, The Sustainable Sites Initiative, www.sustainablesites.org, 2007.

**4.5** Bioswale at the High Point neighborhood, a redevelopment project of the Seattle Housing Authority. Design by Mithūn. Photograph © Roger Williams.

Building on the success of LEED standards and other green building tools, the Initiative improved and expanded existing standards for landscape and site components. Existing standards encouraged worthwhile activities such as water conservation and the use of native plants but did not go into the same detail or depth as building standards. The PDC engaged its interdisciplinary experts from design, science, and engineering, synthesizing knowledge from those fields to expand the breadth and flexibility of green building products.

By structuring new channels for dialogue among researchers, practitioners, and public agencies, the Sustainable Sites Initiative aimed to develop a national standard that outlined the overarching characteristics of a sustainable site, regardless of location or typology; established reference points for landscape performance; and offered new methods and metrics to increase recognition and incentives for sustainable site practices. The Initiative extended the standards to new markets by bringing increased relevance to landscape architects, civil engineers, and land managers, as well as to the large project portfolios they design and construct.

The PDC guided the Sustainable Sites Initiative and five expert subcommittees to explore soil, hydrology, waste and materials, vegetation, and human well-being in greater detail. The PDC established ten initial goals for the Sustainable Sites Initiative:

1. Establish a standard for sustainable site-related planning, design, construction, operations, and maintenance practices with clearly defined, measurable baseline thresholds for attaining sustainability.
2. Advance efforts to define and measure sustainable site development, which enhances the relationships between natural and built systems.
3. Link research and practice, so that knowledge gained strengthens and supports both.
4. Develop and advance best practices to accelerate change in the marketplace.
5. Strive for market transformation by encouraging

adoption of sustainability standards through market incentives.
6. Strive to accomplish an integration of the Sustainable Sites Initiative into existing tools, which improve sustainability in buildings and landscapes.
7. Explore future options for developing a stand-alone site tool.
8. Promote awareness of best practices and sustainability standards and their relevance in the marketplace.
9. Assess and quantify the value of ecosystem services preserved or gained through use of best practices.
10. Identify and quantify cost savings associated with specific best practices used in lieu of conventional practices.

These original ten goals were narrowed down to the four in Table 4.1.

## THE PRINCIPLES

Just as the LEED program built on knowledge about building efficiency that had evolved since the 1970s, the Sustainable Sites Initiative grew from the theory—originally espoused by the late Ian McHarg in his 1969 book *Design with Nature*—that landscapes could be designed by using nature as a guide.[3] It also grew from the regenerative design ideas pioneered in the 1970s and 1980s by the late John Lyle, professor of landscape architecture at Cal Poly Pomona, and summarized in his 1994 book, *Regenerative Design for Sustainable Development*.[4] Both McHarg and Lyle advocated that designed systems should replicate the ecological performance of natural systems. A good example of this would be bioswales constructed like natural wetlands in order to detain, cleanse, and infiltrate runoff—mimicking the performance of natural wetlands (Figure 4.5).

Drawing on this rich history of design and environmental theory, the PDC wrote the following set of principles to guide decisions that involve areas of uncertainty in a way that is scientifically and philosophically responsible and consistent.

## Do No Harm

Make no changes to the site that will degrade the surrounding environment. Promote projects on sites where previous disturbance or development presents an opportunity to regenerate ecosystem services through sustainable design.

## Precautionary Principle

Be cautious in making decisions that could create risk to human and environmental health. Some actions can cause irreversible damage. Examine a full range of alternatives—including no action—by being open to contributions from all affected parties.

## Design with Nature and Culture

Create and implement designs that are responsive to economic, environmental, and cultural conditions with respect to the local, regional, and global context.

## Use a Decision-making Hierarchy of Preservation, Conservation, and Regeneration

Maximize and mimic the benefits of ecosystem services by preserving existing environmental features, conserving resources in a sustainable manner, and regenerating lost or damaged ecosystem services.

## Provide Regenerative Systems as Intergenerational Equity

Provide future generations with a sustainable environment supported by regenerative systems and endowed with regenerative resources.

## Support a Living Process

Continuously re-evaluate assumptions and values and adapt to demographic and environmental change.

## Use a Systems Thinking Approach

Understand and value the relationships in an ecosystem and use an approach that reflects and sustains the contributions of ecosystem services; re-establish the integral and essential relationship between natural processes and human activity.

## Use a Collaborative and Ethical Approach

Encourage direct and open communication among colleagues, clients, manufacturers, and users to link long-term sustainability with ethical responsibility.

## Maintain Integrity in Leadership and Research

Implement transparent and participatory leadership, developing research with technical rigor, and communicate new findings in a clear, consistent, and timely manner.

## Foster Environmental Stewardship

In all aspects of land development and management, foster an ethic of environmental stewardship—an understanding that responsible management of healthy ecosystems improves the quality of life for present and future generations.[5]

To convert these principles into design guidelines, the Sustainable Sites team incorporated the ecosystem services concept. Environmental economists have adopted the term "ecosystem services" to describe those benefits that the environment provides to humans for free, which humans would have to find ways to provide for themselves if the environment ceased to provide them.[6] These services include products such as breathable air; fishable, swimmable, and drinkable water; regulation of atmospheric gases; nutrient and waste cycling; eco-tourism; and a host of others (Table 4.2 and Figure 4.6). Depending on who is conducting the study, there are many categories of ecosystem services that economists have begun to monetize in order to demonstrate the need to incorporate both the diminishment and enhancement of these services into our economic system.[7]

The specific ecosystem services addressed in the Sustainable Sites guidelines and performance benchmarks include global and local climate regulation, air and water cleansing, water supply and regulation, erosion and sediment control, hazard mitigation, pollination, habitat functions, waste decomposition and treatment, human health and well-being, food and renewable non-food

**TABLE 4.2** ECOSYSTEM SERVICES

Ecosystem services are goods and services of direct or indirect benefit to humans that are produced by eco-system processes involving the interaction of living elements, such as vegetation and soil organisms, and non-living elements, such as bedrock, water, and air.

Various researchers have come up with a number of lists of these benefits, each with slightly different wording, some lists slightly longer than others. For the purpose of developing performance criteria for practices that will protect or regenerate these benefits, the members of the Sustainable Sites Technical Subcommittees and staff reviewed and consolidated the research into the list below of services provided by natural ecosystems. The goal of the sustainable site is to protect, restore, and enhance such ecosystem services wherever possible through sustainable land development and management practices.

1. Global climate regulation

   Maintaining balance of atmospheric gases at historic levels, creating breathable air, and sequestering greenhouse gases

2. Local climate regulation

   Regulating local temperatures, precipitation, and humidity through shading, evapotranspiration, and windbreaks

3. Air and water cleansing

   Removing and reducing pollutants in air and water

4. Water supply and regulation

   Storing and providing water within watersheds and aquifers

5. Erosion and sediment control

   Retaining soil within an ecosystem, preventing damage from erosion and siltation

6. Hazard mitigation

   Reducing vulnerability to damage from flooding, storm surge, wildfire, and drought

7. Pollination

   Providing pollinator species for reproduction of crops or other plants

8. Habitat functions

   Providing refuge and reproduction habitat to plants and animals, thereby contributing to conservation of biological and genetic diversity and evolutionary processes

9. Waste decomposition and treatment

   Breaking down waste and cycling nutrients

10. Human health and well-being benefits

    Enhancing physical, mental, and social well-being as a result of interaction with nature

11. Food and renewable non-food products

    Producing food, fuel, energy, medicine, or other products for human use

12. Cultural benefits

    Enhancing cultural, educational, aesthetic, and spiritual experiences as a result of interaction with nature

Source: *Guidelines and Performance Benchmarks, The Sustainable Sites Initiative*, www.sustainablesites.org, 2009.

4.6 Taylor 28 is a downtown Seattle apartment project that features permeable paving and a series of urban rain gardens. Design by Mithūn. Photograph © Mithūn, Juan Hernandez.

products, and cultural benefits.[8] These services are linked to specific actions that are considered as prerequisites and credits for Sustainable Sites (Table 4.3). The prerequisites and credits involve site selection, pre-design assessment and planning, site design, construction, and operations and maintenance. The system establishes uniform, consistent standards for the nation, but also adjusts to the regional variations of climate, soils, and plants.

## THE STATUS

The USGBC intends to continue to participate and collaborate with the Sustainable Sites team and anticipates incorporating the final Sustainable Sites benchmarks and guidelines into future iterations of LEED. Sustainable Sites standards and guidelines can apply to all landscapes, including commercial and public sites, residential landscapes, parks, campuses, roadsides, recreation centers, and utility corridors (Figures 4.7 to 4.12). In writing the standards, we struggled with the words "landscape" and "site," which have different meanings. We used them interchangeably but not together as in "landscape site."[9]

4.7 The Dell at the University of Virginia collects stormwater from the campus and beyond. The project involves "daylighting" a stream that had been buried. Design by Nelson Byrd Woltz Landscape Architects. Photograph by Will Kerner.

The preliminary "Standards and Guidelines for Sustainable Sites" report was released for public comment in November 2007. The preliminary report featured more than two hundred recommendations for the design and construction of sustainable sites. The report stressed the positive environmental impacts of landscapes and has been greeted with both significant support and constructive criticism. The guidelines were downloaded from the Web more than fifteen thousand

**TABLE 4.3** SUSTAINABLE SITES PREREQUISITES AND CREDITS

### 1. Site Selection                                                    21 possible points

Select locations to preserve existing resources and repair damaged systems

**Prerequisite 1.1:** Limit development of soils designated as prime farmland, unique farmland, and farmland of statewide importance

**Prerequisite 1.2:** Protect floodplain functions

**Prerequisite 1.3:** Preserve wetlands

**Prerequisite 1.4:** Preserve threatened or endangered species and their habitats

Credit 1.5: Select brownfields or greyfields for redevelopment (5–10 points)

Credit 1.6: Select sites within existing communities (6 points)

Credit 1.7: Select sites that encourage non-motorized transportation and use of public transit (5 points)

### 2. Pre-Design Assessment and Planning                              4 possible points

Plan for sustainability from the onset of the project

**Prerequisite 2.1:** Conduct a pre-design site assessment and explore opportunities for site sustainability

**Prerequisite 2.2:** Use an integrated site development process

Credit 2.3: Engage users and other stakeholders in site design (4 points)

### 3. Site Design—Water                                               44 possible points

Protect and restore processes and systems associated with a site's hydrology

**Prerequisite 3.1:** Reduce potable water use for landscape irrigation by 50 percent from established baseline

Credit 3.2: Reduce potable water use for landscape irrigation by 75 percent or more from established baseline (2–5 points)

Credit 3.3: Protect and restore riparian, wetland, and shoreline buffers (3–8 points)

Credit 3.4: Rehabilitate lost streams, wetlands, and shorelines (2–5 points)

Credit 3.5: Manage stormwater on site (5–10 points)

Credit 3.6: Protect and enhance on-site water resources and receiving water quality (3–9 points)

Credit 3.7: Design rainwater/stormwater features to provide a landscape amenity (1–3 points)

Credit 3.8: Maintain water features to conserve water and other resources (1–4 points)

### 4. Site Design—Soil and Vegetation                                 51 possible points

Protect and restore processes and systems associated with a site's soil and vegetation

**Prerequisite 4.1:** Control and manage known invasive plants found on site

**Prerequisite 4.2:** Use appropriate, non-invasive plants

**Prerequisite 4.3:** Create a soil management plan

Credit 4.4: Minimize soil disturbance in design and construction (6 points)

Credit 4.5: Preserve all vegetation designated as special status (5 points)

Credit 4.6: Preserve or restore appropriate plant biomass on site (3–8 points)

Credit 4.7: Use native plants (1–4 points)

Credit 4.8: Preserve plant communities native to the ecoregion (2–6 points)

Credit 4.9: Restore plant communities native to the ecoregion (1–5 points)

Credit 4.10: Use vegetation to minimize building heating requirements (2–4 points)

Credit 4.11: Use vegetation to minimize building cooling requirements (2–5 points)

Credit 4.12: Reduce urban heat island effects (3–5 points)

Credit 4.13: Reduce the risk of catastrophic wildfire (3 points)

### 5. Site Design—Materials Selection                                 36 possible points

Reuse/recycle existing materials and support sustainable production practices

**Prerequisite 5.1:** Eliminate the use of wood from threatened tree species

Credit 5.2: Maintain on-site structures, hardscape, and landscape amenities (1–4 points)

Credit 5.3: Design for deconstruction and disassembly (1–3 points)

Credit 5.4: Reuse salvaged materials and plants (2–4 points)

Credit 5.5: Use recycled content materials (2–4 points)

Credit 5.6: Use certified wood (1–4 points)

Credit 5.7: Use regional materials (2–6 points)

Credit 5.8: Use adhesives, sealants, paints, and coatings with reduced VOC emissions (2 points)

Credit 5.9: Support sustainable practices in plant production (3 points)

Credit 5.10: Support sustainable practices in materials manufacturing (3–6 points)

### 6. Site Design—Human Health and Well-Being          32 possible points

Build strong communities and a sense of stewardship

Credit 6.1: Promote equitable site development (1–3 points)

Credit 6.2: Promote equitable site use (1–4 points)

Credit 6.3: Promote sustainability awareness and education (2–4 points)

Credit 6.4: Protect and maintain unique cultural and historical places (2–4 points)

Credit 6.5: Provide for optimum site accessibility, safety, and wayfinding (3 points)

Credit 6.6: Provide opportunities for outdoor physical activity (4–5 points)

Credit 6.7: Provide views of vegetation and quiet outdoor spaces for mental restoration (3–4 points)

Credit 6.8: Provide outdoor spaces for social interaction (3 points)

Credit 6.9: Reduce light pollution (2 points)

### 7. Construction          21 possible points

Minimize effects of construction-related activities

**Prerequisite 7.1:** Control and retain construction pollutants

**Prerequisite 7.2:** Restore soils disturbed during construction

Credit 7.3: Restore soils disturbed by previous development (2–8 points)

Credit 7.4: Divert construction and demolition materials from disposal (3–5 points)

Credit 7.5: Reuse or recycle vegetation, rocks, and soil generated during construction (3–5 points)

Credit 7.6: Minimize generation of greenhouse gas emissions and exposure to localized air pollutants during construction (1–3 points)

### 8. Operations and Maintenance          23 possible points

Maintain the site for long-term sustainability

**Prerequisite 8.1:** Plan for sustainable site maintenance

**Prerequisite 8.2:** Provide for storage and collection of recyclables

Credit 8.3: Recycle organic matter generated during site operations and maintenance (2–6 points)

Credit 8.4: Reduce outdoor energy consumption for all landscape and exterior operations (1–4 points)

Credit 8.5: Use renewable sources for landscape electricity needs (2–3 points)

Credit 8.6: Minimize exposure to environmental tobacco smoke (1–2 points)

Credit 8.7: Minimize generation of greenhouse gases and exposure to localized air pollutants during landscape maintenance activities (1–4 points)

Credit 8.8: Reduce emissions and promote the use of fuel-efficient vehicles (4 points)

### 9. Monitoring and Innovation          18 possible points

Reward exceptional performance and improve the body of knowledge on long-term sustainability

Credit 9.1: Monitor performance of sustainable design practices (10 points)

Credit 9.2: Innovation in site design (8 points)

Source: *Guidelines and Performance Benchmarks*, The Sustainable Sites Initiative, www.sustainablesites.org, 2009.

**4.8** Water conservation and stormwater system for Sidwell Friends School, Washington, D.C. Design by Andropogon Associates, Ltd. Courtesy of Andropogon Associates, Ltd.

**4.9** Wetlands, rain garden, and teaching pond at the Sidwell Friends School. The wetlands are functionally separate from the rain garden and pond. Courtesy of Andropogon Associates, Ltd.

times between November 2007 and January 2008, and the PDC received more than four hundred and fifty substantive comments on the preliminary report.

The feedback from the public comment period, as well as additional research into the metrics of success, were incorporated into the draft guidelines and performance benchmarks.[10] Additionally, case studies that demonstrate and document

specific sustainable landscape techniques were published in November 2008, and were available for a second public comment period. "Final" standards and guidelines were published in December 2009, with weights attached to each credit. At the same time, pilot projects were initiated to test the system. As a result of the pilot projects, the standards, guidelines, and credit weighting system will be adjusted. The pilot phase will be complete

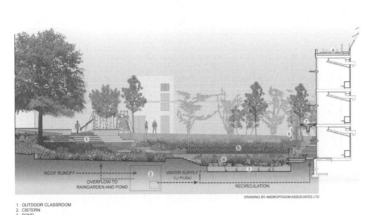

1. OUTDOOR CLASSROOM
2. CISTERN
3. POND
4. RAIN GARDEN
5. WETLANDS FOR WASTEWATER TREATMENT
6. TRICKLE FILTER WITH INTERPRETIVE DISPLAY
7. RAMP TO SECOND FLOOR ENTRY
8. GREEN ROOF

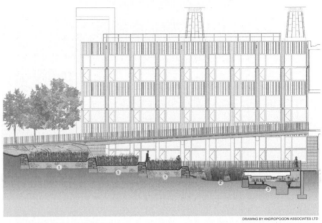

1. WETLANDS FOR WASTEWATER TREATMENT
2. RAIN GARDEN
3. POND

**4.10** Water treatment systems in the terraced courtyard of the Sidwell Friends School. Collaboratively designed by Andropogon Associates, Ltd., Natural Systems International, and Kieran Timberlake Associates. Courtesy of Andropogon Associates, Ltd.

Urban Agriculture - Planting Beds

Green Roof

Solar Panels

Roof Leaders

Aeration Course

Trickle Filter & Interpretive Kiosk

Biology Pond

Treatment Wetlands

Rain Garden "Flood Zone"

Settling Tank

Basement Tanks and Filters for Grey Water Storage

Rainwater Cistern

⬤ Wastewater System

⬤ Stormwater System

4.11 The terraced court-
yard of the Sidwell Friends
School. Courtesy of
Andropogon Associates, Ltd.

4.12 Students at the rain gar-
den and pond of the Sidwell
Friends School. Courtesy of
Andropogon Associates, Ltd.

at the end of 2012 and will result in a reference
guide, which will provide weighted credits in order
to allow for project evaluation, comparison, and
recognition.

The ambition of Sustainable Sites is grand: to
create a landscape equivalent to the LEED building
standards. However, the potential benefits for the
planet, and the world in which we live, are equally
grand.

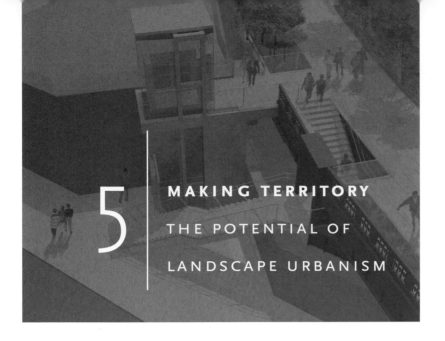

# 5 MAKING TERRITORY
## THE POTENTIAL OF
## LANDSCAPE URBANISM

The Dutch invented the word *landschap*, which migrated into English as our "landscape." In its Dutch root, *land-schap* refers to a territory made by people. In English and in the Romance languages, landscape and its translations, such as the Italian *paesaggio*, often refer to a view, frequently a rural one. However, a deeper meaning refers to the integrated cultural and natural processes of a place. In this sense, at its origin, landscape has more in common with the Italian *territorio* than with the more frequent translation, *paesaggio*. Similarly, the French *terroir*, originally a wine production term, refers to spatial characteristics of climate, soil type, and topography that create the specific qualities of a place as adapted by people. The landscape architect Günter Vogt defines *terroir* as "the exact appropriateness of a specific place, with all its hidden qualities."[1]

The Dutch constructed much of their nation from low-lying lands below sea level (Figure 5.1). They created busy cities and rich farmlands from lakes, marshes, and river channels as they protected significant natural areas. As a result, the concept of creating land is central to the Dutch culture.

As my nation, and much of the world, continue to urbanize, we face issues similar to those that have challenged citizens of The Netherlands throughout their history. How do we construct livable spaces that are more dense? How do we make places in challenging environments? How do we inhabit a warmer planet with rising coastlines? How do we maintain productive farmlands and preserve significant habitat for other species? As we address such questions, the idea of landscape, of making territory, will surely become more central to our culture, as well as to other cultures.

In the process, landscape architecture can lead the design and planning disciplines. This leadership is especially essential for the health and vitality of urban regions. As more of us live in cities, the quality of our built environment grows in importance. Landscape architecture in many ways occupies the ground between architecture and urban planning while overlapping with both. As a result, landscape architecture helps bridge the rule-making orientation of the planners and the form-making emphasis of the architects. The emerging subfield of Landscape Urbanism presents additional bridging potential.

More humans live in cities now than at any time in history. As the world's population continues to grow, the planet becomes more urban. Meanwhile, our ecological literacy expands, and we recognize that urban and suburban places are ecological systems. We understand landscapes as syntheses of natural and social processes. This knowledge gives rise to a new urbanism, one where people are viewed as part of nature, one

5.1 Farmland in the IJssel-meerpolders, the Netherlands. Photograph by Frederick Steiner.

where "the city is of the country"[2] or "the city is of the territory."[3] This new urbanism is grounded in ecological literacy and in understanding the territory of the city.

We describe the resulting urban form and the way we view that form as Landscape Urbanism. This term was coined by architect Charles Wald-heim and advanced by a small band of North American landscape architects and urbanists, including James Corner, Chris Reed, Nina-Marie Lister, and Dean Almy.[4] Waldheim, Corner, and Reed are former students of Ian McHarg, and his ecological advocacy certainly influences their ideas and work. However, this younger generation seeks a more urban and more design-based approach than that of their mentor. Landscape Urbanists suggest the landscape should replace buildings and transportation systems as the principal organizing structure in urban design. Networks and complexity are embraced in order to establish frameworks for urban change.

In addition to McHarg, Landscape Urbanists have been inspired by the work of the Dutch firm West 8. Early North American examples of Land-scape Urbanism include Field Operations' Fresh Kills and High Line projects in New York City and

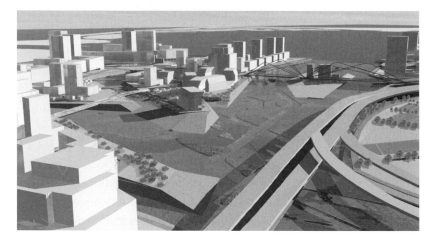

StossLU's entry in Toronto's Lower Don Lands invited competition (Figure 5.2).

Landscape Urbanism represents a fundamental shift in how we view the health of our cities. In the nineteenth century, increasing knowledge about disease and environments gave rise to sanitary engineering and urban parks (Figure 5.3). In the twentieth century, concern about the pollution of water and air resulted in new national environmental laws, which improved water and air quality. Now, we see how ill-conceived development threatens public health. This should give rise to an ecological infrastructure movement comparable to the sanitary engineering movement of the

5.2 Lower Don Lands proposal, Toronto, Canada: a new metropolitan precinct whose urban form is structured by the dynamic ecologies of the reconstituted Don River marsh. © StossLU.

**5.3.** Prospect Park, Brooklyn, New York. Design by Frederick Law Olmsted Sr. and Calvert Vaux. Photograph by Frederick Steiner.

nineteenth century and the water and air quality laws of the twentieth.

How then should we conceive this form? Seven key axioms contribute to Landscape Urbanism:

- Cities and landscapes change constantly.
- Technology connects us to each other and our environments in new ways, changing how and where we live.
- Sense of place and sense of region produce distinct regional cultural identities.
- Certain regional identities foster creativity.
- Landscape-based urban design involves the repetition of patterns across scale.
- Design and planning disciplinary boundaries blur in Landscape Urbanism.
- Cities and landscapes are resilient ecosystems.

### CITIES AND LANDSCAPES CHANGE CONSTANTLY

Traditionally, ecologists contended that systems moved toward a steady state. In what is called "new ecology," systems are viewed as in a perpetual state of flux.[5] As ecologists devote increased attention to studying landscapes and cities, this

shift in view is reinforced. In newer cities, like Phoenix, where development occurs at the rate of an acre (.405 ha) an hour, a pace sustained for more than three decades (before the Great Recession of 2007–2010), change is apparent to even the most casual observer (Figure 5.4). In more ancient cities, like Rome, renewal and restoration transform large neighborhoods into constant construction zones.

Following Vienna's lead, many European cities replaced their ancient defensive walls with parks and open spaces. Changing military technology transformed urban space, generally for the better, as, for example, the park around the historic city center of Krakow, Poland. In Italy, Lucca's walls remain. However, trees were planted where soldiers once stood, changing the walls from a place for fighting to a space for recreation (Figure 5.5).

A consequence for Landscape Urbanism is that change should be a consideration in design and planning. Certain places are designed for a narrow purpose to last through time—a house of worship, a memorial, a park, or a library, for instance. Even such places as these evolve, as technology alters library use or a changing neighborhood affects a church parish. Other places require even more flexibility and adaptability—where we work,

**5.4** Development in the Phoenix metropolitan area. Photograph by Frederick Steiner.

**5.5** City Wall Park, Lucca, Italy. Photograph by Frederick Steiner.

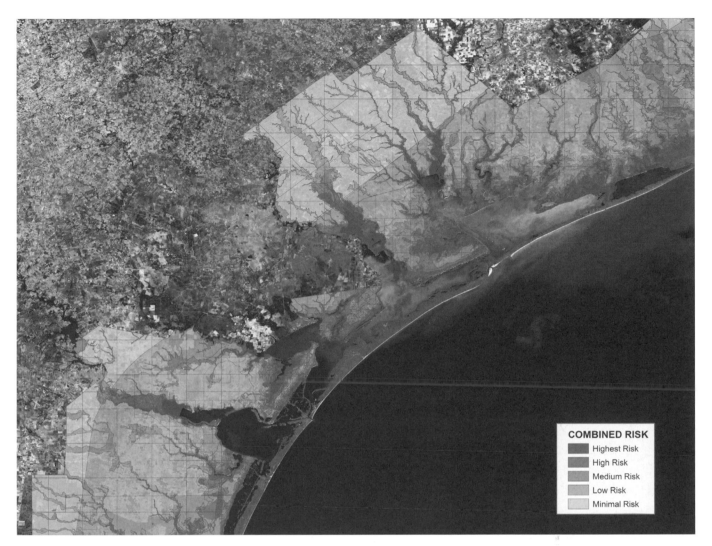

**COMBINED RISK**
- Highest Risk
- High Risk
- Medium Risk
- Low Risk
- Minimal Risk

**5.6** The use of GIS to illustrate risk along the Texas Gulf Coast. Among the risk factors being addressed are historic hurricane tracks, high wind risk areas, storm surges, significant flooding events, rise in sea elevation, economic impacts, demographic vulnerability, growth patterns, and loss of wetlands, marshes, and barrier islands. Map by James L. Sipes, AECOM. Courtesy of AECOM.

sleep, eat, and recreate. These places change from external forces, such as technology, and from within, as we inhabit them through time.

## TECHNOLOGY CONNECTS US

Technology is an instrument of human adaptation. The Internet, laptop computers, geopositioning systems, and cell phones with built-in cameras alter our lives today as much as television and refrigeration did in the previous generation. We can Google a new acquaintance and learn more than many conversations might reveal. We watch television on a clear afternoon at Sky Harbor International Airport in Phoenix to learn a storm front will reach our destination in Texas before we do. Climate data collected at the same

airport report the warming of nighttime temperatures over the past decades.

We can use Google Earth or ArcGIS Online to explore places close to home or far away. This can be a helpful tool for design and planning. We can make a virtual site assessment before an actual visit. By zooming in and out with Google Earth, we can get an initial impression of the site's character and context. We may also revisit the site after departing. This is especially helpful when working with distant places. Through Google Earth, we can visit the projects of others to help us learn from their experiences.

A consequence for Landscape Urbanism is that connecting technologies should be embraced in design and planning. Geographic Information System (GIS) provides another clear example of a connecting technology (Figure 5.6). Through

GIS, we can map and compare social and natural information spatially. As a technology devoted to the organization and application of geographic information, GIS is capable of revealing relationships and patterns across the urban landscape. These relationships and patterns help us visualize processes that affect the livability of cities and regions.

## PLACE AND REGION CREATE IDENTITY

A sense of place enhances urban livability. Local places are embedded within regions. Together, a sense of place and of region contribute to distinct cultural identities. Austin possesses a different identity from Houston, as Pittsburgh does from Philadelphia, and Rome from Milan. The interplay between the built environment and natural processes creates this sense of place (Figure 5.7).

A consequence for Landscape Urbanism is that designers and planners should reinforce regional and local senses of place. In his book *Native to Nowhere* (2004), University of Virginia planning professor Tim Beatley writes about the challenges of sustaining places in this global age. He suggests how places can be strengthened through history and heritage and good community design.[6] According to Beatley, the natural environment, pedestrian places, art, shared spaces, multi-generational communities, and wise energy use all play important roles in place-based design.

## SOME REGIONS FOSTER CREATIVITY

Some regional identities are more powerful and conducive to creativity than others. We write poems and songs to San Francisco and Rome. The skyline of New York City appears in many films, as does its Central Park and Brooklyn Bridge. We know the canals of Amsterdam and Venice, the beaches of Rio and Miami, the architecture of Florence, and Seattle's rain, even if we have never been there (Figure 5.8).

5.7 Roma. Photograph by Frederick Steiner.

A consequence for Landscape Urbanism is that design and planning should reinforce creative regional identities. We need to learn to design with rain, to plan with poetry. A promise of Landscape Urbanism is to connect urban living to nature in thoughtful and artful ways.

To fulfill this promise, we need to understand the rhythms of the seasons. We must study the rocks of the region and how they fashion the terrain and direct the flows of water. We need to learn about the depths and the colors of the soils and how they influence plant growth. We must become familiar with our trees and shrubs, our birds and bees, and our native fishes and mammals.

## PARTS BECOME WHOLES AT HIGHER SCALES

We can fulfill the promise to join urban living to nature carefully and artfully through viewing design on multiple scales. More than a half century ago, Kevin Lynch wrote about approaching design through "additive structure," where the "basic unit is rigidly standardized, inflexible [like a brick]. The flexibility lies in the myriad ways in which the constellation of units may be patterned, and in the interchangeability of parts. The total pattern is not highly organized, but is rather additive in nature: growth of units at the periphery

5.8 The Duomo, Florence, Italy. Photograph by Frederick Steiner.

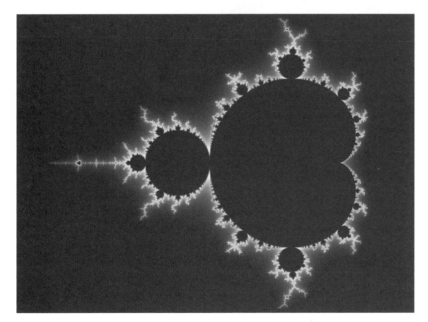

5.9 Fractal of Mandelbrot set. Courtesy of Dr. Wolfgang Beyer, Munich, Germany.

metric shape that forms building blocks in nature (Figure 5.9).

For Landscape Urbanism, a consequence is that designers and planners should understand Lynch's ideas about environmental adaptability and additive structure in urban design, as well as principles of fractal geometry. Fractals and additive structures can be helpful to conceive form across scales. Fractals form patterns. Designing with these patterns will result in forms that fit a place. Designers might also complement or play against these patterns consciously, as they address and form adaptive complex systems. The resulting designs can enhance existing patterns through the addition of new, though complementary, elements.

does not change the structure at the center."[7] Lynch introduced this concept in a 1958 article on "environmental adaptability," which he defined as the capacity that enables the organization of urban space to adapt to the changes in function, concentration, and communication. More recently, fractal theory suggests that the world consists of self-similar systems. A fractal is a geo-

## SEVERAL DISCIPLINES CONTRIBUTE

Landscape Urbanism blurs the boundaries between the disciplines traditionally involved in the design and planning of the urban built environment—architecture, landscape architecture,

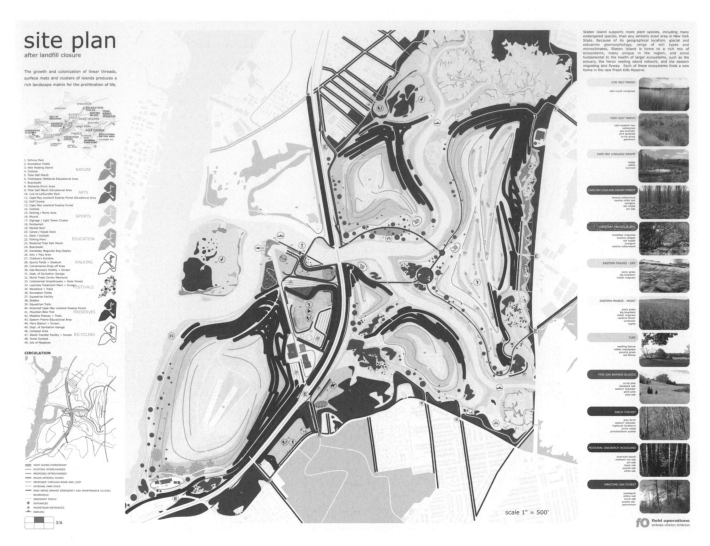

5.10 Fresh Kills Competition, New York City. Design by Field Operations. © James Corner Field Operations.

planning, civil engineering, law, historic preservation, and real estate. Arguably, architecture played a leadership role in traditional urban design. For Landscape Urbanism to advance, landscape architecture should be expected to be a leader in theory and practice.

The Fresh Kills Project mentioned earlier provides an example. A key innovation is that James Corner and his Field Operations colleagues embraced change in their design, eschewing a set end state for a more dynamic, flexible framework of possibilities grounded in an initial "seeding," that is, the careful construction of key elements that help guide the growth of the project. Located in the New York City borough of Staten Island, Fresh Kills covers some 2,200 acres (890 ha) and was formerly the largest landfill in the world. Much of the debris from the September 11, 2001,

terrorist attacks on the World Trade Center was deposited there. The Field Operations plan suggests how the landfill can be converted into a park three times larger than Central Park. The plan involves the restoration of a large landscape and includes reclaiming much of the wetlands that existed on the former dump site. In addition to landscape architecture, the planning required the expertise of ecologists, social scientists, traffic specialists, soil scientists, and hydrologists (Figure 5.10).

A consequence for Landscape Urbanism is that design and planning needs to be based on collaboration and mutual respect among disciplines. This requires respect for both the place-making and the rule-making aspects of Landscape Urbanism. The art of making places should be balanced with the necessity for rules in urban places. Architects need to learn to communicate with attorneys, and engineers with landscape architects. Planners should learn the languages of ecology and economics, as both ecology and economics contribute to our knowledge of home.

## CITIES AND LANDSCAPES ARE RESILIENT

Finally, cities are increasingly viewed as resilient ecosystems. Resilience is a concept and a theory with growing appeal in the disciplines of ecology and planning, and it has considerable relevance for Landscape Urbanism. According to the ecologist Lance Gunderson and his colleagues:

Resilience *has been defined in two different ways in the ecological literature, each reflecting different aspects of stability. One definition focuses on efficiency, constancy and predictability—all attributes of engineers' desire for fail-safe design. The other focuses on persistence, change and unpredictability—all attributes embraced and celebrated by evolutionary biologists and by those who search for safe-fail designs.*[8]

The first definition is tied to standard ideas in ecology, which emphasized equilibrium and stability. The second definition emerges from new ecology, which focuses on non-equilibrium and the adaptability of ecological systems.[9] Pickett and Cadenasso suggest that the latter is appropriate "to urban ecosystems, because it suggests that spatial heterogeneity is an important component of the persistence of adaptable metropolitan regions."[10]

The application of resilience to urban ecosystems is largely the result of the two National Science Foundation-funded, urban long-term ecological research (LTER) projects in Phoenix and Baltimore.[11] Cities are anything but stable and predictable systems. The urban LTERs reinforce our growing appreciation for changing and adapting systems.

To a large degree, the interest from American planners in resilience emerged post-September 11, 2001. The principal leaders are Lawrence Vale of the Massachusetts Institute of Technology and Thomas Campanella of the University of North Carolina at Chapel Hill.[12] Although ecologists have speculated about the application of resilience theory to urban planning, up to this point there has been scant connection between the ecological and the planning resilience research.

Vale and Campanella link resilience to disasters, noting, "Urban disaster, like urban resilience, takes many forms."[13] Furthermore, they observe, "Many disasters may follow a predictable pattern of rescue, restoration, rebuilding, and remembrance, yet we can only truly evaluate a recovery based on special circumstances."[14] Thus, urban resilience is linked to the specific qualities of the place where it occurs.

Vale and Campanella distinguish natural disasters from those caused by people. Natural disasters include those resulting from fire, earthquake, flood, drought, volcano, hurricane, tsunami, and epidemic disease. Human disasters result both from accidents and deliberate, place-targeted events.[15] In many ways, Hurricane Katrina in 2005 and the 2008 Sichuan Province earthquake illustrate how poor planning and design can exacerbate the human consequences of a natural event. For example, the loss of wetlands along the Gulf Coast contributes to the deleterious consequences of hurricanes. The protection of such wetlands and the creation of new marshes would provide greater safety for coastal residents. Likewise, better building codes and more careful site planning would save lives during earthquakes in Sichuan.

Vale and Campanella build their perspective on the considerable body of work done by American planners on the topic of disaster. One of the few times the American public turns to planners is in the wake of tragedy. Might not resilience also be a helpful concept for guiding metropolitan regions in times without disaster? Such regional resilience would be based on enhancing social capital, creating knowledge capital, and protecting natural capital.

A consequence for Landscape Urbanism lies in the potential to connect ideas about resilience from ecology to those in planning. In doing so, we can create healthier urban landscapes that can adapt to change and foster creativity.

## LANDSCAPE URBANISM DESIGN AND PLANNING

These seven axioms suggest three approaches to the design and planning of urban landscapes. The first involves grand gestures, which are intended to completely transform a city or a region. The second is to initiate change throughout a region by studying and incrementally adjusting environmental processes. The third approach is that of an individual designer or a school of designers and artists who, through a lifetime of work, can transform a city or region.

### THE "BIG PLANS"

The first of these can be characterized as the "make no little plans" approach. It was the Chicago architect Daniel Burnham who made that famous statement, saying that little plans "have no magic to stir men's blood. . . . Make big plans; aim high in hope and work." Burnham and the sons of Frederick Law Olmsted Sr. and their friends certainly heeded this proclamation. Their City Beautiful plans for Chicago, San Francisco, and Washington, D.C., are their legacy to us (Figure 5.11).

Whereas Burnham's big plans were based on

architecture and roadways providing the essential building blocks, with big parks and ribbons of green along boulevards playing an important, supportive role, the senior Olmsted presented an alternative grand scheme. Olmsted, with Charles Eliot, conceived a whole new system, which they called the "Emerald Necklace," for the Boston metropolitan region. Their vision remains today

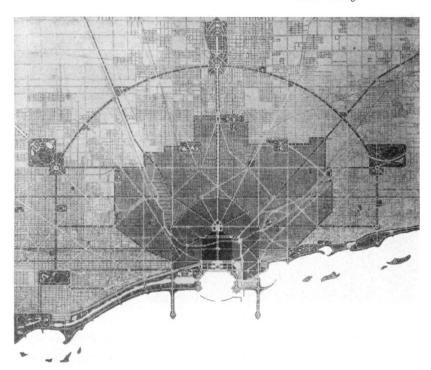

**5.11** Plan for Chicago, 1909, showing the general system of boulevards and parks existing and proposed. Co-authored by Daniel Burnham and Edward H. Bennett. Courtesy of The Commercial Club of Chicago.

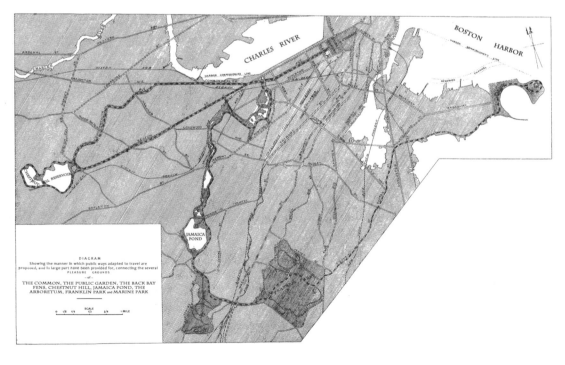

**5.12** Emerald Necklace in Boston. Plan by Frederick Law Olmsted Sr. and Charles Eliot. Courtesy of the National Park Service, Frederick Law Olmsted National Historic Site.

**5.13** 27th Avenue Solid Waste Management Facility, Phoenix. Design by Michael Singer and Linnea Glatt. Photograph by Frederick Steiner.

as the connected green space enjoyed every day by the citizens of Boston (Figure 5.12).

Another grand vision was created for the City of Phoenix with the 1985 establishment of the Phoenix Arts Commission when Terry Goddard was mayor. The public art master plan commissioned by that agency provides a remarkable vision of using the infrastructure of the place to create an identity for the region.

Indeed, this identity has even worked its way into literature. In Don DeLillo's 1997 *Underworld*, set in Phoenix and New York, the icon chosen to represent New York is Brooklyn's Ebbets Field. To represent Phoenix, the author chose an unusual but extremely successful project that came out of the city's public art master plan, the 27th Avenue Solid Waste Management Facility (Figure 5.13). "The landscape made him happy. It was a challenge to his lifelong citiness but more than that, a realization of some half-dream vision, the other-

ness of the West, the strange great thing that was all mixed in with nature and spaciousness, with bravery and history and who you are and what you believe and what movies you saw growing up."[16]

## CHANGE BY INCREMENTS

The second approach, incrementalism, provides an alternative approach to big plans. In the Phoenix region, more than forty years ago, an architecture studio at Arizona State University launched a vision known as Rio Salado. The vision to transform the dry Salt River bed, which had been abused by gravel mining and random dumping, into a linear open space and flood control system was quickly championed by the dean of the college, Jim Elmore, who advocated the Rio Salado vision for decades. Incrementally, the idea took root in Tempe and Phoenix.

If we take Jim Elmore's vision of the Rio Salado, pull back, and look at it as Olmsted might have, we can imagine a "Turquoise Necklace" for the Phoenix metropolitan area, with the Rio Salado connected to the Indian Bend Wash on the east, the Agua Fria River on the west, and the Central Arizona Project canal on the north (Figure 5.14). Such connections, a primary focus of the Public Art Program, have the potential to create a Turquoise Necklace over time for the Phoenix region.

Cities from Hong Kong to Phoenix are getting hotter, prompting residents to grow more concerned about controlling temperature. The urban heat island effect, or what some climatologists are calling the "urban heat archipelago," reduces comfort in already warm cities. Those of us who live in hot cities should be concerned about how we use black asphalt in our public infrastructure projects. Knowledge about climate and materials can transform, incrementally, how we view our region. What can artists, landscape architects, and architects do with such knowledge? We can transform a region bit by bit, parking lot by parking lot, street by street, one sidewalk at a time, by using more appropriate surfaces and planting more trees. I think, if Vitruvius were around today,

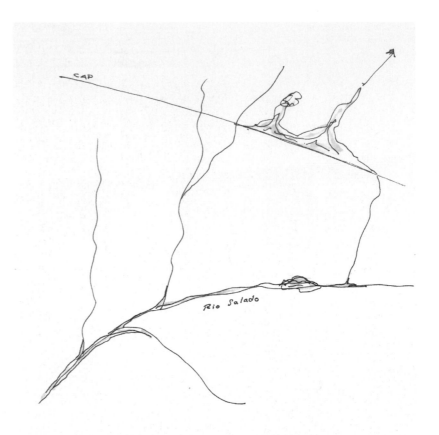

**5.14** The Turquoise Necklace for metropolitan Phoenix. Drawing by Frederick Steiner.

**5.15** High Line Project, New York City. The High Line's dramatic curve westward along 30th Street is augmented by an access point, with the stairs intersecting the structure and rising up through it. © James Corner Field Operations, and Diller Scofidio + Renfro. Courtesy of the City of New York.

**5.16** The High Line, New York City. Photograph by Frederick Steiner.

**5.17** Entrance to Arid Zone Trees nursery, Queen Creek, Arizona. Design and photograph by Steve Martino.

he would write an eleventh book on architecture, one on parking lot design.

A more recent Landscape Urbanist example is the High Line Project in Manhattan.[17] The Regional Plan Association and the Friends of the High Line advocated that an abandoned rail line weaving through twenty-two blocks in New York City should be converted into a 6.7-acre (2.7-ha) park. They promoted the 1.45-mile (2.33-km) long corridor as a recreational amenity, a tourist attraction, and a generator of economic development. In 2004, the Friends of the High Line and the City of New York selected Field Operations and Diller Scofidio + Renfro to design the project, which opened with considerable popular and critical enthusiasm in June 2009. The High Line design suggests a model for how abandoned urban territories can be transformed into community assets (Figures 5.15 and 5.16). James Corner writes, "The result is an episodic and varied sequence of public spaces and landscape spaces set along a simple and consistent line—a line that cuts across some of the most remarkable elevated vistas of Manhattan and the Hudson River, each view unfolding through an otherworldly synthesis of motion."[18]

## TRANSFORMATION OVER TIME

There is a third approach I call the "cumulative effect," whereby a single designer or a school of designers transform a city and large landscapes over time. Consider the influence of Antonio Gaudí on Barcelona. What would Barcelona be if Gaudí had not lived? I would argue that there are parallel examples in other regions. For instance, in the Phoenix area, emergent schools of architecture and landscape architecture could potentially have similar long-term consequences. The work of Will Bruder, Wendell Burnette, and the Jones Studio in architecture, as well as Steve Martino, Christy Ten Eyck, and Michael Dollin in landscape architecture, indicates such interwoven schools of thought (Figure 5.17). Clearly, as Gaudí was shaped by Barcelona before he contributed to its identity, these Arizonans are products of the Sonoran Desert.

## PROSPECTS

We live in an urban world that grows more urban all the time.[19] Increased urbanization in the twenty-first century requires the talents of architects, landscape architects, and planners to shape and reshape places. Much building will be required in new and renewed places. This provides an opportunity for massive transformation of cities and regions. Landscape Urbanism offers a fresh approach to city design and regional planning where people give back to the natural world, rather than destroying it. Instead of viewing the world as a giant sink to deposit our waste, we need to invest our wisdom in creating living landscapes.

# LESSONS FROM
# PAUL CRET, IAN MCHARG,
# AND GEORGE MITCHELL

Although famously proud of all things native, Texans have boldly imported lead-ing architects and planners from around the world. This is especially evident in the skylines and cultural institutions of Houston, Dallas, and Fort Worth.

Texans recruited Paul Philippe Cret and Ian McHarg to undertake ambitious, influential projects. Both Cret and McHarg were professors at the University of Pennsylvania. The Beaux-Arts architect Cret emigrated from France and had returned to serve his homeland with distinction in the First World War. The landscape architect-planner McHarg moved to Philadelphia from Scotland (by way of Harvard) after rising through the ranks from pri-vate to major in the British Army during the Second World War.

In 1930, the regents of the University of Texas commissioned Cret to prepare a campus master plan. The resulting plan helped define the image of the university as Cret led its realization by collaborating on nineteen buildings in the heart of the campus.

In the 1970s, McHarg's Philadelphia-based firm Wallace, McHarg, Roberts and Todd was recruited to prepare plans for Austin and The Woodlands, north of Houston. The Austin plan influenced growth in the city's western suburbs for years to come. The Wood-lands was the most socially and ecologically ambitious new community plan of the 1970s.

The Texans behind such recruitments are equally interesting. George Phydias Mitchell, the developer of The Woodlands, was born to Greek immigrant parents and had earned a petroleum engineering degree from Texas A&M University. His knowledge of geology attracted him to McHarg's natural science–based approach to planning.

We can learn from Cret, McHarg, and Mitchell's innovation and creation. They pre-sented bold visions for the future, which have been pursued with dedication and persis-tence. Their work presents inspiration for alternative paths for design and planning that could certainly benefit Texas but have much broader possibilities for other regions.

1933

UNIVERSITY OF TEXAS

*Plan of Development*

PAUL PHILIPPE CRET
CONSULTING ARCHITECT

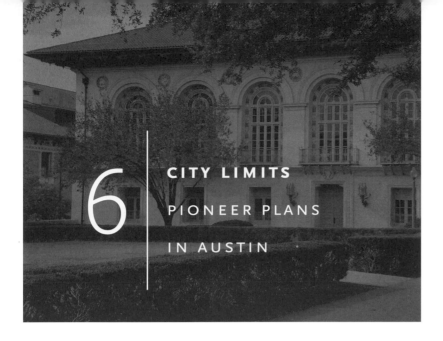

# 6 | CITY LIMITS
## PIONEER PLANS
## IN AUSTIN

inhabit a city that is reluctantly urban. My workplace and homeplace lie within the Austin city limits. Deep in the heart of Texas, Austin simultaneously stands as the state capital and as a state of mind. The city epitomizes Texanness while providing a contrast and a foil for the rest of the state. Texans call Austin "our Athens" (in contrast to College Station, the Sparta of Texas).

Since its founding, Austin has been more liberal than the rest of the state. Most Texans favored slavery. Led by the large German population, Central Texas opposed it. The opposition included Sam Houston, who refused to take an oath of allegiance to the Confederacy. In his *Journey Through Texas*, Frederick Law Olmsted Sr. painted a bleak picture of slavery and applauded the alternative economical model of the German settlers. Olmsted fondly described Austin with its "fine situation upon the left bank of the Colorado. Had it not been capital of the state . . . it would still have struck us as the pleasantest place we had seen in Texas. It reminds one somewhat of Washington; Washington, *en petit*, seen through a reversed glass."[1] Of course, Austin is no longer small and is now a larger city than Washington, D.C.

During the spring and summer, the largest urban bat population in North America lives under a downtown bridge in Austin. Named for the former governor, the Ann W. Richards Congress Avenue Bridge spans the Colorado River. The river was dammed for flood control, creating Town Lake, which was renamed to honor Lady Bird Johnson in 2007. Between March and November, from 750,000 up to 1.5 million bats dramatically emerge from under the bridge around sunset in search of food, consuming from 10,000 to 30,000 pounds of insects each evening. The beloved Congress Avenue bats do much to reduce the city's mosquito population. Downtown, unfortunately, also provides habitat to thousands of large black/dark purple birds called "grackles" (*Quiscalus quiscula*). The noisy swarms of these creatures were uprooted from the university campus, then the state capitol complex, before taking up residence downtown. Austinites coexist with both the cherished bats and the despised grackles.

Within this natural and cultural context, several urban and green design innovations have been generated by the City of Austin, such as its Green Building Program and the Great Streets Initiative. Through the city-owned utility, Austin Energy, builders and architects receive incentives to incorporate energy conservation and sustainability into their residential, commercial, and multi-family projects. Great Streets presented a bold vision to revamp the quality of downtown through improved sidewalks, street trees, and transit.

**6.1** Above top: 2nd Street, Austin, Great Streets proposed design and after image. Above bottom: Great Streets master plan for 306 blocks of downtown Austin, 2nd Street represented in the plan. Design by Joint Venture with Black + Vernooy and Kinney & Associates.

Austin's record of realizing its innovative ideas is mixed. Since its beginnings in 1985, the Green Building Program has achieved considerable success and influenced other initiatives, including the USGBC's LEED program. By contrast, the implementation of Great Streets has been more limited, with only a few city blocks realized as of late 2010 (Figure 6.1). In many ways, it is easier to address one single building at a time than a whole block, which usually involves several landowners and complex (and expensive) urban infrastructure.

Cities evolve through the cumulative impacts of many plans and designs, as well as numerous unplanned and undesigned activities. Unintended consequences flow from both designed and unplanned actions. Two famous plans, completed four decades apart, have influenced the growth of the University of Texas and the City of Austin. The first occurred as one of the final, most complete representative works of the École des Beaux-Arts in America. The second occurred at the height of the Environmental Decade of the 1970s and represents an important advance in ecological planning.

Paul Cret prepared the plan for the University of Texas campus in 1933. Cret was one of the most prominent architects in the United States from the first decade of the twentieth century through the 1930s. During the latter half of the twentieth century, his reputation plummeted with the rise of the International Style. The Modernists opposed the Beaux-Arts tradition, and Paul Cret bore the standard for the French school in America.

Cret first entered the École des Beaux-Arts in his home city Lyon, France. In 1896, he won the Paris Prize, enabling him to study at the most important architectural school in the world at the time: the École des Beaux-Arts in Paris. He came to the United States in 1903 to teach at the University of Pennsylvania (Penn).[2] Except for his service in the French Army during the First World War, he stayed in Philadelphia until he dropped dead on a job site in 1945. While teaching and directing the architecture atelier at Penn, Cret maintained a robust practice in Philadelphia, designing such buildings as the Pan American Union in Washington, D.C. (1907–1917), the

Indianapolis Public Library (1917), and the Detroit Institute of the Arts (1920–1927)[3] (Figure 6.2). The University of Texas plan was undertaken at the height of his career.

The plan for the Lake Austin area was prepared by Ian McHarg and his Wallace, McHarg, Roberts and Todd (WMRT) colleagues in 1976. McHarg was the most prominent environmental planner and landscape architect in the world during the 1970s. After apprenticing as a landscape architect in his native Scotland, he served in the British commandos during the Second World War. Afterward, McHarg studied landscape architecture and city planning at Harvard University, a school then dominated by Walter Gropius and the Bauhaus.[4]

In 1954, McHarg went to Penn, where he taught until his death in 2001. While teaching, writing, and chairing the landscape architecture and regional planning department, McHarg (like Cret) maintained a vigorous, Philadelphia-based practice. His firm, Wallace, McHarg, Roberts and Todd, was responsible for many plans, including those for the Twin Cities Metropolitan Region of Minnesota (1969), the Denver metropolitan region (1971–1972), The Woodlands, Texas (1973–1974), and the Toronto waterfront (1976) (Figure 6.3).

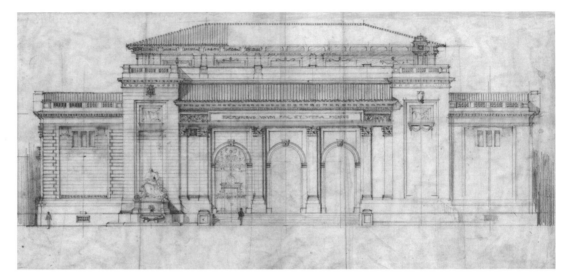

**6.2** Pencil drawing by Paul Cret of his design for the Pan American Union Building in Washington, D.C., 1910. Cret designed the building in association with Albert Kensley. It was Cret's first important commission. Courtesy of the Architectural Archives, University of Pennsylvania.

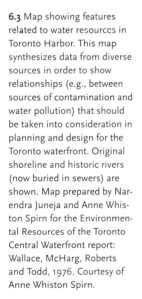

**6.3** Map showing features related to water resources in Toronto Harbor. This map synthesizes data from diverse sources in order to show relationships (e.g., between sources of contamination and water pollution) that should be taken into consideration in planning and design for the Toronto waterfront. Original shoreline and historic rivers (now buried in sewers) are shown. Map prepared by Narendra Juneja and Anne Whiston Spirn for the Environmental Resources of the Toronto Central Waterfront report: Wallace, McHarg, Roberts and Todd, 1976. Courtesy of Anne Whiston Spirn.

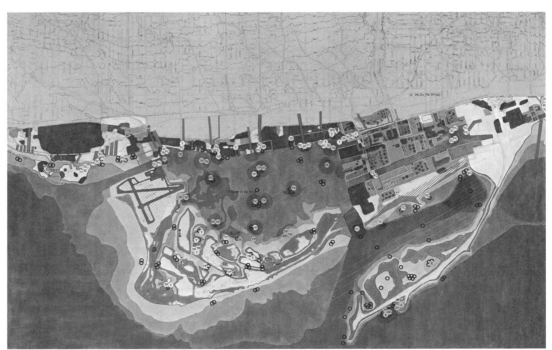

What can the plans for Austin, Texas, put forth by these two Philadelphia-based immigrants, teach us about the nature of city-making? We will look at each plan in some detail and then reflect on the larger significance of each for the present state of the city.

## THE EYES OF TEXAS

Texans aim high, and, early on, they set their sights on a great state university. In fact, the state constitution mandated a university of the "first class." Bolstered with oil revenue from state trust lands, a permanent university endowment fueled the construction of a physical plant worthy of these aspirations. Paul Cret's plan and subsequent buildings for the Texas campus were preceded by the noteworthy work of others, including that of the inventive architect Cass Gilbert and the Dallas architect Herbert Greene (Figure 6.4). But it was with Cret that the university found an architect who matched its confident enterprise.

The Texas Board of Regents engaged Cret as consulting architect in March 1930, a post he retained until his death fifteen years later. In addition to his 1933 comprehensive development plan, Cret participated in the design of nineteen campus buildings, as well as many terraces, retaining walls, and inner-campus roads.[5]

Cret's "Report Accompanying the General Plan of Development" contains careful analyses of the existing buildings, previous plans (most notably those by Gilbert), and the site.[6] The plan also presents a clear vision for the future (Figure 6.5). His scheme respects precedent and context while charting a bold, new course of action. Cret's work is deeply rooted in Beaux-Arts design principles.[7]

Beyond the historicist façades, Beaux-Arts architects like Cret gave careful attention to the relationships among buildings. They organized these relationships to build physical communities. Although (to my knowledge) Cret never used the word explicitly, this approach is "ecological"— that is, concerned about the relationship between organisms (in this case, an academic organism) with each other and with their environments.

6.4 Battle Hall, University of Texas at Austin. Design by Cass Gilbert. Photograph by Frederick Steiner.

Cret's plan consisted of large, carefully rendered, watercolor plans and perspective drawings, as well as a written report (Figure 6.6). His scheme sought to achieve an "elastic formal plan," derived from the writings about architecture as a "civic art" by Werner Hegemann and Elbert Peets.[8] According to Tulane University architecture historian Carol McMichael:

*Formality was achieved by grouping buildings around courts and arranging those groups about axes. Elasticity was achieved by "organic extensions" of existing and projected buildings and by the creation of secondary courts around the primary one at the center of the campus. The whole composition was guided by goals of "interrelation, balance, and symmetry." Interrelation was directed toward realizing elasticity; balance and symmetry, toward formality.[9]*

Cret helped realize these goals through his participation in the design of many buildings on campus. He made generous use of Texas limestone in those buildings, connecting the halls of learning to the bedrock of the region (Figure 6.7).

Cret viewed the plan as flexible and adaptable, writing, "a general plan prepared today will have to be modified from time to time, to take account of changing conditions."[10] He recognized, "To make an elastic formal plan is by no means an easy matter."[11]

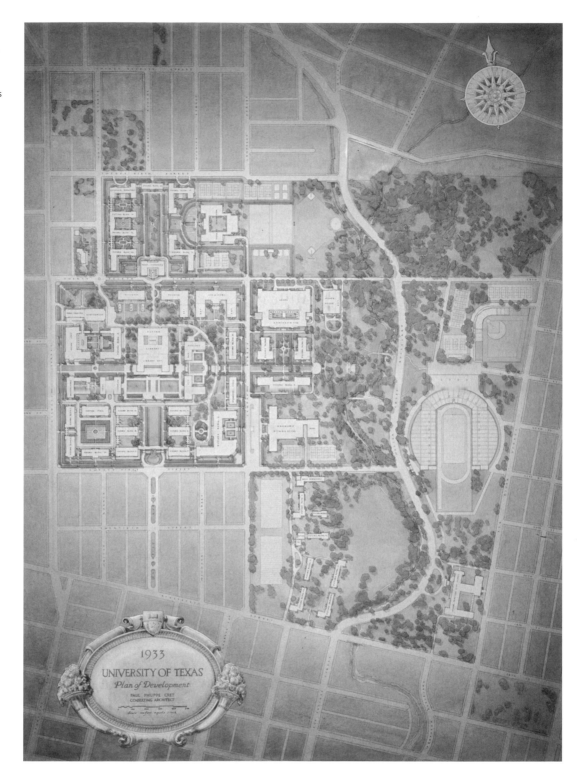

**6.5** Paul Cret plan of development for the University of Texas (1933). Courtesy of the Alexander Architectural Archive, University of Texas Libraries, University of Texas at Austin.

The plan pays careful attention to site conditions and the relationship of the campus to the City of Austin. Vistas, open spaces, the east-west orientation of the central campus, sun angle and weather conditions, breezes, and topography contribute to the arrangement of buildings and circulation systems. Cret used indigenous live oak trees, which would grow to be large in stature, to frame the malls to the south, west, and east of the Main Building (Figure 6.8). Traffic flow between the university and the City of Austin is an important, recognized challenge. Because the Jefferso-

LESSONS FROM CRET, MCHARG, AND MITCHELL | 71

nian north-south, east-west grid of the campus is shifted from the original south-west to north-east grid of the city, the tenuousness of the connections is exacerbated.

Cret envisioned the stream, Waller Creek, running along the east side of the campus, as an important opportunity to link the campus to the city. "This element of the campus," he wrote about the Waller Creek corridor, "can be developed into a most attractive feature, without entailing large expenditures."[12]

One of the most noteworthy aspects of Cret's plan is its acknowledgment that change is inevitable. He presented careful provisions for growth. In particular, Cret recognized that sports would be an important driver of campus change. He observed, "The future of intercollegiate athletics, and especially of the exhibition games requiring very large accommodations for the public, is a subject of great controversy."[13]

## NATURE'S DESIGN

Plans to expand the football stadium in 1969 generated "great controversy" indeed. The expansion plans encroached upon the Waller Creek

6.6 Paul Cret's watercolor perspective of future development of the University of Texas campus (1933). Courtesy of the Alexander Architectural Archive, University of Texas Libraries, University of Texas at Austin.

6.7 Longhorn on limestone wall at the Texas Union, University of Texas at Austin. Photograph by Frederick Steiner.

corridor. Student activists, including many from the School of Architecture, chained themselves to trees and bulldozers, and the Austin environmental movement was born (Figure 6.9). As the city expanded in the early 1970s, its leaders initiated the Austin Tomorrow Plan. A centerpiece of that process became Ian McHarg's *Lake Austin Growth Management Plan*.[14] Although several others from WMRT were involved in the creation of the plan (most notably, Michael Clarke), it is still identified locally as "the McHarg Plan." Local leaders report that the firm was retained because of McHarg, and the plan reflects the principles put forth in his landmark book, *Design with Nature*.

In 1974, the Austin City Council authorized the preparation of a plan for the 92-square-mile (238-km²) area encompassing Lake Austin and the

**6.8** Live oaks on the University of Texas at Austin campus. Photograph by Frederick Steiner.

**6.9** University of Texas student protesting the stadium expansion plans, 1969. Courtesy of *The Daily Texan*.

watersheds of its tributaries. Located to the west of the then city limits, the planning area covered an oak-dominated undulating terrain situated over the Edwards Aquifer. Austin, then as now, was growing; in fact, it has doubled in population every twenty years since 1895. The Lake Austin area was clearly fated for new growth but also possessed significant environmental amenities (Figure 6.10). According to McHarg and his colleagues, how and where growth "occurs will have a profound effect upon life and property and the Area's irreplaceable natural resources. The consequences of unplanned and uncontrolled growth will be felt not only by those persons living in the Lake Austin Area, but by a much larger population residing in the City of Austin and Travis County who will bear the costs of degraded environments and those actions required to deal with such conditions."[15]

Such ideas were new for cities and counties in the early 1970s. The Clean Water Act had passed in 1972, and the nation was in the middle of what became known as the "Environmental Decade." The momentum began with events such as the passage of the National Environmental Policy Act in 1969, signed into law on New Year's Day 1970 by President Richard Nixon, as well as the first

Earth Day, then Earth Week, in April 1970. Published in 1969, *Design with Nature* was central to this movement, and the leaders of Austin wanted to put McHarg's ideas into action.

Whereas Cret's plan for the campus may be interpreted as an implicitly applied human ecology, McHarg and his compatriots applied ecology to their management plan explicitly. Whereas Cret proposed an "elastic formal plan" with "organic extensions," McHarg advocated more of an "elastic organic plan" with "formal extensions." Cret's extensions were primarily buildings and green spaces; McHarg's were infrastructure and green spaces.

The Lake Austin plan consisted of a careful analysis of development trends, the determination of facilities and services necessary to accommodate that development, a detailed inventory of the natural environment with particular attention to the suitabilities for future growth, conservation and development principles, and suggested public policies to manage growth. Water quality received considerable attention in the WMRT plan, especially as it related to the sensitivity of the vast Edwards Aquifer.

McHarg's premise was that by studying the

natural environment, one could identify certain opportunities for development as well as constraints. The constraints could eliminate some land uses while restricting others. This range of development opportunities and constraints corresponded with three proposed zones for the planning area: conservation, limited development, and development. The rules for each zone were "based upon a philosophy that land use and development controls should be as few in number and as uncomplicated as possible so that they may be effectively administered by a public agency and understood by the private sector."[16] Like Cret, WMRT advocated elasticity, a flexibility guided by clear principles.

McHarg contended that "natural regions" could be translated into "planning regions." As a result, he defined four physiographic regions for the Lake Austin area, tailoring the three zones (conservation, limited development, and development) for each region (Figure 6.11). That is, the guidelines for the development zone in one region (for example, the Lake Austin Corridor Region) differed from the other three physiographic regions (e.g., the Plateau Region, the Hill Region, and the Terrace Region). Specific public policies were recommended for the planning area to guide future land use, open space, water supply, sewage collection and treatment, and highway construction and improvements.

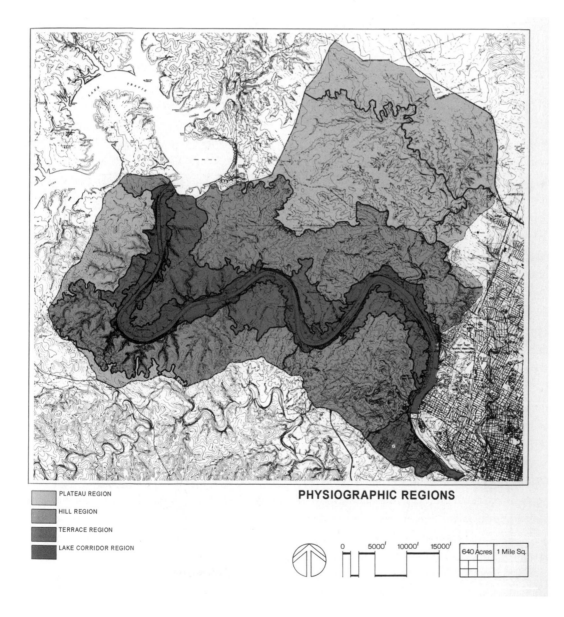

PHYSIOGRAPHIC REGIONS

PLATEAU REGION
HILL REGION
TERRACE REGION
LAKE CORRIDOR REGION

**6.10** Physiographic Regions, *Lake Austin Growth Management Plan.* Prepared by Wallace, McHarg, Roberts and Todd for the City of Austin (1976). Courtesy of Wallace Roberts & Todd.

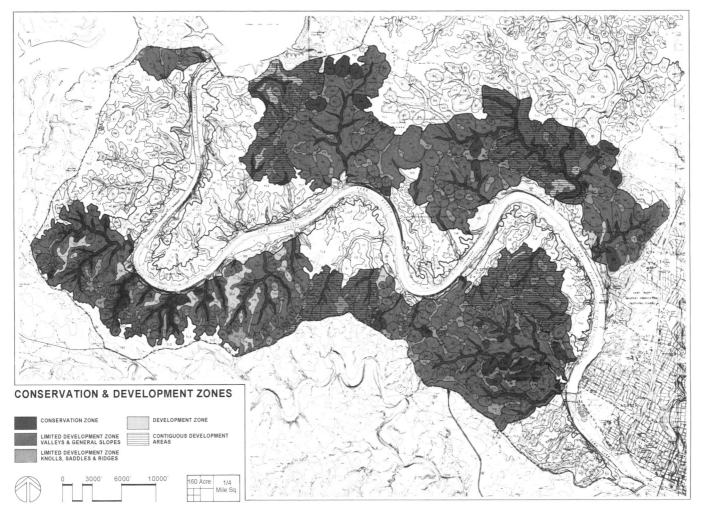

**CONSERVATION & DEVELOPMENT ZONES**

- CONSERVATION ZONE
- LIMITED DEVELOPMENT ZONE VALLEYS & GENERAL SLOPES
- LIMITED DEVELOPMENT ZONE KNOLLS, SADDLES & RIDGES
- DEVELOPMENT ZONE
- CONTIGUOUS DEVELOPMENT AREAS

0    3000'    6000'    10000'

160 Acre    1/4 Mile Sq.

**6.11** Conservation and Development Zones, *Lake Austin Growth Management Plan*. Prepared by Wallace, McHarg, Roberts and Todd for the City of Austin (1976). Courtesy of Wallace Roberts & Todd.

The plan has had varying influence in the Austin metropolitan region that continues to the present. Parts of the area covered by the plan were subsequently incorporated as separate jurisdictions (West Lake Hills and Rollingwood). These towns adopted several development and conservation standards and, as a result, some suburban neighborhoods in these jurisdictions reflect many of McHarg's proposals. A former West Lake Hills City Council member told me that the WMRT plan and *Design with Nature* provided "guiding lights for decades." In other places, his ideas were pursued less vigorously. Yet throughout the Austin metropolitan region, the plan is still used as a basis for ongoing discussions and debates about environmental planning, growth management, and smart growth policies.

## THE BOOKENDS OF AMERICAN MODERNISM

Paul Cret was a Beaux-Arts architect. He was also a modern, literate man with broad, international experiences and connections, whose later buildings clearly exhibited the influences of the Congrès Internationaux d'Architecture Moderne, or International Modern, movement. Ian McHarg entered Harvard with academic Modernism in full bloom. Until his death, he retained a modernist belief in the wisdom of science as a basis to guide decision-making. Still, he shared his mentor Lewis Mumford's skepticism about the International Style. Mumford valued the variety of urban settlements, which responded to specific political and environmental conditions. He was wary of the one-style-fits-all approach of the Modernists. Cret continued to use the Beaux-Arts method to design while experimenting with modern visual motifs, such as spare surfaces. McHarg grounded his method in modern processes, while abandoning the notion that a single style was appropriate across the globe.

Louis Kahn connected Cret with McHarg. Kahn was Cret's most famous student, and he worked in Cret's firm. Kahn was also McHarg's colleague, collaborator, and friend. Although he marinated in Modernism after Cret's death, Kahn does not fit neatly in the modern camp.

Cret worked with the University of Texas campus for a decade and a half. McHarg was directly involved in Austin for two years, but four of his former students (Austan Librach, Pliny Fisk, Kent Butler, and, most recently, I) have been involved with design and planning initiatives in Austin for almost thirty years. Kahn influenced a generation of architects, including many who continue to teach and practice in Austin. What influence do the ideas, designs, and plans of Cret, McHarg, and Kahn exert on the nature of the city?

A lot, but too little.

Between the poetic core of the campus and the woody hills around Lake Austin lies a bumpy mess of a city. In his plan for the campus, Cret pinpointed the ugliness near the state capitol as a significant urban design issue. He wrote: "The whole problem of the capitol grounds and its approach has never been the object of an adequate study, although of great importance to the City of Austin. As this problem is of interest to the state, the city, and the university, it is to be hoped that it will be placed some day in competent hands."[17]

Some seventy years later, one still hopes.

Even though Austin regularly ranks high on "most livable" city polls, its urban fabric generally reveals many of the woes facing other American cities. On its way from Mexico to Canada, Inter-state 35 divides the African-American and Latino populations from the whites. These divisions reflect economic and ethnic segregation. Traditionally, blacks and Hispanics have lived apart—north and south—from each other in Austin, too.

The city lacks affordable housing, and traffic clogs highways and streets. Neighborhoods are under siege by transportation engineers who want to expand highways. Cars and trucks bump along city streets pockmarked with potholes. Giant billboards and utility lines loom above, and business signs blaze in competition for the senses. Power lines cut through majestic oaks, scarring their canopies. Large, vacant lots dot the city center, while suburbs sprawl out at the periphery.

The natural environment of hills, valleys, streams, the Colorado River, and lush vegetation remains quite beautiful. More urban infill development is in and near downtown, a commuter rail line opened in 2010, and additional transit is being planned.

In the meantime, in spite of the challenges, each day I leave my office in a building designed by Paul Cret on the campus he planned. On my way home, I pass a sign welcoming me to the "Edwards Aquifer Environmentally Sensitive Area." My limestone house just inside the Austin city limits was built among the live oaks in 1980, four years after the Wallace, McHarg, Roberts and Todd plan was completed for this area. Each evening, an opossum visits the backyard with her offspring. As I jog in the morning along a stream that is connected to a larger greenway system, I often spot deer and sometimes even a fox.

Such are the fruits of designing with nature. Through the use of ecology to help inform design, we can better shape our surroundings to respond to the opportunities and constraints of the natural world. We can begin to live with nature.

# 7 | THE WOODLANDS
## THE ECOLOGICAL
## DESIGN OF A NEW CITY

After watching postwar suburbs sprawl across the landscape during the 1960s, a handful of developers, architects, and planners argued that Americans could do better. New communities, they claimed, could be built in harmony with nature and be open to people of all races and religions. Jobs would be close to homes, and all buildings would be well-designed. Idealism was these planners' driving force, even if some of the things they planned fell short of their aspirations or now seem odd. Their enthusiasm was fueled in particular by two new communities that had been developed during the 1960s—Reston, Virginia, and Columbia, Maryland (Figure 7.1). Even federal policy makers became interested, and in 1970, Congress passed the HUD Title VII Urban Growth and New Community Development Act, which guaranteed up to $50 million in support if a developer met specific social and environmental goals. As a result of the Civil Rights movement, the social goals of the HUD new community law addressed equal opportunity, discrimination, and the lack of diversity and fair housing. Because the National Environmental Policy Act had just been signed into law, a thorough environmental impact review was required for the new communities to achieve federal approval.

Eventually, thirteen new communities were approved for loan guarantees by the federal gov-ernment under the Title VII program. An additional three were funded by a related New York State program. Ten states were represented in all, most of them east of the Mississippi River. Texas, however, had three federally funded new communities—Flower Mound near Dallas, the San Antonio Ranch, and The Woodlands near Houston. All thirteen communities had ambitious social and environmental goals, but the individual focuses varied, such as the emphasis in Soul City, North Carolina, on African-Americans and the new-town-in-town initiatives in New York City (Roosevelt Island), New Orleans (Pontchartrain), and Minneapolis (Cedar-Riverside). Like The Woodlands, most of the other projects were on green-field sites.

Twelve of the HUD Title VII new towns defaulted on their loans and went bankrupt. The one exception was The Woodlands, sitting only a short distance away from the unplanned sprawl of Houston. Even now, almost four decades later, one might ask the question: Why was The Woodlands different?

I have a personal interest in the answer to that question. Title VII changed my life. In 1971, I began working for an idealistic Dayton, Ohio, homebuilder named Don Huber. His family was famous for building Levittown-like suburbs. Huber himself experimented with modular building techniques and initiated partnerships with church groups to build homes in African-American communities. I went to work for him designing brochures for his housing projects and taking pictures of 5,000 acres (2,023 ha) of rolling Ohio farmland northwest of Dayton. On this land, Huber dreamed of building a new community unlike Levittown or his family's own Huber Heights.

Don Huber decided to pursue a Title VII grant and hired a crusty Harvard MLA named Gerwin Rohrbach to lead the effort. Because I knew the 5,000 acres (2,023 ha) well, Rohrbach appointed me as his administrative assistant. One of my jobs was to give tours of the property, dubbed "Newfields," to the prospective master planners we interviewed. A bunch of old codgers from The Architects Collaborative came from Cambridge; Hideo Sasaki and Stuart Dawson also flew in from Massachusetts. The Simonds brothers, John and Philip, of the Environmental Planning and Development Partnership, traveled from Pittsburgh. Gyo Obata and Neil Porterfield of HOK arrived

from St. Louis. And then there was O. Jack Mitchell and his Omniplan colleagues from Houston. One afternoon, while I was driving the architects Harry and Ben Weese around in my VW bug, we interrupted a pair of naked hippies in a cornfield.

"Don't see that in Chicago," Harry Weese observed.

Like eleven others, Newfields defaulted on its federal loan (leaving its old cornfields in production, but not by hippies, for years afterward).

What made The Woodlands different? The short answer is George P. Mitchell, Ian L. McHarg, and Houston.

Huber was a Dayton homebuilder, George Mitchell a Texas oilman. The difference in the level of capital they could apply was substantial. Huber's goals were lofty, but his experience was grounded in local homebuilding. Mitchell, not constrained by prior development experience, followed the lead of his consultants, most notably Ian McHarg, known for his advocacy of the use of ecology in design and planning. And, of course,

**7.1** Aerial view of Reston, Virginia. Design by William J. Conklin and James S. Rossant for the developer Robert E. Simon. Photograph by James S. Rossant, FAIA.

Houston was growing in the 1970s, while Dayton was not.

In the mid-1970s, I entered the University of Pennsylvania to study with McHarg. By this time, planning for The Woodlands was well underway, and the development was already being recognized as the most successful of the Title VII new communities. The Woodlands is often touted as one of the most complete and comprehensive examples of McHarg's ecological planning method.[1] In fact, McHarg himself repeatedly made this claim in his books, *A Quest for Life* and *To Heal the Earth*.[2] Still, one wonders how much of the positive commentary was hype, and just how successful The Woodlands is from today's perspective.

Cornell professor Ann Forsyth, who has conducted the most thorough critical assessments of The Woodlands to date, dubbed it an "ecoburb."[3] By that she meant that The Woodlands is greener than other American suburban communities, but initially was a suburb without transit accessibility to central Houston. However, because of the jobs located in The Woodlands, it has grown to be more like a small city. Today, we might call developments like Prairie Crossing near Chicago an "ecoburb." However, although still a suburb, Prairie Crossing is linked to Chicago by train. In this regard, it is similar to older suburbs like Riverside, Illinois. Forsyth divides the planning of The Woodlands into five phases: early ideas from the mid-1960s to 1970; ecological design and the involvement of planners from Columbia, Maryland, 1970 to 1974; Title VII in operation, 1975 to 1983; community building, 1983 to 1997; and post-Mitchell growth since 1997.[4] The less critical "inside story" by the former CEO of The Woodlands Operating Company, Roger Galatas, presents a similar time line.[5]

## DESIGN WITH NATURE AND MONEY

George Mitchell was born in Galveston in 1919 to Greek immigrant parents. He remained committed to Galveston throughout his life, helping to restore many of its historic structures that had been destroyed by the 1900 hurricane. Mitchell majored in petroleum engineering with an emphasis in geology at Texas A&M, and after graduation, he went to work for the Stanolind Oil and Gas Company (now Amoco) before spending the Second World War in the Army Corps of Engineers. Following the war, he went into the oil drilling business with his brother. Their successful venture eventually became Mitchell Energy & Development Corp. Then, in the early 1960s, George Mitchell began to experiment with land development as a way to diversify the energy business.

In 1964, Mitchell purchased 50,000 acres (20,234 ha) of land north of Houston owned by the Grogan-Cochran Lumber Company; 2,800 acres (1,133 ha) of this purchase became the seed of what became a 27,000-acre (10,927-ha) new community.

Most Title VII new communities were in the 5,000- to 8,000-acre (2,023- to 3,237-ha) range, but the expansive acreage put together by Mitchell signaled the scope of his ambition. Mitchell consulted with several Houston area architects and planners, hiring Robert Hartsfield away from one of those firms—CRS. A Penn graduate, Hartsfield introduced Mitchell to McHarg's *Design with Nature*. Mitchell also sought out the advice of James Rouse, who had developed Columbia, Maryland, and later hired several people who had worked for Rouse on that pivotal new town. In her writing, Ann Forsyth describes the similarities between Mitchell and Rouse, such as their business acumen and their idealistic commitment to interfaith cooperation and understanding, as well as the similarities between their resulting new towns. She also makes an important distinction, noting in her book *Reforming Suburbia: The Planned Communities of Irvine, Columbia, and The Woodlands* that "Rouse's response [to community planning] had been to explore the potential for social science to solve the problems of city building; Mitchell, eventually, looked to the natural sciences and, in particular, ecology as it was being translated into environmental planning and landscape architecture in the late 1960s and early 1970s."[6] Given Mitchell's background in geology, this is not surprising.

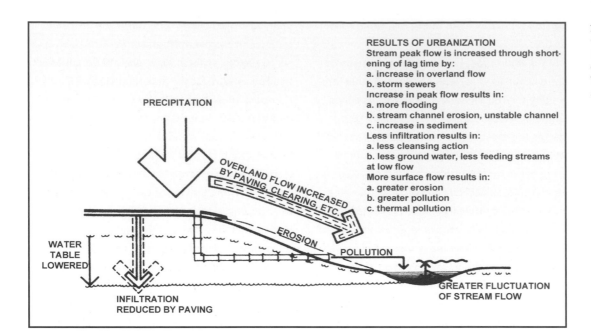

PRECIPITATION

OVERLAND FLOW INCREASED BY PAVING, CLEARING, ETC.

WATER TABLE LOWERED

INFILTRATION REDUCED BY PAVING

EROSION

POLLUTION

GREATER FLUCTUATION OF STREAM FLOW

**RESULTS OF URBANIZATION**
Stream peak flow is increased through short-ening of lag time by:
a. increase in overland flow
b. storm sewers
Increase in peak flow results in:
a. more flooding
b. stream channel erosion, unstable channel
c. increase in sediment
Less infiltration results in:
a. less cleansing action
b. less ground water, less feeding streams at low flow
More surface flow results in:
a. greater erosion
b. greater pollution
c. thermal pollution

**7.2** *The Woodlands New Community Ecological Plan.* Diagram showing the results of "typical" urbanization by Wallace, McHarg, Roberts and Todd.

The first meeting between Mitchell and McHarg was transformative for both men. "I suggested to Mitchell that the most critical factor was cash," McHarg wrote, adding, "God smiles on ecological planners."[7] Or, as Mitchell later restated it, "God smiles on ecological planners, when you make a profit."[8]

McHarg suggested using the natural drainage system of The Woodlands site to structure development. This would, he noted, help reduce the risks of flood damage. Ever the geologist, Mitchell asked, "All right, natural drainage works, but what does it mean to me?"

"First, George, it means you'll get $50 million from HUD and, second, it will save you even more money," McHarg responded. "For instance, you won't have to build a storm drainage system. This will save you $14 million for the first phase alone." And so McHarg converted the oilman into an ecologist.[9]

Wallace, McHarg, Roberts and Todd proceeded to produce a series of four extraordinary reports to guide the planning and design of The Woodlands (Figure 7.2). One of these reports, an ecological inventory, resulted in an ecological plan, guidelines for site planning, and land planning and design principles for the first phase of development.

With money and ecology forming the bedrock of the project, Mitchell's staff and team of consultants, which included economic and marketing specialists Gladstone Associates, master planner and architects William Pereira Associates, and engineers Richard Browne Associates, prepared plans and obtained approvals. After The Woodlands received its commitment from HUD in April 1972, "infrastructure construction assumed a feverish pace" for the 1,750-acre (708-ha) first "village," called Grogan's Mill.[10] The new community officially opened on October 9, 1974.

Through the rest of the 1970s, development continued as one by one the other Title VII new communities failed. During this same period, the relationship between HUD and The Woodlands became an uneasy one. For example, disagreements occurred over financial management, project organization, affirmative action, and low- and moderate-income housing. Beyond the difficulties with HUD, Mitchell faced other economic challenges, chief among them the Arab oil embargo and the resulting sag in Houston's real estate market. Still, despite the setbacks, Mitchell's Woodlands Development Corporation soldiered on with staff reorganization and financial readjustments.

In 1983, the Title VII status of The Woodlands ended, directly affecting the amount of affordable housing in the new community. (As Forsyth notes, most of the federally subsidized housing was built before 1983.) The change came during a period of slow national economic growth. As the price of oil dropped, the Houston economy especially suffered. Regardless, development in The Woodlands continued. Several key employers, among them Hughes Tool and Anadarko Petroleum, moved to The Woodlands. Schools, places of worship, and other key institutions, such as the Cynthia Woods Mitchell Pavilion and the Houston Advanced Research Center, opened. As a result of The Woodlands Country Club, with its three golf courses, the new community became associated with golf.

In 1997, the population of The Woodlands exceeded 50,000. That same year, Mitchell sold The Woodlands Corporation and all of its assets to a partnership of Morgan Stanley and Crescent Real Estate Equities for $543 million.[11] The 2000 Census recorded a population of 55,649. As growth continued into the twenty-first century, the Rouse Company, developers of Columbia, Maryland, purchased a 52.7 percent interest in The Woodlands.[12] Currently, it is one of the most desirable places to live in the Houston metropolitan region. The real estate values have increased and are among the highest in the region.

## THE PINEY WOODS

Given these changes, what are the prospects for the future of The Woodlands? And what will be its lasting legacies? The first thing one notices when driving into The Woodlands from the ugly suburban sprawl around its borders is, well, the woodlands. Every year the residents of The Woodlands are asked what they like most about their community and, according to George Mitchell, every year they respond "the woods."[13] As recommended by McHarg and his colleagues, large stands of loblolly pines and associated oaks, sweet gum, hickory, tupelo, magnolia, and sycamore trees have been preserved. In the Title VII plan, 3,909 acres (1,582 ha) were to be set aside as open space. Eventually, 8,000 acres (3,237 ha)

of the total 27,000-acre (10,927-ha) community will become open space. This land includes public park and preserve land, as well as five private and two public golf courses.

As anyone who has lived in the area very long knows, heavy rains and flooding are a frequent occurrence in and around Houston. To reduce the negative impacts of this excess of water, McHarg's strategy called for, first, the use of natural drainage systems to control stormwater; second, the minimum clearing of native vegetation; and third, limited use of impervious surfaces. This strategy has proven successful, and, as a result, residents of The Woodlands have not been negatively affected by floods.

Wildlife habitat is an auxiliary benefit of large areas of native plants and connected natural corridors (Figure 7.3). Waterfowl, turtles, and small mammals are plentiful in the riparian areas along streams and around The Woodlands' lakes. Residents also report seeing coyotes, a species particularly adaptive to changing habitat conditions.

For his 1994 master's thesis, MIT planning student Russell Clive Claus wrote "a retrospective critique" on the use of ecology in The Woodlands' planning.[14] He used principles from landscape ecology to assess The Woodlands and found it lacking. He argued that several of the ecological principles "that underscored the planning phase are flawed by today's standards and would have been counterproductive to the achievement of contemporary conservation goals." Furthermore, he noted that The Woodlands Corporation "failed to pursue the ecological vision encapsulated in the early planning phase."[15] In defense of The Woodlands plan, the landscape ecology principles did not exist in 1974 when the plan was prepared. It was McHarg, in fact, who helped provide the interdisciplinary collaboration that contributed to the development of landscape ecology. However, Claus' criticism about the failure of the developers to pursue the early ecological planning vision is accurate. Anyone who has ever been involved in a long-term, large-scale planning project can attest to the challenge of sustaining idealism and vision. Claus' thesis reminds us that ecological science

**7.3** Housing and open space at The Woodlands, Texas. Photograph by Frederick Steiner.

and ecological design continue to evolve. Some mechanism to incorporate new ecological knowledge into The Woodlands' ongoing planning and design would have been a really significant innovation. Still, no development as expansive as The Woodlands has incorporated this newer science or design in its planning.

Several smaller-scale conservation developments, such as Prairie Crossing, Illinois, and Dewees Island, South Carolina, have incorporated newer ecological knowledge. In addition, the U.S. Green Building Council's LEED for Neighborhood Development and the Sustainable Sites Initiative, discussed in Chapter 4, display considerable promise for influencing how new communities are planned and designed.

## THE WOODLANDS AND DIVERSITY: MIXED SUCCESS

People classified by the U.S. Census as "white" are now a minority in Texas. Conversely, according to the 2000 Census, 87.5 percent of The Woodlands population is "white non-Hispanic." So one might well ask if the idea of racial diversity, which was a dream for new towns during the 1960s and a goal HUD established for Title VII communities, was ever really likely in The Woodlands. Pre–Title VII Columbia has achieved a good level of diversity, but then this Maryland development is located in the Washington, D.C., region, while The Woodlands is in Texas, where integration of housing remained an explosive issue even in the 1970s.

One remarkable aspect of The Woodlands in this regard is that George Mitchell appeared to be sincerely committed to diversity. He championed efforts to eliminate discrimination in housing sales based on race or religion. In the early years, the range of housing prices was more inclusive than in the later years of development. In addition, HUD supported a better mix of housing before withdrawing its support for low income housing in 1983, a move Mitchell called "very disappointing."[16] The prices of the homes in The Woodlands, rather than overt discrimination, appear to have limited the racial diversity. Although it is possible to purchase condominium units in the lower $100,000s, single-family builder homes starting above $200,000 and custom homes costing into the millions dominate The Woodlands real estate market. Galatas reports that The Woodlands Corporation currently does not address the lower 40 percent of Houston's housing market.[17]

Mitchell was more successful in encouraging religious diversity. According to Forsyth, Mitchell was attracted by Rouse's experiment of bringing various faiths together.[18] Mitchell consulted with Catholic, Jewish, and Protestant leaders and formed The Woodlands Religious Community Incorporated, now called Interfaith.[19] This organization assumed many social planning and social services responsibilities in the new community and has overall been a positive force. For example, when a group of evangelical Christians organized a commemoration for the first anniversary of 9/11 that excluded Muslims and Jews, Interfaith held a more inclusionary event in The Woodlands.

### KEEPING UP APPEARANCES

George Mitchell exhibited considerable devotion to The Woodlands for more than forty years, even after he sold the project. His was not a get-rich-quick scheme. Galatas reports that Mitchell said, "I didn't want to sell The Woodlands, . . . [it] is a great project and I was very proud of it."[20] At the time of the sale, Mitchell was seventy-eight years old. If he had been fifty years old in 1997, he told Galatas, he would not have sold The Woodlands Corporation.[21]

As a result of Mitchell's leadership, The Woodlands is more than a bedroom suburb. It

has indeed become a community, albeit a rather "upscale" one, with newer buildings and neighborhoods closer in character to other contemporary affluent suburbs than to a more rustic ecological ideal. Homes continue to sell well, including those in the million-dollar range.[22] The retail establishments and golf courses indicate an affluent citizenry. Walkways and bike paths meander through The Woodlands, connecting homes to work, shopping, school, and recreation (Figure 7.4). The community's proximity to Houston's main airport and Interstate 45 has made it attractive to business and industry. In fact, Mitchell sited The Woodlands with the location of the airport and interstate in mind.[23] In the beginning, his goal was to provide employment opportunities for at least one third of residents within the community.[24] As of 2004, there were thirty thousand jobs in The Woodlands, which represents a good jobs-housing balance.[25] Employment near homes has reduced somewhat the number of commuters in the Houston metropolitan region. Mitchell originally expected Houston to annex The Woodlands and was disappointed that The Woodlands residents resisted annexation. He remained hopeful about the prospects for annexation, but in late 2006, an agreement was reached with Houston that will make The Woodlands self-governing in 2014.[26]

The New Urbanists have renewed public and developer interest in new communities. However, they tend to ignore the American new communities of the 1960s and 1970s and use earlier eras of town planning as their precedential touchstones. Real differences exist between the visions of the New Urbanists and the earlier generation of American new community planners. New Urbanists advocate for front porches and straight streets. There are few front porches and many winding roads in The Woodlands. Except for an early bibliography put together by Elizabeth Plater-Zyberk, the New Urbanists have paid scant attention to The Woodlands or any other American new community of the 1960s and 1970s. The New Urbanists focus on a specific design aesthetic first and place a strong emphasis on circulation and connectivity second. A few leading New Urbanists

**7.4** Separation of walking, jogging, and biking trail from roadway in The Woodlands, Texas. Photograph by Frederick Steiner.

even express open hostility toward environmentalism (although this is becoming more muted as sustainable design moves more into the mainstream). Most New Urbanist completed developments are more New Suburban than urban. They are affluent neighborhoods that have been developed with economic and aesthetic goals at the forefront, rather than for environmental protection or social equity.

The new communities of the 1960s and 1970s equally emphasized environmental and social concerns. Landscape design prevailed over architectural design. In The Woodlands, transportation systems may have catered to the automobile, but roadways were designed to fit the terrain. Pedestrian and bike trails weave through the piney woods, connecting residential neighborhoods to shopping and office areas. Design standards effectively control signage, and utilities are buried and hidden from sight.

The building architecture in The Woodlands is, well, suburban in appearance. Perhaps this is why its design has not attracted much interest from the New Urbanists or the broader architectural community. In this regard, The Woodlands can be compared to two other Wallace, McHarg, Roberts and Todd projects from the early 1970s: Amelia Island in north Florida and the Austin, Texas, neighborhood where I live. Amelia Island presents similarities to The Woodlands in both landscape and building design, although new developments during the past decade display a noticeable New Urbanist influence. As I noted in the previous chapter, my Austin neighborhood developed following the Wallace, McHarg, Roberts and Todd Lake Austin Growth Management Plan of 1976.[27] Although in my neighborhood it is the oaks that are preserved rather than pines, the residential and retail structures, as well as the street patterns, display similarities to their cousins in The Woodlands.

## PROSPECTS

So how exactly does one judge The Woodlands nearly forty years on? In the environmental and economic realms, The Woodlands can point to many successful achievements. Its social record, however, is more disappointing, with only modest racial diversity. Over time, The Woodlands has become a more affluent, more exclusive community. Its landscape design is accomplished and pleasant, but its building architecture lacks innovation and excitement.

But then there is the dream. The Woodlands began as a dream, and one can imagine another dream that builds from it. One can imagine a new community in the future that sets aside even more land as open space, transcends competence in landscape design, and advances an architecture that is both livable and inventive. This new community would draw on the most up-to-date knowledge in ecological science and ideas from ecological planning. The developer would possess the business acumen and stamina of George Mitchell. The new community would be linked to the world by rail and internally through bike and pedestrian trails. All new buildings would be built to platinum LEED standards, and schools would have windows. The community would also be dedicated to achieving social equity and racial diversity.

George Mitchell helped change planning, design, and development practice in Texas (Figure 7.5). As he reflected, "When we started planning The Woodlands, there wasn't the architecture or land planning talent to design and build a new

town in Houston. That's why I hired ten people from Columbia, plus some of their consultants and talent from all over the nation, like McHarg. Now there's the talent in Houston, but it would be impossible to assemble the land for a new community like The Woodlands."[28]

We can also be inspired by George Mitchell's idealism. A success in the oil and gas business, he did not need to venture into the risky business of building a new community. But he did, largely because of his belief that we can do a better job designing our built environment. Now in the first urban century, with more than half the world's population living in city-regions for the first time in history, we need to pursue this ideal with a renewed commitment. As we have become a more urban planet, many more people have joined us in the urban regions, with more on the way. As our numbers have increased, we face a future with finite or declining land, water, and energy resources. The Woodlands is not perfect, but George Mitchell's vision illustrates the practical reality of dreaming big. The big dreams of the future will likely involve redeveloping large sections of existing cities and suburbs. Such infill should build on advances in our understanding of urban ecosystems.

**7.5** Integration of development with nature at The Woodlands, Texas. Photograph by Frederick Steiner.

# III
# EMERGING
# URBANISM
# IN TEXAS

Texas grows increasingly urban, but its citizens cling to a rural ethos. The state's wealth flows from its natural resources, famously oil, gas, and rangeland, but also water. Texas possesses rich aquifers, many rivers, and coastal expanses. As these resources have been harnessed for settlement, their natural beauty has eroded.

Such is the case with the Trinity River in Fort Worth and Dallas. While San Antonio and Austin converted rivers into community assets, the urban Trinity became visually and chemically degraded. The citizens of Fort Worth and Dallas have begun to reverse this situation and transform the riverway into an urban oasis. Most notably, acclaimed Spanish engineer Santiago Calatrava designed three spectacular bridges to span the Trinity parkway in Dallas.

The transition to greater urbanity poses challenges. In Austin, the University of Texas attempted to recruit renowned Swiss architects to design a new art museum. These efforts were thwarted by two members of the university's board of regents who rejected the contemporary art museum design, favoring a more traditional look. In the wake of the resulting controversy, the university retained a leading landscape architect to design the plaza at the museum.

Conversely, enlightened patrons in Dallas enlisted two of the most important contemporary architecture firms in the world to design new venues in the city's arts district. In addition, a rising star from Portland renewed and expanded the arts magnet high school in the district. Although the architecture sparkled, the landscape design for the district sputtered. Still, a site design emerged that should eventually contribute to the urbanity of Dallas.

Urban designers in Texas and elsewhere are challenged to connect city places to their regional context. Lady Bird Johnson understood this dilemma. She advocated the use of native plants as a device to link people to their place. Native wildflowers along the highways and native trees in city parks reinforce the intrinsic character of a place. They also attract native birds and mammals. Lady Bird Johnson showed us how we can retain the essence of a region, even as it grows more urban.

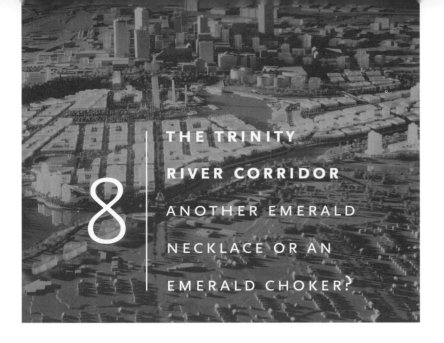

# 8 THE TRINITY RIVER CORRIDOR

## ANOTHER EMERALD NECKLACE OR AN EMERALD CHOKER?

Flying east from Tucson into the Dallas–Fort Worth region in August 2002, my Southwest Airlines neighbor asks, "Is that real grass? I haven't seen a deciduous tree since moving to Arizona a decade ago."

Indeed, the landscape below has changed from brown to green over the past hour, and more and more clouds join us in the air—a storm is moving up from the Gulf. Verdure ribbons replace the arroyos etched into the parched Southwest terrain.

The dendritic patterns of these ribbons dominate the settlements, ranches, and farms laid out by the rugged Texas pioneers. As we enter the Dallas-Fort Worth metropolitan region, the hydrological forces yield somewhat. Still, the influence of water remains a strong force. Dams hold back, or attempt to, flood water; large lakes collect drainage from acres of land; smaller ponds challenge golfers, provide amenities for suburban residents, or are the remnants of the agricultural past; channelized streams direct flows to where we humans want them to go; and water towers dot the landscape, indicating nodes of settlements.

In this mosaic, a large river is evident. Controlled, or under the illusion of control, the river—the Trinity—appears like a green artery, collecting the nutrients of many tributaries (Figure 8.1).

As we descend, I make a quick diagnosis. The great naturalist Aldo Leopold once observed, "One of the penalties of an ecological education" is to see more clearly "a world of wounds."[1] I see the wounds of the Trinity River. Once the heart of a massive ecosystem stretching from near Oklahoma to the Gulf of Mexico, the urban Trinity is "a pale shadow of its natural self: straightened and channelized, severed from its floodplain by levees, polluted with bacteria and traces of long-banned chemicals, and flowing in dry seasons only with big infusions of treated wastewater from sewage plants."[2]

How can the wounds be healed? The answer to that question will not only restore the health of the river but also could contribute much to the quality of the Dallas-Fort Worth "Metroplex" region for years to come. The condition and fate of the Trinity mirrors that of many rivers throughout the nation and much of the world. Over the past century, we harnessed hydrology in a Promethean project to control drainage for human needs, inflicting much injury in the process.[3] Through this "project," nature was viewed as a vast cornucopia of resources to be engineered for human use.

Others see the wounds, too. Several prescriptions have been offered to heal the river. However, the remedies have garnered sharp criticism. At the time my plane landed in August 2002, two efforts in particular exemplified this debate: the City of Dallas Trinity River Corridor Project and the American Institute of Architects *Dallas Trinity River Policy*.[4]

## ARGUMENTS OVER "VISION"

The Trinity and its tributaries cross much of North and East Texas. Including the tributaries, its total length is 710 miles (1,143 km). Two of the main forks of the Trinity meet near downtown Fort Worth, then flow east to Dallas. Beyond Dallas, the Trinity crosses ranches, farms, and forests before entering Galveston Bay. The river flooded frequently early in the history of Dallas and Fort Worth. Its control was important to enable the growth of both cities. But with control came the loss of the river's character as it flows through Fort Worth and Dallas.

The Dallas Trinity River Corridor Project builds on a long history of plans and proposals stretching back to landscape architect George Kessler's 1911 "A City Plan for Dallas" through the 1962 Springer Plan formulated by the city's planning department to the 1997 Texas Department of Transportation "Trinity Parkway Major Transporta-

tion Study" (Figure 8.2). These plans and studies proposed parks and parkways, flood control and water resource management, levee construction and levee expansion, greenbelts and greenways, open spaces and in-fill developments, a "town lake," and wetlands. The river has long been a magnet for ideas, and in 1998, Dallas voters approved a $246 million capital bond program for improvements within the corridor. Ron Kirk, Dallas mayor at the time (and later, President Barack Obama's trade representative), championed the initiative. The bond program, in turn, prompted the city to develop its master implementation plan and establish the Trinity River Corridor Project.

This plan served as "a footprint" toward realization of a vision touted by supporters as "Distinctively Dallas." Mindful of the successes of Town Lake (now Lady Bird Lake) in Austin and the River Walk in San Antonio, Dallas leaders advocated the creation of a central park that would strengthen the civic identity of the city. The 1998 implementation plan, led by engineering

**8.1** A vision for the Trinity River through Dallas. Courtesy of Wallace Roberts & Todd.

firm Halff Associates, included lakes, recreational amenities, gateways, design criteria, trail alignments, and "landscaping" guidance. (The plan's authors clearly viewed landscaping as planting, rather than landscape design and planning in the broader sense.) The plan did result in the engaging idea to create a series of "signature bridges" to be designed by Santiago Calatrava (Figure 8.3).

Meanwhile, after the approval of the 1998 bond package, several compatible studies and plans were launched to address more specific elements in the corridor, including a new highway to release congestion into downtown to be supported by

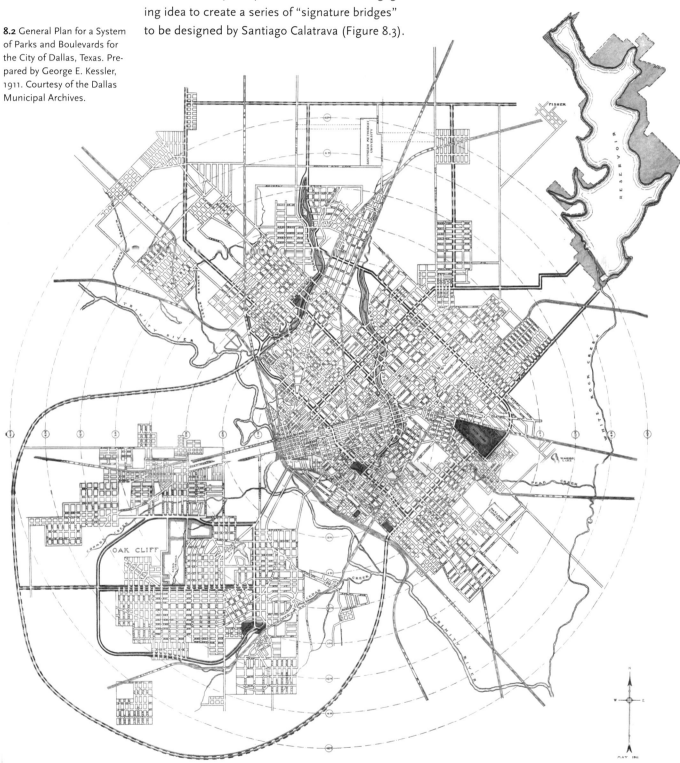

**8.2** General Plan for a System of Parks and Boulevards for the City of Dallas, Texas. Prepared by George E. Kessler, 1911. Courtesy of the Dallas Municipal Archives.

tolls and a town lake (or lakes) for recreation. These auxiliary efforts have, among other things, resulted in bringing the Calatrava bridge concept closer to fruition. To date, funding for the design of two bridges has been raised, thanks largely to the generosity of local philanthropists. For instance, the Hunt Petroleum Company donated $12 million. As a result, the city granted the company the naming rights for one bridge, which is now called the Margaret Hunt Hill Bridge, in honor of the Hunt family matriarch.

However, the city's implementation plan angered many Dallas residents, in particular those active within the local environmental community. Two elements were singled out for criticism: a high-speed, four- to eight-lane limited access tollway and one or more recreational lakes.

The Trinity River Corridor Project studied several routes for the proposed tollway. One option would follow the Trinity within the levees, resulting in a major reconfiguration of the floodplain. Other options would place the tollway outside the levees, lessening the environmental impact on the floodplain but possibly costing more to build. Some proponents dubbed the tollway a "parkway," but even with "landscaping," eight lanes represent a major thoroughfare. Inside the

levees, the flat floodplain offers an opportunity for future expansion, and American highways have a tendency to fill up quickly with gridlock, triggering a call for more lanes.

The central criticism of the proposed lakes was that they were to be "off channel." In other words, the lakes would use an alternate water source, such as treated sewage, rather than the Trinity River. A rationale for the off-channel lake was water quality. The Trinity River contains high levels of chlordane, a pesticide found to be toxic to humans. However, an off-channel lake would not solve this pollution issue, but merely avoid it. An alternative solution might be to clean up the river, and a first step could be the planning of a series of small lakes and interconnected wetlands to help address problems with water quality.

Such criticism, observed Rebecca Dugger, director of the city's Trinity Project, does not fall on deaf ears and has affected evolving elements of the project. "The ideas on what to do with the Trinity are as numerous and varied as there are people in the Metroplex," Dugger said. "These decisions about what to do with the waterways and the roadway cannot be made without taking into consideration our partners and their cost-sharing contributions."[5] Still, she said, the city

8.3 Calatrava Bridge, Trinity River, Dallas. Courtesy of Wallace Roberts & Todd.

must progress on parts of the project even while debates continue about other elements that make up the city's larger scheme: "We have to go forward now, while the bond funds are available and our window of opportunity is still open, refining as we go but beginning to implement our plans."[6]

In reaction to the controversy resulting from the city's plan, the Dallas chapter of the American Institute of Architects organized an eight-member advisory panel of urban design leaders. According to panel member Kevin Sloan, "This group tried to be objective, an independent voice. We worked like a studio jury, listening to various voices, both for and against the implementation plan."[7] The chapter also sponsored a three-day symposium to discuss the implementation plan, and in January 2002 issued the AIA *Dallas Trinity River Policy* (with a November 2001 date, a delay reportedly resulting from internal debate about the level of criticism to include in the policy). A separate report written by the advisory panel—published as an addendum to the chapter's official policy statement—differed slightly from the policy statement and, in general terms, was more critical of the city's implementation plan.

Overall, the AIA Dallas policy statement supported the City of Dallas' major objectives for recreation, flood control, economic development, and traffic relief. The advisory panel, however, was critical of placing the tollway inside the levees, observing that this placement would "extinguish conventional recreational uses from occurring in any meaningful way." In addition, the panel warned, the tollway "becomes an inner liner isolating the park" from the city. The panel also criticized the lake proposal, noting it would be "inadequate to accommodate recreational issues."

Recreation was a central issue because it had been a major element of the marketing strategy for the bond package approved by Dallas voters. The panel agreed with the environmental community that "splitting the river channel to bypass the lake is artificial, unnatural and inconsistent with contemporary thinking, which emphasizes the creation of low-maintenance, self-sustaining environments."[8]

As for AIA Dallas' official *Trinity River Policy*,

the chapter's executive committee distilled its critique of the city's implementation plan to its observation that the city's efforts suffered from a "lack of a grand vision."[9] The advisory panel took that criticism a step further by stating that the city must reformulate its plan after consultation with an urban planner, a landscape architect (with built experience in river corridors), and an urban economist. An economic assessment study undertaken by the city, the panel stated, "is erroneously fragmented in its view dismissing the opportunity to envision the project's economic and urban design component as a contiguous whole."[10]

Although meant as a middle ground, the AIA policy statement—and the advisory panel's report—became a lightning rod for criticism from advocates for the City of Dallas' plan. One proponent noted in the *Dallas Morning News* that the AIA's policy was "put together by people who don't understand the river."[11] An obvious retort is that the implementation plan was put together by people who don't understand cities—or ecology, for that matter. Sloan, one of the authors of the advisory panel's report, noted that when Frederick Law Olmsted Sr. was asked to attack Boston's Back Bay mosquito problem, he created the regional park system known as the Emerald Necklace.[12] With the city's implementation plan, the process is reversed, Sloan observed, adding that a grand opportunity is being squandered for a plan where the parts don't create a whole. He went on to note that, where the city's plan treats landscape as mere decoration ("landscaping"), Olmsted, by contrast, advocated landscape design that performed an artful synthesis of nature and culture.[13] Sloan suggested that the existing implementation plan has the potential to choke the remaining life out of the Trinity River.[14]

## OPPORTUNITIES FOR A BROADER PLAN

Many questions flow from the city's implementation plan and the AIA Dallas policy statement, as well as the many other documents and press reports. These questions continue to be debated, discussed, and studied to the present. For exam-

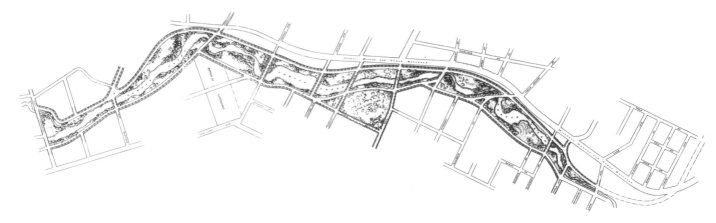

8.4 Plan for the Development of Turtle Creek Parkway, Dallas, Texas, from "A City Plan for Dallas." Prepared by George E. Kessler, 1911. Courtesy of the Dallas Municipal Archives.

8.5 Aerial drawing of the Trinity River Vision Project, Fort Worth. Courtesy of Trinity River Vision Authority.

ple, if a tollway is necessary, why not construct it outside the east levee in an already industrial area? Or, perhaps, expand the east levee; build a couple of lanes with views to the river? West of the west levee (on the poorer side of town), would not a Canada Drive (the main thoroughfare) that looks more like the Turtle Creek Boulevard (a main road through the wealthier slice of Dallas) be a positive addition to westside communities that would also increase traffic capacities (Figure 8.4)? What is the potential role of the successful Dallas Area Rapid Transit (DART) rail system in the Trinity corridor? Inside the levees, why not build smaller lakes and wetlands that make use of the natural channel? Why not follow the example George Kessler created with the delightful Exall Lake in Highland Park in the early twentieth century?

Outside Dallas, other segments of the Trinity were being addressed more sensitively. In Fort Worth, the 2002 Gateway Park Master Plan advocated a downtown that featured the riverfront[15] (Figure 8.5). Meanwhile, the North Central Texas Council of Governments promoted a program called "Common Vision" for the Trinity River, which emphasizes safety, clean water, recreation, the preservation and restoration of natural systems, and diversity.

In Dallas, too, there was hope in the early twenty-first century of creating a design that would highlight the river and promote its restoration. Heeding the AIA Dallas call for a grand vision, Mayor Laura Miller asked AIA Dallas, the Dallas Institute of Humanities and Culture, and the Dallas Plan Organization (a nonprofit group formed in 1992) to organize a private sector task force and commission a study of the Trinity. Mayor Miller intended the study as a review of the city's implementation plan to either confirm its direction or recommend other directions, all in the hope that the study could produce a grand vision that would unify a divided community. The mayor requested that a transportation planning consultant participate in the study to review transportation assumptions. The task force assembled a diverse selection committee, which chose two fine firms based in Cambridge, Massachusetts—Chan Krieger & Associates and Hargreaves Associates—to work on the plan. The study proposed a compelling vision for parks along the Trinity that garnered considerable public support.[16] *A Balanced Vision Plan for the Trinity River* encompassed more than 2,000 acres (809 ha) of the river corridor, including the floodway, the floodplain, and adjacent neighborhoods and business areas.[17]

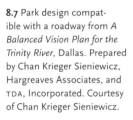

**8.6** Rendering of Trinity River Corridor improvements, Dallas. Prepared by Chan Krieger Sieniewicz, Hargreaves Associates, and TDA, Incorporated. Courtesy of Hargreaves Associates.

**8.7** Park design compatible with a roadway from *A Balanced Vision Plan for the Trinity River*, Dallas. Prepared by Chan Krieger Sieniewicz, Hargreaves Associates, and TDA, Incorporated. Courtesy of Chan Krieger Sieniewicz.

The plan addressed several concerns raised around previous plans. The toll road between the levees was reduced from eight lanes to six and four, depending on the location along the corridor. The plan suggested that the highway be depressed into the top of the levee itself to make it less obtrusive. The planning team also recommended raising the levee by two feet (0.61 m). Rather than one large lake near downtown, two mid-sized lakes and more wetlands were suggested. The enhanced plan would cost $110 million more than the 1998 Halff Associates plan[18] (Figures 8.6 and 8.7).

The Krieger-Hargreaves vision combined five essential components:

1. Flood protection
2. Environmental restoration and management
3. Parks and recreation
4. Transportation
5. Community and economic development

The design team concluded that these five elements needed to be combined "in a way that achieves an appropriate balance."[19]

## ONE STEP FORWARD, TWO BACK

Dallas civic leader Gail Thomas championed the Krieger-Hargreaves scheme. Because it relied on significant public involvement, the *Balanced Vision Plan* enjoyed broad support among diverse interests in Dallas and was approved by the city council in 2003. However, the plan was strongly identified with Mayor Laura Miller, whose popularity had declined. The city had a popular plan but an unpopular mayor who was destined to serve only one term.

Eventually, the Army Corps of Engineers mounted strong opposition to placing any portion of the tollway on top of the levee. They cited the levees that failed in New Orleans after Hurricane Katrina to drive home their position. Business and community interests opposed the tollway outside the levee. Another round of studies was commissioned by another set of consultants. The most reasonable compromises were advanced by HNTB, a firm known for context-sensitive transportation.

HNTB's Dallas office prepared a land-use plan for the areas outside the levee to complement the

**8.8** Model for the Trinity Uptown Project, Fort Worth. Courtesy of Trinity River Vision Authority.

**8.9** Wind turbines for the Trinity River, Dallas. Courtesy of Wallace Roberts & Todd.

park vision advanced by the Krieger-Hargreaves team. HNTB sought to reconnect North and South Dallas, establish the role of economic development along the Trinity River, create a vibrant central city, establish the Trinity River floodplain as the "front yard" of the city (paralleling the Krieger-Hargreaves suggestion), and enhance the city's urban form to increase the appeal of urban life.[20] HNTB also worked out an idea with the Army Corps of Engineers and the Texas Department of Transportation to locate the controversial portion of the tollway adjacent to the inside of the levee on new fill that would be added as the levee was raised to improve flood protection.

Progress appeared to be at hand. Wallace Roberts & Todd (WRT) was brought in to refine the park visions inside the levee. Then, Dallas City Council member and University of Texas Law School graduate Angela Hunt, a critic of Mayor Miller and an opponent of the tollways inside the levee, led an effort to have the issue placed on the November 2007 ballot. Hunt adopted a populist approach with the slogan, "Keep *their* toll road out of *our* park."[21] The election became quite contentious, with the Dallas chapter of the AIA opposing Hunt's proposition. The pro and con campaigns posed challenges with a "no" vote supporting the implementation of the plan and a "yes" vote stopping its implementation. On November 6, Dallas voters rejected Council member Hunt's initiative to kill the tollway. As a result, the massive Trinity River Corridor project proceeded as planned with

enhanced flood controls; the riverside park with lakes, trails, promenades, and green spaces; the preservation of the Great Trinity Forest south of downtown; an equestrian center; and the other recreational amenities envisioned by the Krieger Hargreaves team.[22] "We're going to have a project that's going to be the greatest in this nation, it's going to be a park where there's no parallel," Dallas Mayor Tom Leppert declared the Wednesday after the election.[23]

Meanwhile, as Dallas' plans sputtered, Fort Worth forged ahead. Building on its gateway planning and the North Central Texas Council of Governments' common vision, Fort Worth's 2003 Trinity River Master Plan encompasses 88 miles (142 km) of waterways flowing through the city's neighborhoods, including the Trinity Uptown Project (Figure 8.8). This project envisions a town lake and a bypass channel for flood control. The estimated cost is $435 million, which will be funded by federal, city, county, and water district sources, as well as tax increment financing. In addition to flood control, the Trinity Uptown Project will create new parkland, as well as space for ten thousand residents and businesses with sixteen thousand new jobs.[24]

The Trinity projects continue to move slowly toward realization in both cities (still more smoothly in Fort Worth). In Dallas, where the project's price tag has risen to more than $2 billion, WRT with CH2M HILL and others continue to

guide the implementation plan, now covering 20 miles (32.2 km) of the Trinity River and approximately 10,000 acres (4047 ha). Final approval by the U.S. Army Corps of Engineers for the tollway inside the floodway levees has slowed the Dallas project. Meanwhile, WRT has refined the Trinity Lakes Park design and proposed new ideas, such as wind turbines along the levees, to produce energy. The WRT effort is led by Ignacio Bunster-Ossa, who was involved
in the earlier, failed planning efforts as a sub-consultant. He has the rare second-chance opportunity for a planner to re-engage in a project and give it a new life. Bunster-Ossa notes that projects like the Trinity provide opportunities to create "green infrastructure" in cities while connecting urban nature to larger regional natural systems, especially along river corridors (Figure 8.9).

The Trinity projects in Dallas and Fort Worth present good models of how regional concerns, in this case flooding, can be used to improve the environment while presenting new opportunities for recreation, transportation, and community development. The Dallas project in particular illustrates the challenges of realizing such a model.

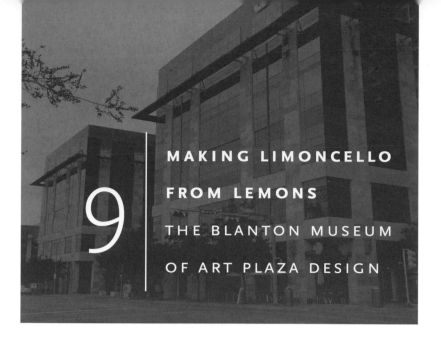

# 9 MAKING LIMONCELLO FROM LEMONS

## THE BLANTON MUSEUM OF ART PLAZA DESIGN

My position in Austin became available as a result of the "Blanton Controversy." In 1999, the bold Swiss architects, Herzog & de Meuron, produced a preliminary design for the Blanton Museum of Art that offended two members of the University of Texas Board of Regents[1] (Figure 9.1). These regents wanted a red-tiled roof. They sought a return to the style of the pre–Second World War Paul Cret–designed portions of the campus. When the regents fired the architects, School of Architecture dean Lawrence Speck resigned. In addition to being an outstanding teacher and accomplished scholar, Speck leads the Austin office of a large Texas firm.[2] He views architecture as a public enterprise, observing, "It's for everybody."

The building skin holds special interest for Larry Speck, a sixth-generation Texan, who identifies ten concerns relating to exterior structure and sustainability:

> sun control
> natural ventilation
> daylighting
> connection to the outdoors
> thermal insulation
> moisture control
> microclimatic zones
> structural efficiency
> materials choices
> energy sources[3]

The juggling of these concerns is evident in his works, such as in the two CSC buildings flanking Austin City Hall with sunscreens and the craftful use of limestone (Figure 9.2). These are my favorite buildings in Austin, perfect in almost every way: scale, materials, and the way they capture light. As often as I drive through downtown, the buildings are always a delight, day and night. They are humble, yet accomplished, examples of how an architect contributes to the fabric of a city. Larry Speck's Regional Modernism reflects both a deep understanding of Texas and a contemporary approach.[4]

Speck had advocated for and contributed to a campus master plan that influenced the Herzog & de Meuron flap. Cesar Pelli & Associates, led by University of Texas alumnus Fred Clarke, with Balmori Associates, prepared the master plan, which was adopted by the regents in 1999. The plan resulted from widespread concern for the quality of the post–Second World War architecture on campus. Meanwhile, the prewar campus, largely the result of Cret, continued to be loved by the alumni, the public, and, as evident from the Blanton Controversy, the regents. The Pelli plan sought to create a framework to encourage future architecture more like Cret's and less like the Modernism of the late twentieth century. In this regard, the University of Texas campus reflected concerns about collegiate architecture that existed across the nation.

**9.1** Proposal for the Blanton Art Museum, University of Texas at Austin. Design by Herzog & de Meuron.

**9.2** CSC Building, Austin. Design by Lawrence Speck, PageSoutherlandPage.

The regents, who opposed the Herzog & de Meuron design, used the Pelli plan to justify their position. Advocates of the Swiss firm's Blanton design, including Speck, argued that this represented a misreading of the Pelli plan. The planners had not intended to eliminate creative design, rather only to make it fit better in scale and proportion. Herzog & de Meuron never had an opportunity to refine their design to better adjust to the Pelli plan.

## LANDSCAPE ARCHITECTURE TO THE RESCUE

The Blanton Museum of Art, well under design in fall 2002, came to provide hope for some creative interventions. After the Herzog & de Meuron donnybrook, Blanton director Jessie Hite reached out to several members of the art and design community. A former architecture dean, Hal Box, offered several suggestions on the Cret-faithful, red tile roof design of Michael McKinnell from Kallmann McKinnell & Wood. I joined three fellow architecture faculty members for several hours of discussion with Hite. The ground rules were simple: given the sensitivity toward the building's exterior appearance, we would avoid external building aesthetics and focus on functional considerations. My colleagues made several constructive suggestions about the interior spaces and the importance of exhibit design. Hite clearly took these ideas to heart and would retain Pentagram to design the exhibit spaces.

The Kallmann McKinnell & Wood design had one clear advantage over the Herzog & de Meuron concept. The Swiss firm's design was a sleek, slender one-story building. McKinnell split the program, creating two taller, two-story buildings below the pitched roofs. The space between the two buildings framed the view of the state capitol to the south. The area could become both an important southern gateway to the campus and a significant urban space in a city lacking in urbanism.

I suggested that the university hire a leading landscape architect to design the space, perhaps in cooperation with an environmental artist. Hite immediately took to the idea because, among other factors, engaging a landscape architect and an artist could energize lagging fund-raising efforts for the museum.

Pat Clubb, vice president for facilities, asked me to prepare a list of the top ten landscape architects, Blanton curator Annette Carlozzi identified four significant environmental artists. The university planners contacted the firms on my list of ten and requested a statement of qualifications. Four were selected for interviews: Hargreaves Associates, Reed Hilderbrand, Robert Murase, and Peter Walker and Partners.

I met Michael McKinnell, a co-designer of Boston's Brutalist City Hall, for the first time as we interviewed the four finalists in 2003. He impressed me with his humility and sincerity. He understood the controversy surrounding the Blanton over the dismissal of Herzog & de Meuron and projected himself as a journeyman architect determined to do the best possible job for his client. He clearly saw the opportunity to elevate the project through the urban and landscape design of the plaza.

A large committee of university administrators, Blanton staff, and project architects would select the landscape architect, who would in turn choose the artist. George Hargreaves and Mary Margaret Jones interviewed first, displaying stunning work and rich collaborative experience with universities, artists, and architects. Jones had graduated from Texas A&M University, but had spent her first year at the University of Texas in Jester Hall across from the Blanton site. Her thoughtful student days perspective attracted support from several committee members. Hargreaves' campus plan for the University of Cincinnati had been transformative (Figure 9.3). He stressed that "university leadership is essential" in campus planning and that it was the landscape architect's job "to create a compelling vision."

**9.3** Portion of the University of Cincinnati campus resulting from the master plan prepared by Hargreaves Associates. Photograph by John Gollings and Hargreaves Associates. Courtesy of Hargreaves Associates.

Doug Reed and Gary Hilderbrand's work impressed the committee as well. They frankly admitted that they were "surprised by the scale of the project." Michael McKinnell in particular was captivated by their work and declared that if they were not selected for the Blanton project, Kallmann McKinnell & Wood would identify another project for them soon.

While Reed Hilderbrand's work was mostly in the Northeast, Robert Murase's projects focused on the Pacific Northwest. As a landscape architect and a sculptor, he presented a challenge for the Blanton staff, who had already selected Vito Acconci, Jackie Ferrara, Mel Chin, or Valeska Soares as potential environmental artists for the project. The staff's fear was that Murase would compete with artists on the project.

Peter Walker and Partners, on the other hand, had thoroughly researched all four artists and offered thoughtful comments on the suitability of each one. Walker was with a client in Switzerland and had unsuccessfully tried to rearrange the interview, but his firm was ably represented by his associates Doug Findlay (the president of the firm) and Sarah Kuehl. The Blanton staff was impressed with Walker's work on the Nasher Sculpture Center in Dallas, while the architects Michael McKinnell and Mark DeShong spoke positively about their past collaborations with Walker.

I felt the day was a triumph for landscape architecture. Doug Findlay observed, "A campus is never complete." Whoever was selected for the Blanton, I felt the four firms convinced the university leadership of the importance of landscape architecture, which would result in more work in the future.

The committee selected Peter Walker and Partners, who, in turn, chose Mel Chin to be the environmental artist. Over the next month, the university prepared to make the big announcement of Walker's involvement, only to discover that we were about to be upstaged by his selection for a project in New York City. Our press office delayed the news release about the hiring of Peter Walker to design the Blanton Plaza because of the announcement that he had been selected with

architect Michael Arad to design the World Trade Center Memorial in New York City during the first week of 2004.

Later in January, Walker and Mel Chin, as well as Walker associates Doug Findlay and Sarah Kuehl, began the design process for the Blanton Plaza. The basement room in the LBJ School of Public Affairs filled with architects, museum staff, and university officials.

Michael McKinnell said, "The buildings are there to create the plaza."

I noted that it would become an important pedestrian entry to the campus.

"Entrances need to have a sense of drama," Walker commented. "There's a need for a formal understanding of the campus by an increasingly informal student body."

Overall, Walker inspired the assembled group and set an ambitious direction for the plaza design. He and Mel Chin presented their initial ideas for the Blanton Plaza to the project architects and university administration on February 10, 2004. Walker created a more park-like character than the bare plaza suggested in the original McKinnell design. He suggested a forest of about one hundred mature cedar elms in rows 20 feet (6 m) apart that would open to reveal the dramatic vista of the state capitol to the south. Chin suggested contributions to the park that would emphasize social and natural connections with the region. Walker observed that the campus might be "the last idealistic place in which students will live." As a result, the campus should provide opportunities for powerful memories.

"I have a long association with dirt," Chin said, "because I'm from Texas. Connections to a place can be made through art."

Walker and Chin explained how the central Texas region provides cultural and natural inspirations for their emerging landscape design. Pat Clubb expressed a couple of concerns. First, the University of Texas at Austin viewed itself as an international institution. As a result, regional associations could be perceived as too localized. Second, Chin's scheme to create art based on found objects from parks seemed a stretch. She was especially concerned about his idea of "talk-

**9.4** Larry and Mary Ann Faulkner Plaza, Blanton Museum of Art. Design by Peter Walker and Partners Landscape Architecture. Photograph by Frederick Steiner.

ing rocks" that would interpret the symbolism of the found objects.

I defended the link to the region, explaining that landscape art needed to respond to natural regional constraints to survive. Furthermore, the university was of this place. The found objects and talking rocks also failed to convince me, though. The university leadership decided not to pursue Chin's ideas, but did implement the Walker design (Figure 9.4).

### BALANCING ACT

As dean, I simultaneously move between projects far and wide. The day after Walker and Chin's presentation, Michael Garrison and I met with a group of community activists led by Mack McCarter of the Shreveport-Bossier Community Renewal Project. Like the Blanton, the Shreveport initiative involved making the most of a challenging situation. The Shreveport leaders possessed

an idealistic agenda to foster stronger communities through care. They had acquired the sixteen-story downtown Shreveport Petroleum Tower to restore and sought to convert this historic symbol of the oil industry into the group's international center for community renewal. Michael Garrison devoted a studio course to explore how the Petroleum Tower could be restored as an example of green design, using solar panels, taking advantage of outside lighting, and recycling its wastewater (Figure 9.5). McCarter plans to make the Petroleum Tower part of a 260,000-square-foot (24,155-m²) building, which will be the largest zero-net energy building in the South when finished.

Mack McCarter is an ordained minister who abandoned traditional preaching when he looked out at his white flock and realized, "I wasn't doing much to change the world." He returned home to Shreveport, joined an African-American congregation, and set about changing a city that had experienced a steep economic decline. Shreveport was founded in 1836 at a key point along the Red River that provided a route into the heart of Texas and beyond into Mexico. Oil was discovered in Shreveport in 1906 and the city boomed as the headquarters for Standard Oil. From the late 1940s through the 1950s, the *Louisiana Hayride* radio show, which helped advance several musical careers, originated from Shreveport's Municipal Auditorium. Since the oil and gas industry downturn in the 1980s, the city has experienced economic recession and population decline. McCarter attracted idealistic attorneys, dentists, pro golfers, architects, and others to help pursue his mission of improving poor communities in Shreveport and nearby Bossier. With $2.6 million from the Robert Wood Johnson Foundation from 2001–2007, they established the Shreveport-Bossier Community Renewal Project. Eventually, McCarter enlisted former President Bill Clinton as an ally in his efforts and subsequently changed the organization's name to Community Renewal International.

McCarter advocated three approaches. The first was to create connections in communities through care and visibility. His "We Care Team" practiced "random acts of caring." More than ten thousand people in Shreveport and nearby Bossier proudly wear "We Care" buttons.

Second, McCarter established haven house centers in distressed neighborhoods. The goal was to make friends and to create safe havens block by block. The third approach was to establish a series of Friendship Houses, which McCarter calls "ICUS" or internal care units. McCarter wanted these havens and Friendship Houses to rebuild social capital in his region.

## EXPANDING THE SCOPE OF THE BLANTON PLAZA

In March 2004, several university officials and I met with Peter Walker and two of his colleagues to discuss redesigning Speedway Boulevard, a major north-south road through campus. The Blanton Museum resulted in closing the south end of

Speedway and opened the opportunity to convert the roadway into a pedestrian mall through campus. In tandem, the East Mall portion of the campus could be renovated.

Walker, Doug Findlay, and Sarah Kuehl explained their assessment of existing pavement, trees, grades, entries, and movement (Figure 9.6). At the time, two-thirds of the area was paved, with the balance planted. Walker proposed to reverse that ratio. He presented ideas for a new campus landscape vocabulary. Walker noted that because of the variety of building styles and sizes, the landscape needed to hold things together. Several small plazas along Speedway were designed to serve as places to congregate and to eat.

The most complicated challenges for the design were access for delivery trucks and bike routes through the campus. Walker addressed

**9.5** Petroleum Tower, Shreveport, Louisiana. The goal of the design was to become the first platinum LEED building in Louisiana. Model by Joel Nolan and JohnPaul McDaris.

**9.6** Speedway and East Mall plan. Design by Peter Walker and Partners Landscape Architecture. Courtesy of Peter Walker and Partners Landscape Architecture.

these issues, as well as maintenance, lighting, and planting. Speedway would become a future pedestrian spine and a new green artery through the campus.

He presented his designs for the Blanton Plaza, Speedway Boulevard, and the East Mall to an enthusiastic university leadership. In particular, President Larry Faulkner and Vice President Pat Clubb expressed strong support for transforming the campus landscape into a greener haven. From New Haven, Fred Clarke also embraced the idea, viewing it as a positive implementation of the Pelli plan.

While in Austin for the Speedway project, Walker gave a lecture to students addressing the topic of minimalism in landscape design. He summarized his early accomplishments as a young partner of Hideo Sasaki and his longstanding interest in contemporary art. In the mid-1970s, Walker began applying his knowledge of minimalism and post-minimalism to landscape architecture. Over the next two decades, this work grew in scale and complexity. He found his work "playing against the natural order of things," as he sought to "define space in the simplest possible way."

"How do you express flatness?" Walker asked the students. Flatness is difficult to achieve outdoors, but is necessary in order to make "nature evident in an abstract way," according to Walker. He used these past explorations to explain his collaboration with Michael Arad on the World Trade Center Memorial, "Reflecting Absence." Walker made frequent references to his work in Japan, where the culture is especially supportive of garden design and of minimalist gestures.

Walker's plaza design for the new Blanton Museum of Art has been warmly received. Speedway and East Mall will be transformed into significant pedestrian corridors as a result of the design of Peter Walker and his colleagues. Soon after the Blanton opened, I visited the plaza with Walker and Bill Powers, the former law school dean and new university president. Looking back to the vista of the state capitol created by Walker's allée of trees, I explained to Bill Powers how Austin's grid shifted at this point to true north-south, and how the Blanton Plaza built on this arrangement.

"So this is what you landscape architects do," President Powers observed.

# 10

## TRUE URBANISM

## THE DESIGN OF

## PERFORMANCE PARK

## IN THE DALLAS ARTS

## DISTRICT

The Dallas Arts District Plan, which I worked on between 2004 and 2007, presented a challenge in balancing the egos and visions of two strong architects, Lord Norman Foster and Rem Koolhaas. Early in the design process, Dallas civic leader Deedie Rose suggested a site designer be involved. She reports that the architects "appeared startled" by this idea and volunteered to do the site design themselves. They indeed located their buildings, but Rose and others continued to press for a landscape architect. Each architect recommended a different American landscape architect, and each was interviewed. However, neither architect could agree on the other's choice. The site design committee asked the architects to come back with someone they could agree on, and they selected the French landscape architect Michel Desvigne. This proved to be an unfortunate choice, given the highly regarded and accomplished Dallas work of Peter Walker and Hargreaves Associates, as well as the local office of SWA and the local firm MESA (Figure 10.1). Fortunately, the Dallas Center for the Performing Arts had engaged JJR principal Deb Mitchell, a very competent designer who knows Dallas well, to work as landscape architect of record with Desvigne.

Foster and Koolhaas' Office for Metropolitan Architecture (OMA) had received their commissions after high-profile searches to create a new Dallas Center for the Performing Arts. The Center was to be located within the Arts District, for which Hideo Sasaki had prepared a master plan in 1982. "The genius of the Sasaki plan," according to Dallas architect Duncan Fulton, "was the clarity of its vision" and its intense focus on Flora Street as "a primary organizing element."[1] Anchored on the west by the Dallas Museum of Art and the new Nasher Sculpture Center, designed by Renzo Piano and Walker, the district features the Morton H. Meyerson Symphony Center, designed by I. M. Pei in 1989 along Flora Street, the main drag of the district (Figure 10.1). The Nasher is a masterpiece of architecture and landscape architecture (Figure 10.2). The Meyerson, on the other hand, is what *Dallas Morning News* architecture critic David Dillon called a "mixed bag, . . . a piece of sculpture meant to be admired rather than embraced."[2] On the east, a new performing and visual arts magnet school was built as an addition to the historic Booker T. Washington High School. The architect, Brad Cloepfil of Allied Works Architecture of Portland, Oregon, produced an inspiring arts school that both created lively new spaces and restored the stately old building. A final structure, informally called the "third venue" and officially known as the Dallas City Performance Hall, would fill in the district. To design the performance hall, the City of Dallas selected SOM, a less adventurous choice than either Foster or OMA

**10.1** Nasher Sculpture Center, Dallas. Design by Renzo Piano Building Workshop and Peter Walker and Partners Landscape Architecture. Courtesy of Peter Walker and Partners Landscape Architecture.

**10.2** Dallas Arts District Overview. Photograph by Iwan Baan. Courtesy of the Dallas Center for the Performing Arts.

**10.3** Margot and Bill Winspear Opera House. Design by Foster + Partners. Photograph by Nigel Young/Foster + Partners.

and a lost opportunity to engage an important Texas architect. The Dallas City Performance Hall was funded by a 2006 bond program. Construction for the parking structure below the 750-seat hall began in 2008. The hall is planned to open in 2012.

Lord Norman Foster designed the Margot and Bill Winspear Opera House to seat twenty-two hundred for performances by the Dallas Opera, the Texas Ballet Theater, and touring Broadway productions. On the outside, the opera house is a big red drum with a giant canopy, touted for dubious environmental benefits. Foster's team had proposed a similar canopy for a commission in Hong Kong, which received a less-than-enthusiastic response. The climatic differences between Hong Kong and Dallas underscore the environmental skepticism of the canopy, which seemed to move from continent to continent regardless of climate or culture. I like the red drum, a bold statement that fits Dallas.

Rem Koolhaas and his OMA colleagues designed the Dee and Charles Wyly Theatre,

located across Flora from the Winspear Opera House. The design was led by OMA's Joshua Prince-Ramus, rather than Koolhaas. At least Prince-Ramus was more present in Dallas than Koolhaas. Then again, Spencer de Grey led the Winspear effort instead of Foster. However, he stayed with Foster, while Prince-Ramus spun off from OMA in the middle of the project, resulting in consternation from their Dallas patrons.

OMA designed the Wyly to seat six hundred. The twelve-story cubic tower houses various performing arts organizations like the Dallas Theater Center, the Dallas Black Dance Theatre, and the Anita N. Martinez Ballet Folklorico. Koolhaas and Prince-Ramus emphasized verticality and transparency in their design of the building. They placed the lobby on the fourth floor with the performance space at ground level so that it could be seen from the street. Deedie Rose and others found the placement of the lobby awkward. OMA responded by creating two ground levels: the performance space at street level and the lobby off a

**10.4** Dee and Charles Wyly Theatre. Design by REX/OMA. Photograph by Ken Cobb. Courtesy of JJR, LLC.

**10.5** Elaine D. and Charles A. Sammons Park. Design by Michel Desvigne in collaboration with JJR. Courtesy of JJR, LLC and the AT&T Performing Arts Center.

plaza sculpted into the earth. This scooped-into-the-ground plaza posed significant challenges for the site design, including handicapped and emergency access, microclimate amelioration, and plant growth. In the end, a memorable and rather marvelous outdoor space was created.

The Foster and OMA buildings formed the "flashy centerpieces" of the $275 million Dallas Center for the Performing Arts[3] (Figures 10.3 and 10.4). The Winspear and the Wyly followed the model established by the Meyerson: pieces of sculpture to be admired, rather than the brilliant connection of architecture and landscape achieved at the Nasher. They are, however, imaginative sculptures. The design for the landscape, by contrast, remained vague. Desvigne presented concepts based on his desire to deconstruct the American grid (Figure 10.5).

As it became clear that site planning would

pose a challenge and Desvigne appeared uninterested in the specifics of this place, two of Dallas' leading arts patrons, Deedie Rose and Howard Rachofsky, asked me to get involved in 2004.

In October 2005, I met with Howard Rachofsky, Doug Curtis of the Dallas Center for the Performing Arts, Deb Mitchell, and Bas Smets of Michel Desvigne Paysagistes, Paris. The former hedge fund manager Rachofsky wore an Italian lime green suit and a shiny white designer t-shirt. We reviewed schematic designs for the Dallas Center for the Performing Arts. I expressed concern that the devils of drainage, materials, and plant details remained unresolved. Progress had been slow, but Smets appeared open to suggestions and committed to the project. More progress was necessary because groundbreaking for the project was to occur early the following month.

I took a 6:30 a.m. flight to Dallas in January 2006, to participate in a site design workshop for the Dallas Center for the Performing Arts. The workshop was held at the offices of Good Fulton & Farrell with Rose, Rachofsky, and Dallas philanthropist and civic leader John W. Dayton participating. The focus of the workshop was the most recent site plan by Michel Desvigne Paysagistes, represented by Justine Miething of Paris. Some of the other participating designers included: Deb Mitchell of JJR (the landscape architects of record), Spencer de Grey of Norman Foster + Partners (architects of the Margot and Bill Winspear Opera House), Joshua Prince-Ramus of OMA (architects of the Wyly Theatre), Claire Kahn of WET Design (fountain designers), and Duncan Fulton of Good Fulton & Farrell (architects of the underground garages and architects of record for the Annette Strauss Artist Square). Although the lighting and fountain designs were imaginative, the landscape architecture, led by Michel Desvigne, seemed to have regressed. The young, charming Miething was new to the group and spoke scant English. The energy and optimism of Bas Smets was missing. Desvigne's deconstructed American grid design appeared shallow and tragically vague, as the architecture concepts of OMA and Foster advanced with depth and detail.

Construction had begun. Ideally, site design should frame other elements. In this case, the design for the site would be produced last, limiting its possibilities.

Although the Dallas Center for the Performing Arts site plan was finally making some progress by April 2006, much, too much, I felt, remained unresolved. I urged my Dallas friends to push our Paris consultants for more concrete designs. By this time in the process, it was clear, Deb Mitchell was providing the bulk of the site design contribution and single-handedly contributing substance to the design for the site.

Critic David Dillon covered the Arts District design process for the *Dallas Morning News* with considerable insight and detail. In 2005, he noted that Performance Park, as the open area was named, was the "glue that will hold [the] various architectural fragments together." But, he continued, Desvigne's "dreamy sketches . . . had little connection to Texas or Dallas."[4]

On Thursday, September 14, 2006, Dillon published an article on the unveiling of the Arts District park design. He wrote: "Dallas has been waiting nearly three years for a major new park in the downtown Arts District. . . . [Y]et, Performance Park turns out to be more miniature golf course than grand civic space, with water hazards, tiny fairways, everything except the flags for pin placement."[5] Dillon criticized French landscape architect Michel Desvigne's lack of commitment to Dallas, observing that the landscape design did not rise to the level of the architecture by Norman Foster and OMA for the Center for the Performing Arts buildings. He praised some functional aspects of the site plan and correctly credited JJR for "virtually all the heavy production work."

In November 2006, the site planning committee met for a full day to rethink concepts and to explore suggestions by Dillon (who was invited to participate after his scathing "miniature golf" critique) and architect/landscape architect Kevin Sloan. We were especially concerned about how the landscape related to building elements such as Foster's giant canopy around the opera house and the scoop in front of OMA's theater. Although late in the process, we established a set of nine principles to guide the revision and the completion of the site design:

1. Create spatial relationship of ground plane to canopy.
2. Establish strong spatial edges and connections.
3. Simplify ground plane to create design consistency.
4. Arrange elements in response to three primary canopy bays.
5. Locate larger trees outside the canopy.
6. Increase green surfaces.
7. Use water as connector across Flora Street.
8. Continue to clarify and refine the grid.
9. Reduce competition with buildings.

This chapter is the most difficult, even painful, for me to write. Good, generous people devoted their time and, in notable cases, their fortunes to make things right. Yet, we fell short. Entering the design process, I was not an admirer of either Foster or OMA. However, these architects were passionate, even brilliant. I came to appreciate, even like, their designs. Larry Speck is an enthusiast of Foster's large canopy, and perhaps Larry convinced me with his arguments about its architectural merits. Maybe I am just a sucker for red. Although neither of the "star architects" appeared at any of the meetings I attended, their representatives were smart and professional in the best sense of the word.

Desvigne never seemed to grasp an American concept of landscape, especially in an urban context, which is a pity. Certainly, there have been amazing recent examples of urban landscape design in Europe, including France. For instance, in Paris, Parc André-Citroën, designed by Alain Provost and Gilles Clément, and Patrick Blanc's Le Mur Végétal at Musée du quai Branly display considerable imagination (Figures 10.6 and 10.7). However, no such genius emerged for Dallas. A flexible space did result, an open canvas for future innovation. Although flexible, Performance Park does fit the context created by the new buildings and helps connect them.

Meanwhile, a team that included Carter & Burgess, Hargreaves Associates, Chan Krieger & Associates, and Good Fulton & Farrell completed a thoughtful master plan for downtown parks in Dallas. This plan set in motion a significant increase in downtown parks and public spaces. The planning team also suggested new strategies for parking and integrated transportation systems. The plan was both pragmatic and ambitious, characteristics missing from the Desvigne site plan.

The prospects for the Arts District will be enhanced if connected to other transportation and open space systems, such as those suggested in the Downtown Parks Plan. Dallas took quick action on that plan, commissioning prominent landscape architects to design a series of downtown parks. For instance, Houston's James Burnett designed a 5.2-acre (2.1-ha) park on the new deck covering the Woodall Rodgers Expressway adjacent to the Arts District. This park will help connect the new arts venues to redeveloping areas north of the expressway.

10.6 Parc André-Citroën, Paris. Photograph by Frederick Steiner.

10.7 Le Mur Végétal, Musée du quai Branly, Paris. Photograph by Frederick Steiner.

**10.8** Aerial view of the Booker T. Washington High School for the Performing and Visual Arts. Design by Allied Works Architecture. Courtesy of Dallas Independent School District.

**10.9** Interior of the Booker T. Washington High School for the Performing and Visual Arts. Design by Allied Works Architecture. Photograph by Jeremy Bittermann.

Through the Arts District design process, I came to realize, again, just how difficult urban landscapes are to design. The role of the landscape architect is too frequently marginalized and the budgets for sites reduced through the design and construction processes. In contrast to other design disciplines, landscape architects have less control of their work because they work with materials that change with time. For example, the industrial designer controls the form of specific items, such as fountain pens and chairs. But for design, as the scale increases from specific project, to building, to larger building, on to groups of buildings with open spaces and transportation systems, complexity increases. Architects attempt to maintain control of building design, but admit that much change occurs through the construction process and even more as the building is inhabited.

Buildings adjust to climate and create microclimates. Landscapes depend on climate to evolve forms and patterns through time. The design of landscapes requires an understanding of environmental processes and an appreciation for change. Landscapes embody complexity. They have many moveable parts that change daily, seasonally, and over time. As a result, landscape design requires balancing many factors. To perform such balancing, designers cannot be fixed on a single, predetermined solution. Rather, they must possess the skill and creativity to consider many possibilities. They must be able to connect living organisms to their built and natural environments to create regenerative urban systems.

"Nature is the subject matter and medium of our daily work," Günter Vogt observes about the practice of landscape architecture.[6] The designers of the Center for the Performing Arts exiled nature, especially the natural nature of Dallas, to the margins. They appealed instead to the human nature of Dallas to build great monuments. The exception, and genuine jewel of the district, is Brad Cloepfil's Booker T. Washington arts magnet school (Figures 10.8 and 10.9). Something old is preserved and enhanced, while something new is added that is both fitting and original.

Several generations have unearthed and interpreted Hadrian's Villa outside of Rome. Although we have no written record of Hadrian's intent, physical remnants of the structures he conceived remain. When I walk among those ruins, I wander about the landscape he willed. At best, with the Dallas Arts District, we have a good structure, thanks to Kevin Sloan, Deb Mitchell, David Dillon, and the amazing patience and generosity of Howard Rachofsky and Deedie Rose.[7] Both possess considerable experience dealing with—sometimes famously stubborn—artists, architects, and landscape architects. Their endurance produced frequently brilliant results. In this case, their efforts with others led to a $15 million gift from Sammons Enterprises for Performance Park (which became the Elaine D. and Charles A. Sammons Park) in September 2008. The Sammons gift will help realize the coherent structure for outdoor spaces around the Winspear Opera House and the Wyly Theatre. My hope is that future generations will improve upon this structure and elevate it to the grandeur that Norman Foster and OMA's teams put in place for the buildings.

# 11 LEGACIES

As chair of the Lady Bird Johnson Wildflower Center's planning committee, I became engaged in a messy zoning fight involving a developer, Stratus Properties, pitted against the Save Our Springs (SOS) Alliance in 2002. The SOS Alliance led the effort to create an ordinance (also called SOS) limiting impervious surfaces in new development over the Edwards Aquifer. However, the development community convinced the state legislature to grandfather properties with prior planning approvals. This weakened the SOS Ordinance and set off numerous battles before the Austin City Council and in the courts. Stratus Properties had tangled with SOS in the past, but the company had a young, new CEO, Beau Armstrong, who claimed to have turned over a new environmental leaf. Armstrong brokered an agreement with the city to develop his property with the 15 percent SOS impervious surface maximum, even though that property had received a grandfather exemption from the SOS Ordinance.

The Lady Bird Johnson Wildflower Center sits on an edge of the Stratus property. Armstrong offered to donate 105 acres (42 ha) to the Wildflower Center in exchange for the center's support. He no doubt saw the Wildflower Center as a valuable amenity. In turn, Wildflower Center director Bob Breunig committed to seek approval from the Center's board, on the condition that Stratus use native vegetation, green building technologies, and other environmental provisions, in addition to keeping the impervious surfaces below 15 percent. Armstrong and the board agreed.

The 1,253-acre (507-ha) Stratus property is located on the vulnerable Barton Springs recharge zone in southwest Austin and, even though 15 percent was the standard that SOS advocated, its leadership opposed the agreement among the city, Stratus, and the Wildflower Center. SOS preferred confrontation and litigation over negotiation and planning. They had moved from the center of Austin politics to its fringe. Still, the SOS Alliance remained most capable of turning out large numbers of angry citizens. Hundreds jammed the city council's hearings on the Stratus proposal with one meeting ending at 3 a.m.

Eventually, the city council would approve the Stratus agreement with a 6-to-1 vote. Earlier, however, after one of the late night hearings, several principal participants essentially agreed that they had to stop meeting like this and find common ground. Both sides agreed on the necessity to protect the Edwards Aquifer but differed on tactics. Bill Bunch of the SOS Alliance and Bob Breunig asked me and the School to convene an informal group, which we dubbed the Great Springs of Texas Partnership.

The Partnership sought to develop strategies for protecting, preserving, and conserving this

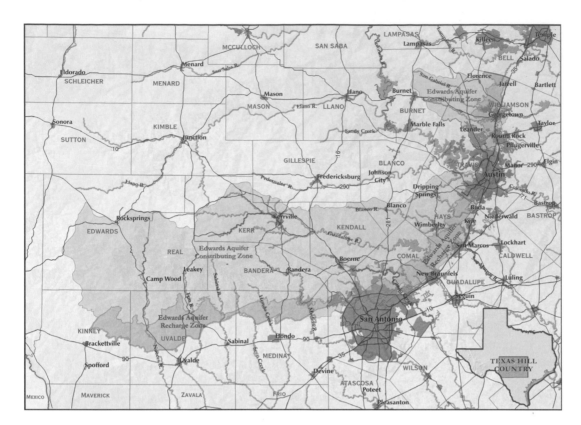

11.1 The Central Texas Hill Country region, known for its unique character, rolling hills, scenic beauty, natural springs, karst aquifers, heritage ranches, and fragile ecosystem. Courtesy of the Hill Country Alliance.

special landscape. In any other state (or in much of the world), this region would have been set aside long ago as a state or national park. The relatively small New Jersey protects its wonderful Pine Barrens region, but mighty Texas has not mustered the will to preserve a comparable landscape. Another partnership between developers and environmentalists, the Hill Country Conservancy, purchases conservation easements and land fee simple in environmentally sensitive areas. The Hill Country Conservancy joined our informal group as well.

Given the culture and traditions of Texas, the only way the Edwards Plateau will be protected is to purchase large parts of it, either through fee simple or easement acquisitions. How to expand the scale of such endeavors became a focus of our organizational meetings through the fall of 2002. We attempted to create an open forum among groups with common interests, but frequently divergent tactics. Our approach was to meet and discuss the areas of agreement, then try to find ways to address areas of conflict.

Design and planning schools at public universities need to play multiple roles. We are viewed

by many as an honest broker of information. As a result, we could collect, analyze, and disseminate information about the Great Springs region (Figure 11.1). We could also convene meetings in a nonpartisan setting. We could study best practices about large-scale conservation efforts and suggest the applicability to the Great Springs region. Several participants in the Partnership were also involved in the Envision Central Texas project (see Chapter 13), and eventually our activities merged. Early on, the Great Springs group agreed that we should use the Geographic Information System (GIS) to map the environmentally sensitive areas in the region and pursue funding to purchase important conservation lands. The mapping came to fruition through the greenprinting effort of the national nonprofit Trust for Public Land and Envision Central Texas, with help from the School of Architecture faculty and students. Funds were raised for purchasing easements and fee simple lands through city and county bond initiatives, as well as through efforts by nonprofit organizations, most notably the Hill Country Conservancy. In addition, another group, the Hill Country Alliance, continues to explore more ambitious preservation options for the whole Hill Country area covering some seventeen counties.

## FISCAL CONSTRAINTS

As the 2002–2003 academic year came to an end, I addressed some budget challenges. In the decade before, as then-Governor George W. Bush took office, the state provided 50 percent of the School's budget. That support had dropped to below 18 percent by 2003. As a result of further state cuts, I had to implement a 5 percent cut for the coming two years (2003–2004, 2004–2005), which translated into around a $300,000 reduction for the School of Architecture. State funding for faculty travel was temporarily suspended, and each vacant position underwent considerable scrutiny for several weeks. Although a challenge, I endeavored to protect people and programs. We offered far fewer summer courses in 2003, and we reduced slightly the number of courses for the 2003–2004 academic year.

We were not the only ones with budget challenges. At our May 9, 2003, board meeting of the Lady Bird Johnson Wildflower Center, Dr. Bob Breunig outlined the financial difficulties brought on by reduced visitation and membership. A key to recovery was to make the Center's gardens a stronger draw.

"When going through hell, keep going," one of the board members observed in typical Texas fashion.

Even wheelchair-bound by a stroke, Mrs. Johnson maintained the idealism that made her a beacon for optimism. She stressed a national agenda for the Wildflower Center, observing, "Wherever I go in America, the land speaks in its own language, in its own regional accent."

We later received the unwelcome news that Dr. Breunig had resigned his position as Wildflower Center executive director to assume similar responsibilities at the Museum of Northern Arizona. Breunig was sorry to go, but he had deep ties to Arizona. I would miss him not only at the Wildflower Center, but also as a collaborator in the Envision Central Texas and Great Springs Partnership. Although public and nonprofit institutions across the United States faced financial and leadership issues in the first decade of the twenty-first century, money was not a limiting factor elsewhere. But even in places of wealth, change challenges the status quo.

## A WORLD AWAY

Later in the month during which Breunig had resigned, I fly to Saudi Arabia to lecture at the King Fahd University of Petroleum and Minerals in Dhahran. My neighbor on the plane from Dallas to La Guardia tells me that members of the royal family of Morocco are University of Texas alumni.[1]

I drift off to sleep and awake over the Sahara Desert, or the Desert du Sahara as the video screen announces, somewhere in western Egypt. It is midday, and small white clouds stretch as far as the eye can see. Their shadows dot the sands below. My fellow passengers keep their window shades down and watch censored images of alcohol, crucifixes, and cleavage on their little video screens. I'm transfixed by the grandeur outside the window.

The landscape changes with traces of water. It looks like Arizona until we fly over ancient settlements approaching the Nile. A fierce, dark green corridor forms rectilinear geometries in contrast to the curving surrounding hills. We are over Luxor, then the Red Sea.

At dusk, after clearing customs, then a passport check by the *mutawwai'in*, Saudi's religious morality police, I fly from Jeddah to Damman.[2] Small, vegetated hills appear like islands in the sand.

At King Fahd University, the "First Symposium on the Development of Academic City Planning Programs and Professional Practice in Saudi Arabia" opened with a prayer. Six photographers documented every aspect of the opening ceremony. The symposium featured lively discussions about the future of planning in the Kingdom and the relationship of the discipline to associated professions, especially architecture and civil engineering.

The King Fahd campus was designed by the Texas architects Caudill Rowlett Scott, later known as CRS, in 1965 (Figure 11.2). Founded after the Second World War in College Station, CRS became best known for its business acumen and programming techniques. The King Fahd campus is bold and imposing, but rather harsh and Brutalist with massive amounts of concrete. Most of my Saudi counterparts had earned degrees from American universities. With my Saudi hosts, I had several interesting discussions about planning and architecture, as well as the current football season and American politics. I met Dr. Saleh Al Hathloul, "the godfather of planning and architecture in Saudi Arabia" and was interviewed by the *Saudi Gazette*. Professor Michael Batty of the University College London's Bartlett School of Architecture presented a prescient paper on planning education with an IT/GIS focus.[3] He stressed the importance of networks and data and public participation, noting the value IT and GIS could play in urban regeneration through e-democracy.

As Westerners, neither Michael Batty nor I could visit the holy cities. However, there were many presentations about Mecca and Medina, so I felt almost as if I had been to both. One speaker observed, "The residents of Mecca, like those of Rome, have adapted to pilgrims. Before oil, pilgrims were a significant source of income for local residents who would move their family into a single room during Ramadan to rent the rest of their home out. Now, the pilgrims tend to be poorer than the local Saudis."

This posed a planning challenge for the king of Saudi Arabia in his capacity as "Custodian of the Two Holiest Places." The speakers at the symposium, scholars and practitioners alike, suggested many solutions to house and feed pilgrims while accommodating a growing population in a desert environment.

The most striking aspect of the symposium, and the visit in general, was the absence of women. I had participated in a symposium in the United Arab Emirates in 1999, and women

had participated, segregated during the formal events, but free to mingle during social events. I recall a woman behind a veil giving a PowerPoint presentation. Initially, she had computer problems, as did others at the conference, but she quickly gained confidence. She had intense blue eyes gazing out from under her black burka and from behind the veil. She moved the mouse with a black-gloved hand. She seemed young, but spoke strongly, focusing on her work—"user responsive, environmentally sensitive housing." Like other Arab speakers, she read her paper. They call unread presentations "American talks."

On a visit to Turkey, I found women in control of the Istanbul Technical University. But in Saudi Arabia, the Prophet Mohammed's words were literally enforced, "If a man and a woman are

**11.2** Tower at King Fahd University of Petroleum and Minerals. The plan for the university was prepared by Caudill Rowlett Scott, known as CRS, of Houston, Texas. CRS was founded in 1946 by Texas A&M University architecture professors William Caudill and John Rowlett, who were joined by their student Wallie Scott in 1948. Photograph by Hasanullah Shah.

alone in one place, the third person present is the devil."

I saw women in *abaya*, the traditional loose black robe, and *hijab*, the head covering, on the streets and even in the hotel, but not at King Fahd University, where professors spoke fondly of their women mentors in the United States.

My hosts displayed considerable hospitality. One afternoon, they arranged for Michael Batty and me to see parts of the city. Our guide was Omar Ashoor, an architecture student who had been born in Florida, where his father had studied computer science. Omar wanted to do an internship in the United States. Even though he was a U.S. citizen, given the post-9/11 political situation, his prospects had dimmed.

He asked what we wanted to see. Something historic and traditional, we responded. "Impossible," Omar responded. "Before oil was discovered in the 1930s, Damman and Khobar were small fishing villages. Dhahran didn't even exist. It would take a couple of hours to reach anything that existed before oil."

We went to a shopping mall instead. The physical structure of the mall was pure contemporary American suburbia. About half of its contents was familiar, the other half completely foreign.

"Young people love the mall," Omar reported.

"Why?" we asked.

"We can check out girls," he answered.

I looked around at the veils and *abaya* and wondered out loud, "How?"

Omar paused for a moment, chuckled, and said, "We have our ways."

My Saudi neighbor on the Damman to Jeddah leg of the return flight had visited the United States twice and seen three cities: Orlando (for fun with his family), Los Angeles (for business with Chinese and Korean manufacturers of children's clothes), and Las Vegas (an extension of the LA trip due to one of his Chinese-American associates). He had stayed at the Luxor in Vegas. I wondered whether he had been dressed there as he was now in the plane, in a white, ankle-length *thobe* and the white traditional headdress, the *kaffiyeh,* with dual black rope headband. The flight was hot, and many men removed their *thobe* and

sat in white *sarwal* briefs with towels covering some of their bodies. Women remained covered in black.

As we left Saudi air space, taking off from Jeddah to New York, the Saudi women, one by one, stood up and proceeded to the toilet. They emerged transformed in Western dresses or skirts, with their *abaya* neatly folded under their arms.

## HOPE BLOOMS

Back in Texas, I participated in various board of directors activities at the Lady Bird Johnson Wildflower Center, including executive, director search, and planning committees. Landscape architect Gary Smith, a leading botanic garden designer, was developing the new landscape master plan, and he led the planning committee through a brainstorming session. Gary asked, "What is the Central Texas ecological garden?"

Mrs. Johnson once observed, "Where flowers bloom, so does hope." This sentiment helped inspire our discussions about a new plan for the Wildflower Center gardens (Figure 11.3).

To increase the possibilities for the design of the Wildflower Center's gardens, we recruited Andropogon Associates' Carol Franklin to lecture on ecological aesthetics. She noted that botanical gardens need to be designed as a "series of journeys" that "bring drama to the place." Nature is very bold, she observed, and our ecological designs should be as bold.

Finding a replacement for Breunig involved several dinners with finalists and Mrs. Johnson. As a result of her stroke, she could not walk and was hesitant to speak in public. Yet, she followed the details of each conversation. When she wanted to ask a question, she found a way. The Secret Service agents stood guard, ever vigilant. Former presidents and first ladies are shadowed by Secret Service agents for life. Mrs. Johnson treated her agents, like everyone else, as extensions of her family. They were clearly fond of her.

The first time I met her, after I joined the Wildflower Center board and before her stroke, Mrs.

Johnson gave me a hug and said, "You're family now." As the search committee queried the candidates at Fonda San Miguel or some other favorite eatery and watched the reactions of the stoic agents, I could see that they were family, too.

Fall is a good time to see the bones of a garden. In October 2004, the center board welcomed new executive director Susan Rieff to her first board meeting, where Gary Smith described the new master plan for the Wildflower Center gardens. Although the plan is a good start, Gary observed, quoting the landscape architect Narendra Juneja, "the proof of the pudding is in the eating, not in the recipe."

## ON THE ROAD AGAIN

At the 2004 American Society of Landscape Architects (ASLA) meeting in Salt Lake City in late October, I met the luminous Terry Tempest Williams at the Landscape Architecture Foundation's annual fundraising gala at the McCune Mansion. With Peter Walker and his wife and colleague Jane Gillette, we talked about the role of landscape architecture in creating a better world. Williams writes passionately and politically about landscapes with intimate, even erotic, detail about the characteristics of places. Williams quizzed us about the contributions of landscape architects and prospects for the future. In her stirring keynote talk the next morning, Williams observed that landscape architects are "not only place-makers but also bridge-builders" and "if we have open space, we have open time," and that "nature lives by the same grace as us."

From the ASLA meeting in Salt Lake City, I flew to New York City for the Urban Land Institute (ULI) conference to participate in the Sustainable Development Council activities. The ULI is organized around interest areas councils. As an academic fellow, I selected the Sustainable Development Council for my involvement.

The ULI conference coincided with the 2004 presidential election. I watched the results outside the NBC news studio at Rockefeller Center

**11.3** Lady Bird Johnson Wildflower Center Gardens Master Plan. Design by W. Gary Smith.

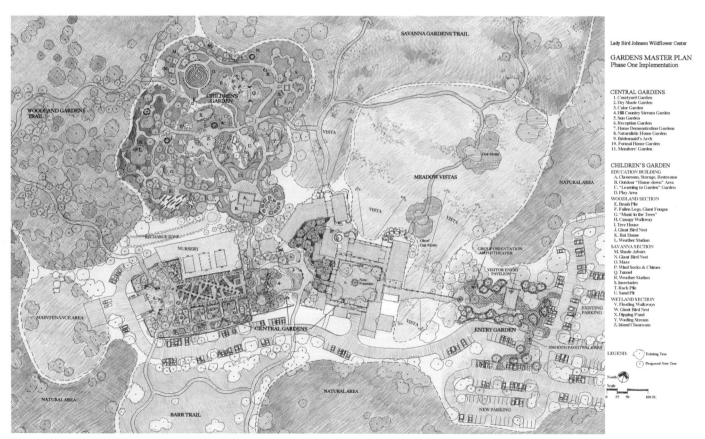

11.4 Lady Bird Johnson Wildflower Center. Design by Overland Partners. Photograph by Bruce Leander.

until the outcome became obvious. Afterward, former President Bill Clinton entered the vast Hilton ballroom like a rock star to deliver his post-election reflection to the ULI gathering. Consisting mostly of developers, bankers, lawyers, and other conservative-leaning real estate types, the warm reception for the former president surprised me. Dress-for-success women in business suits shed their jackets, stood on their folding chairs, and screamed their hearts out. Among his many insightful observations, President Clinton noted that the demographic group that exhibited the biggest jump in support for the Kerry/Edwards ticket from the 2000 elections was well-educated, fifty- to sixty-year-old white males. In his first non-campaign speech after the election, President Clinton appeared gaunt and thin as a result of his recent surgery. Still, his intelligence and charisma remained intact, as did his wit and charm.

## LADY BIRD JOHNSON: A FORCE FOR NATURE

The following autumn, I again attended the Lady Bird Johnson Wildflower Center Board meeting. We discussed strategic planning and budgetary issues. Susan Rieff noted that the board "needed to catch the color" of Mrs. Johnson's dreams, which had stimulated environmental awareness across the nation. To this end, the board began

discussing a possible merger with the University of Texas, an idea that had Mrs. Johnson's whole-hearted endorsement. We agreed to keep these discussions confidential, which we did for months as the process was dragged out by legal issues.

In May and June 2006, the Wildflower Center Board of Directors and the University of Texas Board of Regents agreed on the merger. The 279-acre (113-ha) Wildflower Center became part of the School of Architecture and the College of Natural Sciences (Figure 11.4).

Claudia Alta Taylor Johnson, who we knew better as Lady Bird, is an under-heralded heroine of the American environmental movement (Figure 11.5). Her death on July 11, 2007, in her Austin home resulted in a revival of recognition of her significant contributions. "Like the flowers in the fields she loved," Bill Moyers observed at her funeral, "Lady Bird was a woman of many hues." She helped spark an interest in the quality of our surroundings that led to many of the clean air and water laws that we now take for granted. She also brought the environmental movement back home to Texas.

In May 1965, Lady Bird Johnson convinced her husband to convene the seminal White House Conference on Natural Beauty. That event assembled the environmental leaders of the time, including Laurance Rockefeller, Stewart Udall, and Ian McHarg. The conference helped elevate the environment to national prominence, as policy makers interacted with leading scientists, landscape architects, and planners. Panels of environmentalists, businesspeople, citizens, and elected officials debated a variety of topics, such as tax policies that would encourage conservation and ways in which the federal government could assist communities to preserve landscapes. At the conference, Mrs. Johnson asked the question: "Can a great democratic society generate the drive to plan, and having planned, execute projects of great natural beauty?"

Mrs. Johnson viewed "beauty" broadly. For her, beauty was not mere decoration. Rather, beauty resulted from the wise use of land and water, plants and soils. Pollution is not beautiful. The conference that she helped conceive and convene, and in which she enthusiastically participated, signaled a new awareness of our connections with nature. The White House provided leadership, and the proceedings resulting from the conference provided the framework for the environmental decade that followed. As a result of Mrs. Johnson's influence, some two hundred new laws relating to the environment were enacted during the Johnson administration, with more to follow under President Richard Nixon.

Lady Bird Johnson is best known for her advocacy of highway beautification and wildflowers. As first lady, she lobbied Congress to improve the scenic quality of our nation's roadways, protect the redwoods, and block the damming of the Grand Canyon. After she returned to Texas, she did much to improve the quality of her beloved Austin. For example, she helped establish Town Lake Park in the heart of Austin and then opposed the efforts of city leaders to name the park after her. Two weeks and a day after Mrs. Johnson died at the age of ninety-four, the Austin City Council changed the name of Town Lake to Lady Bird Lake with the support of the Johnson family.

Every day, hundreds of joggers, walkers, cyclists, skaters, fishers, boaters, and bats enjoy Austin's green center. North America's largest colony of urban bats calls the Ann W. Richards Congress Avenue Bridge across Lady Bird Lake home. Nearby, at Barton Springs, endangered salamanders swim with Austinites in a common habitat.

The sole institution she agreed to carry her name is the Lady Bird Johnson Wildflower Center, which she founded in 1982 with the actress Helen Hayes. The Wildflower Center is devoted to native plant research and education. Mrs. Johnson observed that native plants provide the "signatures" of regions. Native wildflowers evolve in the unique climate and soils of a particular place. Wildlife depends on such plants for survival.

The Wildflower Center is both a display garden and a research institution. Its gardens illustrate how wildflowers can enhance our everyday lives. Its research programs advance our understanding about ecological restoration, green roofs, and sustainable site design. The buildings at the Wildflower Center are a pioneering example of sustainable architecture (Figure 11.6). Mrs. Johnson directed the young Overland Partners architects to fit the buildings into the landscape so as to appear that they had been placed there by God.

Perhaps because she was a woman, or maybe as a result of her aversion to self-promotion, Lady Bird Johnson has not yet received the recognition

11.5 Lady Bird Johnson among the wildflowers. Photograph by Frank Wolfe. Courtesy of the Lyndon Baines Johnson Library and Museum.

**11.6** Observation tower and rainwater collection cistern, Lady Bird Johnson Wildflower Center. Design by Overland Partners. Photograph by Bruce Leander.

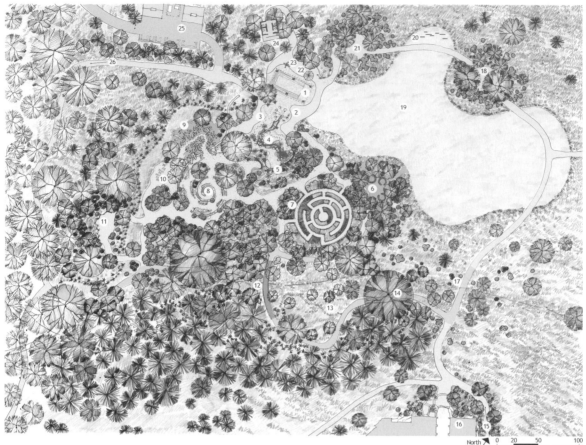

FEATURES:
1. Pavilion
2. The Earth Is a Sieve
3. Dinosaur Tracks
4. Central Texas Stream
5. Hill Country Grotto
6. Giant Bird Nests
7. Metamorphosis Maze
8. Fibonacci Spiral
9. Texas Stumpery
10. Hopscotch
11. Wildlife Blind
12. Bridge
13. Stepping Stones
14. Treetop Wind Chimes
15. Entrance Ramp
16. Library Building
17. The Ford
18. Cedar Elm Classroom
19. Play Lawn
20. Buffalo Sculpture
21. Classroom
22. Cistern
23. Hoerster Windmill
24. Restroom
25. Storage/Maintenance
26. Woodland Trail

North   0   20   50   100

**11.7** Children's Garden, Lady Bird Johnson Wildflower Center. Design by W. Gary Smith.

she deserves as a major environmental figure. Or, perhaps, the focus of her passions—beauty and wildflowers—are viewed as "soft" and not as pressing a concern as water or air pollution or global climate change. We should pause to better understand her message.

Her agenda was much larger, much more profound than it might first appear. A beautiful world cannot be polluted, nor can it be unjust.[4] A Southern woman, Mrs. Johnson supported the Civil Rights leadership of her husband, and she was especially interested in the Wildflower Center's educational outreach programs to minority kids. Gary Smith designed a new Children's Garden at the Wildflower Center to build on Mrs. Johnson's vision (Figure 11.7).

Native wildflowers are a visual manifestation of natural processes in a region. They are an outgrowth of geological time and natural selection. We face the loss of too many natural landscapes in our world. Unfortunately, in spite of Mrs. Johnson's noble efforts, American highways grow uglier by the day. Lady Bird Johnson's life should remind us of another path to the future—one of beautiful landscapes, where native flora and fauna thrive. Mrs. Johnson greened from the heart of Texas. We need to renew her vision for natural beauty as a framework for a more civil society.

# IV | NEW REGIONALISM IN TEXAS AND BEYOND

This section presents Texas examples of regional and landscape planning. Although Texas-based, these efforts relate to broader, renewed interest in regionalism. As Lady Bird Johnson taught us, each region is imbued with special qualities, displayed in flora and fauna that distinguish it from other places. An understanding of those characteristics is the first step toward appreciating the region where we live. Ultimately, the biggest challenge of regionalism is learning to think on a large scale and to take actions on that level.

Texans maintain considerable pride in their heritage. They also identify with the places where they grew up and/or live across the state. However, they are challenged to link their life choices with the incremental destruction of the landscape and heritage that they claim to cherish.

I devote much of this section to Central Texas, the region where I live and work. As I noted in the previous chapter, Hill Country portions of this region would be a national or state park in most countries. Much of the Blackland Prairie in the region would be protected as prime farmland. But this is Texas. And, this is what makes the story interesting.

The Austin region is part of a bigger urban conglomeration called the Texas Triangle, one of the eleven fastest growing megaregions in the United States. Although each megaregion possesses its own unique ecology, culture, and politics, they can each learn from one another. Megaregions, and the metropolitan areas that they encompass, hold the prospect to fuel American prosperity.

# 12 | THE GREEN HEART OF TEXAS

The Edwards Plateau forms a bright green crescent across central Texas, which is visible from space. This limestone formation provides a rich source of groundwater. Called the "Hill Country" because of its undulating terrain, this woody region is also quite scenic. Productive black prairie soils lie to the east of the plateau toward the Gulf of Mexico. At the interface between the plateau and the prairie, many springs exist. These springs have attracted settlements since the days when American Indians dominated the landscape. Hispanic priests founded missions near these springs as part of their efforts to convert native people to Christianity. Waves of immigrants from Spain, Germany, and the southern United States found the springs conducive to settlement and established many towns along the plateau-prairie interface. The springs also feed several significant rivers that flow from the Hill Country across the Coastal Plain to the Gulf. This region includes two of the fastest growing metropolitan areas in the United States: San Antonio and Austin.

Austin is today one of the most popular places in the United States to live and work (Figure 12.1). *Forbes* magazine ranked Austin first out of 239 metropolitan areas nationwide for jobs, income, and good business growth.[1] Austin's popularity as a place to live and conduct business attracts young, high-tech, and well-educated people to the region. In his book defining the "creative class," Richard Florida ranks Austin as the second highest among the forty-nine most creative metropolitan areas in the United States.[2] More recently, Florida ranked Austin first as America's most creative place in metropolitan regions with populations of more than a million people.[3]

The ecology and natural resources of the Central Texas Hill Country contribute significantly to the attractiveness of the region (Figure 12.2). As with so many other places, the environmental quality, which has been so appealing, is in jeopardy of major degradation as a result of growth, especially if meaningful regional planning and growth management controls are not instituted soon. There are clear choices and distinctions in selecting where, within the region, people and businesses should locate. But governments, especially county governments, in Texas have limited authority to direct those choices to the most environmentally sensible and socially equitable places.

Interesting geological forces created the physical context for Richard Florida's model habitat for the creative class. In the western portion of the metropolitan region, the Edwards and Glen Rose limestone formations rise abruptly in the landscape and are downcut by rapidly flowing streams and valleys in an area known as the Balcones Canyonlands (Figure 12.3). The land is rocky and difficult to settle, yet highly desirable for its scenic

12.1 Barton Springs with downtown Austin in the background. Photograph by James M. Innes.

beauty and its habitat value. The rolling Blackland Prairie, which begins on the eastern side of the Canyonlands, supports a highly productive landscape of agriculture and forest land. The prairie is also attractive for rapid suburban growth.

The most noteworthy regional feature in the western Canyonlands is the karstic, cavernous Edwards Aquifer and its contributing watershed area. Barton Springs, which is the primary hydrologic discharge point of the aquifer, is one of many of the Great Springs of Texas. The springs are all linearly aligned on the eastern edge of the Balcones Escarpment, or Fault Zone, which separates the Edwards Limestone from the Blackland Prairie. Barton Springs is at once a critical habitat for endangered species (two aquatic salamanders) and a recreational swimming facility of legendary quality and scale. The springs are 984 feet (300 m) long with a year-round temperature of 68 degrees F (20 degrees C) and an average discharge rate of 396 gallons (1,500 l) per second or 32 million gallons (1.2 million l) per day. Barton Springs represents the cultural hearth of Austin (Figure 12.4). A virtual barometer of the quality of life and environment of Central Texas, the larger aquifer is highly sensitive to contamination from

12.2 Autumn in the Texas Hill Country near Bandera. Photograph by Larry Ditto.

hazardous materials spills and urban runoff pollution in general. To the south, the City of San Antonio supports the largest population in the world (1.3 million people) solely dependent on groundwater (another unit of the Edwards Aquifer) as a drinking water source.

Rainfall is plentiful across the region, and the karstic aquifer recharges clean water rapidly in good supply. Thin soils cover the limestone and during thunderstorms water runs off quickly and flash floods result.

## THE EDWARDS AQUIFER

The Edwards Aquifer (Figure 12.5) is one of the most productive carbonate aquifers in the United States, supporting the development of a strong and diversified economy through Central Texas.[4] The aquifer extends for 261 miles (420 km) underlying a portion of two growing urban regions, San Antonio and Austin.[5] Between 1960 and 1980, the population through the Austin-San Antonio corridor expanded by 53 percent, more than twice the national average.[6] Rapid growth continues to the present. The population of Austin has doubled every twenty years since 1895 with a steady annual growth rate of 3.47 percent. As with many other Sunbelt locations, Central Texas economic prosperity has been fueled by, and is at the expense of, accessible and inexpensive water supplies. The Hill Country exemplifies many locations throughout the southern and southwestern United States where resource managers and planners struggle to provide sufficient supplies of high quality water at a pace capable of sustaining apparently unquenchable developmental demands.

One must preface a discussion of the Edwards Aquifer by first clarifying its lateral extent and unique hydrological nature. The aquifer extends through ten counties of south Central Texas and is separated into three relatively independent hydrological systems: the San Antonio Segment, the Barton Springs Segment, and the Northern Edwards Segment.[7] The San Antonio Segment extends for 175 miles (282 km) and, together with its associated catchment basin, covers more than 7,997 square miles (20,712 km[2]).[8] As the first groundwater reserve to receive sole-source designation under amendments to the Safe Drink-

**12.3** A panoramic view of the Austin skyline is framed by wooded hills as one looks eastward from a roadside overlook. A portion of these woodlands comprises the city's Vireo Nature Preserve dedicated to the Balcones Canyonlands Preserve. Photograph by Matt McCaw, 2005. Courtesy of the City of Austin.

**12.4** Barton Springs Pool. Photograph by Frederick Steiner.

ing Water Act, the San Antonio Segment is often referred to as the Edwards Aquifer when, in fact, the aquifer continues to the northeast for an additional 75 miles (121 km). This portion of the aquifer, the Austin region, is subsequently separated into the Northern Edwards and Barton Springs Segments, falling prey to a similar body of issues and concerns that characterize the San Antonio portion, but with a slightly less imperative tone. Through its SOS Ordinance, Austin acted to limit development over the recharge and contributing zones of the aquifer. Although implementation of the ordinance has been spotty, at least there is a policy framework for protection in contrast to San Antonio, which has some separate initiatives but no comprehensive policy framework. Austin also took leadership in purchasing aquifer lands both through city bond measures and nongovernmental initiatives such as those by the Hill Country Conservancy, a coalition of environmental and business interests. In 2000, similar efforts

began in San Antonio as well with a $1/8$-cent sales tax increase that generated $45 million for acquisition of lands in the Edwards Aquifer recharge and contributing zones, as well as $20 million for watershed lands. In 2005, these efforts expanded when San Antonio voters approved an additional $1/8$-cent sales tax increase yielding $90 million more to protect the aquifer.

The landscape of the Hill Country provides a visible display of the aquifer. The aquifer's principal zone for recharge is the Balcones Fault Zone, a highly fractured, southeast-facing escarpment extending for 180 miles (290 km).[9] The Balcones Escarpment is a transitory terrain separating the Edwards Plateau to the north and west and the Blackland Prairie to the south and east. The Hill Country rises to approximately 2,297 feet (~700 m) and is dominated by woodlands of oak, cedar, and mesquite, along with some grasslands.[10]

In addition to the rich groundwater, the rivers and streams flowing through the Hill Country contain considerable water of value to people and

**12.5** Hamilton Pool, a karst grotto and swimming hole located 30 miles (48.3 km) west of Austin in the Texas Hill Country. Once an underground river, part of the Edwards Aquifer, the surrounding limestone cliffs arch over the pool to form a partial roof. Photograph by Dave Wilson.

other organisms. From central Austin to the west into the Hill Country, a series of constructed lakes control flooding and provide water for human uses. These lakes provide good water, especially for Austin, but the flows below the earth's surface are special and essential for San Antonio's future. Within the zone of high-angle, parallel faulting of the Balcones Escarpment, water exists under confined and unconfined conditions.[11] Streams flowing toward the Gulf come in contact with the exposed Edwards Limestone and lose as much as 100 percent of their baseflow,[12] providing upward of 85 percent of the aquifer's recharge. The remainder of the recharge results from direct infiltration of precipitation on the outcrop.[13] There is a general consensus that current aquifer charge via pumpage and springflow is in excess of aquifer recharge through the San Antonio Segment.

Back in 1982, the Barton Springs Segment had experienced no identifiable groundwater declines associated with pumpage.[14] Large water-level fluctuations in the area were attributed to natural variations in recharge and discharge.[15] In 1985, approximately thirty thousand people in the Barton Springs Segment depended on the aquifer for their water supply. By 2004, though, some fifty thousand people depended on the Barton Springs Segment of the aquifer as their sole source of drinking water.[16]

Portions of the Northern Edwards Segment have actually "outstripped the available supplies of water for municipal and domestic needs," as the metropolitan area witnessed dramatic increases in population and groundwater withdrawal.[17] One exception to this dramatic increase in groundwater use is the City of Austin. With proximity to the Colorado River and the system of lakes created to control floods, the city has never become heavily dependent upon groundwater reserves and maintains a progressive aquifer protection program.[18] However, for most areas of the Northern Edwards Segment and the region as a whole, groundwater use in excess of available supply is an ever-present concern.[19]

Groundwater quality concerns for the Edwards Aquifer are focused primarily on: (1) protection of the aquifer's recharge zone to minimize potential contamination; (2) protection of the surface water quality in streams traversing the recharge zone; and (3) maintenance of the aquifer's freshwater level to stabilize saltwater intrusion.

The development proposals for San Antonio Ranch, a proposed new town situated over a portion of the recharge zone north of San Antonio, were credited with initiating public concern for the recharge zone in the late 1960s and early 1970s. As the issues unfolded, citizens responded to the disquieting revelations that existing regulations were extremely inadequate and ineffective in protecting the recharge zone, and their personal understanding of the aquifer as a multi-faceted resource was limited. Although a lawsuit to prevent the development eventually failed in May 1973,[20] the San Antonio Ranch debate did result in improved analysis of the resource, more stringent recharge zone regulations, and increased public attention on the aquifer's vulnerability to contamination. With these developments, the Edwards Aquifer had clearly attained status as both an invaluable resource and a potent political issue.

The current pumpage rate from the Edwards Aquifer is considered to be at or even slightly above the sustainable yield, as measured in critical drought times. As the Central Texas region continues to grow rapidly, the spring-dependent water resources are increasingly in jeopardy from cessation of flow and degradation of water quality.

## THE BALCONES CANYONLANDS

The Spanish explorers called the terraced, limestone hills northwest of present-day Austin, *balcones*. The Balcones Canyonlands provide homes for literally dozens of endemic rare, threatened, and federally listed endangered species—insects, plants, amphibians, and songbirds (Figure 12.6). Their remarkable biodiversity results in large part from the geologic history of the highly porous limestone bedrock, thin soil mantle, highly adaptive plant communities, and mild, mesic climate that have evolved over the last million or more years.

This biodiversity, as well as the nesting habitat of the endangered Golden-cheeked Warbler and Black-capped Vireo, led to the innovative Balcones Canyonlands Conservation Plan (Figure 12.7). The plan was among the first regional multi-species habitat conservation plans by the U.S. Fish and Wildlife Service. Secretary of Interior Bruce Babbitt advocated habitat conservation plans to help achieve the goals of the Endangered Species Act. Issued on May 2, 1996, the plan was developed by a multidisciplinary team led by University of Texas Community and Regional Planning professor Kent Butler. The plan consists of a permit issued to Travis County and the City of Austin. It has been a model for other locally based habitat conservation plans.[21] The Balcones plan took a comprehensive biological approach, considering state-listed species in addition to those federally listed. It represents, according to Tim Beatley, "a tenuous balancing of development and environmental interests."[22] This coalition has held up well. Beatley calls the Balcones Canyonlands Conservation Plan "impressive in a number of respects," including its multiple species focus and its regional geographical scale.[23]

As a result of the plan, the county and city created the Balcones Canyonlands Preserve. The habitat preserves will consist of a minimum of 30,428 acres (12,314 ha) of endangered species habitat in western Travis County. As of 2010, 27,906 acres (11,293 ha) or 91.7 percent of the preserve land had been acquired.[24]

## THE BLACKLAND PRAIRIE

On the eastern side of the Austin metropolitan region, the rich deep soils of the Blackland Prairie begin to the east of the Balcones Canyonlands. This prairie landscape supported considerable agricultural and forest production for more than a century. Dense woodlands are also common, and flowing streams make the area a highly desirable place to live. The agricultural economy and heritage of prairie agricultural lands in particular have been severely challenged in the last two decades by suburban growth. In a ten-year period in the late twentieth century, more than 1.3 million acres (565,000 ha) of farmland and ranchland was converted to urban-suburban development in Texas,

**12.6** A closer look at this view of the wooded hills around Bull Creek reveals the signs of development into the wildlands. The area is referred to as the Wildland Urban Interface. The extension of homes, power lines, roadways, and businesses outward from the city core brings with it challenges for managing wildlands for endangered species' habitat and water quality and quantity. Photograph by Melody Lytle, 2003. Courtesy of the City of Austin.

**12.7** Male Golden-cheeked Warblers (*dendroica chrysoparia*) set up territories upon arrival to an area and begin to sing. They sing to signal to other males the location of their territory boundaries, which often causes other males to counter-sing. They also sing to attract females for breeding. The Warblers were listed as an endangered species in 1990. Habitat loss and fragmentation are considered the primary threats to their survival. Courtesy of the U.S. Fish and Wildlife Service.

and the rate persisted and increased in the next five years, with 333,592 acres (135,000 ha) of additional high-quality farmland lost. In fact, Texas lost more agricultural land than any other state in the United States during this period.[11]

The challenge for this area today is to balance protection of agricultural lands against the inherent attractiveness of the landscape for suburban residential growth. Extensive new water supplies are currently proposed for development and transport into this area, from just outside the Austin and San Antonio metropolitan regions, to accommodate the next wave of suburban growth.

## CIVIC ENVIRONMENTALISM

Largely on account of the need to protect endangered species habitat and water resources, but also for human use and enjoyment, the Austin region has developed an extensive network of parks and greenbelts that shelter the springs and streams and provide considerable opportunities for hiking and nature study. Between 1997 and 2007, Austin and associated governmental units in the region have acquired more than 49,000 acres (19,800 ha) of land for habitat conservation and recreational use. In 2006, both Austin and Travis County passed bond measures to purchase more open space. Hays County to the south followed suit in 2007 with its own open space bond program.

A measure of Austin's strong civic environmentalism is the extensive acquisition of metropolitan parkland in the eastern part of the region, away from the critical habitats and springs, but closer to the neighborhoods and communities traditionally populated by lower income and minority people. The benefits of public lands to the health and community and quality of life of all populations are beginning to be recognized by residents and businesses alike.

A continuing challenge for the Austin metropolitan region, as is often the case when one city dominates the economic and political base, is to cooperate and share equitably in future infrastructure investments to serve a growing suburban population that extends well beyond the central city limits. These and related issues were the motivation for a significant regional planning initiative: Envision Central Texas.

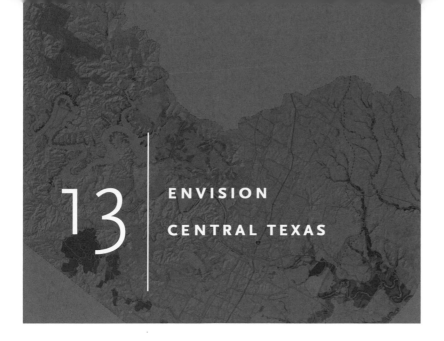

# 13 | ENVISION CENTRAL TEXAS

One of the first people I met upon arriving in Austin in August 2001 was Dr. Bob Breunig, the executive director of the Lady Bird Johnson Wildflower Center. We had known each other in Arizona. Breunig and I visited often to discuss planning for the Wildflower Center and the rapidly growing region. Suburban sprawl threatened the integrity of Mrs. Johnson's dream.

The building complex at the Wildflower Center is state-of-the-art sustainable design. Designed by a young team of University of Texas–educated San Antonio architects, Overland Partners, the buildings drew on the German, Hispanic, and Anglo traditions of Central Texas.[1] Breunig admired the buildings, but he was concerned that the landscape design did not display the same innovation. He advocated for a new landscape master plan that would elevate the landscape while alleviating the impacts of suburban sprawl. The Wildflower Center is situated over the Edwards Aquifer in a part of the city where growth has been especially contentious. The Center helped mitigate this growth both by adding new lands to its gardens and research areas and by providing models for the use of native plants and water conservation.

Breunig and I also became involved in a larger community effort to take on the suburban sprawl issue in early 2002. Two prominent citizens, Lowell Lebermann and Neal Kocurek, invited me to

lunch at the Headliners Club atop the then Bank One (currently Chase Bank) Building in downtown Austin. The Headliners Club was a deal-making headquarters where the men's room displays a panoramic view of the city, and headlines of local newsmakers from LBJ to the younger George Bush adorn the hallways. I had moderated an evening panel at the Headliners Club on sustainability featuring Gus Garcia, Austin mayor at the time; civic leader Robin Rather; and then *Texas Monthly* publisher Mike Levy. The forum degraded into a donnybrook, after Levy launched into a long diatribe against former Mayor Kirk Watson's administration. About the only thing that Levy said that made sense to me was that "it is is a sin if you can make a difference and don't take an action." That evening reinforced the idealism and chaos of Austin, where architectural, growth, and environmental issues are vigorously debated. For instance, after one heated session during the design of City Hall, its architect, Antoine Predock, observed that Austin was "terminally democratic." I also learned about the challenges of panel moderation in Austin and the importance of the Headliners Club.

## "WE BETTER GET OUR ACT TOGETHER"

The positive, straightforward Kocurek (an engineer with a Ph.D., an entrepreneur, and the president and CEO of the St. David's Health Care System) invited me to join a new effort, "We're calling it the Central Texas Visioning Project."

"We're fixin' to do things differently than past efforts," added Lebermann, a former city council member who had been active in the Austin Tomorrow Plan in the early 1970s. "A highlight of that effort was that Scottish fellow from Philadelphia who convinced us to start planning with nature," Lebermann recalled Ian McHarg's involvement fondly.[2] Lebermann was called Austin's "Green Panther" because of his environmental activism. He owned a beer distributorship and was blind from a gunshot accident when he was twelve. A handsome young aide, in sport coat and tie, from the UT Kappa Alpha fraternity acted as Lebermann's eyes.

Lebermann and Kocurek explained that where past planning efforts had focused on Austin and ignored outlying areas, the Central Texas Visioning Project would address all five counties in the metropolitan area (Bastrop, Caldwell, Hays, Travis, and Williamson).

"Whatever Austin and Travis County came up with, the other four counties would oppose," Kocurek explained.

"As would the state legislature," Lebermann added.

"Why only the five counties? Why not the whole Austin-San Antonio corridor since it shares the same hydrology and transportation systems?" I asked.

"We considered that, but felt we could accomplish more focusing on the Austin metropolitan region," Kocurek said, with Lebermann adding, "We're fixin' to double our population in the next twenty years from its current 1.25 million, so we better get our act together."

They foresaw a large board of directors, too large in my opinion. Before leaving Phoenix, I had been involved in an ill-fated regional planning effort that had been doomed by an attempt to involve every possible interest. The result had been a meaningless, compromised process.

"We will involve the best consultants in the nation, Fregonese Calthorpe, to help guide our

efforts so we produce a vision with legs," Kocurek declared. A "Group of Eight" regional leaders had been meeting to structure the process. Kocurek and Lebermann wanted me to join that group.

"We're going to raise 2 million dollars for the effort," Lebermann added.

I recalled the many regional planning efforts I had conducted with students for under $10,000, many with lasting influences in Washington, Idaho, Colorado, and Arizona. I agreed to join the Central Texas Visioning Project. In addition to Fregonese Calthorpe Associates, we retained the services of local civic leader Beverly Silas to be executive director and of EnviroMedia, an agency devoted to environmental and health-related causes, to handle public relations. EnviroMedia convinced the assembled seventy-member board at an early meeting that our name was dull. We renamed the effort Envision Central Texas (ECT), rather unimaginatively echoing Fregonese Calthorpe's previous Envision Utah undertaking.

We held board meetings throughout the five-county region, such as in San Marcos, the county seat for Hays County and home of what was then called Southwest Texas State University (subsequently renamed Texas State University).[3] Much effort was devoted to building a strong foundation and to presenting Envision Central Texas to the public. EnviroMedia conducted a region-wide survey that revealed transportation issues as the biggest problems facing the region. A series of focus groups underscored this problem, but related it to population growth and quality of life issues. A bus tour was organized for the media, along with press releases and briefings, an attractive Web site, and newspaper inserts.

Executive director Beverly Silas and chair Neal Kocurek put a public face on the process and coordinated the monthly board meetings. Silas and Kocurek met with all the city and county elected officials in the region (several of whom served on the ECT board) and raised $2 million. They also led our executive committee's weekly conference call meetings. The executive committee represented diverse, even divergent, interests and included regional leaders, such as former mayors, county judges (the head of the County

Commissioners' Court is called "county judge" in Texas), neighborhood advocates, environmentalists, and business leaders, who were pro and con on locally controversial issues such as light rail.

As Arizona State University political theorist Richard Dagger notes, "Campaigns to curb urban sprawl have met with firm and well-financed opposition."[4] An example of a well-financed and strongly supported campaign to positively manage growth provides a welcome contrast. Envision Central Texas presents just such an example of regional visioning that may also be viewed as an application of human ecology with implications of design for civic environmentalism.

### BUILDING A COMMON VISION

In 2002, the Austin metropolitan region, which is defined by the central city and the five surrounding counties, had a population greater than 1.25 million people (which rose to more than 1.5 million by 2007). The region had grown by 47 percent from 1990 to 2000 and was projected to attain a population of 2.75–3.0 million by 2030.[5] The five-county region covers 3,980 square miles (10,308 km²), of which approximately 1,157 square miles (2,997 km²) were developed in 2000. Regionally, the population density is very low—only 318 people per square mile (113 people/km²)—but it is expected to double in the next 20–30 years. Greater Houston is relatively denser with 550 people per square mile (212 people/km²) in 2006. If only the urbanized parts of the Austin area are considered, then the density in 2000 was 1,080 people per square mile (417 people/km²). Inside the City of Austin, the population density increases to 2,396 people per square mile (925 people/km²) in 2006. This is less than cities like Houston or Phoenix, hardly known for their density, let alone large East Coast cities like New York where, in 2006, the population density was 27,083 people per square mile (10,456 people/km²).

Astonishingly, the Austin region lacked a growth plan. Envision Central Texas, a private, nonprofit organization, was launched in 2001 to help fill this void. Although not a government agency, ECT receives funding from several local governments. The board of directors, designed to reflect the broad range of constituencies concerned with growth, includes business, government, neighborhood, environmental, and social equity groups. The board retained the regional planning firm Fregonese Calthorpe Associates as consultants to guide the process. John Fregonese is the former planning director of Portland Metro in Oregon. Peter Calthorpe is a leading New Urbanist architect.[6] Fregonese Calthorpe Associates and the Envision Central Texas board sought to create a vision uniting the Austin metropolitan region around common strategies that would help ensure that the area's natural resources, economic vitality, social equity, and overall quality of life would be preserved and enhanced, even in the face of rapid growth.

To accomplish these objectives, an extensive public process was organized that involved workshops where hundreds of participants worked together to build future growth scenarios for the Central Texas region. At each workshop, participants worked within a small group. They used a map and game pieces representing various development types to share perspectives on land use, transportation, and environmental issues. John Fregonese and his team interpreted this information to build scenarios to compare with a base-case scenario.

As the scenario development process began, Envision Central Texas solicited proposals for small test sites (approximately 20–200 acres or 8–81 ha) to be used as examples for local planning within the context of the larger, unfolding regional vision (Figure 13.1). The concept was to illustrate a variety of typical situations in the region. Fregonese took the lead with the scenario design, and his partner Peter Calthorpe's architecture firm, Calthorpe Associates, developed these site-specific designs. The community test site designs were to assist in the eventual implementation of the regional vision.

Following the workshops, Fregonese Calthorpe Associates compiled the data and created the maps produced in the small groups through

## Residential over Commercial

**13.1** Residential over commercial design guidelines from East Austin Featherlite Test Site Workshop. Design by Calthorpe Associates. Courtesy of Envision Central Texas.

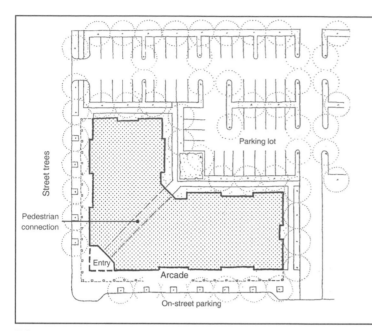

- Orient retail and residential entries to face public streets and sidewalks

- Encourage pedestrian connections from parking areas to building entries at public streets

- Provide visitor drop-off areas and on-street parking at public building entries

- Locate parking to the rear of the building away from public view

- Provide street trees along driveways, drive aisles and pedestrian connections

- Provide a minimum of 1 tree per 5 parking stalls

- Screen trash enclosures from public view with a fence and landscaping

Plan

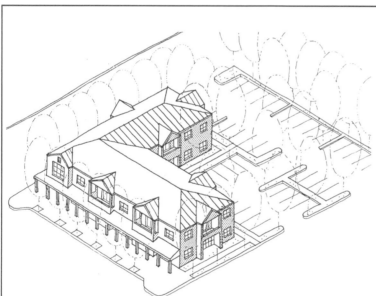

- Provide outdoor dining terraces with tables, chairs, and other furniture to bring activity to the street

- Encourage architectural expression of building entry features

- Provide roof forms such as hips, gables or mansards

- Screen mechanical equipment from view

- Minimum 2-story building wall along public streets is required

- Provide residential entries or lobbies with access from public street

Axonometric

GIS (building on a GIS database created by the University of Texas at Austin School of Architecture). Scenario planning, a tool for assessing the consequences for development and conservation in an uncertain world, was the theoretical basis for the process.[7] Scenario planning is "a systemic method for thinking creatively about possible, complex, and uncertain futures."[8] Scenarios are "plausible stories of what might unfold in the future."[9] Fregonese distinguished this type of planning from traditional planning, noting that scenarios are used to develop a vision and, unlike a static plan, provide a set of strategies that can respond to changing conditions.

Four initial scenarios resulted, a range of possible development types to direct future land use and transportation systems in different patterns and arrangements. Economic, land use, and transportation models were incorporated into the scenarios. Existing conditions and trends, such as current and planned transportation corridors, were considered. Similarly, critical natural resources, such as aquifer recharge zones below the Edwards Plateau and productive agricultural lands in the Blackland Prairie, were taken into account during the visioning process. The four scenarios were formulated to reveal classical differences in growth policies and resultant development patterns, based on citizen guidance and expressed opinions at the regional workshops.

Scenario A is the "business-as-usual" projection (Figure 13.2). This scheme spreads another 1.25 million people across the landscape in patterns similar to recent developments, using transportation systems already approved. Most residents would live in single-family houses built on previously undeveloped land, and most jobs would be located in the central city. As a result, people would continue to commute to work by car. The next 1.25 million people would live on 732 square miles (1,895 km²) of additional land at a population density of 1,323 people per square mile (511 people/km²) in the urbanized areas.

In Scenario B, most new growth would surround major roadways, both new and existing (Figure 13.3). Housing and job growth would occur throughout the five counties. Some redevelopment would occur in existing neighborhoods. Overall, most residents would still live in single-family houses. Regional transportation options would include toll roads, new express bus routes, a commuter rail system, and a central light-rail system. The next 1.25 million people would live on approximately 301 square miles (780 km²) of additional land at a density of 1,714 people per square mile (more than 662 people/km²) in the urbanized portions of the region. In simple terms, this scenario reflects how the region would evolve if controlled by the more progressive developers. Economic concerns would dominate, but growth would follow rational corridors.

With Scenario C, growth would occur in both existing communities and emerging new towns (Figure 13.4). Current towns and cities would gain jobs and residents, but even more mixed-use

**13.2** Potential growth scenario A. Courtesy of Envision Central Texas.

**13.3** Potential growth scenario B. Courtesy of Envision Central Texas.

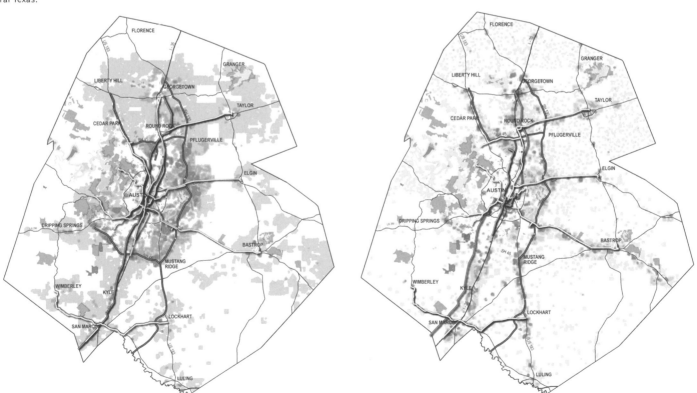

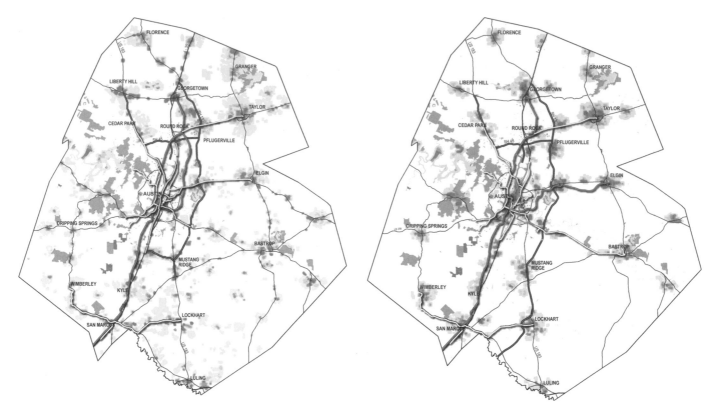

development would result in fewer residents in single-family houses. New towns would be built along major roads and railways, preserving open space and undeveloped land between communities. The next 1.25 million people would live on 267 square miles (692 km²) of additional land at a density of more than 1,756 people per square mile (692 people/km²) in the developed areas. Because of its focus on new towns, this scenario reflects an architectural approach to urban development. As a result, economic concerns are balanced with livability and quality of life.

In Scenario D, most growth would occur in existing towns and communities (Figure 13.5). More land would remain undeveloped than in other scenarios, with about one-third of new households and two-thirds of new jobs located on currently developed land. Regional transportation options would include toll roads, and extensive commuter rail, light-rail, and express bus lines. The next 1.25 million people would live on approximately 132 square miles (342 km²) of additional land at a density of more than 1,939 people per square mile (749 people/km²) in the urban areas in the region. Because of its emphasis on infill

development, this scenario embodies a smart-growth approach advocated by the planning profession. As with Scenario C, economic interests would be balanced with social concerns, but in this scenario with less land urbanized and more land for open space.

The four scenarios were analyzed for planning consequences relating to land development, agricultural and rangeland conversion, new development over the aquifers, annual weekday travel time per person, housing options (e.g., single-family vs. multi-family), infrastructure costs for new development, and regional transportation options. Indicators were established for each of these impacts, so that citizens, elected officials, and planners could compare the consequences of pursuing each scenario. Meanwhile, Calthorpe Associates developed the site-specific designs for six actual local places across the region in Bastrop, East Austin, Lockhart, Pflugerville, Dripping Springs, and the McNeil Junction area between Austin and Round Rock (Figures 13.6 and 13.7). These test site designs helped residents visualize different possible future community developments.[10]

**13.4** Potential growth scenario C. Courtesy of Envision Central Texas.

**13.5** Potential growth scenario D. Courtesy of Envision Central Texas.

In October 2003, the four scenarios were presented to the public in an extensive region-wide survey. Surveys were distributed in all the local newspapers and were available over the Web. More than twelve thousand surveys were returned. The purpose was to assess public preferences for the scenarios and the consequences. The results were analyzed, and the Envision Central Texas board crafted a common vision, which was then brought back to the community in early 2004. The scenario that received the most favorable responses throughout the region was Scenario D, in which most new growth would occur in existing towns and built-up areas (Table 13.1).

As we prepared to publish a preferred scenario based on the survey, Neal Kocurek died sud-

## Garden Apartments

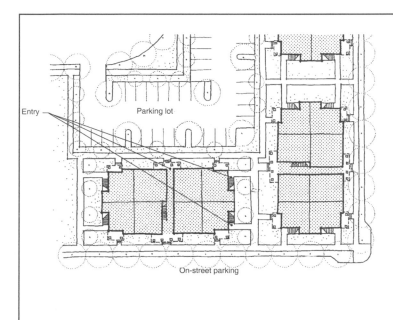

- Minimum 30' separation between neighboring buildings

- Locate parking to the rear of buildings away from public view.

- Provide pedestrian connections from parking areas to building entries at public streets.

- Minimize the number of access drives and curb cuts to parking.

- Provide a minimum 15' landscape separation between parking and residential units.

- Encourage use of on-street parking for visitor parking

- Screen trash enclosures from public view with a fence and landscaping.

Plan

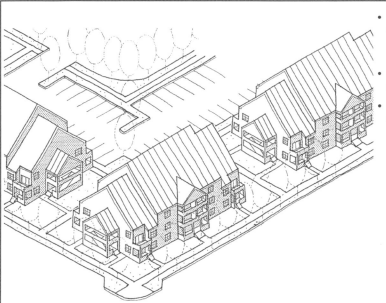

- Require entry porches for ground floor units which have direct access to public streets with 10-foot minimum clear width

- Provide balconies for above grade units facing the street

- Minimum 2-story building wall along public streets is required

**13.6** Garden apartments design guidelines from East Austin Featherlite Test Site Workshop. Design by Calthorpe Associates. Courtesy of Envision Central Texas.

Axonometric

denly on Monday, March 29, 2004, at the age of sixty-seven. As the leader of Envision Central Texas, Kocurek displayed an extraordinary level of wisdom and patience. He contributed a level of civility to public discourse that I have rarely encountered. Kocurek left a significant void in the Austin leadership, both for his vision and for his kindness.

As we recovered from Kocurek's passing, a vision for the region was developed from the survey and distributed in May 2004.[11] The preferred vision projected a total urbanization between Scenarios C and D (Table 13.2 and Figure 13.8).

The vision report presented seven strategic roles for Envision Central Texas:

- Encourage land-use planning to be considered as an integral part of future transportation planning, whether it involves roadways, transit, bicycle lanes, or pedestrian sidewalks.
- Assist communities in developing and integrating regional economic development goals into their local strategies for business development and encourage regional cooperation.
- Advocate for initiatives that achieve a balanced geographical distribution of housing and jobs throughout the region.
- Demonstrate and model positive examples of increased density and mixed use that have been achieved by public-private partnerships in concert with local planning processes.
- Analyze the best practices in the United States in creating a regional open space funding plan that provides fair compensation to landowners.
- Assist communities in developing goals that will close the gap for the underprivileged and underserved populations, particularly in the areas of health, education, housing, jobs, and transportation.
- Recognize projects and initiatives that demonstrate best practices for achieving the regional vision.[12]

To pursue these roles, seven implementation committees were organized. These committees included transportation and land-use integration;

**STREET SECTIONS**

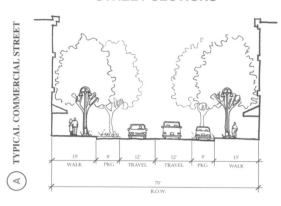

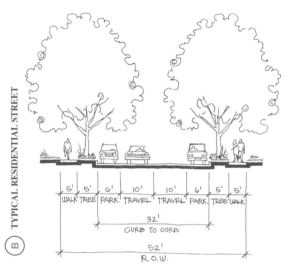

13.7 Street section guidelines from Lockhart Test Site Workshop. Design by Calthorpe Associates. Courtesy of Envision Central Texas.

**TABLE 13.1** RESULTS OF CITIZEN SURVEY

(Percentage of 12,000 responses voting in favor of Scenario D)

| | |
|---|---|
| Best use of land | 57 percent |
| Best use of agricultural land | 55 percent |
| Best to serve future transportation needs | 67 percent |
| Best to serve overall quality of life | 47 percent |

Source: Envision Central Texas.

economic development coordination; housing and jobs balance; density and mixed use; open space funding; social equity; and best practices recognition. These committees began their work in late summer/early fall of 2004. For example, in September 2004, the transportation and land-use integration committee organized a transit-oriented development (TOD) symposium. The TOD symposium included national and local leaders and was held in advance of an election by Austin voters on a commuter rail initiative. The symposium was well attended, and the November 2004 commuter rail vote passed resoundingly with 62.2 percent of the voters supporting the initiative. The initial 32-mile (51-km) rail now connects Austin with suburban Leander and includes nine stations, ideal TOD sites. The line opened in early 2010 with more rail lines in various stages of planning and approval.

In January 2005, Austin Mayor Will Wynn proposed an "Envision Central Texas" bond election. The mayor's goal was to implement the Envision Central Texas vision by funding open space acquisition and inner-city infrastructure improvement. Will Wynn was one of the founding members of

the Group of Eight that Kocurek and Lebermann introduced to me at the Headliners Club. Mayor Wynn sought to help implement the preferred Envision Central Texas vision through the city's bond election. As a member of the bond advisory committee, I attended many meetings through 2005. For instance, one Monday evening in late October, a number of citizens testified about community needs, including open space, affordable housing, urban infrastructure, great streets, a new library, and neighborhood centers. At another meeting, a coalition of skateboarders made an especially compelling presentation. Instead of filibustering, a technique favored by the more established groups, the skateboarders simply had their, mostly dreadlocked, companions stand in support. Following the presentations, our advisory committee discussed our recommendations to the City Council for the bond package.

The Envision Central Texas goal to increase the amount of open space in the region would move toward realization through bond initiatives in Austin, Travis County, and Hays County, as well as conservation efforts by the Hill Country Conservancy. In addition, ECT contributed to a regional greenprint prepared by the Trust for Public Land in cooperation with the University of Texas and others.[13] As noted in Chapter 11, our informal Great Springs of Texas Partnership helped pave the way for this GIS mapping initiative. The first greenprint was completed for Travis County in

**TABLE 13.2** AMOUNTS OF POSSIBLE ACRES OF URBANIZED LAND COMPARED TO 2000

| Indicator | Total Urbanized Acres | Incremental Acres |
|---|---|---|
| 2000 | 740,563 | — |
| Scenario A | 1,208,842 | 468,278 |
| Scenario B | 932,982 | 192,418 |
| Scenario C | 911,340 | 170,777 |
| Scenario D | 825,346 | 84,783 |
| Preferred | 863,611 | 123,048 |

Source: Envision Central Texas.

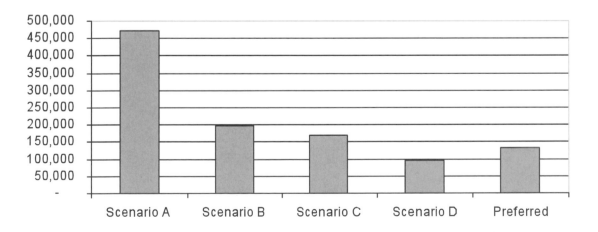

## Land Consumption in Acres

13.8 Land consumption in acres. Courtesy of Envision Central Texas.

2006 (Figure 13.9). Designed to help local governments and communities make informed decisions about land conservation, the model balanced water quality/quantity, recreational opportunities, environmentally sensitive areas protection, and cultural resource preservation. Even before the Travis County greenprint was completed, Envision Central Texas had begun raising funds to apply the Trust for Public Land model to the other three counties in the region. In 2009, greenprints were completed for Bastrop, Caldwell, and Hays Counties.

On Saturday, November 19, 2005, some five hundred people participated in ECT's State Highway (SH) 130 Summit, which was co-hosted with the Austin-San Antonio Corridor Council, at Texas Disposal System's Exotic Game Ranch near Creedmoor. Watching exotic species, such as aoudad and zebra, on the rolling Texas landscape, I navigated through a buffalo herd to reach the pavilion overlooking the landfills of regional waste. The 89-mile (143-km) state highway east of Austin was intended to help relieve traffic pressure on Interstate 35 and has resulted in significant development opportunities. Speakers at the summit included Austin Mayor Will Wynn and State Representative Mike Kruse. Public television station KLRU producer and host Tom Spencer moderated the event that featured Robert Grow, one of the founders of Envision

**13.9** Travis County Greenprint. Prepared by Envision Central Texas and Trust for Public Land, 2006. Courtesy of Travis County Transportation and Natural Resources.

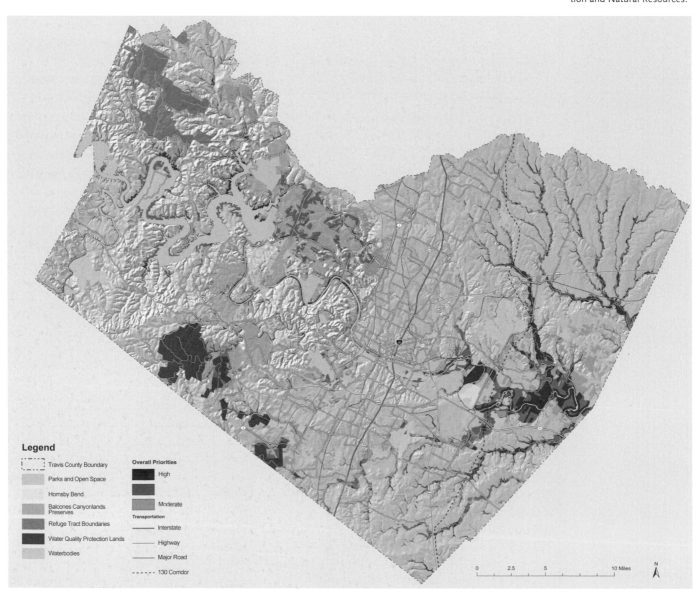

**Legend**

- Travis County Boundary
- Parks and Open Space
- Homsby Bend
- Balcones Canyonlands Preserves
- Refuge Tract Boundaries
- Water Quality Protection Lands
- Waterbodies

**Overall Priorities**
- High
- Moderate

**Transportation**
- Interstate
- Highway
- Major Road
- 130 Corridor

0   2.5   5   10 Miles

N

Utah, as the keynote speaker. Grow noted that "most problems we face are because we think too short-term and too small-scale." Spencer altered Winston Churchill's famous quote, "We shape our buildings, and afterwards they shape us," to "We build our roads, and afterwards they drive us crazy." A few of the potential next steps discussed at the summit included the development of a corridor vision plan, the creation of a toolbox of design concepts for local governments, and the establishment of a management district to guide development.

**NEXT STEPS**

As Austin basked in the Longhorn Rose Bowl victory in the new year, I continued to work with Envision Central Texas and the bond advisory committee in 2006.[14] As incoming ECT chair, I met with board members and local leaders about our agenda for the coming year. On January 9, the advisory committee unanimously recommended to the Austin City Council a $614.8 million bond election that included $144 million for public facilities, $90 million for a new central public library, $92.3 million for open space, $67.5 million for affordable housing, $122.1 million for drainage, and $98.9 million for transportation. Mayor Wynn had appointed the advisory committee to help advance the ECT vision. The open space and affordable housing elements would especially help realize that objective. At our January 9 meeting, we suggested a May election. The advisory committee's recommendations were then considered by the City Council, which decided to trim the bond to $567.4 million and to delay the election until November, at which time the recommendations passed overwhelmingly.

Envision Central Texas continues to convene meetings and conferences around important regional issues such as the SH-130 corridor across the eastern side of the region. ECT hosts an annual Community Stewardship Awards Program, highlighting the best practices across the region. In addition to the regional greenprint, Envision Central Texas partnered with the University of

Texas planning program to develop a Quality Growth Toolbox. This Web-based toolbox provides planners with an interactive compendium of more than one hundred tools, best practices, strategies, and techniques to positively impact growth. The regional metropolitan planning agency, Capital Area Metropolitan Planning Organization (CAMPO), incorporated most of the ECT growth projections into its planning, and local jurisdictions began updating their official comprehensive plans as a result of the vision promoted by ECT. Most notably, the City of Austin decided to prepare a new comprehensive plan in 2009, its first since the 1970s, and selected WRT (Ian McHarg's former firm) as its planning consultant.

In the spring of 2008, Envision Central Texas commissioned an assessment of progress toward the regional vision. The study noted that the region was indeed on track to double in population between 2000 and 2030. The top concerns included: the improvement of transportation systems, the assurance of water availability and quality, and the maintenance of affordable housing. The study indicated that regional business and civic leaders lamented the lack of planning resources and identified the need for greater coordination on regional issues. The authors of the report noted that study participants "believed that the region has made progress toward a number of the goals of the [Envision Central Texas] Vision, [but] there was also a pervasive feeling that Central Texas still faces many of the same issues it did [when the ECT vision was launched] five or ten years ago, only magnified."[15] To break down traditional jurisdictional silos, participants observed that linking economic interests, land use, and transportation is essential for the future of the region.

The study involved interviews with major business and institutional leaders as well as public officials. Focus groups, public workshops, and on-line questionnaires were conducted. Concern about climate change is the most significant issue that emerged in the region since the development of the Envision Central Texas vision.[16] The participants understood the relationship between climate change and energy use. Participants noted that actions toward carbon neutrality and energy conservation are necessary for the Austin region to remain a leader and an innovator.

As an addition to the vision progress assessment, the consultants (TIP Strategies of Austin) prepared organizational recommendations for improving the effectiveness of Envision Central Texas. On one hand, the consultants found "a lack of clarity about the role of Envision Central Texas."[17] On the other hand, they found "broad-based interest in regional issues and a growing awareness of the need for a coordinated region-wide response was . . . a tremendous opportunity for ECT."[18] As a result, the consultants recommended three different approaches for Envision Central Texas: education, advocacy, and action.[19] As Envision Central Texas moves ahead, all three approaches will be considered. One of the challenges will be to maintain the reputation as a non-partisan organization with a record of high-quality, balanced educational programs while moving into advocacy and action.

From improved awareness about planning to greenprinting, Envision Central Texas continues to provide regional leadership. Some advances can be observed in the areas of transportation planning, infrastructure improvement, and open space. Still, much work needs to be done, especially to realize the goals of social equity and more sustainable patterns of growth. Perhaps one of the major accomplishments of Envision Central Texas thus far has been raising awareness of the benefits of regionalism.

"Sprawl is a public problem that requires a public solution," Richard Dagger notes.[20] Suburban sprawl can be viewed as one consequence, one possible future scenario resulting from the urbanization and population trends of this first urban century. Efforts like Envision Central Texas help illustrate different possible paths. The analysis of these alternatives, as well as the careful consideration of the current business-as-usual sprawl, demands an understanding of how we interact with each other, and how our species interacts with other species and the natural world.

Austin has a history of experimentation with innovative planning endeavors, from Austin Tomorrow in the 1970s, through "negotiated growth management" in the 1980s, on to "smart growth" in the 1990s, with mixed implementation results along the way.[21] Other efforts have experienced less success. For instance, the city's Save Our Springs Ordinance, limiting impervious surfaces over the aquifer recharge zone, has been circumvented by developers who had the ordinance weakened by the state legislature. Past efforts have tended to focus on Austin, ignoring the larger region. Envision Central Texas differs because of the involvement of five counties and many smaller cities in addition to Austin. At the very least, Envision Central Texas prompted local citizens to begin thinking regionally.

The Brookings Institution notes that the United States and its economy are now grounded in metropolitan regions like Austin. According to a Brookings study, written by Alan Berube, "America's metropolitan areas are the engines of national prosperity."[22] Perhaps "think globally and act locally" should be extended to "plan regionally." Regional planning should be the creation of knowledge capital, the enhancement of social capital, and the preservation of natural capital. In other words, we need to link Robert Putnam's concern about social capital[23] with broader economic and environmental issues. In doing so, we might realize that we have the ability to create our future—not merely to conform to it.

# 14

## THE TEXAS TRIANGLE MEGAREGION

n the early 1960s, the French geographer Jean Gottmann described a new urban form, "megalopolis," to characterize the network of interconnected cities from Boston to Washington, D.C., along the Atlantic Coast.[1] More than four decades later, scholars are observing ten additional megapolitan regions, called "megaregions," emerging across parts of the United States[2] (Figure 14.1). The Regional Plan Association (RPA) describes megaregions as extended networks of metropolitan centers with their surrounding areas. By concentrating people, jobs, and capital, megaregions could play a decisive role in the increasingly competitive global economy.[3] Spatial development at the megaregional level presents a strategy for confronting economic, environmental, and demographic forces of regional growth that cross the boundaries of individual political or economic entities.

Meanwhile, Robert Lang of the Metropolitan Institute at Virginia Tech introduced a scale between traditional metropolitan areas and megaregions that he calls "megapolitans." According to Lang, a megapolitan combines at least two existing metropolitan areas; totals more than 10 million residents by 2040; derives from contiguous metropolitan and micropolitan areas; constitutes an organic, cultural region with a distinct history and identity; occupies a similar physical environment; links centers through major transportation

infrastructure; forms an urban network via goods and services flows; creates usable geography that is suitable for large-scale regional planning; lies within the United States; and consists of counties as the most basic unit.[4]

The megaregion concept first attracted the attention of policy makers, planners, and academics in Europe and is now gathering attention in North America as well as in Asia. Large-scale spatial planning has been promoted by the European Union, resulting in concepts like the "Blue Banana," a discontinuous corridor of urbanization stretching from Liverpool to Milan. Named for its shape, the Blue Banana contains some 90 million people. A group of French geographers, called RECLUS, led by Roger Brunet, developed the concept. The Randstad Holland is located within this backbone of Europe. The Randstad and the American Megalopolis are the prototypical megaregions. Located in the most densely settled part of Europe, the Randstad includes the major Dutch cities of Rotterdam, Amsterdam, Utrecht, and Den Haag. Although intensely settled and urban, this region also forms the "green heart" of The Netherlands with productive farmland and active recreational corridors (Figure 14.2).

The Texas Triangle is one of the eleven megaregions in the continental United States initially observed by a team from the University of Pennsylvania and the RPA. This megaregion includes

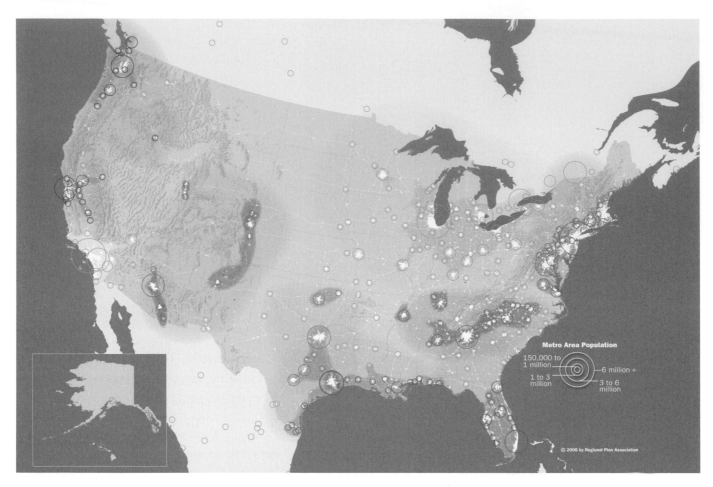

**14.1** America 2050 emerging megaregions. Courtesy of the Regional Plan Association.

**14.2** Dutch pastoral landscape. Photograph by Frederick Steiner.

the metropolitan areas of Houston and San Antonio at its base, Dallas and Fort Worth at the apex, with Austin along the left side of the triangle. Encompassing a total land size of nearly 60,000 square miles (155,399 km²), the megaregion had a total population of 15 million people in 2000 and is expected to grow by an additional 10 million people over the next thirty or so years.[5] This growth poses at least three major challenges. First, consumption will pressure land, water, and other natural resources. Two of the five largest aquifers in the region are projected to have less than 45 percent of currently available water remaining by 2050. Second, the region's population will become more diverse, with significant international in-migration, posing challenging demands on employment, education, health care, and other services. The third challenge will be mobility. National mobility studies show that all of the metro areas in the Texas Triangle have been among the nation's top congested regions for the past two decades.[6] The transportation infrastructure needs major enhancement in order to keep people and goods moving within the region, across the Texas-Mexico border, and along the North American Free Trade Agreement corridor.

To accommodate the anticipated growth in such a vast area, the megaregion approach offers a useful framework for regional planning and policymaking. Nevertheless, there have been debates about whether the Texas Triangle is simply a geometric coincidence or an integrated megaregion. Of the eleven U.S. megaregions, the Texas Triangle has probably invited the most discussion about its boundaries. The different definitions of one or more megaregions in or around Texas all seem plausible. Aside from the triangle version proposed by the Penn and RPA teams, Robert Lang and Dawn Dhavale propose two corridor megapolitans.[7] One is the Interstate 35 Corridor stretching from San Antonio, Texas, to Kansas City, Missouri. The other is the Gulf Coast Corridor from Brownsville, Texas, to Mobile, Alabama, along the Gulf of Mexico. A version of "Texas Hinge" also emerged during the 2006 Megaregion Workshop in Madrid, Spain. Houston forms a hinge between the Gulf Coast Corridor extend-ing from Mexico to the Florida panhandle and the Texas Triangle. Meanwhile, Elise Bright of Texas A&M University questions the very existence of the Texas Triangle megaregion altogether.[8]

## CONCEPTUAL FRAMEWORK FOR MEGAREGION STUDY

### DEFINE A REGION

For planning purposes, a region may be defined by political, biophysical, ecological, sociocultural, or economic boundaries. The megaregion concept expands and builds on the traditional metropolitan region, which often includes overlapping political, ecological, and cultural boundaries.

Political regions constitute civil divisions. They may be defined at scales that are easily recognized, such as state, county, and township boundaries. These types of regions, known also as governmental jurisdictions, define areas that possess certain legislative and regulatory functions that are important to planners. Political regions may also be groupings of areas, such as multi-state regions, that are defined by political entities to serve certain regulatory, policy, and information delivery purposes at the federal level. The U.S. Environmental Protection Agency (EPA), the Census Bureau, and other federal agencies define the United States according to specific regional criteria, often following state boundaries. An underlying assumption for megaregion thinking is that traditional governmental jurisdictions are inadequate in addressing issues such as rapid population growth, protection of large-scale environmental systems, and planning of complex transportation networks.

Biophysical regions may be described as the pattern of interacting biological and physical phenomena present in a given area. Perhaps the most commonly identified type of biophysical region used in planning is the watershed. Since the 1930s, the U.S. Department of Agriculture (USDA) has used watersheds for conservation and flood-control planning. Likewise, the EPA promotes watersheds for regional planning and maintains a Web site (www.epa.gov/surf) called "Surf Your Watershed." Watersheds are important to define for numerous purposes, such as protecting drinking water supplies and identifying wetlands mitigation sites.

Physical regions can be mapped, which makes them attractive to planners (Figure 14.3). Watersheds are mapped by following drainage patterns, which are relatively easy to trace on a topographic map. Physiographic regions are based on terrain texture, rock type, and geologic structure and history. Hydrological and physiographic regions rarely coincide with political jurisdictions or statistical geographies, which impose methodological challenges to planners who need to consider drainage basins and physiographic features for megaregional planning.

Ecological regions are delineated through the mapping of physical information, such as elevation, slope aspect, and climate, plus the distribution of plant and animal species. The EPA defines ecoregions as areas of relative homogeneity in ecological systems and their components. Drawing on the work of Robert Bailey and others,[9] the EPA uses climate, geology, physiography, soils, and vegetation to designate ecoregions. Weather patterns play an important role in ecosystem mapping as well as for planning and natural resource management. Ecological regions, like watersheds, do not line up with political boundaries. Because of their scale, megaregions can encompass such overlapping boundaries while incorporating parts of many ecoregions (Figure 14.4).

Sociocultural regions are elusive to delineation and to mapping. They may be defined as territories that have one or more distinctive traits and provide the basis for people's identities. In the United States, sociocultural regions may span several states, such as the Midwest, the Pacific Northwest, or New England; they can also be smaller areas, which span across political boundaries. For example, the area of northern Indiana and southern Michigan is commonly referred to as "Michiana."

Unlike many phenomena that constitute biophysical regions, people with widely varying social characteristics can occupy a sociocultural region. In addition, human movement in response to seasons means that different populations may occupy the same space at different times of the year. For example, an Idaho rancher will move livestock out of the high country in the autumn to lower elevations along river valleys with warmer temperatures. In winter, the same Idaho mountains attract skiers from settlements located at lower elevations.

Wilbur Zelinsky, a Pennsylvania State University geographer, promoted a wider use of vernacular regions to describe social and cultural components of regions[10] (Figure 14.5). Basically, a vernacular region represents the spatial perception of indigenous people. Because vernacular regions are commonly known and evolved locally through time, they can be described as "popular" regions. According to Zelinsky, regional, ethnic, and historical questions may be answered by exploring vernacular regions. A few American writers have suggested popular regions, such as Ernest Callenbach in *Ecotopia*,[11] which proposes an "ecotopia" from the San Francisco Bay area all the way north to Alaska, and Joel Garreau in *The Nine Nations of North America*.[12]

Geographer Donald Meinig, in particular, pursued Zelinsky's framework and produced detailed studies of the Mormon and Texas cultural regions. Meinig's Texas cultural core overlaps with the Texas Triangle (Figure 14.6). He notes:

*Central Texas [is] defined not so much by its internal cultural character as by the great cities near its corners. If we see it as a great triangle whose sides are the traffic ways uniting the metropolitan areas of its three points, . . . we may . . . take this triangle to be the Core area of Texas in the usual sense of that term: the seat of political and economic power, the focus of circulation, the area of most concentrated development and the most characteristic cultural patterns. . . . [T]he rest of Texas is bound to that core through the mediating functions of Houston, San Antonio, and Dallas-Fort Worth.*[13]

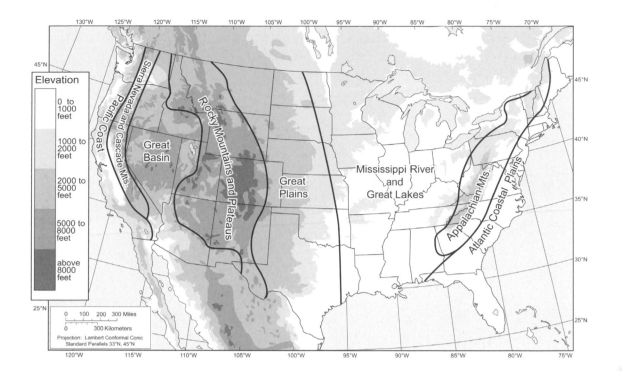

**14.3** Physical regions of the United States. Courtesy of the Arizona Geographic Alliance, Becky Eden, cartographer.

**14.4** Ecoregions of the United States. Courtesy of Robert G. Bailey, U.S. Forest Service.

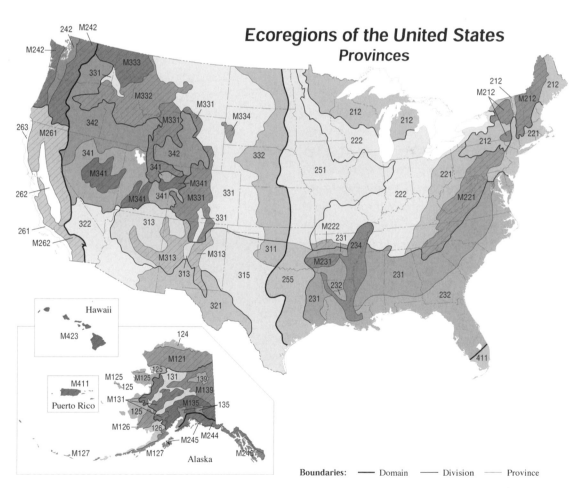

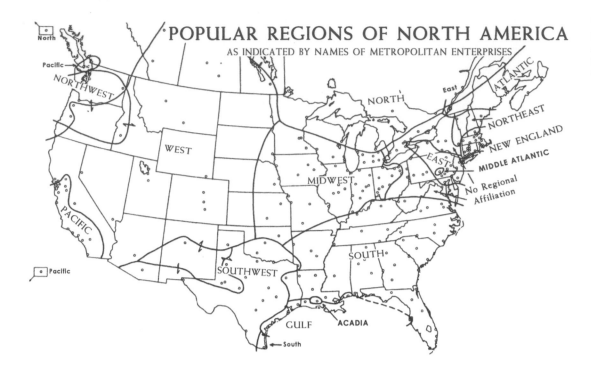

POPULAR REGIONS OF NORTH AMERICA
AS INDICATED BY NAMES OF METROPOLITAN ENTERPRISES

14.5 Wilbur Zelinsky's popular regions of North America, 1980. © Annals of the Association of American Geographers.

Sociocultural regions can be used to create an identity for megaregions. Many megaregion advocates build on and refine Callenbach, Garreau, and Meinig's ideas. For instance, the term "ecotopia" has been adapted for the "Cascadia Ecolopolis" megaregion in the Pacific Northwest.

Functionally, economic regions overlap with sociocultural regions. Economic processes often dominate our views of social processes in regions. For example, daily trips to work, newspaper circulation areas, housing markets, and sports teams may define economic regions. Regions may be branded based on their economic health, such as the Rust Belt in industrial decline in the northeastern United States and the robust Sunbelt in the South and the West.

Agricultural regions are another common delineation of this type; they are often a synthesis of other regional types. Agriculture involves human interactions with the biophysical factors of soil, water, and plants. Climate provides a linkage, a measure of coincidence for the production of food and fiber. Agriculture labels frequently substitute as synonyms for more incorporative regional types: for example, Cotton Belt for the southeastern United States and Corn Belt for the

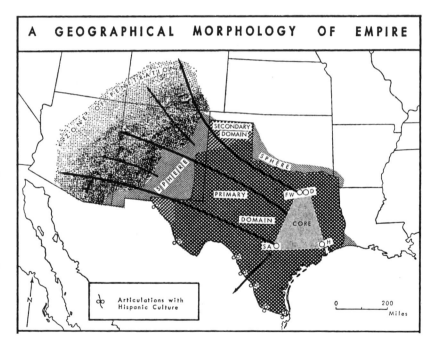

14.6 Cultural core of Texas, identified by geographer Donald Meinig. Courtesy of University of Texas Press.

Midwest, or, even more specific, the Napa Valley of California and the Kentucky Bluegrass region.

The USDA defined new farm-resource regions, breaking away from state boundaries to portray the geographic distribution of U.S. farm production more accurately. The intent is to help analysts and policy makers better understand economic and resource issues affecting agriculture. Megaregions may be viewed as the urban counterpart for

USDA's farm-resource regions because they help us understand economic and resources issues facing urban areas. Like USDA's regions, megaregions move away from state boundaries and are helpful for understanding urban economic issues.

Throughout the United States, metropolitan areas have organized political bodies to address multiple planning issues, including transportation, economic development, housing, air quality, water quality, and open-space systems. These organizations encompass more than one political jurisdiction. Metropolitan Planning Organizations (MPOS) are responsible for planning, programming, and coordinating federal highway and transit investments. In addition to MPOS, other regional entities with planning responsibility include councils of government, planning commissions, and development districts.

Local governments created more than four hundred and fifty regional councils of governments across the United States to respond to various federal and state programs. A board of elected officials and other community leaders typically governs regional councils. For instance, the Portland, Oregon, Metro, an elected regional government for the metropolitan Portland area, guides regional growth through the coordination of land-use and transportation plans. As an elected entity, Metro provides a platform for the Portland metropolitan region of three counties, twenty-five cities, and more than 2.1 million people. Metro's capability to guide growth derives from Oregon's planning law that requires comprehensive plans with housing and land-use goals, as well as urban growth boundaries.

As noted, Robert Lang (with his former Virginia Tech Metropolitan Institute colleague Chris Nelson) advocates for a level between the traditional metropolitan area and the megaregion, which they call "megapolitan."[14] These megapolitans are defined by U.S. Census statistical areas. By increasing scale, megaregions and megapolitans have advantages over traditional metropolitan regions, including both urban complexes and rural hinterlands as well as supporting environmental resource areas.

## TOWARD A THEORY OF MEGAREGIONS

Given these various views from the eyes of different disciplinary beholders, from hydrologists to economists, is there anything really new offered by megaregions? At a minimum, new technologies enable us to reveal more phenomena at larger scales. Remote sensed and satellite photography quite literally allows us to watch natural and cultural forces at continental scales in real time. We can use Google Earth or ArcGIS Online to find images of homes and workplaces almost anywhere in the world. Geographic Information System technology empowers us to combine data to display information in new and creative ways. As a result, megaregions offer the prospect for new *descriptive theories*. We can describe processes, patterns, connections, and networks at larger scales. This enables us to posit ideas about locations of settlements and land uses as well as to suggest why things are located where they are. Megaregions also suggest *analytical theories* at a scale beyond individual cities or metropolitan areas. Megaregions produce mega data concerning transportation, population, land use, environmental, and economic systems. Megaregional research might be considered an application of complexity theory, which suggests that orderly patterns can be discerned in chaotic conditions. As one example, we can analyze the relationship between land-use change and highway capacity. Such relationships can certainly be studied at the community and regional scales, too. However, by enlarging the scale, one can analyze connections, or the lack thereof, among more variability.

The relationship between environmental change and natural disasters provides a second example. For instance, one can analyze the history of hurricanes and/or the potential impact of global climate change on sea level change in the Gulf of Mexico. Such analysis can help identify zones susceptible to flood, sea surge, and wind hazards. The megaregion scale of the Gulf Coast helps us understand climate processes beyond the local, regional, and state levels.[15]

Such analysis can lead to *normative theories*. Both planners and ecologists suggest resilience as a concept for urban settlement renewal after disaster. The megaregion scale might help us understand why one community recovers more quickly than another nearby community after a hurricane, flood, earthquake, tsunami, or wild-fire. We might then be able to derive a resilience strategy that can be prescribed, or at least suggested, for other communities. Resilience means to "bounce back," and analysis might suggest that some communities cannot bounce back, or, conversely, that others should be beyond returning to their pre-disaster state.[16]

Regenerative design and sustainability are two normative theories that can build on resilience, but also suggest ongoing creativity and evolution. According to John Lyle, regenerative design involves "replacing the present linear system of throughput flows with cyclical flows at sources, consumption centers, and sinks." And, furthermore, a "regenerative system provides for continuous replacement, through its own functional processes, of energy and materials used in its operation."[17] Sustainability seeks to balance economic, environmental, and equity concerns. The megaregional scale offers an opportunity to advance regenerative and sustainability approaches because (1) energy and materials processes can be replaced within the larger scaled territory thereby reducing transportation from places farther away, and (2) economic, environmental, and equity trade-offs can be spread out over broader areas.

Megaregional planning presents a new way of approaching large-scale transportation systems, green infrastructure, and economic development. For instance, Amtrak works more efficiently in the Northeast because it connects a series of major population centers. In the Texas Triangle, might similar efficiency be achieved by connecting Dallas-Fort Worth, Houston, and San Antonio by rail? In other words, the megaregion concept suggests a new *procedural theory* for very large-scale planning. Megaregional planning presents a new way of thinking for policy makers and planners. Combined with various regional visioning efforts, such as Envision Utah and Envision Central Texas, megaregions herald a new era of regionalism with

as far-reaching consequences for planning and design as New Urbanism. New Urbanism shifted the way developers, planners, and architects think about neighborhoods and communities. New regionalism can change how we view natural, cultural, and economic processes. In order to pursue this potential, we need to look back and understand how cities and regions have evolved, which can be illustrated through the Texas Triangle.

## URBANIZATION HISTORIES OF THE MAJOR TEXAS TRIANGLE CITIES

The Texas Triangle has three sides measuring 271, 198, and 241 miles (436, 319, and 388 km) in ground distance (Figure 14.7). These distances are quite far to navigate even with modern ground transportation and even considering the Texas

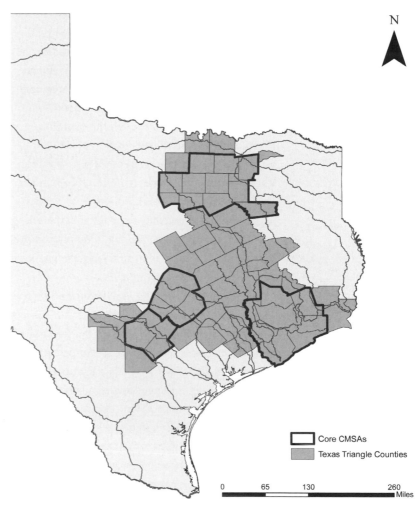

**14.7** The Texas Triangle megaregion, consisting of sixty-six counties. The consolidated metropolitan statistical areas (CMSAs) for San Antonio, Austin, Houston, and Dallas/Fort Worth are also shown. Map produced by Sara Hammerschmidt with data from the U.S. Census 2000 and the Texas Parks and Wildlife Department.

Core CMSAs

Texas Triangle Counties

0    65    130    260
Miles

sense of "bigness." In the nineteenth century, passenger and freight trains connected the major Triangle cities. It was the train connection that boosted the initial growth of the settlements. According to Barry Popik, a New York City etymologist, the term "Texas Triangle" appeared as early as 1936, when the Missouri Pacific (MoPac) Railroad announced its new overnight services from St. Louis and Memphis to link Dallas, Fort Worth, Houston, Austin, and San Antonio.[18] MoPac operated passenger train services across the Southwest in the early years of the twentieth century. "The Texas Triangle" was one section of MoPac's premier name services, the "Sunshine Special."

Today, the Texas Triangle train service no longer operates. Only limited Amtrak connections exist, and these trains are slow because freight is given preference over passengers on the rail lines. Three interstate highways, Interstate 35, Interstate 45, and Interstate 10 have assumed the role of providing intercity connections and delineating the Triangle. To the general public, the term "Texas Triangle" is now probably better known as the tough road trip facing NBA teams against the Dallas Mavericks, the Houston Rockets, and the San Antonio Spurs. Are the Triangle cities economic rivals like their home NBA teams, or do they function as complements? The following is a brief presentation of the functional histories of these cities.

## SAN ANTONIO

The seventh largest city in the United States, San Antonio is located in south central Texas. The 2008 city census reported 1,351,305 people in San Antonio; the 2008 regional data listed a metropolitan population of 2,031,445. Spanish explorers founded San Antonio in 1718 as a supply depot for the missions in East Texas and Louisiana. In 1731, San Antonio gained the distinction of being the first municipality in Texas, established as San Fernando de Bexar. The Mexican Revolution in 1812 marked the start of an unstable political period for the San Antonio area, which climaxed during the war for Texas independence with the iconic Battle of the Alamo in 1836. By 1846, San Antonio's

population had dwindled to eight hundred people. However, after the state of Texas joined the Union, San Antonio emerged as a distribution hub for western migration. Bolstered by German immigration, the population increased to 3,488 people by 1850. By 1860, San Antonio had become the largest city in Texas, and it held this title until the early twentieth century. The formation of the Galveston, Harrisburg, and San Antonio Rail System contributed significantly to San Antonio's prosperity at the time. Nevertheless, by 1930, Houston and Dallas had surpassed San Antonio in size.

During the First World War, Fort Sam Houston became the largest military base in the United States. The military influence drastically changed San Antonio's economic landscape. The once agricultural distribution center of the West was transformed into America's training ground for its soldiers. During the Second World War, more than one third of the total population of the city was military personnel. The population actually doubled during the Second World War. San Antonio's dependency on the military as the main source of employment and the chief economic driver characterized the region's social and economic climate.

As the oldest city in Texas, San Antonio has more recently become a top tourist and convention destination. Tourist attractions include the River Walk, the Alamo and other Spanish missions, and numerous golf courses. The city's convention center sits near the River Walk, which is lined with restaurants and circled by hotels.

## HOUSTON

The City of Houston (2009 city population, 2,242,193; 2009 metropolitan population, 5,728,143) is located in southeastern Texas and is the fourth largest city in the nation. The Allen brothers, Augustus Chapman Allen and John Kirby Allen, founded the Town of Houston on the Gulf Coastal Plain in 1836 and named it after General Sam Houston. The Texas Congress designated Houston briefly as the capital of the Republic of Texas and incorporated the city on June 5, 1837.

The accessibility of water transportation offered Houston strategic advantages. Before the Civil War, Houston was the most interior point with access to the Gulf of Mexico by water. Small river steamships operating on Buffalo Bayou connected the ocean-going ships in Galveston with oxen-drawn wagons in the hinterland. At the turn of the twentieth century, Houston's population had reached 44,683.

In 1900, a hurricane devastated Galveston, the fourth largest city in Texas at the time. The storm on September 8 and 9 resulted in twelve thousand deaths, with at least six thousand in Galveston itself. After the hurricane, Houston became the leading focal point for growth in the state. Galveston rebuilt after 1900 and grew along environmentally sensitive areas of the coastal island, in spite of warnings about hurricane hazards. These predictions came true with Hurricane Ike in 2008, which destroyed much of Galveston again.

Major efforts began after the Civil War to dredge a better ship channel. In 1914 the Houston Ship Channel opened, making Houston a deepwater port, later to be ranked the second largest in the United States. By then, Houston had become a large commercial power, ranking first among Texas cities in terms of commerce and industry. Shipping was a staple industry in the local economy, especially during the Second World War. Houston's economy had changed dramatically after the discovery of oil at Spindletop. To ensure a safe distance from Gulf storms, oil companies built their refineries along the Houston Ship Channel. After the war, Houston used its natural supplies of salt, sulfur, and natural gas to develop one of the largest petrochemical concentrations in the United States. With this industry in place, the city had become a world energy capital by 1970, and its economy, although rapidly expanding from its energy base, is still largely based on oil- and gas-related industries. With a balanced, rich mix of Asian, Hispanic, black, and white citizens, Houston is also quite diverse and cosmopolitan.

## AUSTIN

The City of Austin (2008 population, 757,688; 2008 metropolitan population, 1,705,075) is located in east central Texas, where it straddles the Colorado River at the interface of the Edwards Plateau to the west and the fertile Blackland Prairie to the east. On a site used as a camp for Indian hunting parties, a group of Americans established the village of Waterloo, which became Austin and the capital of the new Republic of Texas in 1839. Austin's first mayor, Edwin Waller, proposed a grid system for streets on the north bank of the Colorado River. This grid is aligned on a northeast-tending ridge between two creek valleys. That structure remains largely intact in the city's downtown. To the north of downtown, the grid shifts to a true north-south structure. Outside this core, streets ramble more organically across rolling hills and around water systems.

After Texas became part of the United States in 1845, Austin became the permanent state capital. St. Edward's University, Austin's first university, was founded by Rev. Edward Sorin of the Congregation of Holy Cross in 1878, and the University of Texas at Austin followed in 1882. Until the early 1970s, the city's economy was dominated by state government and higher education.

Beginning in the late nineteenth century, a series of seven dams was constructed on the Colorado River for water supply, flood control, and hydroelectric power. As a result, manufacturing expanded, the University of Texas grew, and the seeds for the growth of the computer technology industry were planted. Since the 1970s, the city has become an important center for computer technology (with companies such as Texas Instruments, Dell, IBM, Motorola, Samsung, and AMD) and music (with huge events such as the Austin City Limits Music Festival and South By Southwest) and, to some extent, film and television (with Austin-based directors such as Robert Rodriguez and the production of *Friday Night Lights*).

Barton Springs provides a popular year-round swimming pool with its constant temperature and prolific discharge. Its popularity laid the groundwork for a strong local environmental movement affecting city politics and its local and national identity. The Lady Bird Johnson Wildflower Center and other conservation organizations contribute to this "green" orientation. The large academic, high-tech, and student populations supply continued technological innovation, as well as a robust live music scene. Austin is also rapidly becoming a national leader in sustainable building and energy systems.

## DALLAS

The City of Dallas (2010 city population, 1,316,350; 2010 metropolitan population with Fort Worth, 6,477,315) is located on flat prairies along the Trinity River in northeast Texas. The ninth largest city in the nation, its metropolitan population is fourth largest when combined with nearby Fort Worth. John Neely Bryant was the first American explorer settling in the Dallas area in 1841. Rich soil and ample water made the area an ideal place to live. Initially a trading post by the Trinity River, Dallas as a county was officially formed on March 30, 1846, by order of the Texas State Legislature. Soon its role as an inland transportation hub was established when two Texas highways converged there. Providing services in dry goods and grocery stores, shoe and boot shops, and drugstores, Dallas reached a population of about eight hundred by 1860.

Growing as a major rail center in the late nineteenth century, the city now covers 385 square miles (997 km$^2$). Dallas plays a leading role in the petroleum industry, telecommunications, computer technology, banking, and transportation. Companies headquartered in the Dallas metropolitan area include Exxon Mobil, 7-Eleven, Blockbuster, Mary Kay Cosmetics, Southwest Airlines, JCPenney, Comp USA, Texas Instruments, and Zales Jewelry.

## FORT WORTH

Fort Worth (2009 city population, 720,250; 2010 metropolitan population with Dallas, 6,477,315) is also located along the Trinity River, 32 miles (51 km) west of Dallas. At the end of the Mexican-American War in 1849, Major Ripley A. Arnold founded Camp Worth at the Clear Fork and West Fork of the Trinity River. The camp was officially named Fort Worth in honor of General William Jenkins Worth, a hero of the Mexican War. At war's end, the fort was relocated farther west, and settlers took the initial fort area and built department stores, a general store, a hotel, a doctor's office, and a flour mill. Fort Worth also served as an important stop on the way to California for overland mail service and a stagecoach line. Fort Worth, like Dallas, benefited from the natural resources the area had to offer. However, the Civil War caused shortages in money, food, and water supply. Dallas-Fort Worth did not experience strong growth until the arrival of rail connections in the late 1870s.

Evolving from its origins as a cattle drive terminus, Fort Worth retains its Western character. The Stockyards Historic District, for example, preserves and recreates vestiges of the Chisholm Trail and the Texas and Pacific Railway. The city also houses three major art museums: the Modern Art Museum (designed by Tadao Ando), the Kimbell Art Museum (designed by Louis Kahn), and the Amon Carter Museum (designed by Philip Johnson).

Both Dallas and Houston started as distribution centers due to their transportation advantages, with Dallas as a land transportation hub in the inland and Houston as a water transportation hub on the coast. San Antonio and Fort Worth started as military posts, whereas Austin was created in a strategic place as a political-institutional establishment. Some functions overlap among them, especially in recent decades. Nevertheless, in the early days, geographical separation made them more like isolated economic entities than competitors or co-producers.

## ECOLOGICAL SPACE OF THE TRIANGLE

Figure 14.8 illustrates the location of the Texas Triangle and the encompassing ecoregions, as defined by the U.S. Environmental Protection Agency and the U.S. Geological Survey.[19] The metros of Dallas, Austin, and San Antonio are located in and along the edge of the Blackland Prairie and the Edwards Plateau. Houston and other parts of the Gulf Coast lie in the Coastal Plain. Ecological regions in the Coastal Plain are generally perpendicular to the Gulf Coast margin and to the major watersheds and river corridors, as they extend to the coast.

The Blackland Prairie ecological region is a highly fertile and agriculturally productive province composed of fine textured clay soils and only small remnants of a formerly extensive natural prairie. There is still considerable agricultural and ranch land, although urban and industrial growth and development is a persistent challenge to the preservation of the region's intrinsic resources. Located south and west of Austin and San Antonio, the Edwards Plateau ecological region is characterized by a hilly limestone terrain, which is dissected by many spring-fed streams of significant ecological, recreational, and aesthetic values. The Balcones Fault Zone and Escarpment provide a sharp delineation of the Plateau ecological region from the prairie lands to the east. The native vegetative cover is diverse and largely evergreen with juniper and live oak. Most of the region is used for livestock and wildlife management, including hunting.

Together, these resources and their associated amenities provide critical support for the economic stability of the metro areas. Water supplies are developed in the upstream regions immediately west and north of the metros. Agricultural, mining, and other resource-based industries provide a base for many dozens of smaller communities located between the metros. Increasingly, with improved transportation and telecommunication infrastructure, the interstitial zones between the metros are encountering intensive growth and development pressures.

The Houston metro and associated communities closer to the Gulf Coast are situated in the Gulf Coastal Plain ecological region. The terrain is very flat and covered mainly with grassland; forest and savanna-type vegetation prevail in areas

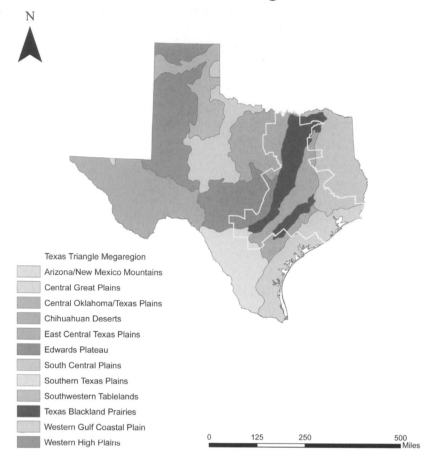

## State of Texas Ecoregions

N

Texas Triangle Megaregion
- Arizona/New Mexico Mountains
- Central Great Plains
- Central Oklahoma/Texas Plains
- Chihuahuan Deserts
- East Central Texas Plains
- Edwards Plateau
- South Central Plains
- Southern Texas Plains
- Southwestern Tablelands
- Texas Blackland Prairies
- Western Gulf Coastal Plain
- Western High Plains

0   125   250   500 Miles

Produced by: Sara Hammerschmidt
Date: May 18, 2009
Data Source: Census 2000 TIGER/Line Data from ESRI,
Texas Parks and Wildlife

**TABLE 14.1** VITAL STATISTICS OF THE TEXAS TRIANGLE REGION

| | Triangle (66 Counties) | 4 Core CMSAS | Texas State | USA |
|---|---|---|---|---|
| Area (sq. mi.) | 57,430 | 25,035 | 268,580 | 3,794,083 |
| Pop. (1,000s) | 14,660 | 12,734 | 20,852 | 281,422 |
| GDP ($million) | 605,458* | 722,832 | 9,749,104 | |
| Percentage of U.S. Total | | | | |
| Area (sq. mi.) | 1.51 | 0.66 | 7.08 | 100 |
| Pop. | 5.21 | 4.52 | 7.41 | 100 |
| GDP | 6.21* | 7.41 | 100 | |

* 2003.

Source: U.S. Census 2000.

**14.8** State of Texas Level 3 ecoregions as defined by the U.S. Environmental Protection Agency and the U.S. Geological Survey. Map produced by Sara Hammerschmidt with data from the U.S. Census 2000 and the Texas Parks and Wildlife Department.

farther inland. Cropland covers a very large portion of this ecoregion. Urbanization and industrial development are the primary agents of change in land cover. The Houston metro population, for example, is expected to grow beyond 8 million in the next twenty-five years.

The combination of the above described areas, flows, and ecoregions helps define the Texas Triangle as shown in Figure 14.9. Encompassing 66 counties and 57,430 square miles (148,743 km²), the megaregion included a total population of nearly 15 million in 2000 (Table 14.1). Much of this population is concentrated in the four core consolidated metropolitan statistical areas (CMSAS): Houston, Dallas-Fort Worth, San Antonio, and Austin.

### THINKING LIKE A MEGAREGION

A megaregion approach means that planning for economic development, environmental protection, and transportation infrastructure should go beyond the conventional practice that has been

typically confined within individual jurisdictions. Take transportation planning as an example: a megaregional approach for transportation planning in the Texas Triangle means that intercity travel between Dallas-Fort Worth, Houston, and Austin/San Antonio becomes an intra-region movement. Currently, MPOS are responsible for transportation demand forecasting and planning for each metropolitan region. The scope of the MPOS' work typically does not go beyond their designated areas. Whereas individual MPOS provide rather detailed pictures of their areas, forces of growth from the interactions among metropolitan areas and between the metro areas and their hinterlands usually fall outside the scope of traditional MPOS. A megaregional transportation plan should, therefore, integrate individual metropolitan transportation plans with consideration of intercity people and goods movements. A new MPO—Megaregion Planning Organization—may be necessary to coordinate the efforts of the existing MPOS and other entities in the megaregion. Such large-scale planning has the potential to concentrate transportation and growth corridors

**14.9** A view of the Texas Triangle produced by the Regional Plan Association and Houston Tomorrow, showing population by census tract for cities around the region. Courtesy of Houston Tomorrow and the Regional Plan Association.

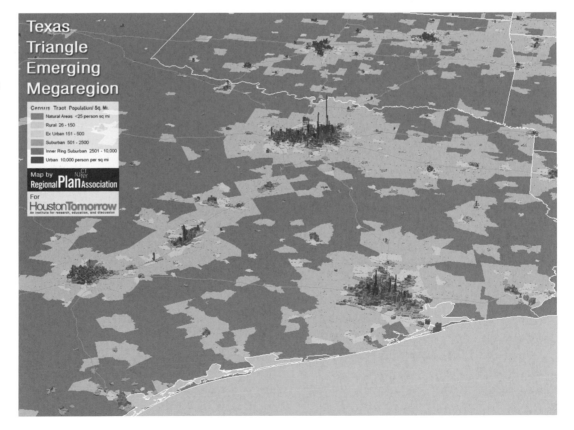

away from environmentally sensitive areas, like the Edwards Plateau, and avoid productive farmlands, like the Blackland Prairie.

Texans think big and the megaregion concept demands large-scale thinking. With 10 million more people living in Texas in the next thirty years, the state has the opportunity to create a globally highly competitive megaregion. If serious education funding issues can be addressed, Texas can emerge as a global exporter of knowledge and culture. The alternative—to become a knowledge importer—is not a positive option for the economy.

The protection of open space is related to water supplies. The Edwards Plateau in particular is essential to San Antonio's future. The springs along the Edwards Escarpment provide a valuable, potentially sustainable, source for many communities. The Texas Triangle is crossed by magnificent rivers, such as the Trinity and the Colorado, which are an important resource for both water and recreation.

Another challenge is connectivity within the megaregion. Currently, the Texas Triangle is dominated by automobile, truck, and air transportation systems. The construction of interstate highways, which are uniquely suited to urban regions stretching 30–80 miles across (48–129

km), enabled the development of late twentieth-century metropolitan regions. But a megaregion encompassing more than 300 miles (483 km) will require a new infrastructure: high speed rail (HSR). Already, European and Asian nations have built HSR systems, and Texas will need to do likewise. HSR should be integrated with expanded urban rail and goods movement. Dallas' leadership with urban rail is a positive step toward diversifying transportation, as are newer rail initiatives in Houston and Austin.

A related challenge concerns the restoration of infrastructure while building new projects for an expanding population. We will need new roadways, bridges, parks, water and sewer lines, utility plants, and wastewater treatment facilities for this first urban Texas century.

This transformation has significant consequences for the people of the Texas Triangle. Social equity, cultural heritage, public safety, and quality of life will be affected. The study of megaregions is a new, evolving area of inquiry, for which theories and methods are still developing. Many related issues in transportation planning, economic and social development, and environmental preservation warrant further study for the Texas Triangle and for other megaregions, nationally and internationally.

# 15 | NEW REGIONALISM

At the Rockefeller family estate in Pocantico Hills along the Hudson River, the Lincoln Institute held a gathering in 2006 entitled "Towards an American Spatial Development Perspective." The focus of the rainy Thursday meeting at the leafy estate just north of New York City was a report prepared by Bob Yaro, Armando Carbonell, and Jonathan Barnett with their Penn planning studio. Sponsored by the Ford Foundation and the Lincoln Institute, the report was inspired by European spatial development schemes, including ones with names like Blue Banana, introduced in Chapter 14.

In Europe, spatial planning emerged as a strategy to influence the distribution of people and activities in areas of various scales. These projected megaregional spatial arrangements suggested metropolitan growth regions in Europe, the center of which seemed to depend on whether German, French, or English scholars drew the scheme. Even though the boundaries vary, spatial planning has become a common platform for European policy makers and planners to give geographic expression to the economic, social, cultural, and ecological policies of the European Union member states.

American planners began to explore the adaptation of the European concept to the United States in the early twenty-first century. The Penn studio was the first realization of this exploration, and the Pocantico conference brought together the key leaders of that studio with American and European regionalists. The Penn study projected that 70 percent of the population growth in the United States and 80 percent of the nation's economic growth would occur in ten megaregions, including the Texas Triangle, by 2050.[1] Subsequently, as a result of Robert Lang's work in Arizona, the Sun Corridor was added as the eleventh megaregion.

The emerging interest in megaregions may be viewed in the context of a renewed interest in regionalism by American architects and planners. Stephen Wheeler identifies five key characteristics of this new regionalism:

1. A focus on specific territories and spatial planning
2. A response to the particular problems of the postmodern metropolitan region
3. A holistic perspective that integrates planning specialties as well as environmental, equity, and economic goals
4. A renewed emphasis on physical planning, urban design, and sense of place
5. A more activist or normative stance on the part of planners[2]

## METROPOLIS 2020: WORKING TOGETHER AS A REGION

While American and European regionalists continued to debate the future mega urban structure of the planet in rainy Pocantico, I flew to Chicago for the Landscape Architecture Foundation's Futures Initiative Symposium. Organized by the University of Illinois at Urbana-Champaign, the symposium addressed "Places of Power" from a multidisciplinary perspective. Speakers explored how politics and economics influence landscape change.[3]

The Chicago symposium continued on Saturday, the fifth anniversary of the September 11 attacks, a date providing clear evidence of how politics can influence the built landscape. The terrorists selected architectural icons that symbolized the economic, military, and political strengths of the United States. In the aftermath of the attacks, architects and politicians debated how to memorialize urban blocks in New York City and rolling fields in western Pennsylvania. The highlight of the Saturday talks was George Ranney, who had also been at the Pocantico Hills meeting. He and his wife, Victoria, had developed the influential conservation-centered community, Prairie Crossing outside of Chicago (Figure 15.1), but his Places of Power talk addressed the Chicago Metropolis 2020 plan. Unlike our very broad-based Envision Central Texas endeavor, Metropolis 2020 was a product of the powerful business elite of the Commerce Club of Chicago. Fregonese Calthorpe Associates provided important consulting services to both of these efforts.

Ranney traced Chicago's planning back to Daniel Burnham's pioneering early twentieth-century effort. Metropolis 2020 expands beyond Chicago to include six counties and some twelve hundred units of local government. Ranney observed that even this scale was inadequate. He noted that fourteen counties should be covered, including two each in Indiana and Wisconsin. The six Metropolis 2020 counties are home to some 8.5 million people. Beginning in 1996, the Commerce Club organized more than two hundred members to explore the issues of unlimited, low-density sprawl; the concentration of poor minorities; the spatial mismatch among jobs, affordable housing, and transportation; and the disparate access to quality growth. The effort resulted in a report in 1999, which was published as a book the following year.[4]

15.1 Prairie Crossing, Illinois. Energy-efficient homes at Prairie Crossing over the human-made pond with native wetland plants. Due to its high water quality, the Illinois Department of Natural Resources uses the pond as a breeding habitat for four endangered fish species. Photograph by Victoria Ranney.

**15.2** Millennium Park, Chicago. Photograph by Terry Guen.

The theme of the effort is "One region. One future." Under the plan three scenarios were developed: business as usual, community leadership, and metropolis vision. In the business-as-usual scenario, more time will be spent just getting around the region from place to place. The metropolis vision recognizes national and global trends. Ranney stressed that aesthetics are critical for the future of the region and, thus, need to be understood and celebrated. The Metropolis 2020 implementation committee consists of forty-five members, half business leaders, and the balance mayors (including the Chicago mayor) and community, labor, and minority leaders. The authors of the report noted:

*To achieve the best possible conditions of living for all the residents of metropolitan Chicago, we, who live in this region, must carry out two tasks simultaneously. First, we must continue to take seriously our lives as members of particular localities within the region, building stronger communities and neighborhoods. Second, we must learn to do something well that we have so far been doing only in bits and pieces, namely, we must think and work together as a region.[5]*

Chicago Metropolis 2020 continues to implement its key recommendations related to public education and child care; transportation, land use, and the environment; neighborhoods and housing; the governance of the region; and the region's economy. As part of this implementation, Chicago Metropolis 2020 works with the Metropolitan Mayors Caucus. In late 2007, this partnership produced a report that suggested housing strategies for three key cities in the region. The group also continues its collaboration with regional transportation, planning, and environmental organizations.

After the conclusion of the symposium, a tour of Millennium Park was offered (Figure 15.2). The City of Chicago had transformed the 24.5-acre (10-ha) unsightly section of Grant Park, consisting of railroad tracks and parking lots, into a dramatic civic lakefront center. The park features the works of several of the most prominent architects, artists, and landscape architects of our time, including Frank Gehry, Anish Kapoor, Kathryn Gustafson, and Piet Oudolf. I had already visited Millennium Park and was meeting my daughter

Halina, who was then living in Chicago, for dinner, so I declined. However, the tour guide was the park's landscape architect, who had received little attention. I was curious to meet her, so I stayed. The landscape architect turned out to be my former Penn student Terry Gwen. She and her late husband, Kevin, had been in the 501 studio I had taught with Ian McHarg and a large supporting cast in 1983. As a result, Halina and I joined the tour.

## AMERICA 2050: SKETCHING A FUTURE

In early July 2007, I sat on the terrace of the Rockefeller villa in Bellagio, overlooking Lake Como, with a small cluster of my fellow citizens (Figure 15.3). The purpose of our gathering was to design a framework for a national plan. Our group, America 2050, undertook this audacious task in a luxurious, verdant place. Thomas Jefferson had initiated such a plan in 1808 as had Theodore Roosevelt in 1908. Our timing seemed about right.

While we met, another group, Global South, grappled with the consequences of climate change on poor, developing countries in the Southern Hemisphere. America 2050 and Global South were part of the month-long, Rockefeller-initiated Global Summit on Innovations for an Urban World in Bellagio. Our Global South colleagues were an angry lot. They were angry at us Americans for not curbing our addiction to fossil fuels. They were angry at us for not recognizing the social and environmental consequences that have resulted from our lifestyles. Some of the most significant problems include growing water scarcity, increased frequency of floods and droughts, higher levels of salinity, and heat waves.

Rajendra Pachauri of the United Nations (UN) Intergovernmental Panel on Climate Change provided a sobering account of the potential con-

**15.3** Rockefeller Foundation Bellagio Center, Lago di Como, Italy. Photograph by Frederick Steiner.

sequences of climate change on the world's most vulnerable regions. Dr. Pachauri explained the necessity for two central approaches to address climate change: mitigation and adaptation. According to the UN, "mitigation involves human interventions to reduce the emission of greenhouse gases by sources or enhance their removal from the atmosphere by 'sinks,'"[6] identified as forests, vegetation, or soils that can reabsorb $CO_2$. The UN defines adaptation as the "adjustments in natural or human systems in response to actual or expected climatic stimuli or their effects, which moderate harm or exploit beneficial opportunities."[7]

Climate change was indeed a topic our group, America 2050, discussed. Our organizer, the Regional Plan Association (RPA), divided us into working groups. One focused on national challenges and obstacles and possible federal roles. Another organizing feature of America 2050 is the impact of megaregions on economic and population growth. Eleven of these metropolitan constellations are expected to receive 80 percent of the national economic growth by 2030.

In Bellagio, we concentrated on three megaregions: the Great Lakes, Southern California, and the Piedmont. I chose to work on my home megaregion, the Great Lakes. This megaregion is also home to the three Cs at the heart of our climate change challenge: coal, cars, and corn. Detroit and the Interstate 75 corridor form the center of the U.S. automobile industry, which originated near the Great Lakes due to the proximity to steel and coal resources. China and the United States contain significant reserves of coal, which is dangerous to mine and dirty to burn, as well as a significant source of $CO_2$. Ethanol, the corn-based fuel additive, has been promoted more recently as a major biofuel source. The Corn Belt has received significant federal subsidies to advance ethanol production, but turning plants such as corn into fuel uses more energy than the resulting ethanol or biodiesel. In addition, nitrogen-based fertilizers, needed to grow corn, contribute much to water quality problems, including the expanding "dead zone" off the Gulf Coast, where oxygen is so depleted that fish, crabs, and shrimp suffocate.

The Great Lakes possess many assets, like old wealthy foundations and well-established research universities. We suggested a federal partnership with regional foundations to significantly boost research on clean-burning coal, more energy-efficient automobiles, and alternative biofuels. We envisioned a "Big 20" research consortium that would build on the Big 10 athletic alliance.

The Great Lakes megaregion also has, well, great lakes and numerous rivers. The megaregion is water-rich, and its water landscapes are popular for fishing, hunting, and boating. Again, federal partnerships with private, state, and local groups could yield many benefits. Ohio's Cuyahoga Valley National Park provides a useful example. The Cuyahoga River, once infamous for catching fire, is now the central feature for the third most visited national park in the system. This success resulted from the National Park Service working with foundations and businesses as well as state and local governments.

A few months later in 2007, I participated in a charrette for young landscape architects, organized by Landscape Forms in Kalamazoo, Michigan. I had traveled from hot humid Texas. The early autumn weather in Michigan was pleasant and comfortable. We suggested that Kalamazoo should start promoting itself as part of the "Cool Belt."

Once a center for innovation, the small city had experienced economic decline. Philanthropy had already provided leadership, much as we had envisioned in Bellagio, by establishing the Kalamazoo Promise in 2005, which committed to pay four years of tuition to any Michigan public college or university for all graduates of any of the city's public schools. This promise resulted in population growth for the old industrial city, as families are attracted to its public schools.

The other topics we had addressed at Bellagio included transportation, megaregion scenarios, social equity, research gaps, and communication strategies. My major contributions came in the areas of land development and preservation. RPA President Bob Yaro and I wrote a white paper on a national framework for conservation,

which we presented to our America 2050 group. We recommended a National Landscape Survey, which would result in a network of preserves. The federal government would lead the survey and the preserve network would be created by federal, state, and local governments working with business, labor, and environmental organizations, foundations, and private citizens.[8] We built on a 1987 map that National Park Service planners had made in Philadelphia (Figure 15.4).

RPA Executive Vice President Thomas Wright wrote a parallel white paper on land development. At Bellagio, we had formed a working group to balance conservation and development. We had refined ideas about the national landscape survey and the network of preserves. We had recommended a National Framework for Conservation and Development to preserve vital landscapes and to create healthy and efficient communities. This framework would depend, in large part, on state growth plans. Such plans would identify appropriate areas for mixed-use, compact communities and provide financial and regulatory incentives for implementation. The plans would help accomplish carbon reduction goals set nationwide.[9]

America 2050's objectives are ambitious, as are those of the Rockefeller Foundation. For example, another session at the Bellagio summit was devoted to architecture, design, and planning education needs to respond to the challenges of urbanization and climate change. Each session brought together around thirty leaders on each topic.

The America 2050 session included Congressman Earl Blumenauer, Atlanta Mayor Shirley Franklin, and New Orleans Director of Recovery Ed Blakely, as well as leaders from civic, business, and environmental groups; the Brookings Institution; the Ford and Lincoln Foundations; four universities (the Universities of Michigan, Pennsylvania, and Texas, as well as the New School); and the *Washington Post*. Our lively group generated many ideas and the structure for a national vision. We concluded that national leadership is a major

**15.4** National Open Space Opportunities. In 1987, a National Park Service team produced a national map, "Potential Protected Landscapes, Local and State Landscape Conservation Areas," that documented landscape conservation efforts underway in the continental United States, outlined here in the lighter shade. Areas protected by the Omnibus Public Land Management Act of 2009 are highlighted in the darker shade. Adapted from National Park Service, Mid-Atlantic Regional Office, Philadelphia. Researchers: Joan Chaplick, J. Glenn Eugster, Margaret Judd, Cecily Corcoran Kihn, and Suzanne Sutro. Courtesy of *Landscape Architecture* magazine.

challenge and were hopeful that leadership would emerge from the 2008 presidential elections.

In his white paper for the summit, University of Michigan historian Robert Fishman traced past national leadership.[10] He began with Thomas Jefferson, whose vision continued through the presidency of Abraham Lincoln. Professor Fishman described the leadership of Theodore Roosevelt, whose ideas contributed to the New Deal policies of his cousin Franklin. National leadership responded to past challenges and contributed to prosperity for many Americans. We now face the interrelated issues of urbanization, population growth, and climate change. Our nation rose to the occasion in 1808 and 1908. The time is indeed again right to plan our nation.

With the election of President Barack Obama, some America 2050 ideas, especially those related to infrastructure, began to take hold as several participants in the Bellagio summit joined his administration. Some progress in the conservation of significant landscapes has also begun. For example, the House and Senate passed the sweeping Omnibus Public Land Management Act of 2009, which was signed into law on March 30 by President Obama. Its 1,218 pages provide deferred maintenance for eight years of not-so-benign neglect by the George W. Bush administration and even codify an important initiative established during the Clinton administration in the 1990s. The Act includes more than one hundred and fifty measures that create more than 2 million acres of new wilderness areas, along with national parks, wild and scenic rivers, historic sites, scenic trails, and other protected public lands.

Although a welcome—and overdue—action, the new law does not go far enough to create a nationwide system of protected landscapes. Some states and regions benefit from new protected areas; many others do not. Although the new act makes the National Landscape Conservation System, created though an executive order by the Clinton administration, a permanent entity, the system is limited to areas administered by the U.S. Bureau of Land Management. As a result, the reach of this national system is not national enough (see Figure 15.4).

Using the Omnibus Public Land Management Act as a foundation, the white paper Yaro and I wrote suggests more comprehensive, bolder next steps.[11] Protecting our lands and natural resources must become a national priority. We must conserve and protect our most precious lands: first, through a National Landscape Survey, and second, through expanding the National Landscape Conservation System to ensure America's future. These landscapes hold a significant place in American history; if we want future generations to enjoy their scenic beauty and safeguard resources, there must be federal action, coupled with state, regional, and local efforts.

# V | LEARNING FROM ABROAD

As architects and planners in one megaregion or one metropolitan area in the United States can learn from each other, so, too, can other places offer lessons for our future. I am fortunate to be involved in two nations with ancient civilizations.

My formal involvement in Italy began after my book, *The Living Landscape*, was translated there in the early 1990s. Its translation surprised me. I had written it as a text for Americans. The translation occurred because the book resonated with Italian planners and architects seeking methods to implement a new law that required provincial-level planning. Italian provinces are roughly parallel to American counties. I studied this law, which opened the door to learning more about Italian history, design, and planning.

Italian colleagues have engaged me in discussions about starting new landscape architecture programs. These discussions have yielded modest progress. By contrast, academic programs have advanced quickly in China, increasing from none in landscape architecture to around seventy in a decade and a half. *The Living Landscape* has also been translated into Chinese—another surprise.

I first came to China in 2005 to help initiate a master of landscape architecture program at Tsinghua University. Laurie Olin had been appointed the first chair of landscape architecture. As part of his appointment, Olin brought in a series of visitors from a list prepared by the Chinese. I was on the list and, thus, became part of the "Olin team." I learned much from resulting visits to China.

# 16 | ENVIRONMENTAL READINGS

## THE ITALIAN DESIGN TRADITION

The day after the 2005 graduation, I left Austin with a group of twelve for a UT Friends of Architecture tour of Roman villas and gardens. Consisting of alumni and patrons of architecture, Friends of Architecture support the University of Texas at Austin School of Architecture programs, and, in return, the faculty provides tours of significant architecture. Most tours concentrate on architecture in Texas cities, so Rome took us quite a bit farther afield. We focused on garden design because Roman gardens reveal much about Italian design ideas and Italians' evolving views about the environment.

After checking in at the Grand Hotel del Gianicolo, we took a quick introductory walking tour of several major attractions under the lucent sky, including the Pantheon, Campo dei Fiori, Piazza Navona, and the Janiculum Hill (Collina del Gianicolo).

The next day, we walked through the Vatican Gardens (Figure 16.1) with official Vatican guide Roswitha Wagner. The gardens compose 15 acres (6 ha), or one-third, of Vatican City, a "paradise on Earth," according to Ms. Wagner. Access is always limited, so that the gardens remain a quiet, reflective place for religious leaders and visitors. However, the gardens had been closed completely until just before our arrival because of the death of Pope John Paul II. We were told our group was among the first to visit in some time. The Vati-

can Gardens date back to medieval times when vineyards and orchards extended to the north of the Apostolic Palace. In 1279, Pope Nicholas II enclosed this cultivated area with walls.

Green parrots circle above the Giardino all'Italiana and the *casino* designed by Pirro Ligorio for Pope Pius IV. In Italy, a *casino* was originally a small villa or pavilion, a summer house built for pleasure. Many themes in Italian garden design were introduced at the Vatican for our visit, including the concept of *otium*, Latin for refined leisure; the use of classical allegories; geometries of plants and water to symbolize the harmony of people with nature; and secret gardens, which were both private to the patrons of the villa and revealed inner truths—"the secret garden in ourselves," in the words of Ms. Wagner.

The next morning, we visited Villa Madama, begun by Cardinal Giulio de' Medici in the sixteenth century (Figure 16.2). One of the first Renaissance villas in the Rome region to be built outside the city, it was designed by Raphael and his students on the slope of Monte Mario. The villa is maintained by the Italian government for official state visitors and is seldom seen by others. Our driver, Silvano, thought we must have connections to Italian Prime Minister Silvio Berlusconi. He was aware that Presidents Bush and Clinton and others had recently visited the villa on the occasion of Pope John Paul II's funeral. We

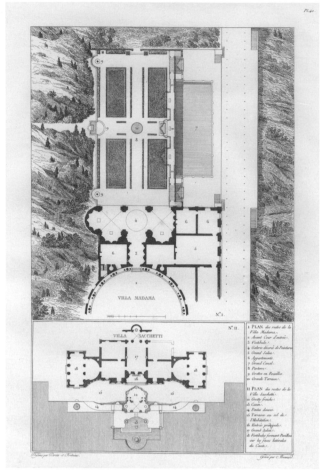

assured him that our visit was focused on architecture, not contemporary politics. Villa Madama is viewed as a precursor to contemporary sustainable design because of the way the building fits in with its natural surroundings, and how it uses the site's microclimate. Villa Madama, with its decorated loggia, garden, and fish pond, is also quite beautiful.

Afterward, we went to Villa Giulia, built in the sixteenth century as a country retreat for Pope Julius III. Several leading Renaissance figures contributed to the design of the villa, gardens, pavilions, and fountains, including architects Giacomo Barozzi da Vignola and Giorgio Vasari, the sculptor Bartolomeo Ammannati, and Michelangelo. Villa Giulia houses the Museo Nazionale Etrusco, with its remarkable pre-Roman collection of antiquities.

We next explored Borghese Gardens by foot in the summer heat. The area had been called the "hill of the gardens" in ancient Roman times.

With the fall of Rome and the abandonment of the aqueducts, the area declined. Noble families began settling the hillsides again during the Renaissance. The large park area now includes museums, the zoo (renamed "the biopark"), and cultural facilities, such as several national academies and schools. We walked through Borghese Gardens to the British School at Rome, designed by Edwin Lutyens in 1911 (Figure 16.3).

On Thursday, May 26, we journeyed outside of Rome to the hill town of Tivoli. We first went to Hadrian's Villa, where the Roman emperor Hadrian—or Adriano, as he is called in Italian—built a sprawling complex overlooking the broad plain stretching toward Rome (Figure 16.4). Hadrian was born in Spain (or of a Spanish family—his birthplace is debated) in 76 AD and was emperor from 117 AD until his death in 138 AD. He made two especially important contributions to world architecture: the Pantheon in Rome and his rural retreat, his *villa urbana*. The retreat, on a plain at

16.1 Vatican Gardens. Photograph by Vincent de Groot (www.videgro.net).

16.2 Villa Madama, designed by Raphael to fit the Roman hillside. Raphael carefully used the solar orientation of the site to guide the design of the villa and gardens.

**16.3** City park at Borghese Gardens, Rome. Photograph by Frederick Steiner.

**16.4** Villa Adriana, Tivoli, near Rome, constructed as a retreat by Emperor Adriano in the early second century. Photograph by Frederick Steiner.

the foot of the Sabine Hills near ancient Tibur, which is modern-day Tivoli, is also a major contribution to landscape architecture. Hadrian's Villa is about 19 miles (30 km) east-northeast of Rome. In ancient times, Roman emperors and nobility left the city during the heat of the summer.

Hadrian wanted his garden to have features from all reaches of the empire representing places he had visited as a military commander. He was also quite enamored with all things Greek, notably, the villas of Alexander the Great. Most Roman villas were derived from Greek precedents, but Hadrian carried this fascination even further by the vast scale of the villa, gigantic even by Roman imperial standards. Built between 118 AD and 134 AD, Hadrian's Villa covers 750 acres (304 ha) and includes about one hundred buildings, plus many gardens, lakes, and baths. Sited just below Tivoli, Hadrian's Villa has been extensively excavated since the seventeenth century. It inspired several Renaissance scholars, artists, and architects (many of whom used it as a source of building materials and decoration).

Afterward, we toured the stunning Villa d'Este gardens in Tivoli, another creation of Pirro Ligorio

(Figures 16.5 and 16.6). Built on top of the ruins of a Roman villa, these gardens were commissioned by Cardinal Ippolito II d'Este (who wanted to become pope) in 1549. Ligorio designed a monumental series of terraces and five hundred fountains. The Neapolitan Ligorio had worked on excavations of Hadrian's Villa from ancient Rome. Ligorio collaborated with the skilled hydraulic engineer Tommaso Chiruchi on the fountains.

16.5 Fountain in the gardens of Villa d'Este, Tivoli. Photograph by Frederick Steiner.

16.6 Villa d'Este. Drawn by Laurie Olin.

**16.7** Villa Aldobrandini, Frascati, Italy. Photograph by Frederick Steiner.

With its representations of the rivers of Tivoli and Rome and many other hydrological marvels, d'Este stimulates both the senses and the mind. Its shady gardens and fountains provided a refuge from the heat in Rome.

On Friday, our Friends of Architecture group first visited the Académie de France à Rome in the Villa Medici. The French Academy is the oldest in Rome, housed in the villa since 1803. Located on Pincian Hill (Collina del Pincio) near the top of the Spanish Steps, the villa and gardens were created, beginning in 1576, by Cardinal Ferdinando de' Medici, who turned the villa into one of the most lavish in Rome. The front is very formal, while the garden façade is less formal but still highly ornamented. In 1801, the Medici sold the villa to the Duke of Parma, who later exchanged it with the French Republic.

After our visit to the French Academy, we traveled south to Frascati in the Alban hills. Frascati is located along a ridge of volcanic hills among a group of thirteen towns called "Castelli Romani." The soil is rich, and the farms are productive. Like the Sabine Hills, the Alban Hills provide an escape for Romans from the summer heat. Located strategically for defense, Frascati housed German troops during the Second World War.

As a result, the area experienced Allied bombing, which took its toll on several villas.

The restoration efforts in Frascati have been extensive and provide a model for historic preservation. Villa Falconieri is a notable example of such renewal because of the extent and detail of building restoration. The villa was constructed between 1548 and 1574, with an addition by Francesco Borromini completed in 1620. The main building has been restored since the war and now is occupied by the European Center of Education. The gardens, however, remain largely in ruin.

We next walked to nearby Villa Aldobrandini, designed by Giacomo della Porta, Carlo Maderno, and Giovanni Fontana (Figure 16.7). The main building, which blends into the profile of the hill behind it, was begun around 1598 and completed around 1603. Here we see a building respond to a major landscape feature, the hill, similar to Villa Madama and Villa d'Este. That same year, construction commenced on the gardens, which were the work of fountain designer and engineer Orazio Olivieri of Tivoli. Between the villa and the hill is the Teatro delle Acque, which once spouted water and played flutes on command by means of a special hydraulic system. At the end of the eighteenth century, the villa passed into the hands of

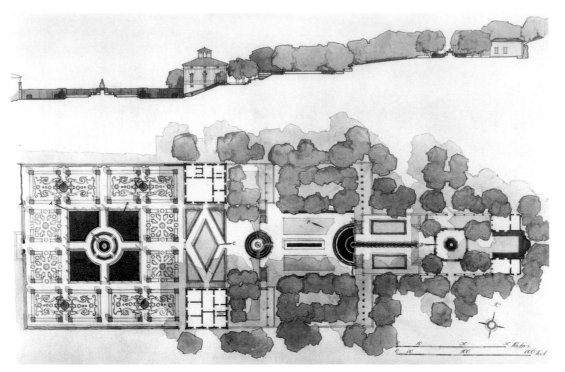

16.8 Plan of Villa Lante at Bagnaia near Viterbo, Italy. Courtesy of the Foundation for Landscape Studies Landscape Collection and ARTstor.

16.9 Villa Lante water chain. Photograph by Frederick Steiner.

16.10 Water table at Villa Lante. Photograph by Frederick Steiner.

the Borghese family. After visiting the gardens and returning to our motor coach at a central piazza in Frascati, an architect on our tour, Bibiana Dykema, looked back at Villa Aldobrandini and noted its considerable "curb appeal."

The next day, we visited Borghese Gallery to see several of Gianlorenzo Bernini's famous sculptures. That afternoon, we set out on our own. I walked around the familiar streets of the Trastevere, then returned up the hill to our hotel to watch a thunderstorm arrive that washed away the heat. A keyhole in the clouds opened, bringing a ray of light across the city.

The following day, we drove an hour north to Bagnaia. Like Tivoli and Frascati, Bagnaia, whose name derives from *bagno*, meaning bath, is a refuge from Rome. The gardens of Villa Lante are an example of the late Renaissance, or Mannerist, phase in Italian design (Figure 16.8). The garden design was clearly derived from other places we had visited, most notably Villa d'Este and Hadrian's Villa. The design is attributed to Giacomo Barozzi da Vignola; however, it is likely he only designed one *casino* and a part of the garden. Tommaso Chiruchi, the hydraulic engineer for Villa d'Este, was involved in the fountain design. Villa Lante was different in many ways from previous villas we had visited because, first of all, there is no grand villa. Instead, the design revolves around two *casini*, which are nearly identical, although they were built by different owners thirty years apart. The *casini* are built in Mannerist style; the first for Cardinal Gianfrancesco Gambara, who commissioned Vignola in 1560; the second by the seventeen-year-old grandnephew of Pope Sixtus V, following the death of Gambara. This youth, made a cardinal by his great-uncle, built the second *casino* and finished the gardens. The gardens clearly do not respond to a dominant building—there is no dominant building. The two *casini* are part of the overall landscape design.

From the village of Bagnaia, one enters through a gate into the first garden space—a perfectly square *parterre*, an ornamental garden on a level surface with paths between the planting beds. The garden is bordered on three sides by high box hedges. On the fourth side, the twin *casini* almost seem more like garden elements than buildings. From the principal *parterre*, one climbs upward through oak trees to a series of terraces and water features (Figures 16.9 and 16.10).

After our visit to Villa Lante, we wove along the hilly roads—getting lost on narrow streets and in hazelnut groves a few times along the way—to Caprarola. Between 1566 and 1569, Vignola had converted a medieval fortress into a Renaissance villa for the Farnese family. Located approximately 25 miles (40 km) northwest of Rome, the villa was commissioned in 1559 by Cardinal Alessandro Farnese, a grandson of Pope Paul III. Vignola worked

on Villa Farnese in Caprarola until his death. The gardens of the villa are as impressive as the house itself, which was constructed as a country house. The building has a pentagonal plan with two façades facing the garden, each with its *parterre* beyond the moat. The lower garden is reached via a drawbridge from the terrace of the *piano nobile*, the "noble floor" and the principal level above the ground in large Renaissance houses. There is a *parterre* garden of box topiary and fountains. A walk through the woods leads to a fountain and then a water chain. At the top of the water chain is a *casino*. More natural woodland surrounds this highly organized area. These uncultivated areas were used for hunting and are often missing from illustrations of Italian gardens.

For me, our journey back to Rome was nostalgic with every turn, every beep of a car horn evoking a memory from the time I lived there. We leaped into a strong surf of history (Figure 16.11). One can touch time in Rome. As names and dates whirled around us, the diamond light, suggestive billboards, and darting *motorini* captured our attention. We walked and talked, ate well and drank remarkable wines, and came to appreciate a place that captures hearts and inspires minds. In Rome and Italy, cooking, wine making, and landscape design are forms of regionalism.

In their masterful study of the interrelationships between architecture and landscape, Clemens Steenbergen and Wouter Reh call Rome "a landscape theater."[1] They note that villa placement was determined by the Tiber valley topography.

**16.11** Piazza Navona, Rome. Drawn by Laurie Olin, July 7, 1981.

This natural structure was reinforced in ancient times by consular roads and the Aurelian Wall. As the city shrank during the Middle Ages, a green belt developed along the wall. These green spaces became prime sites for villas. A series of popes restored the water supply to the city by repairing ancient aqueducts and constructing new ones. Steenbergen and Reh note that these aqueducts "were an indispensable source of water for the villas."[2]

Occupying the higher ground of Rome, the villas provided panoramic views of the city. The elevated position also meant that "the villas were in each other's field of vision."[3] Their placement across the Roman urban landscape followed the arrangement of Renaissance villas in Florence. The Roman villas visually interact with each other, as their patrons and architects had done as well. A community of patrons and architects learned from one another, advancing villa and garden design. They advanced their art by learning from their own projects, from the design of others, and from history. They took advantage of natural conditions in the region, while contributing to an evolving urban landscape of piercing light and seductive color.

## 17

### AUTUMN MOON
### DESIGN AND
### PLANNING IN CHINA

aurie Olin invited me to Beijing as a
visiting professor at Tsinghua University,
where he served as founding chair of
the department of landscape architecture. Two
women with flowers—lilacs and pink roses—
greet me at the airport in September 2005. One
woman, He Rui, is the Department of Landscape
Architecture administrator; the other is the dean's
assistant. A driver takes my bag. Cars come from
everywhere, covering all the paved space. Buicks
appear more plentiful here than at home. It is 6
p.m. on Thursday, and our normally forty-minute
drive across the northern fringe of Beijing takes
an hour and a half in rush hour traffic, slowed
even more by rain. Trees line the highway from the
airport, veiling the fields and buildings on either
side, but as we enter a ring road, the trees soon
give way to urban sprawl.

The following morning, I attend the studio of
the deputy chair of the department of landscape
architecture, Dr. Yang Rui. The studio project is
called "Three Hills and Five Gardens: From Garden to Landscape" (Figures 17.1 and 17.2). The
location is the northwest portion of Beijing, in the
area famous for the imperial gardens of the Ming
and Qing Dynasties. The area has significant
cultural, historic, scenic, and natural value and is
facing intense development pressure.

### YUAN MING YUAN

After studio, Dr. Liu Hailong, a postdoctoral
scholar, takes me to the Old Summer Palace
(Yuan Ming Yuan—one of the five gardens in
the landscape planning studio) near Tsinghua
University (Figure 17.3). Peking University is also
nearby and was once, in fact, adjacent to the Old
Summer Palace but is now cut off by roadways.
"Fragmentation is an important issue," my host
explains, which poses the first challenge for our
studio.

The French and English burned and looted
much of the palace during the Second Opium
War, which lasted from 1856 to 1860. Parts of the
palace have been renovated. The restoration process raises key questions such as: What is authentic, and what do we restore? To what time is the
palace restored? The large green space of the
Yuan Ming Yuan is popular with local residents
and tourists. There are stands where one can have
one's picture taken in (unauthentic) royal robes
against an (unauthentic) imperial background.
After the destruction of the palace buildings and
gardens, farmers settled the area. Displaced by
reconstruction, they (and their descendents)
now manage the grounds and profit from the
concessions.

Many lakes at the Old Summer Palace are now
dry or lowered. The future of the lakes prompts

HYDROLOGY/ECOLOGY
WORKSHOP

**THE CITY AS A
NATURAL SYSTEM**
───────
"WATER AS AN
ESSENTIAL RESOURCE
FOR LIFE"

DEPARTMENT OF

LANDSCAPE ARCHITECTURE

TSINGHUA UNIVERSITY

VISITING PROFESSOR:

COLGATE SEARLE

RON HENDERSON

STUDENTS:

FENGSHUNI

ZHANGSIYUAN

ZHANGYANG

ZHOUXUCAN

LVQI

WANGPENG

ZHANGZHENWEI

CHRISTINA MILOS

2007.06

**Three Hills & Five Gardens**

**17.1** Three Hills and Five Gardens studio site (2007). Courtesy of the Department of Landscape Architecture, Tsinghua University.

**17.2** Panorama of the Three Hills and Five Gardens studio site. Drawn by Xiong Tao in the Qing Dynasty.

much debate among ecologists and conservationists: Should they be lined? How should the edges be treated? In light of Beijing's water supply challenges—the water table has dropped almost 98 feet (30 m) in the past thirty years—should the lakes even be restored at all?

During the peak of the Qing Dynasty, at least under Emperors Kangxi and Qianlong, the Old Summer Palace was open to outside influences.

The section of the Old Summer Palace with European-style buildings and gardens was commissioned by the Qing rulers. Called "Xiyanglou," the European area was designed by F. Giuseppe Castiglione (Italian, 1688–1766) and P. Michael Benoist (French, 1715–1744). Nowadays, tourists capture images of their loved ones in front of Baroque ruins. Change and the opening and closing to outside influences are not recent phenomena. One wonders what tourists three and four

centuries from now will make of current works by Rem Koolhaas, Steven Holl, Paul Andreu, and the other star architects from around the world who have descended on Beijing like locusts.

## OF CRISSCROSSES, CUBES, EGGSHELLS, AND BIRDS' NESTS

Koolhaas and Ole Scheeren of the Office for Metropolitan Architecture (OMA) won the 2002 competition to design the Central Chinese Television (CCTV) headquarters in Beijing's new central business district. The more than 5.9 million-square-foot (555,000-m²) headquarters cover a 25-acre (10-ha) site with two high-rise buildings. The main tower rises 755 feet (230 m) in a continuous loop of horizontal and vertical sections, which Koolhaas calls a "Z Crisscross"; local people note that it looks like "a man brought to his knees." The twisted pile of metal looks like a lowercase "n". The CCTV headquarters combine administration, broadcasting, studios, and production facilities (Figure 17.4). The second tower houses a television cultural center and includes a hotel, visitors' center, public theater, and exhibition center. Chinese New Year's fireworks ignited a devastating fire of the cultural center and hotel in February 2009.

**17.3** Yuan Ming Yuan (Garden of Perfect Brightness, also sometimes called the Old Summer Palace), Beijing. Photograph by Frederick Steiner.

**17.4** CCTV headquarters. Design by Office for Metropolitan Architecture. Photograph by Frederick Steiner.

**17.5** National Centre for the Performing Arts. Design by Paul Andreu. Photograph by Frederick Steiner.

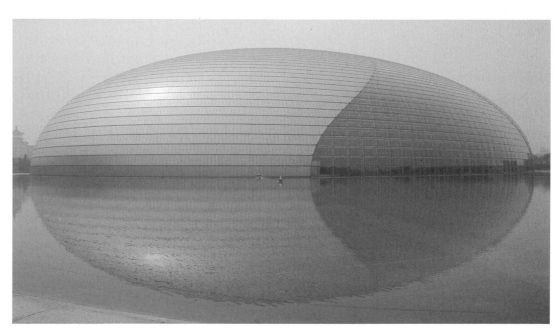

Across town, near the Forbidden City, is the National Centre for the Performing Arts, designed by French architect Paul Andreu. The "Eggshell" is made of titanium and glass. Situated in a park, the oval, silver theater is encircled by water (Figure 17.5). Construction began in 2001 and was completed before the 2008 Olympics. The structure has been called "a crystal drop of water," "a big eggshell," "a boiled egg," and "a colossal turtle egg," among other things.

As OMA's Z Crisscross and Andreu's Eggshell were being built, construction continued on the now-familiar Beijing Olympic facilities, which feature a semi-transparent, cube-shaped national aquatic center and a "nest-like" national stadium. The "Water Cube" was designed by a team of Chinese and Australian architects and engineers, including PTW Architects and the Australian office of Ove Arup. The stunning, $400-million "Bird's Nest" is a joint effort by the Swiss firm, Herzog & de Meuron (who won the design competition for the stadium); China Architecture Design Institute, one of the many prestigious design firms associated with leading universities; and Ai Wei Wei, "the iconoclastic Beijing artist and landscape architect."[1] The Bird's Nest's appearance is created by interlacing steel beam ribbons that enclose the red stadium (Figure 17.6). It quickly became an architectural icon in Beijing with its dramatic, steel beams wrapping around and enclosing the red stadium and green fields.

## TSINGHUA BIG YARD

After my tour of the Old Summer Palace, doctoral candidate Zhuang Youbo and another landscape architecture graduate student show me the Tsinghua campus. During the Boxer Rebellion, several European nations, Japan, and the United States put down the revolt of the Chinese against outside influences. When the rebellion ended in 1901, the Western powers, including the United States, forced China to yield to several demands, including payment for their military expenses. To our credit, the United States decided to return these monies (or at least part of them) to help estab-

17.6 The Bird's Nest stadium from Olympic Forest Park. Courtesy of Tsinghua University Urban Planning and Design Institute.

lish Tsinghua University, initially a prep school to groom young Chinese students for American universities.

Designed by the American architect Henry Murphy, the original campus, now called the "red" campus for its brick rather than its politics, was built on the summer garden grounds of a Qing Dynasty princess. The core was clearly inspired by the Lawn at the University of Virginia and the many central green spaces of American universities that followed Jefferson's example (Figure 17.7). The older Tsinghua campus is a wonderful assemblage of lakes and green spaces.[2] The original core grew, adding areas to the red campus, including a library and the college of science designed by Professor Guan Zhaoye of the Tsinghua faculty.

The newer "white" campus, named for the generous use of tiles, has been built since the late 1980s and is more monumental in scale, with an odd mix of Soviet, American, and Japanese influences (Figure 17.8). Although my hosts might not acknowledge this, the new campus buildings are noticeably influenced by Japanese architecture in general with the massing and cladding of tiles. The entry porch of the architecture building, in particular, is very similar to Arata Isozaki's Gunma Museum of Art from the early 1970s. At that time, Isozaki was in his period of experimenting with "ma," the Japanese character for "space," which is, in fact, a Chinese character with the same meaning.

In addition to the traditional academic buildings and student dormitories, the campus also includes considerable faculty housing, facilities for retired faculty and staff, a primary school, a high school, and shopping areas. Guarded gates control access to the campus. I asked if this is typical for Chinese universities and was told it was and that these work-live communities are called "Dayuan" (Big Yards). Big Yards also exist for large industrial and military complexes. The walls around them, and the walls around most everything, form a crucial element of the Chinese urban fabric. Recently, crowded high-rise office buildings have begun to appear outside the main entrance of the

**17.7** Historic core of Tsinghua University. Photograph by Frederick Steiner.

**17.8** Newer Tsinghua campus. Photograph by Frederick Steiner.

**17.9** The Great Wall. Photograph by Frederick Steiner.

campus of Tsinghua, many built by the university itself, such as the Tsinghua Science Park (which is more like Rockefeller Center than a park).

## THE GREAT WALL

Beijing sits in a basin between the mountains and the sea. As we drive to the Great Wall, we leave the fertile plain, climbing up the mountain to the wall built to divide the cultivated world from that of the nomads. The builders of the Great Wall intended it to be used for defense and it came to define the limits of civilization. As we get closer to the wall, we go through a series of fortified gates, spanning the narrow valleys.

The Great Wall is not a single line but rather a defensive network. Much of it is located along watershed lines (creating a barrier for wildlife, if nothing else). The Great Wall near Beijing was mostly built in the Ming Dynasty. The earlier portions of the wall are from the Qin Dynasty and are to the north and west (Figure 17.9).

Chairman Mao said, "He who doesn't reach the Great Wall is no true man." The Great Wall helps define China, a nation of many smaller walls. Built for defense, it now provides a magnet for tourists. The wall forms a linear ecosystem that incorporates the social and natural systems it crosses, but stands distinct from its surroundings.

## THREE HILLS AND FIVE GARDENS

As we discuss boundaries for the studio site, I ask Professor Yang about the Beijing administrative structure (Table 17.1).

China is organized into twenty-three provinces (with Taiwan as the twenty-third); five autonomous regions; four municipalities, including Beijing (with administrative standing equal to provinces); and two special administrative regions (Hong Kong and Macau). Beijing contains sixteen districts and two counties. In terms of political status, districts and counties hold the same place in the administrative hierarchy. Some districts are renamed counties, reflecting their urbanization. Within districts and counties, there are townships, then villages at the lowest level.

Our first destination is a temple on Fragrant Hill in Xiangshan Park. The entry is crowded, and local citizens try to rent a parking space to us. Walking through this crowded space, I note that, if fragmentation is the first studio challenge, the

TABLE 17.1 BEIJING
ADMINISTRATIVE STRUCTURE.

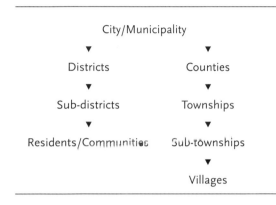

City/Municipality

Districts                          Counties

Sub-districts                    Townships

Residents/Communities      Sub-townships

Villages

second will be how to address the needs of local communities, their economies, and their cultures.

We are greeted by the studio class consisting of fourteen students (nine women and five men), plus an exchange student from Tashkent, Uzbekistan. There are two professors, a postdoc, a Ph.D. student, and me. The landscape architecture graduate students come from architecture, geography, and art undergraduate degree programs. The number of landscape architecture programs in China has grown significantly in the past decade: according to Professor Yang, from none to around seventy—with thirty in schools of architecture, thirty in forestry and agricultural schools, and ten in art programs. Some twenty-five graduate programs and forty-five undergraduate programs now exist.

We visit the Temple of Azure Clouds, called "Biyun Si" by the Chinese, built in the Yuan Dynasty (1331) (Figure 17.10). Women in light blue shirts sweep the grounds with large brooms. The temple consists of a series of courtyards and shrines that progress up a hill. One of the courtyards has a fish pond with goldfish and turtles.

17.10 View from the Temple of Azure Clouds of the Three Hills and Five Gardens studio study area. Photograph by Ron Henderson.

I observe many similarities with Italian gardens—progression, water, axis, and symmetry (Figure 17.11). Natural elements are carefully orchestrated. The progression through the courtyards is orderly and harmonious, with water features marking key spots along the way. There is a clear north-south, east-west axis, with buildings and open spaces organized symmetrically. We stop several times as we climb the stairs to discuss issues of the studio with the students. At one point, Professor Yang observes, "In ancient times, the mountains were occupied by temples; since 1949, by the military."

The main pagoda at the top of the hill displays an obvious Indian influence. The view from the tower's platform provides an amazing panorama of metropolitan Beijing. Looking out across this expansive city, I note that the third studio challenge will be continuity and how to link the past, present, and future.

From the Temple of Azure Clouds, we walk through the park, visiting other sites, including the Zhao Monastery, built in 1780 during the Qing Dynasty for the visiting Sixth Banchan from Tibet. We walk past Beiwu Village, a settlement among the palaces, traditionally for rice production for the emperors. We discuss methods for inventorying water and vegetation resources, as well as the history and economy of the various places in the study area.

**17.11** Design for Garden Compartment in Plan. Giovanni Battista Ferrari, *De Florum Cultura Libri* IV (Rome: S. Paulinius, 1633). Courtesy of Mirka Beneš.

# GROUND WATER SYSTEM
## THE CITY AS NATURAL SYSTEM

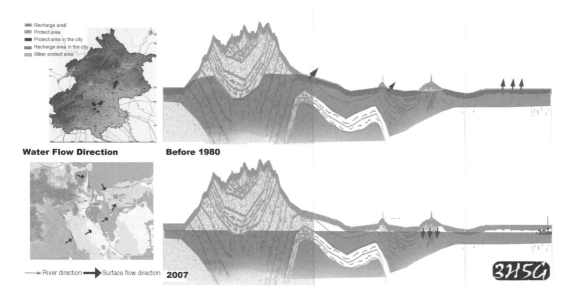

**17.12** Groundwater system of the Three Hills and Five Gardens studio site (2007). Courtesy of the Department of Landscape Architecture, Tsinghua University.

**17.13** Summer Palace, Beijing. Photograph by Ron Henderson.

I suggest the use of transects to help establish common points to compare various data. Most of the Tsinghua student works I have observed are either flat, reflecting the GIS and planning expertise of the faculty, or perspective drawings from the students' backgrounds, mostly in architecture. Landscape architecture uses both plans and drawings. A well-established tool in landscape architecture, transects enable the visualization of a sweep across space, as well as relationships above and below the ground. Landscape architects employ transects to illustrate gradients and linear patterns along which plant communities, animal habitat, and land-use change.

The Tsinghua students begin to apply transects (Figure 17.12). Their transects across the Three Hills and Five Gardens study site enable the students to show the change in topography from the mountains in the west into the valleys. They represent changes in climate, hydrology, vegetation, and land use from the high ground in the west into the flat landscape of urban Beijing.

## YIHE YUAN

For the final stop on our field trip, we enter the Summer Palace (Yihe Yuan, a World Heritage Site and another of the five gardens) through the less-used West Gate (Figure 17.13). Built in the eighteenth century by Emperor Qianlong for his mother, the palace gardens consist of three large lakes. The emperor used the Summer Palace to control water flowing into Beijing. Qianlong, who had a long reign (1736–1796), liked the gardens of South China, so he used many elements from that region. He built three large and three smaller islands on the three main lakes. We walk along the West Causeway (Xi Di), modeled after the Su Di Causeway of the West Lake in Hangzhou. In this less crowded portion of the Summer Palace, we pass several men sunbathing, walkers, and (illegal) swimmers.

By contrast, the 2,388-foot (728-m) Long Corridor is packed with tourists from seemingly everywhere on the planet. China now attracts the fourth most visitors. Many crowd the Long Corridor in anticipation of a fireworks display for the Moon Festival. Clouds cover the moon, and rain feels imminent.

## STUDIO CULTURE

In the next studio meeting, a cultural geography professor from Peking University explains the history of the Five Gardens area. He is enthusiastic, opinionated, funny, and long-winded. He traces the past when individual strong nobles controlled the region, each with his own fortress and flag. In these ancient times, the water flow was very important for drinking, irrigation, and transportation—a recurring theme in his lecture. Temples were built along the rivers. There were many springs back then. Historically, the area was called "Three Hills and One Garden."

The professor says that our study area has five thousand years of human history. Some seventeen hundred years ago, a canal was built across northern present-day Beijing. It provided a connection between the Five Gardens area and the rest of the basin, as did the road from the Forbidden City to the Great Wall. Water—its quantity and quality—will clearly be the fourth studio challenge.

During the Ming Dynasty, the study area became a rice landscape. Villas, gardens, and tombs were built. There are ninety-six tombs for relatives of emperors. Some are for wives; some are for several wives. In all, two hundred people are buried in the ninety-six tombs. There are also seventy-two villas for nobles, according to our Peking University lecturer.

In the Qing Dynasty, the area was also popular among relatives of the emperor. South of the city, the emperor had a large hunting preserve, which was prone to flooding from the Yongding River. As a result, an emperor decided to move the royal hunting preserve from the south to the northwest. Rice symbolized China for this emperor of the south, so he encouraged the cultivation of rice in the area.

The professor shows in an aerial photo from the 1980s that the area was still dominated by rice fields. Historically, there was no wall around the Summer Palace to maintain the connection to the rice fields; instead, there were small hills. He shows a place where rice fields have been replaced by a golf course. The professor describes the intense development pressure on the area and the historical relationship between the lakes and rice, as well as how the two were mutually beneficial. Increasingly, the land around the Summer Palace is being developed, so the lakes no longer benefit from the surrounding rice fields. How to preserve farmland will be the fifth studio challenge. Can the remaining rice fields and other farmlands be preserved?

The situation reminds me of Austin, Phoenix, and other rapidly growing American cities. The Three Hills and Five Gardens area possesses a rich history, abundant natural resources, and great beauty. The Hill Country west of Austin attracts wealthier residents. As new affluent developments spread, they contribute to the degradation of the aquifer and the lost beauty of the landscape. Likewise, people with higher incomes find the low mountains north of Phoenix appealing, with similar negative environmental consequences. The Three Hills and Five Gardens area also attracts the affluent of Beijing, as well as associated commercial development. In addition, the army, the Communist Party, and leading universities occupy significant space in the area, adding to the area's appeal. Meanwhile, farms disappear, water sources dry up, and roadways clog with traffic.

Emperor Qianlong built a water system for both agriculture and pleasure gardens, but he emphasized farming. The trees in the garden were sometimes remnants of the natural vegetation. The pleasure gardens and native trees had benefits for rice production as well as for birds. During Qianlong's time, more villas were built for sons and daughters of the emperor and for government officials, too.

The professor then turns his attention to the Old Summer Palace with three main gardens (Figure 17.14). He notes that the gardens have declined or been converted to unauthentic uses. Historically, garden designs exhibited two basic forms: land surrounding water or water surrounding land.

**17.14** Yuan Ming Yuan (Old Summer Palace), Beijing. Photograph by Frederick Steiner.

The Peking University geographer identifies three main issues facing Yuan Ming Yuan:

1. heritage conservation (the first priority according to the professor)
2. ecological preservation
3. landscape protection

But a more holistic, integrative view is needed. To reinforce the need for heritage conservation, the professor describes a controversy over the name of a subway station that pitted a developer against preservationists. The conservationists wanted to use the historic name. The developer wanted to call it "Century Square," after the time period in which it was developed.

The Five Gardens area was surrounded by military installations and well protected in the time of the emperors. A large pasture existed in the middle of the area for horses to graze. Canals were built from springs in Fragrant Hills to help feed the lakes of the Summer Palace (Figure 17.15). The military poses the sixth studio challenge. It is part of the history and culture of the studio area but it also contributes to its fragmentation and growth.

## PEKING UNIVERSITY

Peking University occupies a military parade area from the Qing Dynasty (Figure 17.16). The American architect Henry Murphy also designed the original Peking University campus. He had become interested in Chinese design while laying out Tsinghua University. As a result, Murphy used more Asian elements in the Peking University campus, like, for example, its garden-like entry gate. However, he did not understand Chinese design very well at that point because he incorporated elements from tombs into campus buildings.

**17.15** Yihe Yuan (Summer Palace). Photograph by Ron Henderson.

**17.16** Peking University campus, Beijing. Photograph by Frederick Steiner.

After 1949, the government decided to locate more universities to the northwest of the city. Today, more than two hundred educational institutions blanket that portion of Beijing.

## ACROSS BEIJING, ACROSS THE WORLD

I am asked frequently if this is my first time in China. I realized that until relatively recently it was practically impossible for an American to visit the People's Republic. Young students do not seem to remember this fact.

I take a taxi across the city to meet my Austin friend Robin Rather and her colleagues for lunch. A giant billboard reads, "the frist landscape of China." A golf course is promoted ("first" was misspelled).

Hurricane Rita was approaching the Texas coast. Less than a month after Katrina, Rita caused half of Houston's residents to evacuate. The storm made landfall near the Louisiana-Texas border. Rita caused $11.3 billion in damage and killed seven people immediately, several more during the evacuation. The region proved to be relatively resilient after Rita, but then the hurricane's main force missed major population centers. Major flooding did not occur, in contrast to New Orleans after Katrina.

## STUDENT WORK

After one of my lectures, I join the other faculty members for presentations from five teams of the studio students. Like all first presentations in a school year, the quality was uneven.

The "nature" team explains that they have collected huge amounts of data. The students cover climate (20 inches, 500 mm, of rain per year in Beijing), vegetation, and water (five watersheds). They state that the biggest challenge they faced was to convert the data to GIS. (No soils or wildlife; very little geology information had been collected so far.) The seventh studio challenge would involve converting GIS data to a standard format and, then, finding patterns within the mapped data.

The students address the numerous water issues facing Beijing. Water once surrounded the city for protection and was also used for drinking, agriculture, transportation, and pleasure gardens. The four water sources now are reservoirs, groundwater, rivers, and grey water.

The "culture" team had divided their task into two parts: history and culture. Heritage protection occurs at three levels in China: national, provincial (Beijing also has that status), and local. The students produce detailed time lines illustrating the rich history of the study area. They focus on gardens, tombs, military installations, literature, temples, and universities.

The "socioeconomic" team covers appearance, land use, users, economic interests, and population. There are more than 17 million people in Beijing, with an average age increasingly getting older. According to this team, the four most important issues facing the study area are:

1. high-tech development
2. real estate development
3. tourist development
4. fragmentation, exacerbated by institutions and the military.

The Three Hills and Five Gardens area is one of the most attractive areas for growth, in part, because of its natural beauty. The concentration of universities attracts high-tech development. Heritage sites appeal to tourists. Meanwhile, governmental and military institutions, which are not accessible to the public, fragment the area. The eighth studio challenge will then be how to cope with development. There is a need for bold vision to mitigate negative consequences. The study area will lose its attractiveness as a place to live and work if growth continues at the current rate.

The "transportation and infrastructure" team notes that commuters are causing traffic jams. The routes for tourism are unclear, and there are traffic conflicts between tourists and commuters. The team addresses bike systems for college students, local residents, and tourists. (The students were at an early stage and had not gotten to water supply, electricity, and other infrastructure systems yet.)

The "management" team divides their work by how the area was managed historically versus today. The students define the differences between villages and street districts. Sometimes the areas overlap; at other times they do not. They also describe the urban planning structure for the area.

We agree that landscape architecture will potentially play a very important role in China's future, with seventy or so new academic programs in the discipline, with the Olympics then on the horizon, and with rapid growth affecting the nation's environments and communities.

Later, in my apartment, I watch the television for news of Rita. Instead, I learn about the second destructive tropical storm in the China Sea within the past few weeks. Both storms bring destruction to the southern coastal areas of China. The Chinese storm is called Damrey, Cambodian for "elephant."

## FORBIDDEN CITY

One Saturday, He Rui, Que Zhenqing, and Mr. Wang, our driver, collect me outside my apart-ment building. Que is an enthusiastic graduate student and a talented designer who helps me with my presentation slides. Mr. Wang drops us off at the Donghua (east) Gate, then we walk around the moat to the front of the Forbidden City, also called the Imperial Palace. Twenty-four emperors lived there. "One had seventy-two concubines," He Rui adds.

From the main gate, we walk south through two gates to Tiananmen Square. Tiananmen is derived from the words for "heaven" and "peace." We walk among thousands of people. After 1949, the new Communist government had expanded the square.

My picture is taken, like that of countless other visitors, under the huge portrait of Chairman Mao Zedong. A Chinese Army guard in green uniform at attention in the foreground. We walk back to the main gate of the Forbidden City. Golden yellow (the emperor's color) and red (for luck and happiness) dominate. We walk through a series of squares and gates. The Forbidden City is rectilinear, and symmetry and geometry dominate these main spaces. As elsewhere in Beijing, all important buildings face south. Golden yellow roofs glisten in the sun (Figure 17.17).

**17.17** Rooftops at Forbidden City, Beijing. Photograph by Frederick Steiner.

Symbolic elements at the end of a roof protect a structure from fire. The roofs are curved to direct rainwater away from the building and thus protect the structure. There is a combination of symbolism and practicality in the buildings. I am persuaded to have an iced latté at the Starbucks inside the Forbidden City. I yield to my hosts' kind desire to make me feel at home. (Subsequently, the Starbucks lost its prime Forbidden City location after a spirited blog campaign to remove it.)

In the east courtyards, we see many artifacts, including several from the Bronze Age, more than three thousand years ago. There is too much to see for one day.

On our return to the Tsinghua Big Yard, Que mentions that the area south of Beijing has not developed as fast as the north, which has more suitable living conditions. The 2008 Olympics were held in the north. Its goal was to be a "green" Olympics, which sought to help create a "green" Beijing. This goal proved to be an uphill battle. The Party had identified the site for the Olympics back in the 1950s, and the site became a big city park after the Olympics. Already in 2005, many trees were being planted. My hosts believed the Olympics would help promote landscape architecture in Beijing and China overall, and, in general, they were correct.

As the "greening" of the Olympics site continued, the Olympic Games faced larger environmental issues, ranging from air quality and the destruction of historical neighborhoods to the improvement of toilets. Much media attention during the Olympics focused on Beijing's poor air quality. To address these issues, the Chinese government closed factories and coal plants near Beijing and explored several options for reducing automobile and truck traffic.[3]

### HUTONG

Professor Yang picks me up, and we drive on the Second Ring Road, which follows the ancient city wall. Liang Sicheng, founder of Tsinghua's School of Architecture, tried to save the wall, but Chairman Mao was opposed to preservation.

Mao wanted to do away with the past and have the wall replaced with modern factories. We pass one of the city's original main gates. Professor Yang explains that the ideal traditional Chinese cities had twelve gates. *Kao Gong Ji* (translated as *The Craftsmen's Record* or *The Book of Diverse Crafts*) is a book about craftsmanship, including the building craft. The book describes city-making principles, making it the oldest statement on urban planning in China and hence one of the first in the world. From the Zhou Dynasty (770–221 BC), the book established principles for the ideal city, which would consist of nine square LI, the traditional Chinese distance measurement. Each LI unit is approximately 0.3 miles (0.5 km). Therefore, the ideal city dimension should be 3 x 3 LI (or 0.9 x 0.9 miles or 1.5 x 1.5 km). Each side of this square city was to have three gates. Thanks to Liang Sicheng, the gate we pass and a few others are preserved.

We visited the Confucian Temple and traditional *hutong* (narrow streets or alleys) neighborhoods. The alignment of traditional courtyard houses, *siheyuan*, form the *hutong* alleyways. These neighborhoods date back to the Yuan Dynasty in the thirteenth century. Traditionally, Yuan *siheyuan* were occupied by a single family. This changed during the Communist era when three or four families moved in, and the neighborhoods began to grow denser. Now, they are threatened by demolition and gentrification. Beijing declared twenty-five *hutong* neighborhoods preservation areas, but still many of these traditional courtyard housing areas are being replaced by new development.

In one *hutong* neighborhood, we visit the Confucian Temple, part of the Imperial College. Construction of the temple began in 1302 and was completed in 1306. Inside the temple courtyard is a seven-hundred-year-old cypress tree from the Yuan Dynasty (Figure 17.18). Because of its imperial past, the temple had declined since 1949. However, at the time of my visit, there was considerable restoration going on in preparation for the forthcoming Olympics. The Confucian Temple and the Imperial College seemed like long dormant seeds coming to life again with the coming Olympics and the thrust of visitors to glimpse into China's deep past.

A bike cab takes us through the gray *hutong* (Figure 17.19). Ordinary people could only use gray for their buildings. Golden yellow was reserved for the emperor. High officials could use red and blue. Except for the *hutong* neighborhoods, much of Beijing is now gold, yellow, red, and blue.

We stop at the courtyard house, also under reconstruction, of Yang Changji, Chairman Mao's teacher and first father-in-law. The typical *siheyuan* has a tree in the courtyard, surrounded by living quarters. As we travel through the neighborhood, I notice communal toilets. Blackboards around the neighborhood are used for official messages and, in Chairman Mao's time, his messages.

## TEACHING FROM A GREEN BOOK

I explore with the studio students how human ecological concepts like habitat, community, landscape, and region might be used with the Three Hills and Five Gardens study area. Different human habitats are prevalent in the area, both historic and contemporary. Communities, such as Beiwu Village, with remnant connections to their recent agricultural past exist. Various landscapes can be found, such as the small mountains with the long views across smoggy Beijing and formal imperial gardens. The Three Hills and Five Gardens study area relates socially and environmentally to the Beijing metropolitan region. Traditionally, the area had been a refuge from urban life, a source of water, and a food source. Increasingly, the study area attracted new development and growth.

During my first visit to China, the student teams continue to refine their work. The nature team focuses on data mapping, nicely combined with site photos illustrating water issues. The students describe the geology, past mining activities, and rock outcrops. They observe that the site could be viewed as an ecotone between

**17.18** Tree in the courtyard of the Confucian Temple, Beijing. The temple was first built between 1302 and 1306, then expanded in 1906. Photograph by Frederick Steiner.

the mountains and the lowlands. The students explain hydrological systems from the national level to the scale of their site. In the summer, people escape the heat of Beijing for the Three Hills and Five Gardens study area because of its higher elevation, water, and vegetation. The nature team makes a nice start with vegetation, mapping plant communities and drawing a plant association structure, consisting of mountain, farm/golf, riparian (rivers and canals), and street vegetation. The students observe that the plant structure was becoming less diverse and simpler. They also collect considerable bird habitat information.

The culture team finds a terrific drawing of the study area from the early twentieth century, but still needs to map their information.

The socioeconomic team focuses on a survey that they had conducted at the Summer Palace. The team members conclude that it is a popular destination, but that tourists do not understand it as part of a larger system. Overall, they find general satisfaction among residents but also concerns about traffic, environmental quality, and rapid development. Like the tourists, residents do not see parts fitting into the larger whole. This group also surveys fellow School of Architecture students and again finds that the various elements of the site were not viewed as connected.

From reviewing the students' works, I identify a final studio challenge: the need to establish an

**17.19** Courtyard housing in Beijing's *hutong* neighborhoods experienced considerable change after 1949. The housing was subdivided to accommodate many families, and living conditions deteriorated. With China's economic growth, families moved into newer neighborhoods, and *hutongs* were destroyed. This destruction prompted a preservation movement. Now, many traditional courtyard houses are being restored and used for new purposes, such as the Ji House Hotel. Courtesy of Kong-Jian Yu.

identity for the study area. The studio can help establish an identity for the Three Hills and Five Gardens area.

## PROJECTS

The weather cools for my last full day in Beijing, but it is clear, and the breeze is fresh. The television reported that Typhoon Damrey had reached the China Coast and had resulted in nine deaths thus far.

The morning before I am to leave, Professor Yang, Dr. Liu, and Ms. Zhuang show me work from the department and the Institute of Resource Protection and Tourism (which Professor Yang directs). Their institute focuses on three types of work: general management plans; plans for protected area systems, including scenic areas; and world and national heritage areas.

First, the three faculty members review the body of work that Professor Yang had conducted since 1997, often with The Nature Conservancy, in Yunnan Province. Their overarching goal was to

create a protected area system of national parks and other conserved places. The first project was for Meili Snow Mountain National Park on the border with Tibet, covering 606 square miles (1,570 km²). The area has rich cultural sites and widespread poverty. Dr. Yang shows me a number of photographs, several of which he has taken himself, which display considerable beauty (Figure 17.20). The institute team developed a 2002 management plan, which created management zones with 245 subareas and 18 policies (Figure 17.21).

Next, Professor Yang's team review their 2004 Yellow Mountain Plan in Anhui Province. The plan covered 59 square miles (152 km²), plus a buffer area. The area attracts some 1.3 million annual visitors to this culturally significant mountain. Hotels at the top and three cable car lines detract from the mountain's scenic and natural qualities. Differences exist over protection and development, resulting in conflicts among national, provincial, and local officials. Against the advice of his national sponsors, Professor Yang sought out the opinions of the local people who were

**17.20** Sacred Mountain from General Management Plan for Meili Snow Mountain National Park. Plan by Tsinghua University Urban Planning and Design Institute. Photograph by Yang Rui (2001).

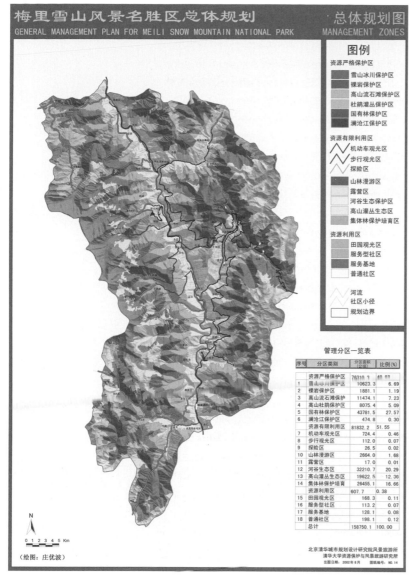

梅里雪山风景名胜区总体规划　·总体规划图
GENERAL MANAGEMENT PLAN FOR MEILI SNOW MOUNTAIN NATIONAL PARK　MANAGEMENT ZONES

图例

资源严格保护区
■ 雪山冰川保护区
■ 裸岩保护区
■ 高山流石滩保护区
■ 杜鹃灌丛保护区
■ 国有林保护区
■ 澜沧江保护区

资源有限利用区
〜 机动车观光区
〜 步行观光区
〜 探险区
■ 山林漫游区
□ 露营区
□ 河谷生态保护区
■ 高山灌丛生态区
■ 集体林保护培育区

资源利用区
■ 田园观光区
■ 服务型社区
■ 服务基地
□ 普通社区

〜 河流
〜 社区小径
□ 规划边界

N

0 1 2 3 4 5 Km

（绘图：庄优波）

管理分区一览表

| 序号 | 分区类别 | 分区面积（公顷） | 比例（%） |
|---|---|---|---|
| | 资源严格保护区 | 76310.1 | 48.07 |
| 1 | 雪山冰川保护区 | 10623.3 | 6.69 |
| 2 | 裸岩保护区 | 1881.1 | 1.19 |
| 3 | 高山流石滩保护 | 11474.1 | 7.23 |
| 4 | 高山杜鹃保护区 | 8075.4 | 5.09 |
| 5 | 国有林保护区 | 43781.5 | 27.57 |
| 6 | 澜沧江保护区 | 474.8 | 0.30 |
| | 资源有限利用区 | 81832.2 | 51.55 |
| 7 | 机动车观光区 | 724.4 | 0.46 |
| 8 | 步行观光区 | 112.0 | 0.07 |
| 9 | 探险区 | 26.5 | 0.02 |
| 10 | 山林漫游区 | 2664.0 | 1.68 |
| 11 | 露营区 | 17.0 | 0.01 |
| 12 | 河谷生态 | 32210.7 | 20.29 |
| 13 | 高山灌丛生态 | 19622.5 | 12.36 |
| 14 | 集体林保护培育 | 26455.1 | 16.66 |
| | 资源利用区 | 607.7 | 0.38 |
| 15 | 田园观光区 | 168.3 | 0.11 |
| 16 | 服务型社区 | 113.2 | 0.07 |
| 17 | 服务基地 | 128.1 | 0.08 |
| 18 | 普通社区 | 198.1 | 0.12 |
| | 总计 | 158750.1 | 100.00 |

北京清华城市规划设计研究院风景旅游所
清华大学资源保护与风景旅游研究所
出图日期：2002年8月　图纸编号：NO.14

**17.21** Management Zones for General Management Plan for Meili Snow Mountain National Park Plan by Tsinghua University Urban Planning and Design Institute.

and culturally significant sites than by degrading those sites for short-term profit.

Professor Yang asks me to contribute a page to a memory book that he had started for the new department. Laurie Olin and Richard Forman's remarks precede mine. This is what I write:

*Without a doubt, China will play a central role in this first urban century. That role might well be one of leadership. To be a leader in this first urban century, any person or nation will need to help the world to understand how to preserve our natural capital, to advance our social capital, and to expand our economic capital. Landscape planning provides the knowledge capital for creating a world that is more equitable, just, healthy, and beautiful. Landscape architecture and landscape planning can help us preserve our natural and cultural heritages, restore the wounds we have inflicted on the earth, and create living landscapes for the future.*

*The establishment of a new graduate degree in landscape architecture is an exciting and worthwhile endeavor. Tsinghua has established a strong bedrock of faculty and students, augmented by an international cast of visitors, led by Professor Laurie Olin. The seeds have been planted for success. The undertaking now requires nurture and care and continued innovation. I am honored to be a part of the process.*

The death toll and economic losses continue to rise in southern China and northern Vietnam as a result of Typhoon Damrey.

We fly back across the darkness and the international date line.

My return trip to China begins on Monday, June 19, 2006, with a 9 a.m. American Airlines flight from Austin to Los Angeles, several hours of layover, then a China Eastern Airlines flight to Shanghai. The next day, I clear customs in Shanghai, which now includes an extra form about avian flu. By the time I reach Beijing, the journey has taken more than twenty-four hours.

With flowers and smiles, He Rui and Mr. Wang greet me and take my bags. We drive on empty expressways through an uncharacteristically quiet city. After twenty minutes, we arrive at the Tsinghua Big Yard. I am deposited well after midnight

opposed to his team's plan. When he suggested the removal of hotels from the mountaintop, Professor Yang became even less popular with local and provincial officials. He argued that Yellow Mountain was a national or even international treasure and that Chinese officials should consider their children and their grandchildren's interests. A local official noted that the outbreak of Severe Acute Respiratory Syndrome (SARS) had hurt tourism and that Professor Yang "was worse than SARS." In the end, Yang was able to win over the local people through determination and logic, and now his team is engaged in several local plans. He was able to show local officials that they had more to gain from protecting environmentally in a second-floor apartment in the building next to where I had stayed the previous September. I hang the flowers upside down on the coat rack in the hall to dry.

After a long, deep sleep, I awake on Wednesday and begin to renavigate Chinese life. The layout of the apartment and the furniture is similar to my previous Beijing apartment. He Rui provides me with juice and bread; the university with toiletries. I do not remember how to work the hot water, which requires turning on the gas. I am afraid if I turn the gas knob the wrong direction, the apartment will explode. I turn on CCTV 9, hoping for World Cup scores, but instead am greeted with a report on avian flu.

The sound of children from the nearby school fills the air. Inside the apartment, it is warm but not uncomfortable, with a gentle breeze demonstrating the benefits of natural cross-ventilation. When I go outside, I feel the heat. My eyes water from pollution. Women carry parasols to shade themselves. A few cyclists wear masks to filter the bad air. I walk across campus to my temporary office in the architecture school (Figure 17.22).

## TSINGHUA SCHOOL OF ARCHITECTURE

At the entry to the School, the six graduating landscape architecture thesis projects are exhibited. As I inspect the boards, one of those students, Lu Han, greets me warmly. She guides me through the projects, five of which evolved from the Three Hills and Five Gardens fall studio. Lu Han had designed a bike route for the area, building on Professor Yang Rui's reminiscences from his student days cycling through the area to Fragrant Hill. Other students had redesigned the lands around the Beiwu Village and the Summer Palace entry area. Que Zhenqing's design addressed the canal system. I recall the walks and talks from my previous visit. Que's solution displayed considerable ecological thought and design ability. In addition to Laurie Olin, Andropogon's Colin Franklin, Colgate Searle of the Rhode Island School of Design, and Ron Henderson (a landscape architect from Rhode Island and Olin protégé) had been visiting faculty for students' thesis committees. Que's project received a 2007 American Society of Landscape Architects (ASLA) student award, one of only six selected internationally in the design category. Overall, the quality of the work was high and displayed both Chinese and American influences. Que's design reflected his Chinese professors' understanding of the history and culture connected with the canal system of the Three Hills and Five Gardens area, as well as the design and representational skills taught by Olin and the American professors (Figure 17.23).

Yang Rui and I meet Dean Zhu Wenyi and my Austin colleague Ming Zhang for dinner at a restaurant across campus. The chain restaurant is called Wahaha, which means "small body laugh loudly"; the particular Wahaha where we have dinner is named Zuiai, which translates to "Drunk Love." My hosts explain that the food is from a region near Shanghai and is thus mild.

We discuss what it means to be a "world class" university (a goal of Tsinghua's president, as if being the best or one of the best in China was not in itself "world class"), the problems of ranking systems, and various architects, including Zaha Hadid and Paolo Soleri. Most of the academic programs of Tsinghua and its rival Peking University, including architecture and planning, have strong American roots and thus similarities with American theory and practices. The ties between the nations were strained after 1949, but never completely broken. Certainly, there were strong Soviet influences from the 1950s through the 1980s. However, the current academic exchanges are especially strong again with the United States, Canada, Japan, and the European Union.

At 9 p.m., Professor Yang drops me back at my apartment where a man greets me to turn on gas for hot water. I awake at 5 a.m. on Thursday morning and call Austin to check in. I smell gas in the apartment, but the warm water in the shower feels good.

During this visit, I adjust more to local, more casual dress (and the weather). I wear more short-sleeve shirts. During my previous visit, it was always coat and tie.

**17.22** Tsinghua University campus. Photograph by Frederick Steiner.

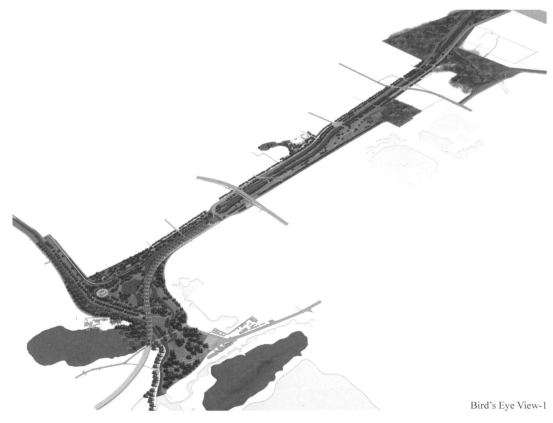

**17.23** Bird's-eye view of Que Zhenqing's master's thesis project. Courtesy of Que Zhenqing.

Bird's Eye View-1

I walk to the office at 7 a.m., noticing changes along the way. The schoolchildren now wear summer uniforms: purple shorts, white shirts, and a red bandana. As I enter the Tsinghua School of Architecture, I notice a young woman with a digital camera taking pictures of the first landscape architecture graduates' exhibit.

I am scheduled to give four lectures during this visit, including two on Italian gardens. The audience includes landscape architecture, architecture, and planning students and faculty from Tsinghua and other universities, as well as practicing designers and planners. I spend much of the rest of the day in the slide library, the School's library, and Googling Italian gardens. I receive many e-mail messages about the Lady Bird Johnson Wildflower Center becoming part of the University of Texas.

## WU LIANGYONG

Around 4 p.m., Ming Zhang and Yang Rui come by my office with Wu Liangyong, "the most distinguished architect and planner in China." He had been away from Beijing during my previous visit. When Liang Sicheng founded the School as a department in 1946, Wu Liangyong became its first faculty member and has been with the university ever since.[4] He recalls several previous unsuccessful attempts to begin a landscape architecture program at Tsinghua.

In 1951, Wu Liangyong met the American landscape architect Tommy Church in San Francisco. Church showed him some projects in the Bay Area. Wu returned to China with a desire to start a landscape architecture degree program within the School of Architecture, but "politics intervened," and contact was cut off with his new American friend. In the early 1990s, Wu tried again to initiate a program with Lynn Miller and his Penn State colleagues. That effort fell short as well.

Professor Wu was clearly happy that a department had been established at Tsinghua and that so many others are being created throughout the nation. "We need landscape architecture to lead the way to solve our regional environmental issues—no other discipline is so well equipped," he declared. "Landscape ecology and landscape planning are crucial for China's future."

## CUAN DI XIA VILLAGE AND TAN ZHE TEMPLE

At 7:30 a.m. on Saturday morning, in a light rain, I meet other "overseas teachers" at Er Xiao Men Gate, the main ceremonial entry to the university, for a field trip to Cuan Di Xia Village and Tan Zhe Temple in the Mentougou District, west of Beijing.

As we step on the bus, we receive a light snack of crackers and wrapped fruit-flavored candies, plus a bottle of water. Thunder threatens but as we move away from Tsinghua, the storm dissipates. Most of the bus passengers are Chinese or of Chinese descent. The rest are from Germany, Italy, Russia, and the United States. Several families joined the field trip, and the children know each other from the Tsinghua primary school. We travel on the West Fifth Ring Road into small mountains topped with pagodas and castles.

As we weave around slower trucks, I realize how impossible this trip would have been a few decades ago. I see a couple playing badminton outside and remember a fellow Cincinnati student, John Tannehill, who helped break down the first Cold War barriers in 1971 through ping-pong diplomacy.

We pass through the immense western suburbs of Beijing, complete with a Sam's Club and a Communist Party compound in a neo-Mussolini style. At a traffic light, the bus pulls up beside a small blue car with a young couple. The woman hands her companion a lint remover. He peels off a layer and throws it out onto the street. He then methodically cleans the lint off his black pants.

Some people sleep on the bus. The kids play in the aisle and in their seats. We pass a huge factory, then a big power plant with two large cooling towers and a third relatively smaller one. The two young girls seated next to me know how to hang their snack bags on a small hook on the seats in front of them. I follow their example. An obviously learning-from-Las-Vegas disco club, with a grotesque, five-story tall crescent façade, appears on the left.

Our bus climbs into higher mountains, these with almost vertical strata. Small garden plots are carved into terraces up the slopes. The river valleys contain little water for long stretches. The scarce water collects in highly eutrophied small ponds along the river. We come upon another power plant, then an expansive reservoir, one of the reasons for the dry river valley at lower elevations. The reservoir appears below capacity, but that does not dissuade the many fishers from flocking to its bank. Vineyards and larger irrigated fields line the highway.

A boy on our bus gets carsick and is attended to by half a dozen adults. Our journey is delayed by a wreck. A badly damaged car is being pulled from a ditch. It had hit a small blue bus. The car's windshield appears to have been hit by the driver's head, but no one along the road appears injured. We pass a sign welcoming us to a "scenic spot," followed by several acres of land scraped bare.

After a cursory security review, we enter Cuan Di Xia Village, which features the country cousins of the urban *hutong* neighborhoods, traditional quadrangle-courtyard housing from the Ming and Qing Dynasties (Figure 17.24). Our two-hour trip from Beijing had taken three hours, so we hurry into the hilly village with busloads of other visitors. Terraces along the slopes indicate the village's agricultural heritage. The current cash crop appears to be tourists.

The village's name means "under the stove," and we eat a "farmer's lunch" in the courtyard of a quadrangle house. The male proprietor looks as though he is indeed a farmer who had recently been out in the field. His are the dirtiest hands of any server I had ever encountered, which causes me some concern as he distributes the double plastic cups for our tea. But he is generous with the beer, which he appears to enjoy himself. The woman of the house keeps the dishes coming in rapid succession, threatening to overload our flimsy table.

We eat from twelve dishes, plus rice, soup, and fried cornbread that tastes like hush puppies. As we leave the house/restaurant, we find Cuan Di Xia Village, a popular destination for Chinese tourists, even more crowded. We depart into the smog after noon toward the Tan Zhe Temple.

**17.24** Cuan Di Xia Village near Beijing provides examples of well-preserved, quadrangle courtyard housing typical of the Ming and Qing Dynasties. Photograph by Frederick Steiner.

We proceed parallel to the river, which is again crowded with Saturday refugees from the city. Many people fish; others just play in the water. Colorful flags and banners mark picnic and parking areas.

We go back through the western suburbs, full of men with no shirts, women in uniforms, cyclists, watermelon stands, taxis, McDonald's restaurants, and high rises, before returning again to the mountains. Passing beekeepers and several incense stands, we arrive at the seventeen-hundred-year-old Buddhist Tan Zhe Temple. Within the temple walls, many vendors sell things—incense, cards, wall hangings, little Buddhas—that bring good fortune, happiness, and fertility. Men offer small caged birds. If they are set free, good luck is ensured. This seems good for the birds, until I realize that they are probably recaught, then recycled for another seeker of a bright future. After an hour of climbing and picture-taking, we return to our bus.

We arrive back at Tsinghua at 5:30 p.m. The light rain returns as I walk to my office to check e-mail. The storm grows more serious as I leave the school for the apartment. The lightning becomes so intense that I take refuge in the shopping center, where a friendly vendor offers me a chair to ride out the storm. I feel for the guys selling watermelons under tarps next to the power substation across the road.

Back in the dry apartment, I turn on CCTV 5 to find a five-year-old overweight boy with a Mohawk playing drums in a pulsating light display with an appreciative audience waving light sabers to the beat.

## AROUND THE BIG YARD OF THE BIG SCHOOL

I awake early Sunday morning. As I take pictures of the gate into my apartment compound, the local Communist Party representative, who usually sits in the small gatehouse, arrives. She's curious but smiles a tacit approval. I take a picture of her blackboard with various announcements.

I walk on the road between the gray brick primary school compound and the adjacent sports field. It is a bit after 7 a.m., but many people are jogging, walking, skipping rope, and exercising. The school grounds are much neater than the surrounding neighborhoods. The school buildings are sturdy and handsome. The Chinese have invested more in their schools than their homes. A boy with a French horn and his mother arrive, then a teacher for a Sunday morning lesson.

At the senior center, a group of mostly women participate in a coordinated exercise with poles. After the primary school, the red brick senior center is the most solid building in the neighborhood. A bird whistles and a human passerby answers his call. Three types of housing dominate the Big Yard: large pre-Revolution courtyard homes for professors, *hutong*-like neighborhoods with smaller homes, and large Socialist-era apartment blocks (Figure 17.25). The larger courtyard houses have been converted for institutional uses. The *hutong*-like areas are used for poorer residents of the Big Yard. Most residents, including me, live in the apartments, which are quite pleasant. Some faculty members now rent out their apartments within the Big Yard and live outside in newer, more spacious housing.

I walk through a small park that leads to the shopping center. A man with a sophisticated electronic gadget is listening to American business news. In the back of a bank, several heavily armed guards supervise the transfer of money into a fortified truck. People walk their small dogs. All the dogs in Beijing seem small. I later learn that dog size is regulated by district location. In the city's main districts, such as Haidian, Dongcheng, and Chaoyang, households are limited to one dog (the one dog policy), 14 inches (35 cm) at the shoulders. Outside these central districts, the dog can be larger although the size is determined by each district. The precedent for this law dates back to the time of the empire, which explains the size and shape of the Pekinese. After the rains, the weather is pleasant, almost cool.

I return to the apartment to fetch some papers I forgot in the morning. I decide to take a different route through a five-story apartment block neigh-

**17.25** Tsinghua University neighborhood. Photograph by Frederick Steiner.

borhood dating from the 1950s to the 1960s. The architecture appears similar to other Socialist-planned neighborhoods from the same era: the same factory-like architecture that can be found in, for example, Warsaw. However, the common areas are generous, and the buildings are sited to take advantage of wind flows and solar access. Around the corner from where I am staying (and where I stayed last time), I discover a small shopping area with a restaurant, a grocery store, and an Internet café.

Back in my office, I write about Giacomo Barozzi da Vignola and Andrea Palladio for my lectures on Italian design; my Chinese hosts expect me to fill some gaps in design history. I recall my memorable evening at Fanzolo di Vedelago with Count Emo, owner of the Palladio-designed Villa Emo. He explained the challenges of keeping the complete villa—the main palace, the auxiliary buildings, the adjacent *borgo* (town), the farm fields, and the irrigation systems—together. Count Emo explained that it was much easier to pass art objects from generation to generation than architecture or landscapes. Especially landscapes, he noted.

Meanwhile, the storm returns to Beijing. By the time I walk back to the apartment, the rain slows to a sprinkle. With the generous canopy over the Tsinghua campus, I keep mostly dry.

A bird begins an unfamiliar call before dawn. In the distance, I hear a faint response. After a while, their conversation is joined by other sounds, other conversations.

The schoolchildren sing their national anthem, as I brush my teeth. I leave a little later than normal and notice all the gates to the primary school are shut. Clearly, tardiness is not tolerated. The school is like a cocoon within the walls of the Big Yard.

A group constructs a full-scale replica of a traditional Chinese building in the atrium of the School of Architecture. Yang Rui gives me a book on the painting, *Qing Ming Shang He Tu*, which is a reproduction of an ancient Chinese landscape scroll (Figure 17.26). "An original living landscape," Professor Yang observes. In the painting, *Qing Ming* refers to a Chinese lunar festival. (*Tu* means "drawing"; *He* means "river"; and *Shang* means "go up.") The scroll depicts a transect, painted by Zhang Zeduan about 980 years ago, from rural to urban, long before the Scottish

biologist and town planner Patrick Geddes' valley section diagram illustrating similar relationships. The drawing describes lively street life and the commercial prosperity along the Bian River, part of China's Grand Canal. Rural-to-urban activities are shown during the Qing Ming Festival in the capital city at the time, Bian Liang, in the Song Dynasty, on both sides of the river canal.

China remains as dynamic as this almost thousand-year-old image. The past shown in *Qing Ming Shang He Tu* is not a romantic, bucolic scene; rather, it is a real slice of life, full of hardworking people. The vibrant population remains, but upon looking closer, one sees what is lost or is being lost. The prime farmland around cities is converted for other uses; the clear views are clouded by haze and/or huge billboards; waters are becoming scarcer and more polluted; buildings and bridges at a human scale are becoming quaint relics. There is hope, however, because a growing number of Chinese recognize these problems.

With He Rui and two AV specialists, I practice my slides. I feel old-fashioned using a slide projector, but I like the quality of transparencies. No one has asked me to give a lecture about the Italian landscape in a while, so I have never scanned those slides.

## ITALY IN CHINA

At 2:30 p.m., I give my first lecture explaining how Italian landscapes are connected to architecture and agriculture, as well as to urbanism and the countryside. I note that Italian garden design is generally identified as one of the three main styles—the others are Chinese and English. I question if a fourth is emerging—an international ecological style, which is place-based, connected to regionalism, and accounts for change over time. I review the Greek influence on the Romans and, in turn, the Roman influence on the Italian Renaissance. I show slides of several key sites from the Roman antiquity, including Hadrian's Villa, a Greek theater in Sicily, the Colosseum, Rome's port city Ostia Antica, and Pompeii. I review the transition between the medieval period and the Renaissance, as well as the Medici's influence in Florence, then Rome. I explain the competing Gothic style in the north of Italy with examples from Milan and discuss these competing styles in the context of the Reformation and the Counter-Reformation. I spend some time on two major Renaissance works in Rome, the Campidoglio and St. Peter's Basilica. I then explore three gardens from the Italian Renaissance—Villa Madama (by Raphael and his students), Villa Farnese at Caprarola (by Vignola), and Villa d'Este (by Ligorio)—and the connections between buildings and gardens.

I introduce the Latin word *otium*, or refined leisure. Clearly, this was not a form of leisure available to all in either ancient Rome or sixteenth- and seventeenth-century Italy. However, the concept of *otium* contributes to our modern notions of vacations and recreation. I conclude by discussing the three principal design features advanced in Italian Renaissance garden design: the geometrical arrangement of plants, the imaginative use of water, and the deployment of space, using axes and vocal points. The lecture goes well, but I could have used more images. The discussion session that follows is the best I have had so far in China. The discussion involves our relationship to nature, the relationship of architecture to landscape, and order in gardens and in cities.

I go home, take off my tie, and put on shorts. The toilet is acting up, always a challenge in a foreign place. The gas smell seems stronger.

Storms sweep through Beijing during the night, making the walk to work Tuesday morning quite pleasant. I notice two things on my walk from the southwest portion of the campus to the southeast. First, many more mixed activities are permitted in streets and on walkways than zoning allows in the United States. Cars, buses, bikes, and pedestrians intermingle freely, yet fiercely. Second, a block from the primary school, a policeman directs cars away from the street leading to the school, thus creating a safe zone with few automobiles. Parents drop their children off at this point, and the kids walk the rest of the way.

That afternoon, I give my second lecture about the Italian landscape. This time I show more Italian villas, including three Palladian ones in the Veneto, which, removed from the papal politics of Rome, tended to be working farms or suburban

retreats. I speak briefly about my time with the last Count Emo, looking at his fields and pump station.

I introduce the English landscape school as a counterpoint to the Italian Renaissance garden, quoting Alexander Pope, who wrote:

*To build, to plant, whatever you intend,*
*To rear the column or the arch to bend,*
*To swell the terrace, or to sink the grot;*
*In all, let Nature never be forgot,*
*Consult the genius of the place in all, . . .*

What we find in England, is the rise of empiricism. That is, nature is not fixed, as in the pattern books in Italy, but in flux. The result is an argument for irregularity in contrast to the rigid geometry expressed in the Italian garden or, on an even grander scale, in France. The three principal proponents of the English landscape school were William Kent, Lancelot "Capability" Brown, and Humphry Repton. Horace Walpole said that William Kent was "born with a genius to strike out a great system from the twilight of imperfect essays. He leaped the fence and saw that all of nature was garden." This sums up nicely a contribution to the English landscape movement (Figure 17.27).

**17.27** View of Turf Bridge in Stourhead Gardens, England. Designed by Henry Hoare II, 1741–1765. Photograph by Mirka Beneš.

I explain the American Academy in Rome, which was founded in 1894 by Charles McKim, Daniel Burnham, Andrew Carnegie, J. P. Morgan, John D. Rockefeller, William Vanderbilt, and Henry Clay Frick—in other words, the two leading American architects of the time and the richest men in the nation. It was modeled after the French Academy and is similar to several other national academies in Rome, including the British School at Rome, the German Academy, the Spanish Academy, the Dutch Academy, and others. The American Academy was inspired by Burnham and Stanford White, who had worked together with artists and landscape architects on the World's Columbian Exposition, or the Chicago World's Fair, of 1893.

The purpose of the Academy is to encourage the study of art, architecture, and the humanities amid the classical tradition of ancient Rome and the Renaissance. One part of the Academy focuses on the arts, the other on the humanities. Each year, it awards around thirty Rome Prizes to Fellows of the Academy, granting a period of residency for six months to two years. Arts prizes are awarded in architecture, landscape architecture, design, historic preservation, literature, musical composition, and the visual arts. In the humanities, Rome Prizes are awarded for archaeology, medieval studies, Renaissance and early modern studies, and modern Italian studies. In addition to Fellows, the Academy hosts senior scholars, or Residents.

The Academy is situated on the highest point within the walls on the Janiculum Hill. The two main centers are a McKim, Mead, and White–designed building and the nearby Villa Aurelia with generous grounds accompanying both buildings. A list of former Fellows includes a Who's Who in American architecture and landscape architecture, including, for example, Louis Kahn, Robert Venturi, Michael Graves, Laurie Olin, and Dan Kiley. I urge my Tsinghua colleagues, considered the elites of their nation, to lead the establishment of something similar in China.

I conclude my lecture with images of Rome and the Italian countryside and add a few remarks about my research in Italy, which focused on con-

temporary design and planning. Like the Chinese, the Italians have an ancient tradition of urban planning. They also developed a style of garden design in the Renaissance, which has been applied to cities and is evident in Paris, Washington, D.C., and elsewhere. Since the early twentieth century, the Italians have enacted good city planning laws and progressive statutes for the preservation of monuments important for their cultural heritage, and since the 1970s, they have put in place measures for planning river basins and regions.

Missing, however, were measures to protect landscapes. Beginning in the 1990s, a new Italian law required plans for provinces (roughly parallel to American counties). The Italians face similar challenges as the United States and China, ranging from water supply to air quality to suburban sprawl issues. They have made a good start and have a strong heritage to build on, as do the Chinese people.

Walking home after the lecture, I am joined by Dr. Liu Hailong, who said he enjoyed my talk (he was being generous) and asked, "As an ecologist, what do you really think about Italian gardens?"

Clearly, I admit, they are not ecological. But, I respond to Dr. Liu, Italian gardens are interesting from an ecological perspective, if viewed in the context of their topographic setting, their water supply, their relationship to villa buildings and villa functions, and how they interact with surrounding human settlements and the countryside. Plus, they are important to cultural heritage. Italian gardens are simply delightful to experience, marvels of human ingenuity.

Later, walking alone, I realize the classic Italian garden provides ideas and inspiration that can be adapted for contemporary designs and plans, even ecological ones.

In spite of another storm, the night is muggy. The mosquitoes discover that I am in Beijing and feast on my arms and legs.

### THE OLYMPICS

The next day, I meet Professor Hu Jie for lunch. He is the chief landscape architect for Beijing Olympic Forest Park, so we talk about the construction process on our walk across from the campus through the Tsinghua Science Park to the "Drunk Love" restaurant with a big golden Buddha in its lobby. During my previous visit, he had sought my advice about how to make a "green" bridge over the Fifth Ring Road more ecological. I advised him to make the green areas as wide as possible so that animals could cross.

Over watermelon juice, a chicken dish, shrimp, vegetables, and a fried pastry, Hu Jie and I discuss publication plans for the Olympic Forest Park project. He would like to have it published in *Landscape Architecture* magazine and present it at the national ASLA conference. Already the project has been published several times in the *Chinese Landscape Architecture* magazine and he has plans for a book. I commit to reading his paper and helping with ASLA. Hu Jie invites me to visit the Olympic Forest Park the following day. In the end, I write the article for *Landscape Architecture*.[5]

Change is not an abstract phenomenon in China. The Chinese understand the dual nature of change: opportunity and danger. Both can be seen in Beijing today. Air pollution can literally be seen on most days. Traffic clogs city streets, with cars and trucks competing with bikes, pedestrians, carts, and donkeys. As once plentiful groundwater sources dry up at a pace of almost a meter a year, water quality degrades. One estimate says that living in Beijing is like smoking seventy cigarettes a day.

Landscape architecture plays a mitigating role in the pollution challenges and the unbridled growth of Beijing. Olympic Green with the Beijing Olympic Forest Park provide a dramatic example of the positive contributions made by landscape architects. The 2.6 square-mile (6.8-km²) Olympic Forest Park, at twice the size of Central Park, is the largest public green space ever built in Beijing. The focus of recent open space development in Beijing has been on greenbelts associated with the construction of the ring roads (all plants, no people) and on street widening. There have been some new parks—most of them linear and associated with former walls and moats or as center-pieces of massive development projects.

Currently, only 41 square miles (107 km²) of parks and 111 square miles (287 km²) of other open space exists in a city of 17 million people, a number expected to exceed 21 million by 2020. Existing parks and open space are heavily used in Beijing. The magnificent Temple of Heaven park is less than half the size of Olympic Forest Park and attracts 17.8 million visitors (12.1 million Beijing residents and 5.7 million tourists) annually, or some 89,000 people a day. Chinese scholars note that the type and distribution of current parks is unreasonable, that connectivity is inadequate, and that there are simply not enough parks. Many Beijing citizens pursue recreation under highway cloverleaves. The green spaces associated with the Olympics elevate the level and quality of new parks in Beijing.

The overall master plan and park design evolved from a series of competitions. Sasaki Associates won the initial 2002 international open competition for the Olympic master plan (Figures 17.28 and 17.29). Unveiled in 2003, the new Olympic Green sought to transform the rapidly growing northern areas of Beijing.

"Our conceptual framework for the plan was developed quickly. Within a few days, we had established the organizing principles," said Alan Ward, who led Sasaki Associates' team with Dennis Pieprz. The basic structure of the plan placed the main stadium off-axis. The main north-south axis of the Olympic Green formed a continuation of Beijing's historic central axis. Ward notes that the scheme was influenced by traditional Chinese garden design, with mounded earth to the north beyond a foreground of water.

The Sasaki design proposal for the Olympic Green sought balance and integration. This balance was poetic and pragmatic. The design balanced East with West, the ancient with the contemporary, development with nature, existing surrounding context with its Olympic Green master plan. The Sasaki concept had three fundamental elements: the Forest Park, the Cultural Axis, and the Olympic Axis.

The Forest Park consists of an area of land north of the Olympic Green central area. According to the Sasaki master plan, the Forest Park was

Beijing Olympic Forest Park

Beijing Olympic Green Central Area

N

to be of grand dimensions, in many ways evoking in scale and function other great city parks of the world, such as the Bos in Amsterdam and Prospect Park in New York. The design of the Cultural Axis and its commemorative plaza in the master plan was intended to be contemporary in its actual expression, rather than a historic replication. The design was to illustrate the manner in which other peoples of the world have adapted to Chinese cultural achievements. Finally, the Sasaki master plan proposed an Olympic Axis that begins within the existing Asian Games stadium, extending northeast through the proposed national stadium, continuing onward to a sports heroes garden, intersecting with the Cultural Axis, then concluding within the Forest Park.

The Sasaki team working on the Olympic Green included the young designer Hu Jie, who had earned his Master of Landscape Architecture at the University of Illinois in 1995. A native of Beijing, Hu Jie was especially helpful with the con-

text and history of the Olympic site, as well as the translation of terms. Led by Ward, the Sasaki entry was also selected for the landscape competition in late 2003, as the basis for the overall landscape scheme.

After the competitions, realization and detailed design became the responsibility of Chinese landscape architects. Hu Jie returned from Boston to Tsinghua University to help establish a new graduate landscape architecture program and now directs the Landscape Design and Planning branch of Tsinghua's Urban Planning and Design Institute. In December 2003, the Beijing Municipal Commission of Urban Planning entrusted the Tsinghua Institute with the planning and the design of the Beijing Olympic Forest Park, the large northern portion of Sasaki's Olympic Green master plan. As a result, Hu Jie took lead responsibility for design, which he continued to have through implementation.

Although many of the new buildings that sprang up around Beijing could just as likely be in

**17.28** The master plan with Olympic Green and the Olympic Forest Park. Courtesy of Tsinghua University Urban Planning and Design Institute.

**17.29** Aerial view of the Olympic Green and the Olympic Forest Park. Courtesy of Tsinghua University Urban Planning and Design Institute.

Dallas or Dubai, the Olympic Forest Park is deeply rooted in the Chinese design tradition. Beginning with the framework established by Sasaki, Hu Jie advanced a distinctively Chinese aesthetic vocabulary with clear American landscape architecture references. Like other designers with cross-cultural backgrounds, Hu Jie was well prepared for this synthesis. In addition to his Sasaki and Illinois experience, he earned a master's degree in landscape architecture from the Beijing Forestry University and a bachelor's degree in architecture from the Chongqing Institute. Hu Jie grew up on the Tsinghua campus where his father was a professor of architecture.

The application of feng shui principles, such as a sheltering hill to the north, and the use of traditional elements, such as ceremonial rocks, reflect the Chinese grounding. The ecological considerations are more American, but then one could make a case that feng shui is a precursor to contemporary site planning and ecological design. "Although feng shui is not followed literally," Hu Jie notes, "its principles are respected and used for inspiration."

The Fifth Ring Road divides Olympic Forest Park into two parts. The northern portion is con-nected to the southern part by a green deck and two roadways under the ring road. The broad 2-acre (0.8-ha) deck, called the Ecological Corridor, includes considerable vegetation and provides connections for pedestrians, cyclists, and wildlife (Figure 17.30). In the northern portion, the plan emphasizes nature restoration. The goal is to recover regional ecosystems by retaining existing landforms and natural vegetation. Few facilities are provided, and visitation is controlled to maintain plant and animal habitat.

The southern portion of Olympic Forest Park, which opened after the Olympic Games, was designed for more active use and for connections with the main Olympic Village. The southern park includes the Olympic venues for tennis, archery, and hockey; the terminal station for the new subway from the historic center of Beijing to the Olympic sites (which may include a shopping venue in the future); and a large outdoor amphitheater. The terminal and amphitheater are located just south of the lake. However, the main features include a dragon-shaped, 301-acre (122-ha) lake and a hill with three peaks constructed with soil and debris from the lake. The main peak rises 158 feet (48 m) above the lake and is cen-

**17.30** Rendering of the Ecological Corridor, which provides a deck over the Fifth Ring Road and connects the northern and southern portions of the Olympic Forest Park. Courtesy of Tsinghua University Urban Planning and Design Institute.

17.31 Workers in 2008 at traditional Chinese rock garden on the main mountain peak at Olympic Forest Park in Beijing. Photograph by Frederick Steiner.

tered around the axis of the Olympic Park and of Beijing itself. A secondary peak southwest of the high point rises 92 feet (28 m) from the lake, with a third, 66 feet (20 m), farther to the southwest. Large granite stones top each peak (Figure 17.31).

As the park was being built, construction continued on the Water Cube and the Bird's Nest. The central spine of the Beijing Olympic Park and the major venues can be viewed from the dramatic, panoramic prospect below the giant rock on the main peak (Figure 17.32). Below the hill, the lake wraps around its base. Beyond the Olympic Village, a sea of construction cranes adorns the Beijing skyline beyond the park. The hillside is heavily planted, as are the banks of the lake. The lake and the vast tree plantations are essential components of the long-term contributions of the Olympic Forest Park (Figure 17.33).

The lake provides a model for water conservation (Figure 17.34). Reclaimed rain and flood water and reused water sources feed the lake. Constructed wetlands clean the water. Parallel water circulation systems replenish water for Beijing in dry seasons and discharge flood water in rainy seasons.

"Water in Beijing is a major challenge," Hu Jie observes. "The water recycling and water quality protection system for Forest Park was designed to become a model for the city."

The new forest will help ameliorate Beijing's climate and reduce the dust that plagues the city. Hu Jie and his team added many new trees and preserved significant clusters of existing trees, resulting in a total of 540,000 trees in the new park. As a consequence, the park featured mature vegetation the day it opened. (This strategy echoes Frederick Law Olmsted and Calvert Vaux's opening of Central Park.)

According to Wu Yixia, the project manager for the Olympic Forest Park, "We were amazed to discover egrets and many other birds in the park's new wetlands, as well as weasels, pheasants, and rabbits on the new mountain slopes. Watching these birds and animals colonize the parks is fulfilling for the design team."

The planting design advocated extensive use of native species with groves of canopy trees and a layer of shrubs massed below. The climate of Beijing can only sustain two plant ecology layers, so tree and shrub and shrub and ground cover strategies are used by landscape architects. Hu Jie

**17.32** The view southward from main mountain peak overlooking Olympic Forest Park's main lake and the Olympic venues with Beijing's skyline visible in the distance. Courtesy of Tsinghua University Urban Planning and Design Institute.

**17.33** Wooded area of Olympic Forest Park looking toward the main mountain peak. Courtesy of Tsinghua University Urban Planning and Design Institute.

and his principal colleagues Wu Yixia and Lu Lu Shan (chief engineer and senior architect) carefully combined these trees and shrubs to create seasonal landscapes (Figure 17.35). The planting plan emphasized the value for avian habitat, the reduction of urban heat islands, and the exchange of oxygen and carbon dioxide.

The Beijing Olympic Forest Park design follows ancient Chinese traditions. As Hu Jie observes, "Confucius connected mountains and waters with a person's character by saying that the benevolent person finds pleasure in mountains; the wise one in water."

The Olympic Forest Park contains ample inspiration for the benevolent and the wise. Over the past three decades, poverty in China fell significantly as environmental degradation skyrocketed. The Olympics offered hope.

As Alan Ward notes, "What happens after the Olympics is most important. Beijing is urbanizing rapidly. As Olmsted and Vaux got ahead of urban growth with Central Park as New York City grew north, so, too, do Olympic Green and the Olympic Forest Park help shape growth as Beijing grows north."

I believe the Bird's Nest will likely persist as an icon in Beijing over time. Even without a permanent use, it attracts thousands of visitors every day. I am less convinced when it comes to some of the other grand architectural monuments, such as OMA's contorted CCTV headquarters. I am confident that the Olympic Forest Park will continue to add great value for the citizens of Beijing for years to come. Families will enjoy a walk around the dragon-shaped lake beneath the giant trees at the base of the hill constructed for the 2008 Olympics.

17.34 The wetland in Olympic Forest Park. Courtesy of the Tsinghua University Urban Planning and Design Institute.

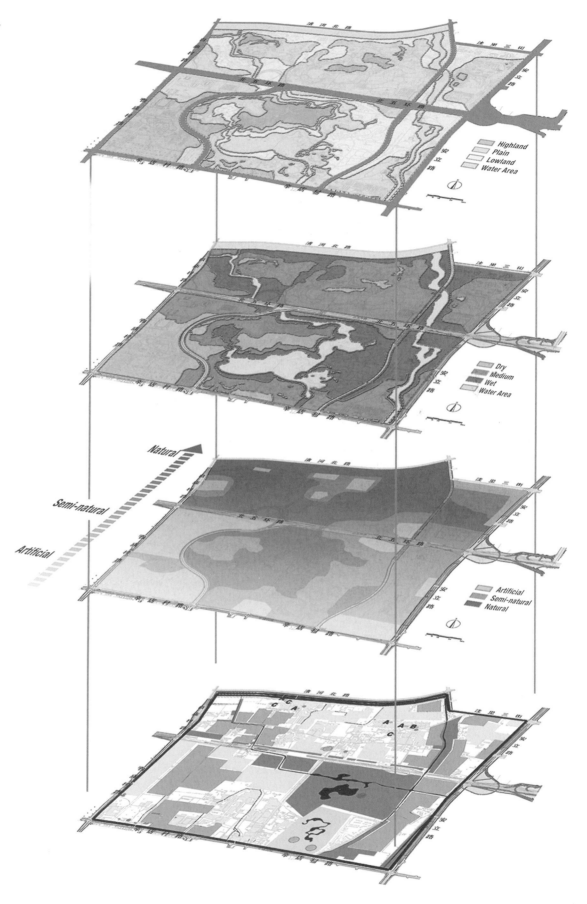

**17.35** An analysis of elevation, humidity, and planting of the Olympic Forest Park design, which included the preexisting site situation. Courtesy of the Tsinghua University Urban Planning and Design Institute.

Highland
Plain
Lowland
Water Area

Dry
Medium
Wet
Water Area

Natural

Semi-natural

Artificial

Artificial
Semi-natural
Natural

After my lunch with Hu Jie, I review several of the Three Hills and Five Gardens student studio projects from the previous fall semester. Although mostly presented in Chinese, the thought processes of the analyses are clear in the drawings and diagrams, as are the students' ideas for planning.

## STORM OF THE CENTURY

A big storm is expected. Professor Yang Rui said the largest rainfall in Beijing's history was predicted for this evening. He offers me a ride back to the apartment and suggests that we stop for some take-out dinner for me, so that I would not need to brave the storm later. I decline because my evening walks are refreshing. With umbrella in hand, I leave the campus for my favorite Hunan restaurant.

After dinner, I enter Beijing's storm of the century. Considerable, piercing rain falls, but fortunately, only sparse lightning strikes during my walk home. Back home, CCTV9 reports the second tropical storm of the season, Jelawat, is expected to affect the southern coast of China. The rains, indeed, come down all night and into the morning, but only a slight drizzle accompanies my walk to school the next morning.

## BEIJING PLANNING EXHIBITION HALL

Ming Zhang and I set off in a cab to the central city. Our first stop is the four-story Beijing Planning Exhibition Hall, which features gigantic models of the city as well as specific districts and projects. The Exhibition Hall occupies a prominent mid-town location, just east of the old Beijing Railway Station in the historic Qianmen neighborhood. It features a large bronze model of the city in 1949 and a 1:750 model of the city as it would become in 2008. This expansive model of the city consumes much of the third floor. One can view the 3,251-square-foot (302-m²) model from the fourth floor or walk around its edges on the third.

Nearly 1,000 lit glass floor panels over aerial photographs of the outer edges of the city form the walking platform. Sections of the city are removed for rebuilding, a constant undertaking.

The city's new central business district, an architects-gone-wild area east of the Forbidden City, has its own, separate wood model, as does the 2008 Olympic Village. The sheer scale of the current urban expansion astounds and numbs the senses for its audacity and ambition. The historic core with its monuments and *hutong* is encircled by high-rises that dwarf the once mighty walls, which defined the city.

The Exhibition Hall includes many galleries, which featured, during my visit, a dream Zaha Hadid apartment for Beijing's future; sculpture and other artworks for past and future Olympics; and a review of twenty years of cooperation between Tsinghua and MIT. Kevin Lynch of MIT began visiting Beijing in the early 1980s and conceived an urban design exchange. After Lynch's death, fellow MIT urban design professor and subsequent Penn School of Design dean Gary Hack and the venerable Tsinghua professor, Wu Liangyong, implemented the studio in 1985, which continues to the present.

The studios typically involve twenty MIT students from architecture, planning, and real estate with ten from Tsinghua's School of Architecture. In 1998 and 2000, Ming Zhang was the teaching assistant for the joint studio, and boards from those years' projects were included in the exhibition. The studio addressed the White Pagoda in 1998 and the Dongbuyaqiao neighborhood in 2000. Ming laments that those remained mostly academic exercises and were not implemented. Still, the works influenced the urban design and planning thinking in Beijing. Reviewing the wisdom and insight of these studios, I am left longing to see more of this type of sensitive place-making implemented by city officials and developers.

The concluding panel in the MIT exhibit features the calligraphy of Professor Wu Liangyong.

After my final lecture during this second visit, Yang Rui, Ming Zhang, and I pass the most recent addition to Tsinghua's white campus, the Sino-

Italian Energy Efficient Building, on our way to dinner. Financed by the Italian government and designed by Italian architect Mario Cucinella of Bologna, with the contribution, as project manager, of Federico Butera from the Milan Polytechnic, the building features a huge, north-facing blue wall. This "green" building showcases the potential for $CO_2$ emission reduction in Chinese architecture, but is visibly "blue" rather than "green" in the white campus. Ming explains that the Italian government donated the building. When Tsinghua officials objected to the blue wall, the Italians explained that was the architect's design. Either the university would accept the design or the Italians would withdraw their funding. The blue wall remains.

Sunny blue skies return to Beijing, as we taxi by the new Norman Foster–designed airport terminal being readied for the Olympics. By the time we leave Beijing at noon, smog blanketed the expansive metropolis. Over Japan, we have watermelon for dessert.

# VI | LEARNING FROM DISASTER

We are a resilient species. We employ design and planning as tools for resilience after disasters. Given the current state of our planet, we will need to refine those tools to ensure that we survive and thrive. September 11 and Hurricane Katrina illustrate the challenges we face and the necessity to respond to disasters, both human-induced and natural.

In anticipation of and in response to disaster, we can mitigate and adapt. Mitigation involves the moderation of the underlying causes of a disaster. Along the Gulf Coast, the protection of wetlands can moderate the force and the intensity of hurricanes.

Adaptation involves adjusting activities to specific uses and situations. Along the Gulf Coast, this includes redesigning houses and other structures so that they can better withstand storm surges. In addition, local ordinances can be adjusted to discourage inappropriate and risky land uses in hazard-prone areas.

The design of mitigation strategies and the planning of adaptation measures contribute to our resilience capacity. Healthy systems respond best. After all, health is the ability to recover from injury, disease, and insult. Resilient places are certainly sustainable. However, resiliency suggests an ability to move beyond sustainability. Systems that mitigate and adapt are regenerative. The design of such systems offers a significant opportunity for architects and planners.

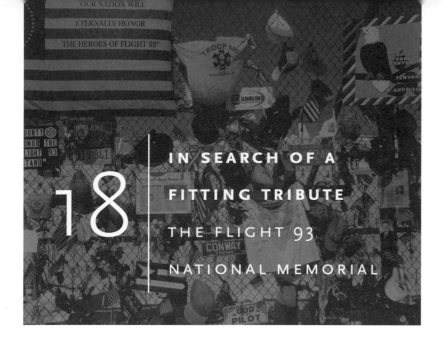

## IN SEARCH OF A FITTING TRIBUTE
### THE FLIGHT 93
### NATIONAL MEMORIAL

A s I sat in a February 2005 Landscape Architecture Foundation executive committee meeting in EDAW's sunny office in Miami Beach, a message reached me from Austin. Helene Fried, the competition advisor for the Flight 93 National Memorial, wanted me to call her in San Francisco.

On route from Newark International Airport to San Francisco, terrorists had taken control and diverted United Airlines Flight 93 toward Washington, D.C. The jet had crashed into a field in Somerset County in western Pennsylvania on September 11, 2001. Of the four planes hijacked that day, Flight 93 was the only one not to reach the terrorists' target. Most probably, the jet was brought down by the courageous acts of its passengers and crew, who had already learned about the other terrorist acts that autumn morning.

My brother John, an FBI agent in San Francisco, had been assigned to the case. I recall the days and nights he had devoted to the effort of piecing together what had occurred on that fateful flight. His involvement had inspired me to enter the competition.

I had never entered a design competition before, and I have a rather time-consuming day job, so as I studied the materials in the official competition packet, I realized I needed help. E. Lynn Miller was directing our new Master of Landscape Architecture (MLA) program and stay-ing at my house. At my red kitchen table, I asked him to join me and showed him my initial idea, which abstracted the flight path of the Boeing 757-200 airplane from Newark to San Francisco on its detour over the Cleveland metropolitan area, toward Washington, D.C., to its crash southeast of Pittsburgh near Shanksville, Pennsylvania. Lynn agreed with the concept, but, looking at my sketch, he tactfully suggested we seek more help, recommending our young colleague Jason Kentner, a lecturer in our new MLA program.

Lynn spent his career at Penn State, where Jason had earned his Bachelor of Landscape Architecture degree before going to Cambridge, Massachusetts, to work for Reed Hilderbrand and pursue his MLA at Harvard. Jason and Lynn possessed a wealth of knowledge about western Pennsylvania. Jason agreed to join Lynn and me.

The Pennsylvania Turnpike (Interstate 70/76) is near the crash site, connecting it with Pittsburgh to the west (an hour driving time) and Washington, D.C./Baltimore (three hours) to the east. According to the U.S. National Park Service, the site "is situated on the Allegheny Plateau between the Laurel Highlands and the Allegheny Mountains."[1] Its winters are cold and snowy with gusty winds.

Almost immediately after the crash and subsequent investigation and clean-up, a temporary memorial appeared, erected and maintained by

**18.1** Mementos left by visitors at the temporary Flight 93 memorial, Pennsylvania. Photograph by Frederick Steiner.

**18.2** Initial sketch for Flight 93 Memorial Competition entry by E. Lynn Miller for the finalist entry by the Jason Kentner, Karen Lewis, E. Lynn Miller, and Frederick Steiner team.

local residents in conjunction with family and friends of the victims (Figure 18.1). Family members also constructed small memorials at the crash site. By 2004, a national memorial had been proposed, which was endorsed by the secretary of the interior on January 14, 2005.

An area was designated for the memorial, which includes approximately 2,200 acres (890 ha), "of which about 1,355 acres (548 ha) include the crash site, the debris field, and the area where human remains were found and those lands necessary for visiting the national memorial."[2] The Park Service notes that the "site is composed of rolling hills dominated by the gentle ridge along its eastern ridge. The central portions of the site are overlain with rocky, thin topsoil that was placed over the site as part of the reclamation of previous bituminous coal strip mining."[3]

Fifty years of surface and subsurface mining significantly shaped and scarred the landscape. Mining buildings and equipment, as well as polluted ponds and soils, are scattered across the site. Two large mining draglines dominate the ridge around the bowl-shaped area that slopes down to the woody edge of the crash site.[4]

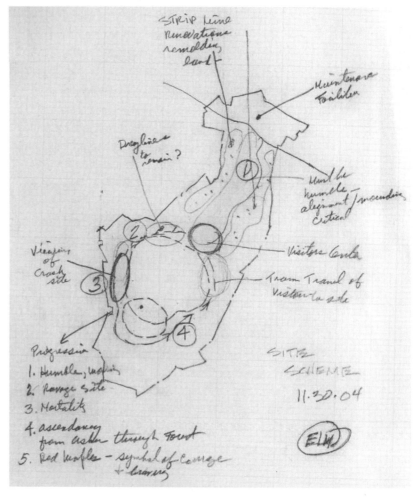

**18.3** A proposed visitor information center, Flight 93 Memorial Competition, finalist design entry by Jason Kentner, Karen Lewis, E. Lynn Miller, and Frederick Steiner. Courtesy of the National Park Service, Flight 93 National Memorial.

Jason, Lynn, and I met, and Lynn presented a scheme that used my concept of tracing the flight path, but he abstracted it substantially and fit the idea to the site (Figure 18.2). He suggested that we make the journey across the 2,200-acre (890-ha) site, the memorial. We discussed making the center for visitors the focus for interpretation. Jason suggested that we needed an architect on the team, especially because of the visitors' center, and he recommended Karen Lewis, whom he knew from Harvard.

Karen, then an architecture lecturer at the University of Kentucky, agreed and quickly we began to think of ourselves in terms of 3 plus 1. Three of us were located in Austin, one in Lexington; three men, one woman; three undergraduate degrees from public universities, one from a private college; three Harvard graduate degrees, one Penn; three from just west of the Appalachian Mountains, one from the East; three landscape architects (if I can be counted as one), one architect; and so on. The four of us came together in Austin over the semester break and into the 2005 new year to complete our entry by the January 11 deadline.

Although our ages range from the late twenties to the early seventies, we jelled quickly as a team.

We read everything we could about the passengers and crew of United Flight 93 and the ecology of the site. After several discussions, Karen produced a bold concept for the visitors' center (Figure 18.3). Purposefully alien to the strip-mined landscape, the space inside recalled the cramped interior of a jet plane. The visitor walked up a ramp that provided glimpses of the sky and the ground, before reaching an overlook to the crash site, called "Sacred Ground" in the competition brief. The building reversed the basic concept of the Vietnam Veterans Memorial in Washington, D.C. Instead of being black and carved into the ground, our visitors' center would be white and rising above the earth's surface toward the sky.

The information center for visitors sat on the highest point of the site and could be viewed from the Lincoln Highway, U.S. 30, on the northern border of the proposed project boundary. We used red maples as symbols for the forty passengers and crew members on the flight, randomly arranging the trees at the entry to the project to signify the passengers coming together in Newark, not knowing each other.

The beginning of the visitor's journey was to be a pleasant bucolic drive on a single-lane road across a rolling, rural landscape restored from its strip-mined past. The road turned abruptly, as did Flight 93 on the morning of September 11. The sharp turn led up the hill toward the visitors' center. Next to the center, another forty red maples formed an organized pattern, symbolizing the coming together of the passengers and crew members to take the plane back from the terrorists. We planned a system of swales and berms, pointing toward Newark, San Francisco, and Washington, D.C., to reclaim the hillside.

From the visitors' center, the path moved along the ridge line to the place overlooking the crash site where the FBI coordinated its investigation. According to the competition guidelines, Sacred Ground was to be reserved for family members of passengers and crew. We proposed two paths from the FBI headquarters. One for visitors paralleling the crash flight moving in front of Sacred Ground, flanked by a grove of quaking aspens. The second path, reserved for family members, moved behind Sacred Ground.

We designed an allée of forty red maples, where family members exit Sacred Ground and reunite with other visitors (Figure 18.4). The paths joined at a small lake and wetland area, then proceeded around a bowl planted with 3,021 white oaks, one for every victim of the 9/11 attacks. On the western side of the road, we proposed 1,776 oaks to celebrate the founding year of our nation. To discourage deer browsing, we put each oak seedling in a translucent planting tube. The path moved around the bowl back up the hill to the visitors' center. At the hilltop, visitors would be invited to leave mementos, before leaving through a woodland, where a final forty red maples were integrated into the forest.

Jason visited the site in December, and we used his photographs as background in the representations for our entry board. We used a color scheme drawn from the competition materials, emphasizing light blues and adding the September red color of the maples. Jet streams crossed the sky above our design, which we called Memory Trail.

The National Park Service and competition advisors posted the 1,059 entries on the Flight 93 Memorial Web site. Jason studied each one

18.4 A proposed red maple allée, Flight 93 Memorial Competition, finalist design entry by Jason Kentner, Karen Lewis, E. Lynn Miller, and Frederick Steiner. Courtesy of the National Park Service, Flight 93 National Memorial.

and was confident that we would be one of the finalists. I only made it to number 797, our entry, and agreed that ours was strong. We convinced ourselves that we would hear by Friday, January 28—one week before the public announcement of the results. That Friday came and went with no news, then the weekend, then Monday. On Tuesday, I flew to Miami, now convinced that we were not among the finalists.

When Assistant Dean Raquel Elizondo called with a message from Helene Fried, I realized that Fried was not calling all 1,059 competitors, but I thought that we were probably receiving an honorable mention. The news that we were one of five finalists elated and surprised me. Fried said that, beyond telling my team members, I needed to keep the news confidential until Friday, February 4, at 4 p.m. EST, when the five finalists would be made public.

After calling Jason, Karen, and Lynn, I floated back to EDAW's conference room. After a few moments, my cell phone rang again. I answered the call from my friend and former Arizona State colleague Laurel McSherry, with Ohio State at the time.

"I have a secret, but you can't tell anyone until four o'clock on Friday," she began, before generously inviting me to join her Flight 93 finalist team.

"Laurel," I responded, "I have a secret, too, but I can't tell anyone until four o'clock on Friday, either."

At 4 p.m. on Friday, I was flying from Miami to an architecture educators' conference in Atlanta. I looked at my watch and told the stranger sitting next to me the news.

When we landed at Hartsfield Airport, I had twelve messages on my cell phone. I spent the next two hours talking to reporters. By Monday, the competition advisors—Helene Fried and Don Stastny—circulated a reminder to the five finalists that the competition rules required us to coordinate press inquiries through them.

After I returned to Austin, I reviewed the entries of the other finalists and the ones who had received an honorable mention. Jason had been prescient, selecting two of the finalists, Laurel's and ours, in addition to one that had received an honorable mention. I found finalist Ken Lum's entry especially interesting because it was an eloquent rendition of my original concept. He had received the call from Helene in the middle of his Master of Architecture thesis committee meeting at the University of Toronto.

In late February, the competition hosted a workshop for finalists, the National Park Service, family members, local officials, and those volunteers who had constructed a temporary memorial in Somerset.[5]

At the workshop, which I could not attend due to a prior commitment, Jason, Karen, and Lynn met other finalists, National Park Service planners, family members, and local officials. In a charrette format, they worked on a management plan for the memorial, which we subsequently refined. Besides learning a little about the personalities of our competitors, we also determined that running a path for family members behind Sacred Ground was infeasible. We also received jury comments to help us refine our final design.

In March, I was scheduled to give a lecture in Cleveland, so I requested approval from the competition advisors to visit the site. They granted permission, but I could only visit areas open to the public, could not speak to the press, and generally had to keep a low profile.

**18.5** View from the temporary Flight 93 National Memorial, looking toward the crash site, Pennsylvania. Photograph by Frederick Steiner.

My brother John and his wife, Sandy, also an FBI agent, had moved from San Francisco to Pittsburgh to be closer to her family and ours. The three of us visited the memorial on a frigid, windy March afternoon. On public roads, we crisscrossed and circled strip-mine ravaged landscape. I shot several rolls of pictures and took a lot of notes before we reached the temporary memorial, constructed and managed by local volunteers, called "Ambassadors." A temporary visitors' center—a shack, really—was surrounded by windswept, snow-covered fields (Figure 18.5). Two giant draglines, witnesses to a recent strip-mining past, dominated the barren northern horizon. Visitors had attached thousands of offerings to a large chain-link fence with billowing flags that formed the western edge of the temporary memorial. Others had scribbled remembrances on the metal guardrails in the gravel parking lot. The names of the forty passengers and crew members had been carved into park benches that looked out to Sacred Ground. Local schoolchildren had made forty ceramic angels that stood on the slope beyond the benches. The place possessed raw power.

I had seen many images of the site and listened to descriptions from my teammates. As I looked across the vastness and over the rolling hills that had been forests, farms, and coal fields, I thought about the horrible sequence of events that brought United Airlines Flight 93 to this place.

Inside the memorial, we were greeted by volunteer Nevin Lambert, who, from his front porch, had witnessed the crash. He had not spoken a word about what he had seen for several months afterward, but was now quite loquacious and even more inquisitive. I had urged John and Sandy to keep our visit discreet, which I assumed would be an easy task for special agents of the FBI. But Nevin persisted. I would be returning to the site in a few weeks for a second workshop, so I told Nevin who we were. He started to cry and hugged John, Sandy, and me, saying, "thank you" over and over again.

I returned to Austin with a lot of images and an even greater sense of making a contribution to a significant event in our history. Lynn, Jason, and I continued to discuss this significance in Austin and through our e-mail correspondence with Karen in Lexington.

At the second workshop at the county courthouse in Somerset, Pastor Larry Hoover led with an invocation in which he observed, "We see new growth, new life on this beautiful spring morning."

Afterward, each team was to present its concept. I spoke for our team. As I rose and looked at the audience, raw emotion filled the eyes of those family members who were waiting for my words. As I described our approach, I tried not to be too distracted by the tears and emotional faces in the audience.

The Stage II jury was announced. It would include several of the victims' family members, as well as leading designers, notably Laurie Olin of Philadelphia and Penn and Julie Bargmann of D.I.R.T. and the University of Virginia. We also learned that other finalists had augmented their teams with new talent: Laurel McSherry had added Andropogon; Warren Byrd had joined Paul and Milena Murdoch.

The meeting concluded with photographs of all the teams on the courthouse steps. Karen, Jason, and I visited Sacred Ground with competition advisor Don Stastny and two photographers from the Heinz Foundation, a major sponsor of the competition. The Flight 93 aircraft had turned

18.6 Remnants from the crash site of United Flight 93, now Sacred Ground. Photograph by Frederick Steiner.

**18.7** The proposed Ambassadors' Overlook from the temporary memorial site, Flight 93 Memorial Competition, finalist entry by Jason Kentner, Karen Lewis, E. Lynn Miller, and Frederick Steiner. Courtesy of the National Park Service, Flight 93 National Memorial.

upside down before hitting the ground at full speed. A ball of fire, the plane crashed into a hemlock grove. A pile of wood chips, mixed with plane chards, remained on the edge of the grove. Family members had constructed small monuments inside the fenced-off area. Don reached down and picked up a small metal fragment to show us (Figure 18.6).

With Karen and Jason, I walked through the hemlock grove. We studied the area and then walked the length of the entire site from U.S. 30 to the temporary memorial. We adjusted our path as we read the landscape. We then returned to Austin and Lexington and worked on the project, while fulfilling our academic responsibilities.

After the end of the school year, Karen moved to Austin for the summer to work on our entry, and we devoted all our waking hours to the project. We hired one architecture and two landscape architecture students to work on the project with the funds the competition had provided. My daughter Halina, a graphic designer (who subsequently completed a Master of Landscape Architecture at City College of New York in 2010), joined us (pro bono) to work on the required project brochure. She ended up contributing to the model-building as well. We produced four models, although only two were required. Jason is a master model-builder. He conceived expressive, imaginative models, constructed with wood sections and trees made from paint brushes. Dean Wellington "Duke" Reiter of Arizona State University joined us for a weekend to help with the design of

a family chapel inside Sacred Ground. We spent considerable time revising our original design for Sacred Ground, adjusting the path and the red maple allée, as well as adding the chapel. The chapel would look into the hemlock grove, where we would redistribute the pile of wood chips and tiny parts from the airplane.

We carefully refined each aspect of our design, including the path, the visitors' center, and the parking areas. We added an overlook off U.S. 30, where motorists could view the memorial without having to drive through the whole site. We named the proposed overlooks. The visitors' center overlook—Lambert's Farm Overlook—was named after Lambert's farm because the front porch of their house was prominent on the horizon, and part of the family's farm would become part of the memorial. We called the spot where family members split from other visitors the "FBI Overlook" because that is where the agents conducted their investigation. From the FBI Overlook, we added a walking path to the temporary memorial, which we named the "Ambassadors' Overlook," in honor of the local residents who had constructed and maintained the temporary memorial (Figure 18.7).

One of my tasks involved Googling wildlife and vegetation species to Photoshop into our final boards. Some time over the past few years, landscape architects have begun to use photographic images from Web sources to display their planting plans. In fact, the Murdoch-Byrd team did this most effectively. One of our innovations was

**18.8** A proposed chapel, Flight 93 Memorial Competition, finalist entry by Jason Kentner, Karen Lewis, E. Lynn Miller, and Frederick Steiner, with advice from Wellington Reiter. Courtesy of the National Park Service, Flight 93 National Memorial.

to use wildlife species and soil types in a similar manner. We also highlighted rare and endangered plant and animal species that would be helped by our design.

The competition required us to propose an implementation team and a budget. We invited EDAW to be our landscape architects of record and they helped us compile a strong group of architects, engineers, and biologists with substantial National Park Service experience. We proposed a $22,347,052 budget to realize the memorial expression component of our plan.

We worked day and night. A FedEx truck picked up our models on June 10. The boards and brochures went on June 14 to meet the deadline on the following day. Lynn flew to Somerset to unpack the models on June 15. The models then went on exhibit for family members, the Stage II jury, and the public from July to September. The jury met in early August, and we waited and waited. We again set arbitrary dates for when we would hear, which, like the last time, came and went. We speculated. Jason was convinced that we had won. I felt, however, that the Murdoch team had the strongest entry, although the central

image of a crescent—reminiscent of the star and crescent symbol of Islam—might prove a fatal flaw.[6]

This time the call, during the morning of August 19, did not bring good news. We learned that the Murdoch team had prevailed. The jury comments revealed that our visitors' center prompted concern—I think, misunderstanding. The stark thin building was not meant to be contextual. The events of September 11, 2001, did not fit that Pennsylvania landscape. The jury noted that the visitors' center could be seen from the whole site, which was our intent. This visibility was not received positively.

A subsequent conversation with jury member Laurie Olin revealed that the lay members of the jury did not understand our models, expecting more literal renditions, and that there was too much information on our boards. Perhaps we should have heeded former *Landscape Architecture* magazine editor Grady Clay's sage advice "to simplify, simplify, then exaggerate."

But I should not wallow in sour grapes. I am quite proud of our Memory Trail. However, it is fair to reflect on what we learned. For me, the biggest lesson was that we underestimated the production time. While other finalists had formed strategic alliances, most successfully Paul and Milena Murdoch with Warren Byrd, we remained steadfastly 3 plus 1. We brought in the three graduate students, my daughter, and Duke Reiter, but the design in the end was ours.

Duke Reiter's ideas were helpful for the chapel design, but, being a dean, he had limited time (Figure 18.8). EDAW helped us with the proposed implementation. However, both EDAW and Duke were not located in Austin, which limited their involvement, even when we sought it. One afternoon, noted architect Arthur Andersson stopped by our studio for an impromptu review. A competition veteran, he offered some useful advice about the color combinations we were using on our boards.

If we had partnered with a firm, we might have communicated our ideas more effectively. We might have also improved our production efficiency and increased our output. For example, I worked on the print machine all night before our deadline. My time would have probably been better spent working on the writing for our brochure. The Murdoch entry was especially thorough and clear in its intent. They produced an attractive, comprehensive, and thick document describing their concept. Academics market their ideas differently than practitioners.

Part of the problem may have also been the lack of memorial objects in our design. We resisted putting names on rocks and sought to make the whole landscape the memorial. As a result, we did not really present a single memorial object, one that was easy to visualize. Rather, by embracing the journey and the landscape, we dealt with movement, time, and change. Our design emphasized restoration, the reclamation of a landscape polluted by decades of strip mining, and the healing of a nation wounded by the 9/11 attacks (Figure 18.9). We sought to honor the bravery of the passengers and crew members of United Flight 93, while creating a place for reflection for their loved ones.

A year later, Karen sent the team a message noting how the experience continued to influence her work. The experience had transformed us all. Karen became an architect who thinks more in landscape terms and scales. I viewed the Flight 93 competition as a way to contribute to our nation's healing. The entry itself was to be that contribution. I never factored in the impact of becoming a finalist. It had brought me and my colleagues much closer to the event. The faces of the victims' family members will stay with me forever.

United Airlines Flight 93 did not crash into an icon like the other planes, but rather "just" in a field. The heroism of those on board prevented the plane from reaching our nation's capital and its presumed target, the Capitol. The field, the landscape, should be transformed to honor their memory.

The National Park Service has worked with victims' families to realize this vision. Considerable progress has been achieved, but seven property owners held out on selling about 500 acres (202 ha) of the 2,000-acre (890-ha) site. Much of this land is contaminated, former strip mines that would have little economic value if the plane had not crashed there. At the urging of victims' families and the *New York Times*, George W. Bush ordered condemnation of these properties in one of the final acts of his presidency. As a result of this use of eminent domain, the Flight 93 National Memorial will be completed in time for the tenth anniversary of the 2001 terrorist attacks (Figure 18.10).

**18.9** Draglines from former strip mining of the Flight 93 National Memorial site. Photograph by Frederick Steiner.

**18.10** Memorial Plaza with a wall following the path of United Flight 93 to its crash site. Design by Murdoch Architects. Courtesy of the National Park Service, Flight 93 National Memorial, and Paul and Milena Murdoch.

We seem to inhabit an age of memorials. Perhaps, people in all times seek to memorialize the key events of their times. In an essay about Gettysburg, Reuben Rainey observes:

*Now we can begin to understand why these aging veterans engaged in such a flurry of monument making on the hallowed ground of the preserved battlefield. Obviously, they wanted to be appreciated and remembered by future generations for their sacrifices and deeds of valor. It was no doubt a great joy to reunite with their former comrades for what would be, for many, one last reunion on this field of glory. They may have indulged in nostalgic hyperbole and the making of myths, but they understood something of great importance. No society can continue to flourish without perpetuating its fundamental values through rituals of remembrance and the making of monuments.[7]*

Lauric Olin has noted, "Memorials are created especially to instill, refresh, and perpetuate memories."[8]

The making of landscapes is thus central to instilling, refreshing, and perpetuating memories. Landscapes, after all, are our most enduring cultural artifacts. Our landscapes far outlast us.

The Gulf Coast was battered by major hurricanes and/or tropical storms every year between 1994 and 2009. In 2005, there were twenty-six named storms, including fourteen hurricanes and seven major hurricanes. On August 29, 2005, Katrina came ashore with winds of 140 miles (225 km) per hour and a storm surge of more than 30 feet (10 m) and affected more than 100,000 square miles (258,999 km²) (approximately the area of Italy).

This force of nature left 527,000 people homeless, resulted in 1,299 casualties, caused more than $250 billion in damages, and flooded 80 percent of the City of New Orleans. More than 30 square miles (78 km²) of marshland in Louisiana and 25 percent of marshes in Mississippi were lost because of Katrina. Experts predict that future hurricane seasons will be even worse because of warmer water temperatures in the North Atlantic.[1]

The Gulf Coast is one of eleven very large, rapidly growing, megaregions, or "megapolitan areas," in the United States. Ten million people live in the coastal communities, in what Robert Lang identifies as the Gulf Coast Megapolitan Area, including more than 5 million in the region's most important metropolis, Houston.[2] The entire megapolitan area, including Houston, is susceptible to hurricanes and flooding, with much of the Gulf Coast region fewer than three feet (0.9 m) above sea level. Considering the fact that the Gulf Coast plays an especially important role in the nation's energy supply, the regular impact of catastrophic weather on communities and the economy is devastating. In addition, as the 2010 Deepwater Horizon explosion and subsequent oil spill illustrates, tapping that energy source adds another layer of vulnerability to the Gulf Coast.

## THE GULF COAST: A TEST CASE FOR RESILIENCE

The ability for urban areas and landscapes to rebound from disaster is termed "resilience." Resilience, from the Latin *resilire* meaning to spring back or rebound, is a concept and a theory with growing appeal in the disciplines of ecology and planning. When rising from traditional concepts in ecology, resilience emphasizes equilibrium and stability. The United Nations defines resilience as the ability to absorb disturbances while retaining the same basic structure and ways of functioning, the capacity for self-organization, and the capacity to adapt to stress and change.[3]

Most recently, concepts of resilience emerge from what is called "new ecology," which focuses on nonequilibrium and the adaptability of ecological systems. The latter is appropriate "to urban ecosystems, because it suggests that spatial heterogeneity is an important component of the

persistence of adaptable metropolitan regions."[4] Cities are anything but stable and predictable systems. Former New Orleans Mayor Marc Morial has noted that the challenge we face "is not only about rebuilding New Orleans and the Gulf Coast, it is about rebuilding a culture, a human system."[5]

Katrina flooded the media, breaking through the levees of our inattention (Figure 19.1). Environmental neglect collided with social inequity on the evening news before the local shooting of the day. Images from the streets of New Orleans, along the coast of Mississippi, and across the interstate highways of the Gulf Coast challenged how we think about our nation and our leaders.

Interest, like oil supply, peaks. Interest, like the tide, subsides. Natural disasters come and go: from Hurricane Andrew in 1992, through the Mississippi floods of 1993, on to the Indian Ocean tsunami of December 2004, and the Sichuan earthquake in May 2008.

Might Katrina be different? Might it present an opportunity for rethinking architecture, urbanism, and regionalism? Could it be the beginning of rethinking humanity's relation to nature in this first urban century? Might the concept of resilience not be helpful for guiding regions like the Gulf Coast even in times without disaster? Might the Sichuan earthquake play a similar role in China?

Ecological understanding can be advanced through mapping and design exercises, but such generative prospects should be viewed as part of a larger network of thinking about how people interrelate with land and water.

At least three natural ecologies coalesce to form the ecotone we call the U.S. Gulf Coast from Florida to Texas: the coast itself, the coastal plain, and the Gulf of Mexico. Water and land interface along the Gulf Coast in many ways and on several levels in this "liquid landscape."[6]

**19.1** Flooding of New Orleans following Hurricane Katrina. Photograph by Smiley Pool, *Dallas Morning News.*

The numerous rivers that empty their loads in the Gulf shape the region in many ways, including its deltas and beaches. The mighty Mississippi drains about 41 percent of the coterminous United States. Its drainage basin encompasses 1,151,000 square miles (2,981,076 km²) in thirty-one states and two Canadian provinces. In addition to the Mississippi, the Brazos, Colorado, and Trinity in Texas; the Rio Grande; the Pearl in Mississippi; and the Suwannee in Florida and Georgia, a total of thirty-three major river systems contribute to the ongoing processes of erosion and deposition.

These changes are but the most recent in a long geologic era stretching back some 200 million years ago when the Gulf of Mexico was formed, as North America broke away from South America and Africa. The Gulf then became the depository for layers and layers of sediment,

which included organic matter (Figure 19.2). Heat and pressure converted this matter into petroleum and natural gas.

In addition to oil and gas, the Gulf Coast has some of the most productive fisheries in the world. These fisheries and the health of the Gulf itself are threatened by increasing nitrogen and phosphates dissolved in the waters. The overloading of these nutrients leads to eutrophication, or the choking-off of oxygen, resulting in hypoxic water. This has led to a huge dead zone in the Gulf, so depleted of oxygen that fish, crabs, and shrimp suffocate. Most of the nitrogen and phosphorous enter the Mississippi basin through upstream runoff of fertilizers, soil erosion, animal waste, and sewage. The increasing demand for corn ethanol fuels the expansion of the dead zone. Some compare the scale of this dead zone to the size of Massachusetts. Its size varies seasonally, and hurricanes and flooding affect the dead zone as well.

The Mississippi River also created numerous deltas with vast, marshy wetlands. Historically, the Mississippi and other rivers deposited their loads when entering the Gulf, resulting in deltas. As the rivers have been straightened and "controlled," their deposition capacity was reduced, with the coastline eroding inland. As a result of coastal erosion, Louisiana has lost 1,900 square miles (4,920 km²) of land, mostly wetlands, since the 1930s (Figure 19.3). Since the 1970s, the rate of loss has accelerated to an average rate of 30 square miles (77 km²) annually. The sedges, marsh grasses, rushes, and bald cypresses of these wetlands provide habitat for many animals.

In addition to indigenous people, the Gulf Coast was settled by three primary population groups: the Spanish in Florida and Texas, the French in Louisiana, and Southern Americans who swept westward from the Carolinas and Georgia with their slave-based plantation culture. Where the dominant early cultural imprint established by the English and the Spanish is clear elsewhere in the United States, the French influence is distinct in Louisiana. The lingering influence of the French is evident in place names, land division, architecture, the law, and food.

**19.2** Coastal marshes near the birdfoot delta of the Mississippi River, Plaquemines Parish, Louisiana, June 2009. Photograph by Jaap van der Salm. Courtesy of Dutch Dialogues/Richard Campanella.

The Creole and Cajun peoples form unique elements of Louisiana's population derived from the French root stock. Historically, Creoles descended from the French and Spanish colonists who settled New Orleans. Over time, the term also applied to mixed-race, French-speaking Roman Catholics in the city. Another distinct group of French origin, the Cajuns, migrated from Acadia, now part of Nova Scotia, to Louisiana when the British took control of Canada in 1755.

The Creoles and Cajuns represent diversity, but there are also significant ethnic divides in the Gulf Coast region. The most significant is between black and white, dating back to slavery and exacerbated by prejudice and poverty ever since. From Florida to Texas, the gulf between rich and poor is

**19.3** The marsh adjacent to Lake Borgne, southeast of New Orleans, is broken up by canals used mostly by oil companies. Photograph by Lori Waselchuk, September 2005.

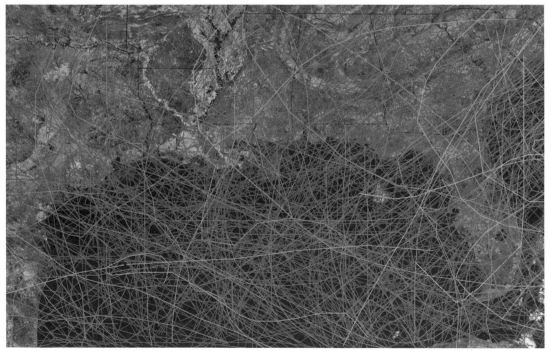

**19.4** Hurricanes in the Gulf Coast between 1851 and 2000. This map, showing all of the severe storms that hit the Gulf Coast from 1851 to 2000, helps illustrate the potential danger associated with living in the region. Map by James L. Sipes, AECOM. Courtesy of AECOM.

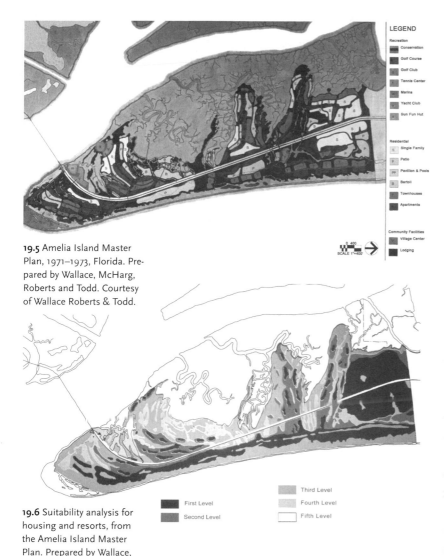

**19.5** Amelia Island Master Plan, 1971–1973, Florida. Prepared by Wallace, McHarg, Roberts and Todd. Courtesy of Wallace Roberts & Todd.

**19.6** Suitability analysis for housing and resorts, from the Amelia Island Master Plan. Prepared by Wallace, McHarg, Roberts and Todd. Courtesy of Wallace Roberts & Todd.

First Level
Second Level
Third Level
Fourth Level
Fifth Level

**19.7** Adaptive architecture principles applied to dune housing, from the Amelia Island Master Plan. Prepared by Wallace, McHarg, Roberts and Todd. Courtesy of Wallace Roberts & Todd.

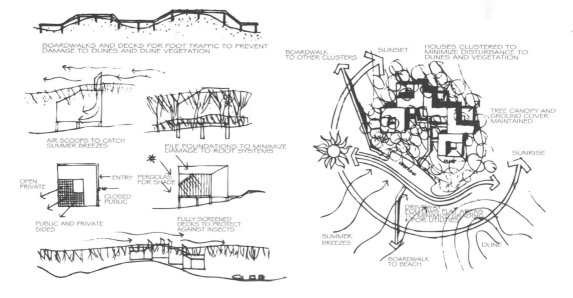

significant and arguably the most entrenched in the nation.

The ecology of the Gulf is diverse and fragile. The ecologies of all places possess diversity and fragility, and the Gulf can help illustrate the challenges we as a species face on this changing planet. Certainly, the U.S. Gulf Coast contains more than its share of environmental threats and social injustices. A key to resilience is the ability to assess vulnerability to environmental threats. Borrowing from the United Nations' definition, vulnerability refers to the degree to which a system is susceptible to, and unable to cope with, the adverse effects of environmental change.[7]

We know much about the threats facing the Gulf Coast. Environmental scientists predicted the consequences of a major hurricane for New Orleans long before Katrina, as social scientists warned about the poor quality of schools in Louisiana and Mississippi. The increased knowledge about these threats presents an opportunity to take ameliorative actions, i.e., ecologically based countermeasures. Through tools like GIS mapping and remotely sensed imagery, we can produce images, much like medical doctors create x-rays of our bodies, that reveal areas of concern.

For instance, Figure 19.4 clearly displays that much of the Gulf Coast is susceptible to hurricanes. We can map the areas most prone to

storm surge with some accuracy. The solution is straightforward: do not develop communities along the coast in places that will most seriously be affected by storms. Reflecting on hurricanes, Ian McHarg suggested exactly that approach nearly forty years ago in *Design with Nature*. He and his colleagues, most notably Bill Roberts, put that theory into practice in the 1971 plan for Amelia Island, Florida.[8] Amelia Island has suffered relatively little damage in the numerous hurricanes that have struck Florida in the past three decades (Figures 19.5 to 19.8).

We can also map flood-prone areas. My hometown of Dayton, Ohio, was mostly destroyed by a flood in 1913. The loss of life and property was significant. In response, civic leaders developed an innovative plan that involved purchasing land and easements in the floodplains and building a series of earthen dams. The areas behind these dams fill with water during storms, but are otherwise used for farming and open space. Dayton has been spared damaging floods since 1913 and also has a large, regional open-space system.

The loss of wetlands results in the decline of biodiversity. It also makes the region more susceptible to hurricanes and floods. Instead of losing wetlands along the Gulf Coast, we should

be adding and restoring such areas. Bruce Babbitt illustrates how the nation has undertaken such a strategy for the Everglades.[9] After Hurricane Andrew struck southern Florida in 1992, there was considerable discussion about the future of the region. The vast Everglades wetlands will play a crucial role in that future. These discussions and debates led to a restoration program based on federal-state cooperation. Although it is too early to declare the Everglades restoration plan a complete success, large wetland areas have been protected as a result (Figure 19.9).

The sources of the pollution contributing to dead zones in the Gulf of Mexico are clear. Our nation has a mixed record of controlling water pollution. We have done an admirable job regulating what are known as "point sources" of pollution as a result of the Clean Water Acts dating back to the 1970s. Our record with "non-point sources," such as those from farming, is not as strong. Non-point sources are creating the dead zone at the mouth of the Mississippi. Best management practices to control such pollution are well known. These practices should be required throughout the Mississippi River Basin in order to restore the water quality of the Mississippi River and the Gulf of Mexico.

**19.9** In many parts of western Broward County, development stretches all the way inland to the remnant Everglades—with very little "buffer" between the fragile wetlands and new communities, schools, and roads. Courtesy of the South Florida Water Management District.

The dead zone, the loss of wetlands, flooding, and hurricanes illustrate how the world changes. They are also well-studied phenomena, which humans have learned how to mitigate and adapt to, even if such strategies have not been widely pursued in the Gulf Coast of the United States. Sea-level rise may be more vexing. We are pretty sure that global climate change will result in sea-level rise, but we are not sure how much.

Mitigation and adaptive strategies are even more speculative but key for human systems to respond to climate change. Clearly, mitigation and adaptation involve design and planning. We can learn from positive precedents. After Katrina, the Dutch were frequently cited as an example of a culture that adapted to the interface between land and sea.[10]

The flood-control system in The Netherlands was in tatters at the end of the Second World War. It was restored, but destroyed again by devastating North Sea storms in 1953, resulting in considerable loss of life and property. The Dutch responded with a comprehensive and expensive system for storm and flood protection (Figure 19.10). With the prospect of sea-level rise, the Dutch are exploring ways to readjust that system.

The Dutch are also well-known for their fairness and tolerance. The Gulf Coast of the United States, by contrast, is an example of intolerance and racism. Hurricane Katrina proved a powerful reminder of the social inequities of this region. Significant investments are necessary for education, housing, social services, economic development, and health care. One equity challenge concerns rebuilding lost homes and businesses. Naturally, after Katrina, people wanted to rebuild their homes in the same place. Should people be encouraged, even receive subsidies, to rebuild in dangerous places? At the very least, the risks should be transparent to individual property owners and public officials.

If we learn from disasters such as Katrina, as the Dutch have from their history of storms and flooding, we can reduce the loss of life and property, as we reduce the impact on what nature will claim, with or without permission.[11]

**19.10** Eastern Scholdt Storm Surge Barrier designed by West 8, who used black and white seashells to provide camouflage for birds, Zeeland, the Netherlands. Courtesy of West 8 Urban Design & Landscape Architecture.

### "RESPONDING TO URBAN COMPLEXITIES": THE 10TH INTERNATIONAL ARCHITECTURE EXHIBITION

The University of Texas School of Architecture was invited to prepare an exhibit for the Venice Biennale. For months, several faculty members and students worked on our Gulf Coast exhibit, emphasizing the theme of resilience, for the 10th International Architecture Exhibition of the Venice Biennale. I traveled to Italy on Tuesday, August 29, 2006, to help with the final installation and to participate in the opening activities.

The 2006 Architecture Biennale, curated by London architect and urbanist Ricky Burdett, differed from past exhibits. Instead of focusing on individual star architects, the Biennale addressed the larger theme of "Cities, Architecture, and Society." The goal was to present an "overview on how architects, planners, and designers are responding to different urban complexities around the world." The exhibits addressed issues such as migration, sprawl, de-industrialization, and social change in the first urban century.[12]

On the plane to Venice, one of my readings was the just-published special issue of *Places*, "Building Community Across the Transect," devoted to New Urbanism. As a long-time user, teacher, and promoter of transects, I read the issue with considerable interest. An article by

Charles Bohl and Elizabeth Plater-Zyberk especially interested me.[13]

Bohl and Plater-Zyberk include a sidebar, "Nature and the City," which features an imaginative axonometric interpretation of Ian McHarg's sea-to-inland transect (Figure 19.11). They state that "urbanists believe the integrity of human settlements should be given equal standing with that of the natural world."[14] I concur. Then they add the specious argument that "environmentalist positions and current regulations both would preclude the building of a new Paris, Rome, Chicago, New York, or Charleston."[15] (They might add New Orleans and Venice.) I would argue that neither environmentalist positions nor current regulations would preclude any of these places, but rather that current environmental knowledge would suggest they be designed differently. In fact, current greening efforts in Chicago and New York suggest that they are already being redesigned. Nature has yet to achieve "equal standing" with human settlement, though.

In their "Nature and the City" sidebar, Bohl and Plater-Zyberk bemoan the call of "environmentalists" to "green the city" because it "will damage the pedestrian continuity associated with successful urbanism."[16] But if such green areas protect an endangered species or help control flooding, so what if pedestrian continuity is inconvenienced? Can truly good landscape architects,

architects, and urbanists not design pedestrian systems to fit the local context?

Bohl and Plater-Zyberk include a regional land-allocation map that suggests growth and open-space areas for the Mississippi Gulf Coast. The GIS maps for the Gulf Coast we produced with EDAW (now AECOM) and the Regional Plan Association (RPA), which were part of our Biennale exhibit, suggest a very different growth pattern. Although I agree with many tenets of New Urbanism, I part company with a sometimes anti-environmental stance, which suggests that urbanism should trump nature.[17] I think that urbanism and environmentalism should be balanced, be given "equal standing." However, placing some urban uses in inherently dangerous locations, such as areas prone to storm surges and flooding, is foolish. As I write this, I look out of a window from a plane at the English countryside with a neat matrix of villages, fields, and woodlands, and I believe that a balance can be achieved.

I arrive in Venice (without some of my luggage) late in the afternoon of August 30. The bag with twenty-five pounds of postcards to distribute at the Biennale arrives, but not the one with my best suit, dress shirts, camera, and toiletries. British Airways supplies the latter. I am not the only one in the lost luggage line, and I wait for more than an hour to file my claim.

**19.11** In ecological analyses, the transect may be used to understand how physical and biological systems interact to create living environments. Ian McHarg's *Design with Nature* (1969) uses this technique to describe the ecozones of a typical stretch of land from beach to inland bay. This sea-to-inland transect by Duany Plater-Zyberk & Company is an axonometric interpretation of McHarg's original. Courtesy of Duany Plater-Zyberk & Company.

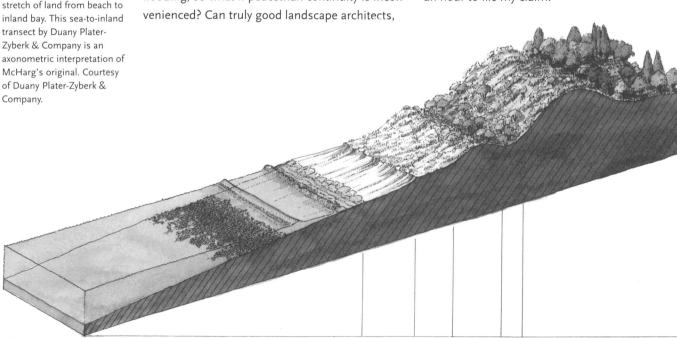

**19.12** Murano, Venice, Italy. Photograph by Frederick Steiner.

As I write my address, the claims agent asks, "Are you an architect?" I look up, and she explains, "You write like an architect," adding that her son wants to study architecture at the University of Venice.

I take a *motoscafo* (motorboat) to my hotel, Casa Sant'Andrea in Santa Croce near the train station and Piazzale Roma (Figure 19.12). The late afternoon sun is low in the sky, which results in a vivid lighting of some building façades and shadows being cast across others as we cross the Laguna Veneta. A converted sixteenth-century monastery, the no-frills Casa Sant'Andrea hotel operates with the "approval of the Venetian Church."

After breakfast the next morning, I am greeted by most of our installation team: Barbara Hoidn, Eric Hepburn, Rachel Brown, and Frank Jacobus. They are moving into Casa Sant'Andrea for the duration of the installation and opening. The hotel is inexpensive, convenient, and clean with a friendly, helpful staff. Barbara Hoidn and I travel on the crowded Route 82 *vaporetto* (water bus) through the scenic Grand Canal, past Jeff Koons' *Balloon Dog (Magenta)* in front of the Palazzo Grassi, to Giardini della Biennale, where our exhibit is being constructed in the Padiglione Italia. Paul Allen's gigantic yacht, *Octopus*, with at least two helicopters, is parked near the garden gate, along with several other impressive boats, in town for the film biennale activities.

Inside the Italian Pavilion, I meet Robert Hegeler and Sven Ulrich from Berlin, who are constructing the armature for our exhibit. Hoidn introduces me to our neighbors: the South Africans and the Irish. For the first time at the Architecture Biennale, the Italian Pavilion features the work of foreigners. We also meet two young Swiss architects from the Federal Institute of Technology Zurich (Eidgenössische Technische Hochschule Zürich) exhibit, who seek Hoidn's advice on how

**19.13** The aftermath of Hurricane Katrina, New Orleans, 2005. Photograph by Tom Fox, *Dallas Morning News*.

to mount their work without creating air bubbles. The maze of exhibits projects considerable positive energy and collaboration.

Our exhibit is more stunning than I expected—the result of considerable work here in Venice, in Berlin, and back in Austin. The visual depictions of Katrina's consequences, featuring *Dallas Morning News* photographs, are especially powerful (Figure 19.13). I think we have done a fine job collecting and representing the work of those involved in actual plans for recovery (including Calthorpe Associates, Fregonese Calthorpe Associates, and WRT), as well as speculations by thirteen other universities. Our team's concepts suggest powerful new ideas for recovery, especially relating to infrastructure.[18] The visual representations are accomplished, clear, and sophisticated.

In the exhibit, we also included the mapping of an environmentally sensitive areas project undertaken with EDAW and the RPA. In this voluntary effort, areas vulnerable to risk from Pensacola, Florida, to Houston-Galveston, Texas, were mapped (Figure 19.14). Existing mapped information for societal risks, flooding, high winds, storm surges, sea-rise vulnerability, and historic hurricane patterns were combined to illustrate levels of vulnerability.[19] Our maps were eventually requested by FEMA as Hurricane Ike approached the Texas coast in 2008. The maps were quite accurate in predicting the areas near Galveston that were most vulnerable.

Mapping is important in addressing the information scarcity issue faced by residents of the Gulf Coast. As noted by University of New Orleans scholars, "Distrust was exacerbated by the lack of information about the city's recovery strategy and how much power would be vested in the plans created. Overwhelmed with the sheer scale of Hurricane Katrina's devastation and with being severely understaffed, city agencies too often failed to convey the basic information residents needed."[20]

Hoidn introduces me to various Biennale officials and then we tour the Giardini grounds to look at other exhibits. The well-lighted Palladian American Pavilion is being cleaned by Italian workmen. The Swedish/Norwegian/Finnish combined Scandinavian Pavilion has three large trees growing through an opening in the ceiling of the main exhibit hall. The British are installing many computers and a lot of A/V equipment with wires running every which way. The French sit outside their pavilion, smoking cigarettes and working on their laptops. The German exhibit focuses on conversions of urban spaces. Although still under construction, the tall floor-to-ceiling translucent photographic columns are visually captivating. The columns also have a series of boxes, which open to the work of architects with their ideas and projects. Clearly, several exhibits represent

a significant investment by their governments. For instance, Hoidn estimated, that the Spanish spent 800,000 Euros on theirs. (We made do with around $200,000.)

In perfect weather, I spend a full day working on touch-up painting, putting up walls, and moving ladders. We listen to Radiohead and a much more upbeat Cuban hip-hop band, Orishas, and the Afro-Cuban Orchestra Baobab. Outside, around a glass box being constructed to mark the entry to the Biennale, Pink Floyd and Queen are played continuously.

I visit the Biennale office from time to time, to check e-mail and to take breaks in the Scarpa-designed courtyard garden. Late in the day, I meet Ricky Burdett, the curator of the Biennale, and Giampaolo Bigarello, the architect overseeing construction on the Italian Pavilion (Figure 19.15).

**19.14** The greatest potential for loss of life related to a hurricane is from storm surges. This map indicates the potential risk from storm surges along the Texas coast near Houston. Map by James L. Sipes, AECOM. Courtesy of AECOM.

STORM SURGE RISK
- Highest Risk
- High Risk
- Medium Risk
- Low Risk
- Minimal Risk

**19.15** Italian Pavilion at the 10th International Architecture Exhibition, Venice Biennale, 2006. Photograph by Al Fadhil.

Saturday is a repeat: beautiful weather, a lot of work. We meet Christian Bruun, a Danish filmmaker from Los Angeles, the curator of the U.S. exhibit. We are curious about the inactivity around the U.S. Pavilion. Christian explains that their materials had not cleared customs and had just arrived—four days late. They will also be addressing Katrina and New Orleans, featuring finalists of national and student *Architectural Record* design competitions. Their work is more site-specific than our more larger-scale regional coverage. We cross-reference each other's exhibits.

Hoidn and I cross the canal to visit the section of the Biennale grounds featuring Austrian, Egyptian, Greek, Polish, and other pavilions. The Greeks are especially friendly and give us a tour of their work-in-progress.

On our route back to the Italian Pavilion, we pass the ever-elegant, seemingly always-eating Belgians. Their pavilion was the first after the Italians' to be established in the early twentieth century. The Belgian Pavilion is located between those of the Dutch and the Spanish, west of the main path leading from the gate to the Italian Pavilion. At a table in front of their structure, the Belgians seem constantly gathered for conversation, wine, food, and smoking.

Ricky Burdett stops by our exhibit with Norman Foster. We discuss Katrina and the lack of progress and vision in the recovery efforts. We take an espresso break, then deliver one hundred and fifty press packets to the Biennale offices at the Arsenale, where we visit the exhibit of sixteen megacities with populations of more than 10 million (actually seventeen cities, but Milan and Turin are grouped together). The exhibit is still under construction in the linear, former rope-making factory. We work late, as many of our crew members will be leaving the next day.

In the morning, we take the waterbus to the Ponte dell'Accademia stop and walk to Campo Santa Margherita, where we join Rita Bertoni of the Biennale staff for a late dinner at a pizza restaurant. She gives us a packet of opening event tickets for our guests. We discuss the history of the Architecture Biennale. An art historian from Milan, Bertoni is enthusiastic about the theme and the changes made this year.

Bertoni's dog, Greta, accompanies us, and someone in our group repeats the observation that there are few public green spaces or trees for dogs in Venice. "True," Bertoni says, "but, no cars either." She notes that Venice once had many more cats, but over time neutering has become more popular, and their numbers declined. Meanwhile, Bertoni reports, the rat population increased. She laments the deleterious consequences of tourism on Venice and of globalization on everything else.

Back in my room, my feet and legs ache.

Over the next several days, we continue to prepare the exhibit and meet with the press and various dignitaries. On Tuesday morning, we are greeted by fog and Wilfried Wang, who arrived the night before. At our exhibit, UT faculty members Wang and Jason Sowell take pictures, and we clean up for the press. Wang calls our exhibit a "mini-biennale within the Biennale." We are interviewed by journalist Laura Larcan and photographed by *La Repubblica*.

That evening Ricky Burdett invites our team to dinner at the Hotel Monaco on the Grand Canal next to Harry's Bar. We are joined by Burdett's graphic designer wife, Mika; Elias and Vallia Constantopoulos (from the Greek Pavilion); Austrian architect Gustav Pichelmann; and

Aldo Cibic, one of the principal designers of the megacity exhibit in the 984-foot (300-m) long Corderie dell'Arsenale. Burdett and Wang had been classmates at the University College London Bartlett School in the 1970s and became lifelong friends. They were especially influenced by Kenneth Frampton, and this influence is evident in the theme and the structure of the Biennale. With the exhibits about 75 percent complete, and with the opening the next morning, Burdett and Cibic excuse themselves after 11 p.m. to return to the Biennale to attend to last-minute details.

The next day the Biennale opens to the press. I enjoy the French Pavilion, which the French team actually inhabits as the exhibit with considerable humor. They are friendly, offer food and wine, and give out yellow t-shirts. By contrast, the British Pavilion is incomprehensible, but flashy. The Australians are clear and thoughtful, as are the Swedes/Norwegians/Finns, who address urbanity in the Arctic. The Danes had cooperated with Tsinghua University on ideas about the future of Beijing. The U.S. Pavilion has come together nicely. An Italian restaurant and an outdoor bar have appeared overnight and illy is providing free coffee for the opening.

After breakfast on September 7, I take a land bus to Venice's Marco Polo Airport for my return flight to Austin. We fly out to the north. Below, the ancient Roman land division remains evident in the productive alluvial fields. We loop out over marshes into the sea, then back around and over Venice, which I can clearly read from this map in the air. The place below is threatened by water and by tourists. I wonder if the natural world were truly given "equal standing" with human settlement, would the situation be different?

As the Biennale opens in Venice, media coverage varies. In Italy and much of Europe, the Biennale is a major feature story. Its focus on cities, rather than buildings, is debated, criticized, and championed. The European media clearly understands.

The *New York Times* architecture critic, Nicolai Ouroussoff, a champion of high style architecture, acknowledges the direction away from "star" buildings toward "urbanism's complexities," but then he focuses on Rem Koolhaas in a September 10 article.[21] Four days later, Ouroussoff follows up with an article that notes how hard it is "to find the architecture" in the exhibit.[22] Whatever disagreements I may have with some New Urbanists, at least they have the gumption to assert architecture's role in the big issues of our time.

# VII | CONCLUSION

## 20 | THE SEDIMENTATION OF OUR MINDS

### PROSPECTS FOR NEW DESIGN THINKING

The 2006 Texas Society of Architects conference was held in Dallas, where I attended a "Patrons on Beauty" panel, moderated by Fort Worth architect Mark Gunderson. Patrons Deedie Rose, Howard Rachofsky, and Ray Nasher discussed their interests in art and architecture. Ray Nasher observed that we "need to consider everything in the built environment from exit signs to landscape architecture" (Figure 20.1). Stressing the importance of comprehensive interdisciplinary cooperation among graphic designers, architects, landscape architects, planners, and civil engineers, Deedie Rose added, "We don't own art or architecture or the land—we're merely caretakers."

Texans, like other Americans, possess a caretaker heritage, a history of giving back, and a tradition threatened by excessive, unplanned, and ugly development. The Philosophical Society of Texas, founded by Mirabeau Lamar, Sam Houston, and others in 1837, was modeled after Ben Franklin's American Philosophical Society. The Republic of Texas was, after all, a nation-state in 1837, and the United States was its model. I participated in the annual meeting of the Philosophical Society of Texas in 2006.

The theme was immigration and highlights included talks by Caroline Brettell of Southern Methodist University and Senators Kay Bailey Hutchison and John Cornyn. The speakers laid out challenges posed by immigration. Population growth in the United States is fueled by births and immigration. New immigrants are changing the face of urban landscapes. During past immigration waves, new residents settled in the urban cores of traditional gateway cities like New York and Chicago. In more recent waves, immigrants are just as likely to settle in the suburban neighborhoods and rural areas of emerging gateway regions such as Dallas-Fort Worth, Atlanta, and Charlotte.

In addition to changing settlement patterns, immigration, population growth, and urbanization are influencing the design and planning professions in numerous ways. As the demographics of Texas and the nation continue to change, design and planning must adjust by understanding and responding to more diverse cultures. As new immigrants are as likely to move to Addison, Texas, as the Lower East Side in Manhattan, one of the challenges for an architect or planner is how to incorporate the values of an immigrant from Mumbai or Guatemala City or Lagos into the North Texas landscape.

So what do we, or, more importantly, what do new architecture, planning, and design graduates do with these opportunities and challenges? What are the barriers faced by architecture and related fields?

Let us begin with architecture.

20.1 Aerial view of the Nasher Sculpture Center, Dallas. Design by Renzo Piano Building Workshop and Peter Walker and Partners Landscape Architecture. Photograph by Timothy Hursley. Courtesy of Nasher Sculpture Center.

Some claim that the star system holds back architecture. I will let you in on a guilty secret: I am actually fond of the star system. We need heroes. Star architects pave new paths and explore new ideas through form. Our architecture heroes are fun, . . . but the system is flawed. Alas, the flaws are manifold. We prop our stars up, then we knock them down. Their personal lives are exposed (Frank Lloyd Wright aside, they are mostly pretty boring). The stars tend to be old, white guys with bow ties, round dark-rimmed glasses, and a penchant for blacks and grays. They also are mostly educated at a few elite schools from Charlottesville, Virginia, to Cambridge, Massachusetts. Their iconic buildings seldom respond to the context of the community in which they are located. Although sometimes lip service is paid to a place, the buildings of star architects look pretty much the same in Beijing, Cincinnati, or Dubai. Celebrity architects produce a brand to be bought and sold.

There is hope. First, we have increasingly more female heroes, including, for example, Zaha Hadid (first woman to win the Pritzker Prize), Merrill Elam, and Billie Tsien. Many Texas graduates—such as Craig Dykers and his Snøhetta colleagues in Oslo and New York City, David Lake and others of Lake|Flato in San Antonio, and the Bercy Chen Studio in Austin—are rising stars in architecture.

The biggest problem with the star system is not the creation of heroes—we need inspiration. Rather, this system limits the role model options open to architects on a narrow design path. Too often, star architects create a brand style, which results in similar-looking buildings no matter where they are located.

There are other options available for architecture especially, but also for the planning and associated environmental design disciplines. Higher education is one other possibility. Could one

imagine a Nobel Laureate in physics not being an academic? Or, consider the number of Pulitzer Prizes in history awarded to academics. Architecture has a long, interesting academic past. We in the academy launched the likes of Paul Cret, Louis Kahn, Robert Venturi, Denise Scott Brown, Charles Moore, Michael Graves, Peter Eisenman, Daniel Libeskind, and many more.

But let me suggest a different path, where the academy is not a launching pad, but the goal. My heroes include other deans who are expanding the scope of their schools, such as Donna Robertson, who has created a landscape architecture degree at IIT; Brenda Scheer, who created a planning degree at the University of Utah; and Gary Hack, who created a new digital design degree at Penn.

Another option for the star designer path of architects is urbanism. There is the so-called New Urbanism, mostly led by architects who romanticize the past, and Celebrity Urbanism, championed by star architects who romanticize the future (Figure 20.2). Famous architects such as Norman Foster, Daniel Libeskind, Zaha Hadid, and Frank Gehry are "increasingly functioning as megascale

**20.2** The Abu Dhabi Cultural Center exemplifies Celebrity Urbanism. Star architects have been commissioned to design spectacular buildings there, such as Frank Gehry's Guggenheim Abu Dhabi, Zaha Hadid's Performing Arts Centre, and the Louvre Abu Dhabi by Jean Nouvel, as well as the Maritime Museum and the Zayed National Museum in honor of the late leader of the United Arab Emirates, H. H. Sheikh Zayed bin Sultan Al Nahyan. Courtesy of Tourism Development and Investment Company (TDIC).

planners."[1] In the process, their brands expand in scale, reminiscent of Modern architecture's forays into city planning. As Celebrity Urbanism grows in popularity, we should recall the deleterious consequences for urban renewal, public housing, and college campuses from the 1950s through the 1970s. There is also the edgier Landscape Urbanism, mostly led by landscape architects, like West 8 in The Netherlands, as well as James Corner and his Field Operations studio[2] (Figure 20.3). There is the pragmatic urbanism (which has yet to reach the status of capitalization), led mostly by planners and urban designers like Dean Almy

(Figure 20.4). Then, there is an emerging thoughtful, creative urbanism, based on environmental and equity concerns, led by architects like Ricky Burdett, as well as a few developers like Diane Cheatham and Ross Perot Jr., in Dallas.

Perot is responsible for Victory Park near downtown Dallas (Figure 20.5). Originally, a rather conservative basketball arena for the Dallas Mavericks in 2001, the 75-acre (30-ha) project on a brownfield site soon expanded into sleek, mixed-use towers. The focal point of the $3 billion development is the thirty-three-story W Dallas Hotel and Condominiums. Diane Cheatham's Urban

**20.3** Landscape Urbanism intervention, proposal for The Cornfield, Los Angeles, aerial montage. © James Corner Field Operations with Morphosis.

**20.4** The work of Dean Almy's Dallas Urban Lab provides an example of pragmatic urbanism. This illustration of a tension wire corridor and substations helps demonstrate the potentials of burying such a stretch of power lines. Courtesy of Dean Almy.

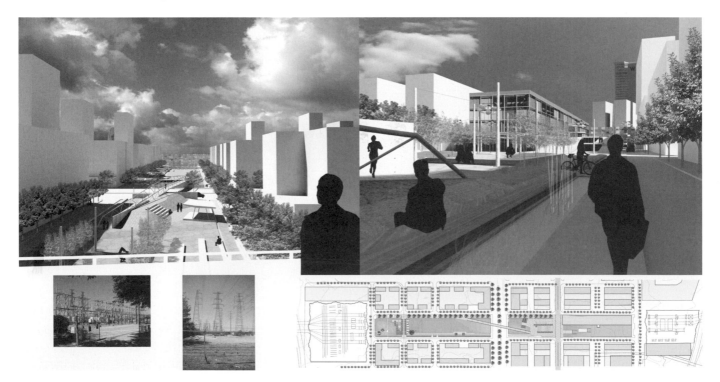

**20.5** Victory Park, Dallas. Photograph by Jeremy Woodhouse.

**20.6** Urban Reserve Master Plan, Dallas. Project landscape architect Kevin Sloan Studio. Courtesy of Kevin Sloan Studio.

A ZONE ONE
1. Entrance
2. Existing Volunteer Tree Canopy
3. Italian Cypress Field
4. Filtration Pond

B ZONE TWO
5. Street - Vanguard Way
6. Dry Side, Desert Willow
7. Wet Site, Bald and Pond Cypress
8. Rain Garden Biofilters
9. Bridges
10. Filtration Ponds

C ZONE THREE
11. Buffalo Grass
12. White Rock Creek Park, Existing

CONTEXT
13. Existing 1950s Subdivision
14. DART Transit Rail
15. White Rock Creek

0 30 60    120

Reserve combines an environmental sensitivity with contemporary architecture (Figures 20.6 to 20.8). Landscape architect Kevin Sloan and architect Bob Meckfessell's plan for the narrow 13-acre (5-ha) site fits fifty lots among a DART rail line, a creek, and an existing neighborhood. Cheatham engaged leading architects with national practices, such as Kieran Timberlake and Tod Williams Billie Tsien, as well as inventive Texans, like Vince Snyder, Dan Shipley, Maria Gomez, and Max Levy.

Another possible future for architecture is sustainability, the green route. From Pliny Fisk to Susan Maxman and Bill McDonough on to Rafael Pelli, architects continue to plow new ground. Leadership in Energy and Environmental Design moved green design from the fringes into the mainstream. Some complain about the constraints established by LEED and other green building standards. However, constraints present opportunities to advance design innovation. "Design depends largely on constraints," Charles Eames observed.

Housing presents architects with another career track. In addition to designing houses for the rich and famous, several architects work in housing for ordinary people and making housing more affordable. For illustration, let us look west

20.7 Urban Reserve street as biofiltration machine. Project landscape architect Kevin Sloan Studio. Courtesy of Kevin Sloan Studio.

20.8 Urban Reserve, Dallas. Project landscape architect Kevin Sloan Studio. Courtesy of Kevin Sloan Studio.

to California and the work of Renee Chow and Teddy Cruz. They have advanced our understanding of housing in suburban spaces and shanty towns. As high-rise housing grows in popularity in cities across the nation, so do opportunities for architects. In New York City, Rafael Pelli pioneered green high-rise housing in his design of The Solaire, a twenty-seven-story apartment tower in Battery Park City that advanced sustainable design when it opened in 2002. Nicolai Ouroussoff reports "an eruption of luxury residential towers" across New York City designed by "international celebrities" like Jean Nouvel, Bernard Tschumi, and Herzog & de Meuron.[3]

Beyond these fields, other options for architecture include materials research (see the work of Sheila Kennedy and Billie Faircloth), the whole-building process (the ideas of Stephen Kieran and James Timberlake), or geeky constructionists like

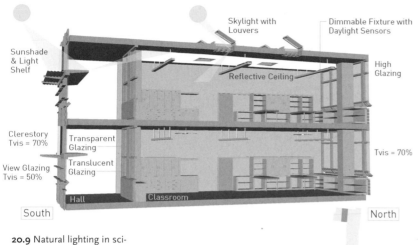

**20.9** Natural lighting in science classrooms, Sidwell Friends School, Washington, D.C. Design by Kieran Timberlake. Courtesy of Kieran Timberlake.

Ken Yeang, Santiago Calatrava, and Ove Arup, who have raised engineering to an art form (Figures 20.9 to 20.11).

A few architects have focused their energies on the poor. Architecture for Humanity founder Cameron Sinclair, Bryan Bell of Design Corps, and John Cary of Public Architecture are just three of them. These architects are charting new synthetic, worthwhile paths that overlap a great deal with community and regional planning.

To take advantage of the challenges and opportunities presented by urbanization, population growth, and immigration, planners need to renew their ties with architecture and landscape architecture. In late November 2006, an architecture

**20.10** Interior hallway, Sidwell Friends School, Washington, D.C. Design by Kieran Timberlake. Photograph © Peter Aaron/Esto.

20.11 Green roof, Sidwell Friends School, Washington, D.C. Design by Kieran Timberlake. Photograph © Peter Aaron/Esto.

graduate student asked me why there were no courses in public participation or social research in the University of Texas School of Architecture. I responded that there are several in our Community and Regional Planning Program. However, we do not make those courses very accessible to students outside that program. Planning programs, including ours at the University of Texas at Austin, that are located in the same school or college as architecture and landscape architecture have an opportunity to contribute much to the future of the built environment. We need to take advantage of this opportunity.

In addition to public participation, planners have developed considerable expertise in land-use law, environmental policy, public health, and transportation systems. This knowledge can be very useful to architects, landscape architects, preservationists, and interior designers. Such knowledge will be expanded by increased interaction.

Landscape architecture has much to contribute as well. To maximize this potential, landscape architects need to increase our understanding of the basic media with which we work—soils, water, and plants—as well as how built elements respond to weather and use. Such ecological knowledge can contribute much to the challenges presented by urbanism.

Which brings us to interior design. We spend much of our lives indoors. There will be a lot more of us living on Earth, we will be living in urban areas, and we will be from more diverse backgrounds. How we spend time indoors will be increasingly important. I think the most important challenge faced by interior design is a lack of theory. For the profession to advance, theory is essential because, after all, there is nothing as practical as a good theory.

The world needs more and better interior designers, architects, landscape architects, and planners. Population, urbanization, and immigration trends demand the knowledge and skills of these professions. I agree with Lewis Mumford, who proclaimed, "trend is not destiny"; however, design and planning hold the potential to chart destiny.

To chart our destiny, we need to consider time more carefully. Perhaps architects should use time rather than space to conceive their work, as Jeremy Till advocates. Time helps define us as a species and is a force in shaping the built environment, whether we pay attention to it or not. Till warns that "an architecture that ignores the everyday will be ignored every day."[4]

Each day connects us to the past and sets the stage for the future. Landscapes and regions connect us to the far reaches of geologic time. Robert Smithson was a keen observer of landscapes and geology. He wrote, "One's mind and the earth are in a constant state of erosion."[5] He also noted that "[t]he magnitude of geological change is still with us, just as it was millions of years ago."[6] Smithson saw sedimentation as the process whereby the earth builds itself and landscapes become more fertile, and thus he advocated similar sedimentation of our minds.

As a child, I drew all the time. Growing up, I never questioned that I would be somehow involved in the visual arts. I liked color and experimenting with paints on various surfaces. Shapes fascinated me to no end, and I enjoyed geometry and playing with angles and lines. As a Boy Scout in a mid-sized manufacturing city, I found inspiration in nature and in urban streets. The Scouts also introduced me to the world of cartography, instilling an appreciation for visual representations of what surrounds us and what we imagine to be around us. We Scouts would chart our course on a map, then hike that path or steer those currents. The map provided a helpful guide, but the walk or the canoe ride down the river always presented a different reality. Upon reflection, the experience combined the preparation and the execution.

During my college years, I found that the physical arrangement of built environments mattered more and more to me, as I witnessed the declines of Cincinnati, St. Louis, Detroit, Cleveland, and Philadelphia—once vibrant cities—before heading west.

The design of our built environment should matter to us all. Our neighborhoods and workplaces affect our health, our welfare, and our happiness. How we design buildings, roads and rails, parks, and water and sewer systems determines energy use and greenhouse gas production. With growing urban populations in Texas, across the nation, and around the world, we will need more roads and parks, homes and offices, schools and rail lines. Often, while driving around Houston, Dallas, and San Antonio, I am reminded of the aspirations of the region of my origins, the Silicon Valley of the early twentieth century, the birthplace of airplanes, automobiles, refrigerators, and cash registers.

We will need to create a new Texas, a new Great Lakes region, a new Italy, and a new China, even as oil and gas resources become more scarce. We need to recreate the built environment while ensuring that we can feed ourselves, drink clean water, and breathe safe air. We will also need to find ways to dispose of our waste without fouling our nests. This will challenge our resolve and tap all our creative reserves.

The future is in our hands.

Architecture matters for that future, as does landscape architecture, community and regional planning, interior design, and historic preservation. The City of Austin provides an ideal incubator for our disciplines. In return, we strive to improve the quality of the city's built environment.

Through programs such as Austin Energy Green Building and Envision Central Texas, as well as institutions such as the Lady Bird Johnson Wildflower Center and the Charles W. Moore Center for the Study of Place (founded at the architect's home and studio after his death in 1993), and our School's Center for Sustainable Development, Austin is at the forefront of sustainable design and planning. The city sports increasingly important, contemporary civic architecture, such as Austin's LEED Gold City Hall, Trustee Hall on the St. Edward's University campus, and the Austin-Bergstrom International Airport; impressive historic structures like the State Capitol and the

20.12 Austin City Hall. Design by Antoine Predock. Photograph by Frederick Steiner.

20.13 Trustee Hall, St. Edward's University, Austin. Design by Andersson-Wise Architects. Photograph by Timothy Hursley.

Main Building on the University of Texas campus; and significant green open spaces, such as Zilker Park, the Balcones Canyonlands Preserve, and the Balcones National Wildlife Refuge (Figures 20.12 and 20.13). And Austin is offering more and more engaging urban places, such as the new plaza at the Blanton Museum of Art. Austin provides places for non-humans to live, too. For instance, the National Wildlife Federation certified City Hall as a wildlife habitat in 2008. Austin is a living laboratory for architecture and design creativity. As participants in the architectural and planning civic dialogue, we contribute to that laboratory as well.

To my regret, I draw much less now than when I was a boy. My surroundings still matter, including city streets and more private places, such as my backyard. A canopy of large, live oaks shades my house and the front and back yards. Birds, raccoons, squirrels, and opossum enjoy the place as much as I do. As I sit under the live oaks and watch a squirrel race along the fence, I am reminded that the quality of the built environment matters to other species, too. We need architecture that beautifully weaves into this web of life.

I am also reminded of how much we are shaped by the light we first see, by the rooms we first explore, and by the leaves and bugs we first encounter. My early memories include venturing into the woods to look for mushrooms with my parents and grandparents, my mom attempting to teach me how to differentiate the poisonous ones. I watched my parents and grandparents harvest watercress from small streams and dandelions that had invaded the lawn.

My paternal grandparents had a small farm in Ohio, not far from the Indiana border along the Old National Road. There, I learned to hunt rabbits and pheasant—one native, the other introduced for sport. My two brothers and I fished in the creek that formed the southern property line of the farm, as well as in a small pond planned by soil conservationists. All kinds of warfare, no doubt, occurred in that pond, between the native fishes and those introduced by conservationists and fishing enthusiasts, but I was unaware of these battles as a boy.

My grandmother taught me much about native plants, especially roots and berries. Memories of her sassafras tea and blackberry cobbler still arouse my taste buds. I learned even more about plants as a Boy Scout, hiking and canoeing through the small hills and winding valleys of southern Ohio and Indiana, in the area where the mighty Wisconsin glaciers ran out of steam, a land of drumlins and terminal moraines.

This foundation served me well as I went to study with Ian McHarg in a quest to learn how to design with nature. McHarg's landscape architecture and regional planning program at Penn had two tracks: one focused on design, which was more site-oriented, and the other on planning, which was more regionally based. I pursued the latter track. Both were grounded in ecology. So my formal training in plants is much more from a community perspective than about individual species.

This perspective has been most helpful, as I have moved and worked around the United States—mostly in the American West—in Europe, in northern Mexico, and, more recently, in China. In each place, understanding native communities provided the key to learning the essence of what makes the region tick. Along the way, I have

had the privilege to contribute to the planning and design of two special institutions, the Desert Botanical Garden in Phoenix and the Lady Bird Johnson Wildflower Center in Austin. This involvement has heightened my awareness of the importance of native plant education and research. It has also made me more aware of the dangers of losing species, as well as the significant opportunities for healing the earth's wounds with a more widespread use of native plants.

Technologies, especially connecting technologies, are transforming human societies. Connectivity involves the ways in which new networks and information systems will alter landscapes and communities, the transfer of knowledge, time, social relationships, and education. Connecting technologies—from the automobile to the Internet—can also divide people and, thus, further fragment landscapes and communities. We constantly attempt to connect through information and transportation technologies.

The world grows smaller as a result. When I returned to China in May 2007, I felt less like a tourist. The great change there became less abstract, more personal. My favorite Hunan restaurant across the street from the Tsinghua Big Yard disappeared and was replaced by a more trendy establishment. Later that summer, I returned to my old Dutch home—Wageningen. The university was abandoning its former home, dispersed and integrated within the city, for a suburban American-style campus with an eclectic collection of bad architecture. Afterward, before joining the Bellagio conference, I visited Milan, where the Polytechnic was expanding its Lecco campus. Being connected enabled me to witness change, as I returned to the same places I had been before.

In May 2008, I returned to Beijing again, this time with my colleagues Wilfried Wang and Ming Zhang and fifteen University of Texas students, flying into the new Norman Foster-designed Beijing terminal. I am now familiar enough to be a guide. We visited the Olympic Forest Park in advance of the Summer Games. We also took a night train to Suzhou, then a bus to Hangzhou. After China, I visited Sardinia once again, then toured Macedonia for the U.S. State Department. Using Google Earth and the Internet, I viewed each place in advance.

Information stored and communicated via computers reveals more and more about our interactions and connections, with each other and with our worlds. GIS, combined with real-time satellite images and the Internet, provides the equivalent of what GIS pioneer Jack Dangermond has called "a central nervous system for the planet." Humans can aspire to provide the brain for that system. How we apply our brains to use these technologies and this information will transform how we live and, therefore, the patterns of our settlements. Beyond the brain, we humans can also contribute our hearts and our conscience to Dangermond's central nervous system. This implies an application of technologies that are fair and transparent to the public.

As the information landscape advances, we can gain a better understanding of our connectivity with nature. For example, satellites can generate daily climate information for settlements. Such information can be mapped through GIS over time. GIS can also be used to overlay climate data on land-use and land-cover maps. This process reveals how we use the land and how what we grow on its surface affects urban climate. In this way, GIS and remote-sensing technologies enable us to visualize relationships. Our ecological understanding advances as we reveal previously unseen connections. These linkages become real when we visit a place and translate the abstraction from a computer map or photograph into the sights, sounds, and smells of everyday life.

We especially gain insights into urban places, as well as the urbanization and population growth challenges we face. The deleterious consequences are all around us, especially obvious to those of us trained in ecology. As Aldo Leopold observed, we live alone in a "world of wounds," and we "must be the doctor who sees the marks of death in a community that believes itself well and does not want to be told otherwise."[7]

Fortunately, we do not have to live as alone as in Leopold's day, but . . . .

How do we go about healing the Earth?

Let us explore one of the consequences of our dominant pattern of growth in the United States—*suburban sprawl*. Suburban sprawl is dispersed, automobile-dependent development outside compact urban and town centers, along highways and in the rural countryside. Such development consumes more land, water, and energy than more traditional settlement patterns. Sprawl fragments open space and tends to be homogenous in appearance. It negatively affects our sense of place, as well as habitats for animals as diverse as the bullfrog and the red fox.

As American cities continue to sprawl, we Americans grow fatter. In 2002, the Centers for Disease Control and Prevention (CDC) reported that some 60 percent of Americans are overweight and at least 18 percent are obese.[8] This issue is garnering increased attention. *Time* updated the CDC-based data in June 2004 and reported that now "two-thirds of U.S. adults are officially overweight, and about half of these have graduated to full-blown obesity."[9] These figures continue to rise and are especially alarming for children. In 2009, the American Academy of Pediatrics reported 32 percent of U.S. children are overweight and linked the growing number of overweight children to their physical inactivity and to community design.[10] Part of the problem of children being physically inactive is the lack of safe neighborhood design that supports walking to school, parks, recreational facilities, and walking just for the sake of exercise. The rates of overweight children and adults are most alarming among African-American and Latino populations.

The lack of walking opportunities and the easy access to fast food are two contributing factors. Thus, the design and planning of our surroundings are important public health issues. Although nothing ever happens quite as planned, if we do not plan for a better future, if we do not take action for positive change, the consequences will be even worse.

For example, in most American cities, there is a lack of safe and accessible sidewalks, crosswalks, and bike paths. Transportation alternatives are limited, with little pedestrian access to buses and transit systems. Parks and recreation facilities are unsafe, unsightly, and not accessible. Shopping areas and services cannot be accessed without automobiles. In addition to obesity, other public health issues have also been linked to suburban sprawl and community design.

The connection between obesity, our health in general, and the design of our built environments should be apparent. As Dr. Richard Joseph Jackson, formerly of the CDC and now a professor of environmental health sciences at UCLA, observes:

*Medicine will not be adequate to deal with the health challenges of the twenty-first century, not even with the help of the sequenced genome and advances in robotic surgery. Even though the United States spends one of every seven dollars on medical care, we will not significantly improve health and the quality of life, unless we pay more attention to how we design our living environments. Healthy living environments include not just a clean and heated kitchen, bath, or bedroom, but also the landscape around us. Health for all, especially for the young, aging, poor and disabled, requires that we design healthfulness into our environments as well.*[11]

We spend more time in cars, over a week more per year than a decade ago. The dependency on automobile and truck transportation leads to increased respiratory problems. Animals and plants are affected by air pollution as well. Many cities across the nation and around the world experience ozone warning days because of traffic. Clogged highways also delay travel times, which can increase our tension and anxiety.

Ecology can enable us to understand the relationship between community design and our health. Landscapes with green corridors for walking and biking provide greater opportunities for their inhabitants to improve their health than those that are dominated by highways.

We can take at least four positive steps toward healing the planet and, in the process, we can save humanity.

*First*, we need to acknowledge the relationship between health and the built environment that is being advanced by the CDC, the Robert Wood Johnson Foundation, *Time*, and others. As we shape our communities, we must be mindful of how they shape us. Our built environment affects our well-being. For example, health and productivity losses associated with indoor air pollution are estimated to cost tens of billions of dollars annually. We need to be committed to creating healthy buildings, interiors, landscapes, and cities.

*Second*, we need to build green. This is a much too important issue to be left to architects and builders alone. Building and construction activities worldwide consume three billion tons of raw materials each year or 40 percent of the total global material use. Buildings use around half of all energy, two-thirds of all electricity, and their construction consumes one-fourth of all harvested wood. The Earth is a source and a sink for everything we use to build and we dispose of afterward. We need to ask: What is the source of each material we use, not only in buildings, but also in what we eat, wear, and watch? Where and how will materials be disposed of after they are used?

*Third*, we must stop sprawling and do a better job restoring and conserving our current built environment. We have a considerable existing building stock that represents an important component of our cultural heritage. We need to preserve and restore what we already have. In doing so, we can help protect wildlife habitats, beautiful coastlines, and prime farmlands from needless destruction.

*Fourth*, we need to think regionally. The model for regionalism introduced in the Preface provides a theory for such thinking. The model is process-based and requires an understanding of natural phenomena, as well as an engagement in policy. I have provided several examples of such new regionalist thinking from Austin to Beijing.

As we add the equivalent of another new nation of people in the United States over the remainder of the twenty-first century, we must restore what we already have. To accommodate a total of 400 million U.S. citizens, as much of the built environment becomes obsolete, we must double the capacity for housing, parks, transportation systems, schools, sewer and water infra-structure, and businesses. We also need clean and efficient energy that can be accessed by peaceful means. We cannot continue to do business as usual. The first urban century demands new transdisciplinary approaches for conceiving our futures. This will require innovation in fields as diverse as journalism, law, teaching, entrepreneurship, gender studies, politics, and science. We also need new forms of creative expression in art, music, and writing. This all suggests an urgency for renewed explorations in human ecology.

I am optimistic about our capability to heal the wounds that are inflicted by our current approaches to urban design and planning.

Ecology is about connections and relationships. Ecological understanding can thus provide an antidote for future shock, and ecologically based design and planning can offer a remedy for suburban sprawl.

The American transcendentalist Henry David Thoreau wrote: "This earth was the most glorious instrument, and I was audience to its strains."

Let us listen to that instrument, enjoy the strains, and learn from them so that we might play the instrument with beauty and precision. In doing so, we can heal the wounds of this Earth and create a healthier, safer, and more creative world for those who will inherit our places.

# NOTES

## CHAPTER 1

1. Vitruvius, *On Architecture* (trans. Frank Granger, Cambridge, Mass.: Harvard University Press, 1931), Book I, Chapter I, 10.

2. Lionel Casson, *Everyday Life in Ancient Rome* (Baltimore: Johns Hopkins University Press, 1998), p. 134.

3. Vitruvius, I, IV, 1.

4. Ernest L. Boyer and Lee D. Mitgang, *Building Community: A New Future for Architectural Education and Practice* (Princeton, N.J.: Carnegie Foundation for the Advancement of Teaching, 1996).

5. Robert D. Putnam, *Bowling Alone: The Collapse and Revival of American Community* (New York: Simon & Schuster, 2000).

6. Peter Calthorpe and William Fulton, *The Regional City: Planning for the End of Sprawl* (Washington, D.C.: Island Press, 2001) and Roger Simmonds and Gary Hack, eds., *Global City Regions: Their Emerging Forms* (London: Spon Press, 2000).

7. Calthorpe and Fulton, *The Regional City*, p. 10.

8. Steven A. Moore, "Reproducing the Local," *Platform* (Spring, 1999): 9.

9. Kenneth Frampton, "Towards a Critical Regionalism: Six Points for an Architecture of Resistance" in Hal Foster, ed., *The Anti-Aesthetic: Essays on Postmodern Culture* (Port Townsend, Wash.: Bay Press, 1983), p. 21.

10. Richard Jackson, formerly of the Centers for Disease Control and Prevention in Atlanta and now professor and chair of Environmental Health Sciences at UCLA, suggests a different fourth "e": exercise.

11. Moore, "Reproducing the Local," p. 8. See also Steven A. Moore, "Technology, Place, and the Nonmodern Thesis," *Journal of Architectural Education* (Volume 54, Number 3, February 2001): 130–139, and Steven A. Moore, ed., *Pragmatic Sustainability: Theoretical and Practical Tools* London: Routledge, 2010).

12. For more discussion about deep structure and deep context, see Anne Whiston Spirn, *The Language of Landscape* (New Haven: Yale University Press, 1998).

13. The leaders of this movement include Peter Calthorpe, Stefanos Polyzoides, Elizabeth Moule, Andres Duany, Elizabeth Plater-Zyberk, and Dan Solomon. In addition to Calthorpe and Fulton's book, see Andres Duany, Elizabeth Plater-Zyberk, and Jeff Speck, *Suburban Nation: The Rise of Sprawl and the Decline of the American Dream* (New York: North Point Press, 2001), and Daniel Solomon, *Global City Blues* (Washington, D.C.: Island Press, 2003).

14. Calthorpe and Fulton, *The Regional City*, p. 279.

15. Duany, Plater-Zyberk, and Speck, *Suburban Nation*, pp. 11–12.

16. See Frederick Steiner, *The Living Landscape* (New York: McGraw-Hill, 2000; paperback edition, Island Press, 2008), and James Burke and Joseph Ewan, *Sonoran Preserve Master Plan* (Phoenix, Arizona: Department of Parks, Recreation, and Library, 1998).

17. Gary W. Barrett and Eugene P. Odum, "The Twenty-First Century: The World at Carrying Capacity," *BioScience* (Volume 50, Number 4, 2000): 363–368.

18. Stewart Brand, *The Clock of the Long Now: Time and Responsibility* (London: Weidenfeld & Nicolson, 1999), p. 8.

19. United Nations Development Programme, United Nations Environment Programme, World Bank, and World Resources Institute, *World Resources 2000–2001, People and Ecosystems, The Fraying Web of Life* (Amsterdam: Elsevier, 2000).

20. Grant Hildebrand, *Origins of Architectural Pleasure* (Berkeley: University of California Press, 1999), p. xvii.

21. George Hersey, *The Monumental Impulse: Architecture's Biological Roots* (Cambridge, Mass.: MIT Press, 1999), p. 183.

22. Stephen R. Kellert, Judith H. Heerwagen, and Martin L. Mador, eds., *Biophilic Design* (Hoboken, N.J.: John Wiley & Sons, 2008), p. vii.

23. Brand, *The Clock of the Long Now.*

24. Jeremy Till, *Architecture Depends* (Cambridge, Mass.: MIT Press, 2009), p. 95.

## CHAPTER 2

1. See Steven Moore, "Architecture, Esthetics, and the Public Health," in Sandra Iliescu, ed., *The Hand and the Soul: Aesthetics and Ethics in Architecture and Art* (Charlottesville: University of Virginia Press, 2008).

2. Stephen M. Wheeler, *Planning for Sustainability* (London: Routledge, 2004).

3. United Nations Commission on Environment and Development, *Our Common Future* (Oxford, U.K.: Oxford University Press, 1987), p. 8.

4. John Tillman Lyle, *Regenerative Design for Sustainable Development* (New York: John Wiley & Sons, 1994).

5. Philip R. Berke, "The Evolution of Green Community Planning, Scholarship, and Practice," *Journal of the American Planning Association* (Volume 74, Number 4, 2008): 404.

6. For more information, see www.solardecathlon.org.

7. John D. Quale, *Trojan Goat: A Self-Sufficient House* (Charlottesville: University of Virginia School of Architecture, 2005), p. 20.

8. Seth Wilberding, "On the Mall, Few Functional Landscapes," *Landscape Architecture* (Volume 98, Number 2, February 2008): 40.

9. M. Garrison, R. Krepart, S. Randall, and A. Novoselac, "The BLOOMhouse: Zero Net Energy Housing," a paper presented at the Texas Society of Architects Annual Conference, October 24, 2008.

10. The next morning, after the accident, I received a call. Texas A&M professor Pliny Fisk had heard about our accident. His A&M Solar Decathlon team was leaving and he offered their help. He did not know that the mishap had occurred in Austin and thought it had happened along the way between Texas and Washington. Pliny offered to load our house or parts of it on the A&M truck. I explained the situation and wished the A&M team success. Pliny generously wished our Longhorn team a successful competition as well.

## CHAPTER 3

1. Witold Rybczynski, *The Perfect House* (New York: Scribners, 2002).

2. See, for instance, S. Barles, "Urban Metabolism and River Systems: An Historical Perspective—Paris and the Seine, 1790–1970," *Hydrology and Earth System Sciences* (Volume 11, 2007): 1757–1769.

3. Arthur C. Nelson, "Leadership in a New Era," *Journal of the American Planning Association* (Volume 72, Number 4, 2006): 393–407.

## CHAPTER 4

1. www.usgbc.org.

2. Ibid.

3. Ian L. McHarg, *Design with Nature* (Garden City, New York: Natural History Press/Doubleday, 1969).

4. Lyle, *Regenerative Design for Sustainable Development.*

5. American Society of Landscape Architects; Lady Bird Johnson Wildflower Center, The University of Texas at Austin; and U.S. Botanic Garden, *Preliminary Report of the Practice Guidelines and Metrics, The Sustainable Sites Initiative* (Austin: The University of Texas at Austin, 2007).

6. Robert Costanza, "Ecosystems Services: Multiple Classification Systems Are Needed," *Biological Conservation* (Volume 141, 2008): 350–352. See also, Stephen C. Farber, Robert Costanza, and Michael A. Wilson, "Economic and Ecological Concepts for Valuing Ecosystem Services," *Ecological Economics* (Volume 14, 2002): 375–392, and Dennis D. Hirsch, "Ecosystem Services and the Green City," in Eugenie L. Birch and Susan M. Wachter, eds., *Growing Greener Cities: Urban Sustainability in the Twenty-First Century* (Philadelphia: University of Pennsylvania Press, 2008), pp. 281–293.

7. Costanza, "Ecosystems Services."

8. American Society of Landscape Architects; Lady Bird Johnson Wildflower Center, The University of Texas at Austin; and United States Botanic Garden. *Guidelines and Performance Benchmarks, Draft 2008* (Austin: Sustainable Sites Initiative, 2008).

9. The shorthand name for the initiative, which was determined early in 2010, reflects the focus of the effort, that is, SITES<TM>.

10. American Society of Landscape Architects et al. *Guidelines and Performance Benchmarks, Draft 2008.*

## CHAPTER 5

1. Günter Vogt, *Miniature and Panorama, Vogt Landscape Architecture Projects 2000–2006* (Baden: Lars Müller Publishers, 2006), p. 167.

2. Lewis Mumford, *The Culture of Cities* (London: Secker and Warburg, 1938).

3. Giovanni Maciocco, *Fundamental Trends in City Development* (Berlin: Springer, 2008).

4. See, for example, Dean Almy, ed., *On Landscape Urbanism, CENTER 14* (Austin: Center for American Architecture and Design, 2007); Charles Waldheim, ed., *The Landscape Urbanism Reader* (New York: Princeton Architecture Press, 2006); Chris Reed, *StossLU* (Seoul, Korea: C3 Publishing, 2007); and Field Operations, Diller Scofidio + Renfro, Friends of the High Line, City of New York, *Design-*

ing the High Line, Gansevoort Street to 30th Street (New York: Friends of the High Line, 2008).

5. Daniel B. Botkin, *Discordant Harmonies: A New Ecology for the Twenty-First Century* (New York: Oxford University Press, 1990).

6. Timothy Beatley, *Native to Nowhere* (Washington, D.C.: Island Press, 2004).

7. Kevin Lynch, "Environmental Adaptability," *Journal of the American Institute of Planners* (Volume 24, Number 1, 1958): 16–24. Reprinted in Tridib Banerjee and Michael Southworth, eds., *City Sense and City Design: Writings and Projects of Kevin Lynch* (Cambridge, Mass.: MIT Press, 1990).

8. Lance Gunderson, C. S. Holling, L. Pritchard, and G. D. Peterson, "Resilience," in Ted Munn, ed., *Encyclopedia of Global Environmental Change* (Hoboken, N.J.: John Wiley & Sons, 2002), pp. 530–531.

9. Botkin, *Discordant Harmonies*. See also David Waltner-Toews, James J. Kay, and Nina-Marie E. Lister, eds., *The Ecosystem Approach: Complexity, Uncertainty, and Managing for Sustainability* (New York, Columbia University Press, 2008), and Richard T. T. Forman, *Urban Regions: Ecology and Planning Beyond the City* (Cambridge: Cambridge University Press, 2008).

10. Steward T. A. Pickett and Mary L. Cadenasso, "Integrating the Ecological, Socioeconomic, and Planning Realms: Insights from the Baltimore Ecosystem Study," in Laura Musacchio, Jianguo Wu, and Thara Johnson, eds., *Pattern, Process, Scale, and Hierarchy: Advancing Interdisciplinary Collaboration for Creating Sustainable Urban Landscapes and Communities* (Tempe: Arizona State University, 2003), p. 34.

11. See http://caplter.asu.edu/ and www.beslter.org.

12. Lawrence J. Vale and Thomas J. Campanella, "The City Shall Rise Again: Urban Resilience in the Wake of Disaster," *The Chronicle of Higher Education* (January 14, 2005): B6–B9, and Lawrence J. Vale and Thomas J. Campanella, eds., *The Resilient City: How Modern Cities Recover from Disaster* (New York: Oxford University Press, 2005).

13. Vale and Campanella, "The City Shall Rise Again," p. B6.

14. Ibid.

15. Ibid.

16. Don DeLillo, *Underworld* (New York: Scribner, 1997), pp. 449–450.

17. Field Operations et al., *Designing the High Line*.

18. Ibid., p. 30.

19. See, for instance, Ricky Burdett and Deyan Sudjic, eds., *The Endless City* (London: Phaidon Press, 2007).

### CHAPTER 6

1. Frederick Law Olmsted, *Journey Through Texas: or, a Saddle-Trip on the Southwestern Frontier; with a Statistical Appendix* (New York: Dix, Edwards & Co., 1857).

2. Carol McMichael, *Paul Cret at Texas: Architectural Drawing and the Image of the University in the 1930s* (Austin: Archer M. Huntington Art Gallery, College of Fine Arts, The University of Texas at Austin, 1983).

3. Ibid. See also "Paul Philippe Cret" in Ann L. Strong and George E. Thomas, eds., *The Book of the School: 100 Years* (Philadelphia: Graduate School of Fine Arts, University of Pennsylvania, 1990), p. 72. For a complete biography, see Elizabeth Greenwell Grossman, *The Civic Architecture of Paul Cret* (New York: Cambridge University Press, 1996).

4. Ian McHarg, *A Quest for Life: An Autobiography* (New York: John Wiley & Sons, 1996). See also Ian L. McHarg and Frederick R. Steiner, eds., *To Heal the Earth* (Washington, D.C.: Island Press, 1998), and Frederick R. Steiner, ed., *The Essential Ian McHarg* (Washington, D.C.: Island Press, 2007).

5. McMichael, *Paul Cret at Texas*.

6. Paul P. Cret, "Report Accompanying the General Plan of Development" (Austin: University of Texas, January 1933).

7. Carol McMichael characterizes Beaux-Arts buildings as "axially and symmetrically disposed particulate plans . . . [with] . . . historicist elevations derived from a careful study of the architectural monuments of antiquity and the Renaissance." Furthermore, she describes the opposition between Cret's "traditional Beaux-Arts" and "modern purist concepts" as "(a) symmetrical, compartmentalized plans vs. asymmetrical, open plans; (b) mass-dominant buildings vs. volume-dominant buildings; (c) particulate masses vs. unified masses; and (d) ornamented surfaces vs. unornamented surfaces." McMichael, *Paul Cret at Texas*, p. 43.

8. Werner Hegemann and Elbert Peets, *The American Vitruvius: An Architect's Handbook of Civic Art* (New York: Architectural Book Publishing Co., 1922).

9. McMichael, *Paul Cret at Texas*, p. 84.

10. Cret, "Report," p. 3.

11. Ibid., p. 4.

12. Ibid., p. 32.

13. Ibid., p. 17.

14. Wallace, McHarg, Roberts and Todd, *Lake Austin Growth Management Plan* (Austin: City of Austin, July 1976).

15. Ibid., p. 2.

16. Ibid., p. 49.

17. Cret, "Report," p. 14.

### CHAPTER 7

1. See, for example, George T. Morgan Jr. and John O. King, *The Woodlands: New Community Development, 1964–1983* (College Station: Texas A&M Press, 1987); Cynthia L. Girling and Kenneth I. Helphand, *Yard-Street-Park* (New York: John Wiley & Sons, 1994); Roger Galatas with Jim Barlow, *The Woodlands: The Inside Story of Creating a Better Hometown* (Washington, D.C.: The Urban Land Institute,

2004); Richard Ingersoll, "Utopia Limited: Houston's Ring Around the Beltway," *Cite* (Volume 31, Winter-Spring, 1994): 10–16; and Peter Wood, "37,000 Woodlanders Can't Be Wrong," *Cite* (Volume 31, Winter-Spring, 1994): 17.

2. Having McHarg on board, however, was not in itself a guarantee for success. With his Wallace, McHarg, Roberts and Todd colleagues, he helped propose two Title VII new communities. The Pontchartrain new-town-in-town in New Orleans never even received HUD approval. Only The Woodlands prevailed.

3. Ann Forsyth, "Evolution of an Ecoburb," *Landscape Architecture* (Volume 95, Number 7, July 2005): 60, 62, 64, 65, 66–67. See also Ann Forsyth, "Ian McHarg's Woodlands: A Second Look," *Planning* (August 2003): 10–13, and Ann Forsyth, "Planning Lessons from Three U.S. New Towns of the 1960s and 1970s: Irvine, Columbia, and The Woodlands," *Journal of the American Planning Association* (Volume 68, Number 4, 2002): 387–417.

4. Ann Forsyth, *Reforming Suburbia: The Planned Communities of Irvine, Columbia, and The Woodlands* (Berkeley: University of California Press, 2005), pp. 161–163.

5. Galatas, *The Woodlands*.

6. Forsyth, *Reforming Suburbia*, p. 164.

7. McHarg, *A Quest for Life*, pp. 256, 260.

8. Interview with George Mitchell, August 24, 2005.

9. McHarg, *A Quest for Life*, p. 264.

10. Morgan and King, *The Woodlands*, p. 52.

11. Galatas, *The Woodlands*, p. xiv.

12. Ibid., p. xvi.

13. Mitchell interview.

14. Russell Clive Claus, "The Woodlands, Texas: a retrospective critique of the principles and implementation of an ecologically planned development" (Cambridge, Mass.: Department of Urban Studies and Planning, Massachusetts Institute of Technology, Master of City Planning thesis, 1994).

15. Ibid., p. 2.

16. Mitchell interview.

17. Galatas, *The Woodlands*.

18. Forsyth, *Reforming Suburbia*, p. 182.

19. Galatas, *The Woodlands*.

20. Ibid., p. 155.

21. Ibid, p. 156. Galatas reports that Mitchell would have preferred to sell his energy interests, but they were entangled in litigation. He sold the energy company about three years after liquidating The Woodlands.

22. Mitchell interview.

23. Ibid.

24. Ibid.

25. Galatas, *The Woodlands*, p. 179.

26. Mitchell interview.

27. Wallace, McHarg, Roberts and Todd, *Amelia Island, Florida, A Report on the Master Planning Process for a Recreational New Community* (Hilton Head Island, S.C.: The Sea Pines Company, 1971) and Wallace, McHarg, Roberts and Todd, *Lake Austin Growth Management Plan*.

28. Mitchell interview.

### CHAPTER 8

1. Aldo Leopold, *Round River: From the Journals of Aldo Leopold*, Luna B. Leopold, ed. (Minocqua, Wis.: North Word Press, 1991), p. 237.

2. Randy Lee Loftis, "Trinity River Ecology Courses Through Politics of Toll Road Debate," *Dallas Morning News* (October 28, 2007).

3. Andrew Karvonen traces the term first to the mythological Greek character Prometheus "who was punished by the gods for stealing fire from the heavens and giving it to the humans," then on to the subtitle of Mary Shelley's 1818 novel *Frankenstein: The Modern Prometheus*, "reflecting the hubris of human attempts to control nature." Andrew Karvonen, *Botanizing the Asphalt: Politics of Urban Drainage* (Austin: The University of Texas at Austin, Ph.D. dissertation, 2008), p. 10.

4. American Institute of Architects, Dallas, *Trinity River Policy* (Dallas, Texas, November 2001).

5. Correspondence with Rebecca Dugger, September 2002. The U.S. Army Corps of Engineers, the Texas Department of Transportation, and the North Texas Tollway Authority are among several public entities that share stakes in the project, along with numerous neighborhood organizations and private landowners.

6. Ibid.

7. Interview with Kevin Sloan, August 2002.

8. American Institute of Architects, *Dallas Trinity River Policy*.

9. Ibid.

10. American Institute of Architects, Dallas, *Advisory Panel Summary Report* (Dallas, Texas, September 2001).

11. David Dillon, "AIA Has a Flood of Protests," *Dallas Morning News* (January 20, 2002).

12. Sloan interview.

13. Ibid.

14. Ibid.

15. The 2002 Gateway Park Master Plan was developed by Texas A&M landscape architecture students. The A&M plan was undertaken concurrently with the larger Trinity River Vision Master Plan, which began in 2001. Prepared by Gideon Toal, the Trinity River Vision Master Plan was completed in April 2003. These plans influence ongoing development and conservation efforts for the Trinity River and its major tributaries in Fort Worth.

16. In *A Balanced Vision Plan for the Trinity River* (December 2003), Chan Krieger, Hargreaves, and others put forth a "grand vision" that attempted to balance "diverse and potentially conflicting goals," addressing flood protection, mobility, recreation, economic development, environmental restoration, and air quality.

17. Ibid.

18. Ibid.

19. Ibid., p. 16.

20. HNTB, *City of Dallas Trinity River Comprehensive Land Use Plan* (Final Report) (Dallas: Trinity River Corridor Project, adopted March 9, 2005). See also www.trinityrivercorridor.org.

21. Bruce Tomaso, "Dallas Vote Exposes Mistrust of Dallas City Hall," *Dallas Morning News* (November 10, 2007).

22. Bruce Tomaso, Dave Levinthal, and Rudolph Bush, "Dallas Voters Endorse Trinity Toll Road," *Dallas Morning News* (November 7, 2007).

23. Dave Levinthal, "Leppert Vows to Deliver on Trinity River Toll Road, Park," *Dallas Morning News* (November 7, 2007).

24. Max B. Baker, "Key GOP Lawmaker Impressed by Project," *Fort Worth Star-Telegram* (August 9, 2007). See also www.trinityrivervision.org.

## CHAPTER 9

1. One regent was the wife of a former Republican governor. The other was a Democrat, but he had been a strong supporter of and campaign contributor for George W. Bush. Subsequently, he unsuccessfully ran for governor. I wrote in "Jacques Herzog" on the ballot for governor in that election.

2. Page Southerland Page had made Larry Speck an offer he couldn't refuse. He had a small, but distinguished, practice. They had a prosperous, but stodgy, Austin practice. They asked him to become their design architect. As a result of his subsequent design leadership in the firm, the practice took off in quality and in creativity.

3. Lawrence W. Speck, *Technology and Cultural Identity* (New York: Edizioni, 2006).

4. Speck is a leader of Regional Modernism in Texas, and many of his former students work in prominent Texas firms noted for their regionally based approach to Modernism, such as Overland Partners and Lake|Flato. The late Texas A&M University architectural historian Malcolm Quantrill uses an intriguing term, "Plain Modernism," in his study of the work of Nova Scotia architect Brian MacKay-Lyons. See Malcolm Quantrill, *Plain Modern: The Architecture of Brian MacKay-Lyons* (New York: Princeton Architectural Press, 2005).

## CHAPTER 10

1. Duncan T. Fulton, "Dallas Arts District," in Sinclair Black, Frederick Steiner, Marisa Ballas, and Jeff Gipson, eds., *Emergent Urbanism* (Austin: School of Architecture, The University of Texas at Austin, 2008).

2. David Dillon, "The Meyerson Turns 15," *Dallas Morning News* (September 15, 2004).

3. David Dillon, "Artistic Differences," *Dallas Morning News* (March 27, 2005).

4. Ibid.

5. David Dillon, "Room to Grow," *Dallas Morning News* (September 14, 2006).

6. Vogt Landschaftsarchitekten, *Lupe und Fernglas, Miniatur und Panorama (Magnifying Glass and Binoculars, Miniature and Panorama)* (Berlin: AedesLand, 2007), p. 47.

7. The Dallas Center for the Performing Arts area opened to the public as the AT&T Performing Arts Center on October 12–18, 2009.

## CHAPTER 11

1. My neighbor is a plastic surgeon who retired to become an attorney. Along the way, he inherited his father's construction company and is sole trustee of a "significant" family trust. His grandfather had immigrated from Rhodes, when it was part of the Ottoman Empire. Despite what his passport says, my neighbor considers himself to be more Greek than Turkish and more Spanish than Greek, even though the family had left Spain five hundred years before. He is traveling to New York City to assess the suitability of a wayward relative to partake in the family trust.

On a visit to Morocco, he and his wife reportedly met a man in the resort elevator as they returned from a round of golf. The man wore a Longhorn T-shirt and he inquired if they had found the golf course suitable.

"Certainly," my neighbor responded.

"We try here in Morocco," observed the Longhorn.

"You're a Texas fan, I see."

"That's where I went to school, as did my children."

"I'm from Dallas," my neighbor reported.

Back in the hotel room, my neighbor's wife pointed to a picture of the king and said, "That's the Longhorn from the elevator."

Later, in the restaurant, the king greeted them again.

"How are you enjoying your dinner?"

"It's delightful, Your Excellency," responded the wife.

"I apologize for not introducing myself more properly on the elevator, but I find it can be unsettling to people, . . . even Texans."

2. See Jan Goodwin's chapter on Saudi Arabia in her revealing book *Price of Honor*, rev. ed. (New York: Penguin, 2003).

3. The editor of the journal *Environment and Planning B: Planning and Design*, Batty's books include *Cities and Complexity* (Cambridge, Mass.: MIT Press, 2005); *GIS, Spatial Analysis, and Modeling*, edited with D. J. Maguire and M. F. Goodchild (Redlands, Calif.: ESRI Press, 2005); and *Fractal Cities*, with P. A. Longley (London: Academic Press, 1994).

4. See Lewis L. Gould, *Lady Bird Johnson: Our Environmental First Lady* (Lawrence: University of Kansas Press, 1999).

**CHAPTER 12**

1. *Forbes*, "Best Places for Businesses and Careers" (May 9, 2003). See online e-magazine: Forbes.com, www.forbes.com/2003/05/07/bestland.html.

2. Richard Florida, *The Rise of the Creative Class: And How It's Transforming Work, Leisure, Community And Everyday Life* (New York: Basic Books, 2002).

3. Aaron Steelman, "Why Cities Grow: Economist Richard Florida Argues that Cities Must Attract Young, Talented Workers—What He Dubs the 'Creative Class'—If They Want to Prosper. Is He Right? And Is there Anything New about this Theory?" *Region Focus* (Fall 2004): 13–16.

4. W. W. Hammond, "Regional Hydrogeology of the Edwards Aquifer, South Central Texas," in E. T. Smerdon and W. R. Jordan, eds., *Issues in Groundwater Management* (Austin: Water Resources Symposium No. 12, Center for Research in Water Resources, The University of Texas at Austin, 1986), pp. 53–68.

5. Austin–San Antonio Corridor Policy Research Project, *The Emerging Economic Base and Local Developmental Policy Issues in the Austin–San Antonio Corridor* (Austin: Policy Research Project Report No. 71, Lyndon B. Johnson School of Public Affairs, The University of Texas at Austin, 1985).

6. Ibid.

7. City of Austin, *Facts and Information on the Northern Edwards Aquifer. Regional Conference on the Edwards Aquifer, North of the Colorado River* (Austin: City of Austin Office of Environmental Resource Management, 1986).

8. C. R. Burchett, P. L. Rettman, and C. W. Boning, *The Edwards Aquifer, Extremely Productive, But . . .* (San Antonio: Edwards Underground Water District, 1986).

9. City of San Antonio and Edwards Underground Water District, *San Antonio Regional Water Resource Study: Summary* (San Antonio: Department of Planning, City of San Antonio, 1986).

10. Stuart Glasoe, Frederick Steiner, William Budd, and Gerald Young, "Assimilative Capacity and Water Resource Management: Four Examples from the United States," *Landscape and Urban Planning* (Volume 19, Number 1, 1990): 17–46.

11. R. W. Maclay and T. A. Small, "Hydrostratigraphic Subdivisions and Fault Barriers of the Edwards Aquifer, South Central Texas, U.S.A.," *Journal of Hydrology* (Volume 61, 1983): 127–146.

12. City of San Antonio and Edwards Underground Water District, *San Antonio Regional Water Resource Study: Summary.*

13. Hammond, "Regional Hydrogeology of the Edwards Aquifer, South Central Texas."

14. R. M. Slade Jr., M. E. Dorsey, and S. L. Stewart, *Hydrology and Water Quality of the Edwards Aquifer Associated with Barton Springs in the Austin Area, Texas* (Austin: Water Resource Investigation Report 86–4036, U.S. Geological Survey, 1986).

15. Rainer K. Senger and Charles W. Kreitler, *Hydrogeology of the Edwards Aquifer, Austin Area, Central Texas* (Austin: Report of Investigations No. 141, Bureau of Economic Geology, The University of Texas, 1984).

16. Slade, Dorsey, and Stewart, *Hydrology and Water Quality of the Edwards Aquifer Associated with Barton Springs in the Austin Area, Texas*; Brian A. Smith and Brian B. Hunt, *Evaluation of Sustainable Yield of the Barton Springs Segment of the Edwards Aquifer, Hays and Travis Counties, Central Texas* (Austin: Barton Springs/Edwards Aquifer Conservation District, 2004).

17. City of Austin, *Facts and Information on the Northern Edwards Aquifer.*

18. Ibid.

19. Glasoe et al., "Assimilative Capacity and Water Resource Management."

20. See Wayt T. Watterson and Roberta S. Watterson, *The Politics of New Communities: A Case Study of San Antonio Ranch* (New York: Praeger, 1975).

21. See Timothy Beatley, *Habitat Conservation Planning* (Austin: University of Texas Press, 1994) and Bruce Babbitt, *Cities in the Wilderness* (Washington, D.C.: Island Press, 2005).

22. Beatley, *Habitat Conservation Planning*, p. 185.

23. Ibid., p. 189.

24. See www.balconescanyonlands.org.

25. United States Department of Agriculture Natural Resources Conservation Service, *National Resources Inventory, 1982–1992* (Washington, D.C., 1995). Online reference: http://www.texasep.org/html/Ind/Ind_2agr_sprawl.html.

**CHAPTER 13**

1. One of Overland's four founders, Rick Archer, served on the search committee that brought me to Austin. He was also president of the School's Advisory Council and active in university alumni activities. Rick graduated valedictorian of the University with a 4.0 grade point average. He was recognized for his academic achievements, service, and leadership and was named Outstanding Student at the University of Texas and National Student Leader of the Year. The other founding partners include Madison Smith, Tim Blonkvist, and Robert Schmidt.

2. See discussion in Chapter 6.

3. The board met near Aquarena Springs. Now part of Texas State University, the springs formerly featured frolicking mermaids, called "Aquamaids," with trained swimming pigs as attractions at a submarine theater. Long before the swimming pigs, Native Americans and Hispanic settlers were attracted to the springs as a source of drinking water.

4. Richard Dagger, "Stopping Sprawl for the Good of All: The Case for Civic Environmentalism," *Journal of Social Philosophy* (Volume 34, Number 1, 2003): 29.

5. Capital Area Metropolitan Planning Organization, unpublished data presenting CAMPO area growth in population, 2003 and 2030 (Austin, Texas, 2005).

6. Calthorpe Associates, "Proposed Urban Design Guidelines, East Austin Rail Corridor, Featherlite, Austin, Texas" (Austin: Envision Central Texas, 2003); Peter Calthorpe, *The Next American Metropolis: Ecology, Community, and the American Dream* (New York: Princeton Architectural Press, 1993); and Calthorpe and Fulton, *The Regional City*.

7. Garry D. Peterson, T. Douglas Beard Jr., Beatrix E. Beisner, Elena M. Bennett, Stephen R. Carpenter, Graeme S. Cumming, C. Lisa Dent, and Tanya D. Havlicek, "Assessing Future Ecosystem Services: A Case Study of the Northern Highlands Lake District, Wisconsin," *Conservation Ecology* (Volume 7, Number 3, 2003): 1–19.

8. Garry D. Peterson, Graeme S. Cumming, and Stephen R. Carpenter, "Scenario Planning: A Tool for Conservation in an Uncertain World," *Conservation Biology* (Volume 17, Number 3, 2003): 359.

9. Peter R. Mulvihill, "Expanding the Scoping Community," *Environmental Impact Assessment Review* (Volume 23, 2003): 45.

10. Calthorpe Associates, "Proposed Urban Design Guidelines, East Austin Rail Corridor, Featherlite, Austin, Texas."

11. Envision Central Texas, *A Vision for Central Texas* (Austin, Texas, 2004). See also www.envisioncentraltexas.org.

12. Ibid.

13. The Trust for Public Land, *The Travis County Greenprint for Growth* (Austin: Trust for Public Land, 2006).

14. Many topics are discussed and debated in the halls of Goldsmith, Sutton, the West Mall Office Building, and Battle, the mostly lovely and significant structures that house the School of Architecture. The faculty, staff, and students rarely mention football, except those returning from Italy and then that's the football played with feet. However, after the Texas Rose Bowl victory on January 4, 2006, we rivaled ESPN in our gridiron discussions. The national championship certainly reinforced a sense of community around the School, on campus, and throughout Austin. Even the delivery of books for my spring course—Environmental Readings—was delayed so that the University Co-Op Bookstore could sell more Longhorn T-shirts and baseball caps.

15. Envision Central Texas, "Central Texas Citizens' Concerns Range from Local Traffic Congestion to Global Climate Change, According to New Envision Central Texas" (news release, July 28, 2008).

16. TIP Strategies, Inc., *Vision Progress Assessment Prepared for Envision Central Texas* (Austin, July 2008).

17. TIP Strategies, Inc., *Organizational Recommendations Prepared for The Envision Central Texas Board of Directors* (Austin, July 2008), p. 1.

18. Ibid., p. 2.

19. Ibid.

20. Dagger, "Stopping Sprawl for the Good of All," p. 31.

21. Kent Butler and Dowell Myers, "Boomtown in Austin, Texas: Negotiated Growth Management," *Journal of the American Planning Association* (Volume 50, Number 4, 1984): 447–458. For a history of Austin's environmental politics, see William Scott Swearingen Jr., *Environmental City: People, Place, Politics, and the Meaning of Modern Austin* (Austin: University of Texas Press, 2010).

22. Alan Berube, *MetroNation: How U.S. Metropolitan Areas Fuel American Prosperity* (Washington, D.C.: The Brookings Institution, 2007), p. 6. See also Mark Muro, Bruce Katz, Sarah Rahman, and David Warren, *MetroPolicy: Shaping a New Federal Partnership for a Metropolitan Nation* (Washington, D.C.: The Brookings Institution, 2008), and Robert Puentes, *A Bridge to Somewhere: Rethinking American Transportation for the 21st Century* (Washington, D.C.: The Brookings Institution, 2008).

23. Putnam, *Bowling Alone*.

## CHAPTER 14

1. Jean Gottmann, *Megalopolis: The Urbanized Seaboard of the United States* (New York: Twentieth-Century Fund, 1961). Gottmann developed the term "megalopolis" from Greek words meaning "very large city."

2. Armando Carbonell and Robert D. Yaro, "American Spatial Development and The New Megalopolis," *Land Lines* (Volume 17, Number 2, 2005): 1–4.

3. Regional Plan Association, *America 2050: A Prospectus* (New York: Regional Plan Association, 2006). See also Catherine L. Ross, ed., *Megaregions: Planning for Global Competitiveness* (Washington, D.C.: Island Press, 2009), and Margaret Dewar and David Epstein, "Planning for 'Megaregions' in the United States," *Journal of Planning Literature* (Volume 22, Number 2, 2007): 108–124.

4. Robert E. Lang and Dawn Dhavale, *Beyond Megalopolis: Exploring America's New "Megapolitan" Geography* (Alexandria: Metropolitan Institute, Virginia Tech, July 2005). With colleagues at the Morrison Institute of Arizona State University and at the Brookings Institution, Lang has advanced the "mega" concept further for the Intermountain West. See Grady Gammage Jr., John Stuart Hall, Robert E. Lang, Rob Melnick, and Nancy Welch, *Megapolitan: Arizona's Sun Corridor* (Tempe: Morrison Institute, Arizona State University, May 2008), and Robert E. Lang, Andrea Sarzynski, and Mark Muro, *Mountain Megas: America's Newest Metropolitan Places and a Federal Partnership to Help Them Prosper* (Washington, D.C.: Metropolitan Policy Program, The Brookings Institution, 2008).

5. Texas State Data Center, *Texas Population Projections Program* (Texas State Data Center and Office of the State Demographer, May 10, 2006), http://txsdc.utsa.edu/.

6. Texas Transportation Institute, *Urban Mobility Study* (College Station, 2005), http://mobility.tamu.edu/.

7. Lang and Dhavale, *Beyond Megalopolis*.

8. Elise Bright, "Viewpoint: Megas? Maybe Not," *Plan-

ning (Volume 73, Number 4, 2007): 46. For a contrasting perspective, see: Kent Butler, Sara Hammerschmidt, Frederick Steiner, and Ming Zhang, *Reinventing the Texas Triangle: Solutions for Growing Challenges* (Austin: Center for Sustainable Development, The University of Texas at Austin, 2009).

9. Robert Bailey, *Ecoregions: The Ecosystem Geography of the Oceans and the Continents* (New York: Springer-Verlag, 1998).

10. Wilbur Zelinsky, "North America's Vernacular Regions," *Annals of the Association of American Geographers* (Volume 70, 1980): 1–16.

11. Ernest Callenbach, *Ecotopia* (Berkeley, Calif.: Banyan Tree, Berkeley, 1975).

12. Joel Garreau, *The Nine Nations of North America* (Boston: Houghton Mifflin, 1981).

13. Donald Meinig, *Imperial Texas, An Interpretive Essay in Cultural Geography* (Austin: University of Texas Press, 1969), pp. 110–111.

14. Robert E. Lang and Arthur C. Nelson, *America 2040: The Rise of the Megapolitans* (Alexandria: Metropolitan Institute, Virginia Tech, 2006).

15. Frederick Steiner, Barbara Faga, James Sipes, and Robert Yaro, "Taking a Longer View: Mapping for Sustainable Resilience," in Eugenie L. Birch and Susan M. Wachter, eds., *Rebuilding Urban Places After Disasters: Lessons from Hurricane Katrina* (Philadelphia: University of Pennsylvania Press, 2006).

16. Frederick Steiner, "Metropolitan Resilience: The Role of Universities in Facilitating a Sustainable Metropolitan Future," in Arthur C. Nelson, Barbara L. Allen, and David L. Trauger, eds., *Toward a Resilient Metropolis: The Role of State and Land Grant Universities in the 21st Century* (Alexandria, Va.: MI Press, 2006), pp. 1–15.

17. Lyle, *Regenerative Design for Sustainable Development*.

18. Barry Popik, The Big Apple (March 12, 2007). www.barrypopik.com/index.php/new_york_city/entry/texas_triangle_dallas_houston_san_antonio/.

19. G. E. Griffith, S. A. Bryce, J. M. Omernik, J. A. Comstock, A. C. Rogers, B. Harrison, S. L. Hatch, and D. Bezanson, *Ecoregions of Texas* (Reston, Va.: U.S. Geological Survey, 2004).

## CHAPTER 15

1. Lincoln Institute of Land Policy, Regional Plan Association, University of Pennsylvania School of Design, *Toward an American Spatial Development Perspective* (Philadelphia: Department of City and Regional Planning, University of Pennsylvania, 2004).

2. Stephen M. Wheeler, "The New Regionalism: Key Characteristics of an Emerging Movement," *Journal of the American Planning Association* (Volume 68, Number 3, Summer 2002): 267.

3. James L. Wescoat Jr. and Douglas M. Johnston, eds., *Political Economies of Landscape Change: Places of Integrative Power* (Dordrecht, The Netherlands: Springer, 2008).

4. Elmer W. Johnson, *Chicago Metropolis 2020* (Chicago: University of Chicago Press, 2000).

5. Ibid., p. i.

6. United Nations Framework Convention on Climate Change, Fact Sheet: The Need for Mitigation (New York, 2007).

7. United Nations Framework Convention on Climate Change, Fact Sheet: The Need for Adaptation (New York, 2007).

8. Frederick Steiner and Bob Yaro, "A Land and Resources Conservation Agenda for the United States," Innovations for an Urban World, A Global Urban Summit, The Rockefeller Foundation, Bellagio Study and Conference Center, Bellagio, Italy, July 2007. See also, Frederick R. Steiner and Robert D. Yaro, "A New National Agenda," *Landscape Architecture* (Volume 99, Number 6, June): 70–77.

9. Thomas Wright, "Land Development and Growth Management in the United States: Considerations at the Megaregional Scale," Innovations for an Urban World, A Global Urban Summit, The Rockefeller Foundation, Bellagio Study and Conference Center, Bellagio, Italy, July 2007.

10. Robert Fishman, "1808–1908–2008: National Planning for America," Innovations for an Urban World, A Global Urban Summit, The Rockefeller Foundation, Bellagio Study and Conference Center, Bellagio, Italy, July 2007. For a comprehensive review of the Bellagio summit, see Neal R. Peirce and Curtis W. Johnson (with Farley M. Peters), *Century of the City: No Time to Lose* (New York: The Rockefeller Foundation, 2008).

11. Steiner and Yaro, "A New National Agenda." Meanwhile, scholars at Peking University have mapped China's landscapes at the national, regional, and local levels. At the national level, Kong-Jian Yu and his colleagues focus on "ecological security." Their maps are based on critical natural processes, which they define as headwater conservation, soil erosion prevention, stormwater management, flood control, desertification mitigation, and biodiversity conservation. Kong-Jian Yu, Hai-Long Li, Di-Hua Li, Qing Yiao, and Xue-Song Xi, "National Scale Ecological Security Patterns," *Acta Ecologica Sinica* (Volume 29, Number 19, October): 5163–5175.

## CHAPTER 16

1. Clemens Steenbergen and Wouter Reh, *Architecture and Landscape: The Design Experimentation of the Great European Gardens and Landscapes* (Bussum, The Netherlands: Thoth, 1996), p. 85.

2. Ibid.

3. Ibid., p. 87.

## CHAPTER 17

1. Thomas J. Campanella, *The Concrete Dragon, China's Urban Revolution and What it Means for the World* (New York: Princeton Architectural Press, 2008), p. 132.

2. See Jeffrey W. Cody, *Building in China: Henry K. Murphy's "Adaptive Architecture," 1914–1935* (Hong Kong: The Chinese University Press and Seattle: University of Washington Press, 2001).

3. Two weeks of test events rehearsed the games in August 2007. Olympic organizers reserved four days during the test events to keep more than a million private vehicles a day off gridlocked Beijing streets. The test was declared only a "partial success." Associated Press, "China Downplays Olympic Environmental Issues" (August 24, 2007).

4. Liang Sicheng and his first wife Lin Huiyin studied architecture at the University of Pennsylvania under Paul Cret. Lin Huiyin's niece is Maya Lin.

5. Frederick Steiner, "Olympic Green," *Landscape Architecture* (Volume 98, Number 3, March 2008): 90, 92–97.

## CHAPTER 18

1. U.S. National Park Service, *Flight 93 National Memorial, Final General Management Plan/Environmental Impact Statement* (Somerset, Pa.: Flight 93 National Memorial, 2007), p. iii–1.

2. Ibid., p. iii.

3. Ibid., p. iii–7.

4. Ibid.

5. I received a call from Joanne Hanley. She asked if I knew who she was. I searched my mind, but couldn't recall.

"How about Joanne Michalovic?"

"Sure, she was my student at Washington State in the late 1970s."

"Well, I'm now Joanne Hanley."

I told her that it was great to hear from her and asked what she was up to.

"I work for the National Park Service and am the superintendent of the Flight 93 National Memorial."

She received special permission from Don and Helene to call me. Joanne had recommended me as a potential juror and was delighted when our team was selected as a finalist. She said that she was looking forward to seeing me at the forthcoming workshop. Unfortunately, I was already scheduled to give lectures in Turin and Florence. Tickets had been purchased and posters printed, so my three teammates participated, while I was in Italy.

6. The crescent symbolism would plague the Murdoch team as they refined their design toward construction drawings. California author and blogger Alec Rawls and Mt. Pleasant, Pennsylvania, resident Bill Steiner (no relation that I'm aware of) spent two years investigating the Murdoch team and concluded that their work was a "terrorist memorial." Rawls called the design "a giant prayer rug." Joanne Hanley and her National Park Service colleagues found that such theories "are plagued with faulty theories and assumptions." See Paul Peirce, "Author Persists in Somerset Memorial Claims," *Pittsburgh Tribune-Review* (July 27, 2007).

7. Reuben Rainey, "Hallowed Grounds and Rituals of Remembrance: Union Regimental Monuments at Gettysburg" in Paul Groth and Todd W. Bressi, eds., *Understanding Ordinary Landscapes* (New Haven: Yale University Press, 1997), p. 80.

8. Laurie Olin, "Memory Not Nostalgia" in W. Gary Smith, ed., *Memory, Expression, Representation* (Austin: School of Architecture, The University of Texas at Austin, 2002), p. 18.

## CHAPTER 19

1. Steiner et al., "Taking a Longer View." For an insightful reflection on Hurricane Katrina's impact on New Orleans, see Stephen Verderber's *Delirious New Orleans: Manifesto for an Extraordinary American City* (Austin: University of Texas Press, 2009). For an explanation of urban development in a risky environment, see Richard Campanella, *Delta Urbanism: New Orleans* (Chicago: American Planning Association Planners Press, 2010).

2. Robert Lang, "Katrina's Impact on New Orleans and the Gulf Coast Megapolitan Area," in Birch and Wachter, eds., *Rebuilding Urban Places after Disaster: Lessons from Hurrican Katrina* (Philadelphia: University of Pennsylvania Press, 2006).

3. United Nations Framework Convention on Climate Change, Fact Sheet: The Need for Adaptation. See also Timothy Beatley, *Planning for Coastal Resilience, Best Practices for Calamitous Times* (Washington, D.C.: Island Press, 2009).

4. Pickett and Cadenasso, "Integrating the Ecological, Socioeconomic, and Planning Realms."

5. Marc Morial, presentation at the "Rebuilding Urban Places after Disaster: Learning from Hurricane Katrina" symposium, University of Pennsylvania, February 2–3, 2006.

6. For more on this region as a liquid landscape, see Anuradha Mathur and Dilip da Cunha, "Negotiating a Fluid Terrain," in Birch and Wachter, eds., *Rebuilding Urban Places after Disaster*, pp. 34–46.

7. United Nations Framework Convention on Climate Change, Fact Sheet: The Need for Adaptation. http://unfccc.int.

8. See Ian L. McHarg, *A Quest for Life*.

9. Babbitt, *Cities in the Wilderness*.

10. See, for example, Han Meyer, Inge Bobbink, and Steffen Nijhuis, eds., *Delta Urbanism: The Netherlands* (Chicago: American Planning Association Planners Press, 2010).

11. Of all the plans produced in the wake of Hurricane Katrina, New Urbanist Peter Calthorpe's "Louisiana Speaks" plan goes the furthest in presenting a long-term community vision based on regional planning. The Calthorpe team engaged more than twenty-seven thousand south Louisiana

citizens, creating a new standard for inclusive planning derived from an understanding of environmental, economic, and social patterns.

12. Marsilio Editori, *Cities, Architecture and Society* (10th International Architecture Exhibition, Venice, Italy: Fondazione La Biennale, 2006).

13. Charles Bohl with Elizabeth Plater-Zyberk, "Building Community Across the Rural to Urban Transect," *Places* (Volume 18, Number 1, Spring 2006): 4–17.

14. Ibid., p. 14.

15. Ibid.

16. Ibid.

17. I'm also skeptical about the tendency toward a limited and deterministic style of New Urbanism. However, Duany makes a compelling case for the restoration of New Orleans by recreating the city's unique building culture. See Andres Duany, "Restoring the Real New Orleans," *Metropolis* (February 2007): 58, 60.

But . . .

After a warm-up talk by former Milwaukee mayor and Congress for the New Urbanism president John Norquist, Andres Duany took center stage at the Lone Star Room in the Frank Erwin Center in Austin, Texas, on March 29, 2007. In his long speech, Duany took subtle jabs at Peter Calthorpe and John Fregonese, claiming that planning in Portland had been a "total failure" (Fregonese had been the director of Portland Metro, and Calthorpe had contributed to a well-known plan for Portland). He also criticized planning efforts that cost "millions" and involved extensive public engagement activities (such as Fregonese Calthorpe's work for Envision Central Texas).

Duany declared that "the poor contribute nothing to environmental problems" because of their limited spending capacity and, furthermore, he wasn't interested in the poor anyway. He also claimed that all post–Second World War planning had failed.

Two days later, as I walked around Town Lake, renamed Lady Bird Lake later that year, with hundreds of other walkers, joggers, cyclists, boaters, fishers, and dogs of all ages, I reflected on how successful Larry Speck and Johnson, Johnson & Roy's 1984 plan for this very spot had been. Many good plans have contributed to Austin's success. Walking around Lady Bird Lake, I realized just how wrong Duany was about planning.

18. Our team included Kevin Alter, Larry Doll, Barbara Hoidn, Jason Sowell, Wilfried Wang, Nichole Wiedemann, and me, as well as several hard-working students and staff members.

19. Steiner et al., "Taking a Longer View."

20. Marla Nelson, Renia Ehrenfeucht, and Shirley Laska, "Planning, Plans, and People: Professional Expertise, Local Knowledge, and Governmental Action in Post-Hurricane Katrina New Orleans," *Cityscape* (Volume 9, Number 3, 2007): 40–41.

21. Nicolai Ouroussoff, "Putting Whole Teeming Cities on the Drawing Board," *New York Times* (September 10, 2006).

22. Nicolai Ouroussoff, "Inside the Urban Crunch, and Its Global Implications," *New York Times* (September 14, 2006).

## CHAPTER 20

1. Joan Ockman, "Star Cities," *Architect* (March, 2008): 60–67.

2. See, for example, Dean Almy, ed., *On Landscape Urbanism*, CENTER 14. New Urbanism, Landscape Urbanism, and other urbanisms are being advocated to reform urban development. Joan Busquets, in collaboration with Felipe Correa and their Harvard students, identifies ten new urban strategies in *Cities X Lines* (Cambridge, Mass.: Nicolodi Editore, Graduate School of Design, Harvard University, 2007). Their ten strategies are: Synthetic Gestures, Multiplied Grounds, Tactical Maneuvers, Reconfigured Surfaces, Piecemeal Aggregations, Traditional Views (New Urbanism), Recycling Territories (Landscape Urbanism), Core Retrofitting, Analog Composition, and Speculative Procedures.

3. Nicolai Ouroussof, "Nice Tower! Who's Your Architect?" *New York Times* (March 23, 2008).

4. Till, *Architecture Depends*, p. 139.

5. Robert Smithson, "A Sedimentation of the Mind: Earth Projects," in Jack Flam, ed., *Robert Smithson: The Collected Writings* (Berkeley: University of California Press, 1996), p. 100.

6. Robert Smithson, "Frederick Law Olmsted and the Dialectical Landscape," in Flam, ed., *Robert Smithson*, p. 170.

7. Leopold, *Round River*, p. 165.

8. Centers for Disease Control and Prevention, "Prevalence of Overweight and Obesity among Adults, United States, 1999–2002." More recent (2006) CDC data indicate that 30 percent of U.S. adults twenty years and older—more than 60 million people—are obese.

9. Lemonick, Michael D., "How We Grew So Big," *Time* (June 7, 2004).

10. Committee on Environmental Health, "The Built Environment: Designing Communities to Promote Physical Activity in Children," *Pediatrics* (Volume 123, Number 6, June 2009): 1591–1598. See also Fritz Steiner and Talia McCray, "We Knew All Along," *Planning* (Volume 75, Number 7, July 2009): 48.

11. Richard J. Jackson, "What Olmsted Knew," *Western City* (March 2001): 12–15. See also Richard J. Jackson, "The Impact of the Built Environment on Health: An Emerging Field," *American Journal of Public Health* (Volume 93, Number 9, September 2003): 1382–1384.

# BIBLIOGRAPHY

*A Balanced Vision Plan for the Trinity River Corridor* (Dallas, Texas, December 2003).

Almy, Dean, ed. *On Landscape Urbanism, Center 14* (Austin: Center for American Architecture and Design, The University of Texas at Austin, 2007).

American Institute of Architects, Dallas. *Advisory Panel Summary Report* (Dallas, Texas, September 2001).

American Institute of Architects, Dallas. *Trinity River Policy* (Dallas, Texas, November 2001).

American Society of Landscape Architects; Lady Bird Johnson Wildflower Center, The University of Texas at Austin; and United States Botanic Garden. *Guidelines and Performance Benchmarks, Draft 2008* (Austin: Sustainable Sites Initiative, 2008).

American Society of Landscape Architects; Lady Bird Johnson Wildflower Center, The University of Texas at Austin; and United States Botanic Garden. *Guidelines and Performance Benchmarks 2009* (Austin: Sustainable Sites Initiative, 2009).

American Society of Landscape Architects; Lady Bird Johnson Wildflower Center, The University of Texas at Austin; and United States Botanic Garden. *Preliminary Report of the Practice Guidelines and Metrics. The Sustainable Sites Initiative* (Austin: The University of Texas at Austin, 2007).

Associated Press. "China Downplays Olympic Environmental Issues" (August 24, 2007).

Austin-San Antonio Corridor Policy Research Project. *The Emerging Economic Base and Local Developmental Policy Issues in the Austin–San Antonio Corridor* (Austin: Policy Research Project Report No. 71, Lyndon B. Johnson School of Public Affairs, The University of Texas at Austin, 1985).

Babbitt, Bruce. *Cities in the Wilderness* (Washington, D.C.: Island Press, 2005).

Bailey, Robert. *Ecoregions: The Ecosystem Geography of the Oceans and the Continents* (New York: Springer-Verlag, 1998).

Baker, Max B. "Key GOP Lawmaker Impressed by Project," *Fort Worth Star-Telegram* (August 9, 2007).

Barles, S. "Urban Metabolism and River Systems: An Historical Perspective—Paris and the Seine, 1790–1970," *Hydrology and Earth System Sciences* (Volume 11, 2007): 1757–1769.

Barrett, Gary W., and Eugene P. Odum. "The Twenty-First Century: The World at Carrying Capacity," *BioScience* (Volume 50, Number 4, 2000): 363–368.

Batty, Michael. *Cities and Complexity* (Cambridge, Mass.: MIT Press, 2005).

Batty, Michael, and Paul Longley. *Fractal Cities* (London: Academic Press, 1994).

Beatley, Timothy. *Habitat Conservation Planning* (Austin: University of Texas Press, 1994).

——. *Native to Nowhere* (Washington, D.C.: Island Press, 2004).

——. *Planning for Coastal Resilience: Best Practices for Calamitous Times* (Washington, D.C.: Island Press, 2009).

Berke, Philip R. "The Evolution of Green Community Planning, Scholarship, and Practice," *Journal of the American Planning Association* (Volume 74, Number 4, 2008): 393–407.

Berube, Alan. *MetroNation: How U.S. Metropolitan Areas Fuel American Prosperity* (Washington, D.C.: The Brookings Institution, 2007).

Birch, Eugenie L., and Susan M. Wachter, eds. *Growing Greener Cities: Urban Sustainability in the Twenty-First Century* (Philadelphia: University of Pennsylvania Press, 2008).

——, eds. *Rebuilding Urban Places after Disaster: Lessons from Hurricane Katrina* (Philadelphia: University of Pennsylvania Press, 2006).

Black, Sinclair, Frederick Steiner, Marisa Ballas, and Jeff Gipson, eds. *Emergent Urbanism* (Austin: School of Architecture, The University of Texas at Austin, 2008).

Bohl, Charles, with Elizabeth Plater-Zyberk. "Building Community Across the Rural to Urban Transect," *Places* (Volume 18, Number 1, Spring 2006): 4–17.

Botkin, Daniel B. *Discordant Harmonies: A New Ecology for the Twenty-First Century* (New York: Oxford University Press, 1990).

Boyer, Ernest L., and Lee D. Mitgang. *Building Community: A New Future for Architectural Education and Practice* (Princeton, N.J.: The Carnegie Foundation for the Advancement of Teaching, 1996).

Brand, Stewart. *The Clock of the Long Now: Time and Responsibility* (London: Weidenfeld & Nicolson, 1999).

Bright, Elise. "Viewpoint: Megas? Maybe Not," *Planning* (Volume 73, Number 4, 2007): 46.

Burchett, C. R., P. L. Rettman, and C. W. Boning. *The Edwards Aquifer, Extremely Productive, But . . .* (San Antonio: Edwards Underground Water District, 1986).

Burdett, Ricky, and Deyan Sudjic, eds. *The Endless City* (London: Phaidon Press, 2007).

Burke, James, and Joseph Ewan. *Sonoran Preserve Master Plan* (Phoenix, Ariz.: Department of Parks, Recreation, and Library, 1998).

Busquets, Joan, and Felipe Correa. *Cities X Lines* (Cambridge, Mass.: Nicolodi Editore, Graduate School of Design, Harvard University, 2007).

Butler, Kent, and Dowell Myers. "Boomtown in Austin, Texas: Negotiated Growth Management," *Journal of the American Planning Association* (Volume 50, Number 4, 1984): 447–458.

Butler, Kent, Sara Hammerschmidt, Frederick Steiner, and Ming Zhang. *Reinventing the Texas Triangle: Solutions for Growing Challenges* (Austin: Center for Sustainable Development, The University of Texas at Austin, 2009).

Callenbach, Ernest. *Ecotopia* (Berkeley, Calif.: Banyan Tree, 1975).

Calthorpe Associates. "Proposed Urban Design Guidelines, East Austin Rail Corridor, Featherlite, Austin, Texas" (Austin: Envision Central Texas, 2003).

Calthorpe, Peter. *The Next American Metropolis: Ecology, Community, and the American Dream* (New York: Princeton Architectural Press, 1993).

Calthorpe, Peter, and William Fulton. *The Regional City: Planning for the End of Sprawl* (Washington, D.C.: Island Press, 2001).

Campanella, Richard. *Delta Urbanism: New Orleans* (Chicago: American Planning Association Planners Press, 2010).

Campanella, Thomas J. *The Concrete Dragon, China's Urban Revolution and What it Means for the World* (New York: Princeton Architectural Press, 2008).

Carbonell, Armando, and Robert D. Yaro. "American Spatial Development and the New Megalopolis," *Land Lines* (Volume 17, Number 2, 2005): 1–4.

Casson, Lionel. *Everyday Life in Ancient Rome* (Baltimore: Johns Hopkins University Press, 1998).

Centers for Disease Control and Prevention. "Prevalence of Overweight and Obesity among Adults, United States, 1999–2002."

Chan Krieger & Associates; TDA, Incorporated; Hargreaves Associates; and Carter & Burgess. *A Balanced Vision Plan for the Trinity River* (Dallas: City of Dallas, December 2003).

City of Austin. *Facts and Information on the Northern Edwards Aquifer. Regional Conference on the Edwards Aquifer, North of the Colorado River* (Austin: City of Austin Office of Environmental Resource Management, 1986).

City of San Antonio and Edwards Underground Water District. *San Antonio Regional Water Resource Study: Summary* (San Antonio: Department of Planning, City of San Antonio, 1986).

Claus, Russell Clive. "The Woodlands, Texas: A Retrospective Critique of the Principles and Implementation of an Ecologically Planned Development" (Cambridge, Mass.: Department of Urban Studies and Planning, Massachusetts Institute of Technology, Master of City Planning thesis, 1994).

Cody, Jeffrey W. *Building in China: Henry K. Murphy's "Adaptive Architecture," 1914–1935* (Hong Kong: The Chinese University Press and Seattle: University of Washington Press, 2001).

Committee on Environmental Health. "The Built Environment: Designing Communities to Promote Physical Activity in Children," *Pediatrics* (Volume 123, Number 6, June 2009): 1591–1598.

Costanza, Robert. "Ecosystems Services: Multiple Classification Systems Are Needed," *Biological Conservation* (Volume 141, 2008): 350–352.

Cret, Paul P. "Report Accompanying the General Plan of Development" (Austin: The University of Texas, January 1933).

Dagger, Richard. "Stopping Sprawl for the Good of All: The Case for Civic Environmentalism," *Journal of Social Philosophy* (Volume 34, Number 1, 2003): 28–43.

DeLillo, Don. *Underworld* (New York: Scribner, 1997).

Dewar, Margaret, and David Epstein. "Planning for 'Megaregions' in the United States," *Journal of Planning Literature* (Volume 22, Number 2, 2007): 108–124.

Dillon, David. "AIA Has a Flood of Protests," *Dallas Morning News* (January 20, 2002).

———. "Artistic Differences," *Dallas Morning News* (March 27, 2005).

———. "The Meyerson Turns 15," *Dallas Morning News* (September 15, 2004).

———. "Room to Grow," *Dallas Morning News* (September 14, 2006).

Duany, Andres. "Restoring the Real New Orleans," *Metropolis* (February 2007): 58, 60.

Duany, Andres, Elizabeth Plater-Zyberk, and Jeff Speck. *Suburban Nation: The Rise of Sprawl and the Decline of the American Dream* (New York: North Point Press, 2001).

Envision Central Texas. *A Vision for Central Texas* (Austin, Texas, 2004).

Farber, Stephen C., Robert Costanza, and Michael A. Wilson. "Economic and Ecological Concepts for Valuing Ecosystem Services," *Ecological Economics* (Volume 14, 2002): 375–392.

Field Operations, Diller Scofidio + Renfro, Friends of the High Line, City of New York. *Designing the High Line, Gansevoort Street to 30th Street* (New York: Friends of the High Line, 2008).

Fishman, Robert. "1808–1908–2008: National Planning for America," Innovations for an Urban World, A Global Urban Summit, The Rockefeller Foundation, Bellagio Study and Conference Center, Bellagio, Italy, July 2007.

Flam, Jack, ed. *Robert Smithson: The Collected Writings* (Berkeley: University of California Press, 1996).

Florida, Richard. *The Rise of the Creative Class: And How It's Transforming Work, Leisure, Community And Everyday Life* (New York: Basic Books, 2002).

*Forbes.* "Best Places for Businesses and Careers" (May 9, 2003).

Forman, Richard T. T. *Urban Regions: Ecology and Planning Beyond the City* (Cambridge: Cambridge University Press, 2008).

Forsyth, Ann. "Evolution of an Ecoburb," *Landscape Architecture* (Volume 95, Number 7, July 2005): 60, 62, 64, 65, 66–67.

———. "Ian McHarg's Woodlands: A Second Look," *Planning* (August, 2003): 10–13.

———. "Planning Lessons from Three U.S. New Towns of the 1960s and 1970s: Irvine, Columbia, and The Woodlands," *Journal of the American Planning Association* (Volume 68, Number 4, 2002): 387–417.

———. *Reforming Suburbia: The Planned Communities of Irvine, Columbia, and The Woodlands* (Berkeley: University of California Press, 2005).

Frampton, Kenneth. "Towards a Critical Regionalism: Six Points for an Architecture of Resistance," in Hal Foster, ed., *The Anti-Aesthetic: Essays on Postmodern Culture* (Port Townsend, Wash.: Bay Press, 1983).

Fulton, Duncan T. "Dallas Arts District," in Sinclair Black, Frederick Steiner, Marisa Ballas, and Jeff Gipson, eds., *Emergent Urbanism* (Austin: School of Architecture, The University of Texas at Austin, 2008), pp. 98–100.

Galatas, Roger, and Jim Barlow. *The Woodlands: The Inside Story of Creating a Better Hometown* (Washington, D.C.: The Urban Land Institute, 2004).

Gammage Jr., Grady, John Stuart Hall, Robert E. Lang, Rob Melnick, and Nancy Welch. *Megopolitan: Arizona's Sun Corridor* (Tempe: Morrison Institute, Arizona State University, May 2008).

Garreau, Joel. *The Nine Nations of North America* (Boston: Houghton Mifflin, 1981).

Garrison, M., R. Krepart, S. Randall, and A. Novoselac. "The BLOOMhouse: Zero Net Energy Housing," a paper presented at the Texas Society of Architects Annual Conference, October 24, 2008.

Girling, Cynthia L., and Kenneth I. Helphand. *Yard-Street-Park* (New York: John Wiley & Sons, 1994).

Glasoe, Stuart, Frederick Steiner, William Budd, and Gerald Young. "Assimilative Capacity and Water Resource Management: Four Examples from the United States," *Landscape and Urban Planning* (Volume 19, Number 1, 1990): 17–46.

Goodwin, Jan. *Price of Honor*, rev. ed. (New York: Penguin, 2003).

Gottmann, Jean. *Megalopolis: The Urbanized Seaboard of the United States* (New York: Twentieth-Century Fund, 1961).

Gould, Lewis L. *Lady Bird Johnson: Our Environmental First Lady* (Lawrence: University of Kansas Press, 1999).

Griffith, G. E., S. A. Bryce, J. M. Omernik, J. A. Comstock, A. C. Rogers, B. Harrison, S. L. Hatch, and D. Bezanson. *Ecoregions of Texas* (Reston, Va.: U.S. Geological Survey, 2004).

Grossman, Elizabeth Greenwell. *The Civic Architecture of Paul Cret* (New York: Cambridge University Press, 1996).

Gunderson, Lance, C. S. Holling, L. Pritchard, and G. D. Peterson. "Resilience," in Ted Munn, ed.-in-chief, *Encyclopedia of Global Environmental Change* (Hoboken, N.J.: John Wiley & Sons, 2002): pp. 530–531.

Hammond, W. W. "Regional Hydrogeology of the Edwards Aquifer, South Central Texas," in E. T. Smerdon and W. R. Jordan, eds., *Issues in Groundwater Management* (Austin: Water Resources Symposium No. 12, Center for Research in Water Resources, The University of Texas at Austin, 1986), pp. 53–68.

Hegemann, Werner, and Elbert Peets. *The American Vitruvius: An Architect's Handbook of Civic Art* (New York: Architectural Book Publishing Co., 1922).

Hersey, George. *The Monumental Impulse: Architecture's Biological Roots* (Cambridge, Mass.: MIT Press, 1999).

Hildebrand, Grant. *Origins of Architectural Pleasure* (Berkeley: University of California Press, 1999).

Hirsch, Dennis D. "Ecosystem Services and the Green City," in Birch and Wachter, eds., *Growing Greener Cities*, pp. 281–293.

HNTB. *City of Dallas Trinity River Comprehensive Land Use Plan* (Final Report) (Dallas: Trinity River Corridor Project, adopted March 9, 2005).

Ingersoll, Richard. "Utopia Limited: Houston's Ring Around the Beltway," *Cite* (Volume 31, Winter-Spring, 1994): 10–16.

Jackson, Richard J. "The Impact of the Built Environment on Health: An Emerging Field," *American Journal of Public Health* (Volume 93, Number 9, September 2003): 1382–1384.

———. "What Olmsted Knew," *Western City* (March 2001): 12–15.

Johnson, Elmer W. *Chicago Metropolis 2020* (Chicago: University of Chicago Press, 2000).

Karvonen, Andrew. *Botanizing the Asphalt: Politics of Urban Drainage* (Austin: The University of Texas at Austin, Ph.D. dissertation, 2008).

Kellert, Stephen R., Judith H. Heerwagen, and Martin L. Mador, eds. *Biophilic Design* (Hoboken, N.J.: John Wiley & Sons, 2008).

Lady Bird Johnson Wildflower Center, American Society of Landscape Architects, and U.S. Botanic Garden. *Preliminary Report of the Practice Guidelines and Metrics, The Sustainable Sites Initiative* (Austin: The University of Texas at Austin, 2007).

Lang, Robert. "Katrina's Impact on New Orleans and the Gulf Coast Megapolitan Area," in Birch and Wachter, eds., *Rebuilding Urban Places after Disaster*, pp. 89–102.

Lang, Robert E., and Dawn Dhavale. *Beyond Megalopolis: Exploring America's New "Megapolitan" Geography* (Alexandria: Metropolitan Institute, Virginia Tech, July 2005).

Lang, Robert E., and Arthur C. Nelson. *America 2040: The Rise of the Megapolitans* (Alexandria: Metropolitan Institute, Virginia Tech, 2006).

Lang, Robert E., Andrea Sarzynski, and Mark Muro. *Mountain Megas: America's Newest Metropolitan Places and a Federal Partnership to Help Them Prosper* (Washington, D.C.: Metropolitan Policy Program, The Brookings Institution, 2008).

Lemonick, Michael D. "How We Grew So Big," *Time* (June 7, 2004).

Leopold, Aldo. *Round River: From the Journals of Aldo Leopold*, Luna B. Leopold, ed. (Minocqua, Wis.: North Word Press, 1991).

Levinthal, Dave. "Leppert Vows to Deliver on Trinity River Toll Road, Park," *Dallas Morning News* (November 7, 2007).

Lincoln Institute of Land Policy, Regional Plan Association, University of Pennsylvania School of Design. *Toward an American Spatial Development Perspective* (Philadelphia: Department of City and Regional Planning, University of Pennsylvania, 2004).

Loftis, Randy Lee. "Trinity River Ecology Courses Through Politics of Toll Road Debate," *Dallas Morning News* (October 28, 2007).

Lyle, John Tillman. *Regenerative Design for Sustainable Development* (New York: John Wiley & Sons, 1994).

Lynch, Kevin. "Environmental Adaptability," *Journal of the American Institute of Planners* (Volume 24, Number 1, 1958): 16–24. Reprinted in Tridib Banerjee and Michael Southworth, eds., *City Sense and City Design: Writings and Projects of Kevin Lynch* (Cambridge, Mass.: MIT Press, 1990).

Maciocco, Giovanni. *Fundamental Trends in City Development* (Berlin: Springer, 2008).

Maclay, R. W., and T. A. Small. "Hydrostratigraphic Subdivisions and Fault Barriers of the Edwards Aquifer, South Central Texas, U.S.A.," *Journal of Hydrology* (Volume 61, 1983): 127–146.

Maguire, David, Michael Batty, and Michael Goodchild, eds., *GIS, Spatial Analysis, and Modeling* (Redlands, Calif.: ESRI Press, 2005).

Marsilio Editori. *Cities, Architecture and Society* (10th International Architecture Exhibition, Venice, Italy: Fondazione La Biennale, 2006).

Mathur, Anuradha, and Dilip da Cunha. "Negotiating a Fluid Terrain," in Birch and Wachter, eds., *Rebuilding Urban Places after Disaster*, pp. 34–46.

McHarg, Ian L. *Design with Nature* (Garden City, N.Y.: Natural History Press/Doubleday, 1969).

———. *A Quest for Life: An Autobiography* (New York: John Wiley & Sons, 1996).

McHarg, Ian L., and Frederick R. Steiner, eds. *To Heal the Earth* (Washington, D.C.: Island Press, 1998).

McMichael, Carol. *Paul Cret at Texas: Architectural Drawing and the Image of the University in the 1930s* (Austin: Archer M. Huntington Art Gallery, College of Fine Arts, The University of Texas at Austin, 1983).

Meinig, Donald. *Imperial Texas: An Interpretative Essay in Cultural Geography* (Austin: University of Texas Press, 1969).

Meyer, Han, Inge Bobbink, and Steffen Nijhuis, eds. *Delta Urbanism: The Netherlands* (Chicago: American Planning Association Planners Press, 2010).

Moore, Steven. "Architecture, Esthetics, and the Public Health," in Sandra Iliescu, ed., *The Hand and the Soul: Aesthetics and Ethics in Architecture and Art* (Charlottesville: University of Virginia Press, 2008).

———, ed. *Pragmatic Sustainability: Theoretical and Practical Tools* (London: Routledge, 2010).

———. "Reproducing the Local," *Platform* (Spring, 1999): 2–3, 8–9.

———. "Technology, Place, and the Nonmodern Thesis," *Journal of Architectural Education* (Volume 54, Number 3, February, 2001): 130–139.

Morgan Jr., George T., and John O. King. *The Woodlands: New Community Development, 1964–1983* (College Station: Texas A&M Press, 1987).

Mulvihill, Peter R. "Expanding the Scoping Community," *Environmental Impact Assessment Review* (Volume 23, 2003): 39–49.

Mumford, Lewis. *The Culture of Cities* (London: Secker and Warburg, 1938).

Muro, Mark, Bruce Katz, Sarah Rahman, and David Warren. *MetroPolicy: Shaping a New Federal Partnership for a Metropolitan Nation* (Washington, D.C.: The Brookings Institution, 2008).

Nelson, Arthur C. "Leadership in a New Era," *Journal of the American Planning Association* (Volume 72, Number 4, 2006): 393–407.

Nelson, Marla, Renia Ehrenfeucht, and Shirley Laska. "Planning, Plans, and People: Professional Expertise, Local Knowledge, and Governmental Action in Post-Hurricane Katrina New Orleans," *Cityscape* (Volume 9, Number 3, 2007): 23–52.

Ockman, Joan. "Star Cities," *Architect* (March, 2008): 60–67.

Olin, Laurie. "Memory Not Nostalgia," in W. Gary Smith, ed., *Memory, Expression, Representation* (Austin: School of Architecture, The University of Texas at Austin, 2002).

Olmsted, Frederick Law. *Journey Through Texas: or, a Saddle-Trip on the Southwestern Frontier; with a Statistical Appendix* (New York: Dix, Edwards & Co., 1857).

Ouroussoff, Nicolai. "Inside the Urban Crunch, and Its Global Implications," *New York Times* (September 14, 2006).

———. "Nice Tower! Who's Your Architect?" *New York Times* (March 23, 2008).

———. "Putting Whole Teeming Cities on the Drawing Board," *New York Times* (September 10, 2006).

Peirce, Neal R., and Curtis W. Johnson (with Farley M. Peters). *Century of the City: No Time to Lose* (New York: The Rockefeller Foundation, 2008).

Peirce, Paul. "Author Persists in Somerset Memorial Claims," *Pittsburgh Tribune-Review* (July 27, 2007).

Peterson, Garry D., Graeme S. Cumming, and Stephen R. Carpenter. "Scenario Planning: A Tool for Conservation in an Uncertain World," *Conservation Biology* (Volume 17, Number 3, 2003): 358–366.

Peterson, Garry D., T. Douglas Beard Jr., Beatrix E. Beisner, Elena M. Bennett, Stephen R. Carpenter, Graeme S. Cumming, C. Lisa Dent, and Tanya D. Havlicek. "Assessing Future Ecosystem Services: A Case Study of the Northern Highlands Lake District, Wisconsin," *Conservation Ecology* (Volume 7, Number 3, 2003): 1–19.

Pickett, Steward T. A., and Mary L. Cadenasso. "Integrating the Ecological, Socioeconomic, and Planning Realms: Insights from the Baltimore Ecosystem Study," in Laura Musacchio, Jianguo Wu, and Thara Johnson, eds., *Pattern, Process, Scale, and Hierarchy: Advancing Interdisciplinary Collaboration for Creating Sustainable Urban Landscapes and Communities* (Tempe: Arizona State University, 2003), p. 34.

Puentes, Robert. *A Bridge to Somewhere: Rethinking American Transportation for the 21st Century* (Washington, D.C.: The Brookings Institution, 2008).

Putnam, Robert D. *Bowling Alone: The Collapse and Revival of American Community* (New York: Simon & Schuster, 2000).

Quale, John D. *Trojan Goat: A Self-Sufficient House* (Charlottesville: University of Virginia School of Architectural, 2005).

Quantrill, Malcolm. *Plain Modern: The Architecture of Brian MacKay-Lyons* (New York: Princeton Architectural Press, 2005).

Rainey, Reuben. "Hallowed Grounds and Rituals of Remembrance: Union Regimental Monuments at Gettysburg," in Paul Groth and Todd W. Bressi, eds., *Understanding Ordinary Landscapes* (New Haven: Yale University Press, 1997).

Reed, Chris. *StossLU* (Seoul, Korea: C3 Publishing, 2007).

Regional Plan Association. *America 2050: A Prospectus* (New York: Regional Plan Association, 2006).

Ross, Catherine L., ed. *Megaregions: Planning for Global Competitiveness* (Washington, D.C.: Island Press, 2009).

Rybczynski, Witold. *The Perfect House* (New York: Scribners, 2002).

Senger, Rainer K., and Charles W. Kreitler. *Hydrogeology of the Edwards Aquifer, Austin Area, Central Texas* (Austin: Report of Investigations, No. 141, Bureau of Economic Geology, The University of Texas, 1984).

Simmonds, Roger, and Gary Hack, eds. *Global City Regions: Their Emerging Forms* (London: Spon Press, 2000).

Slade Jr., R. M., M. E. Dorsey, and S. L. Stewart. *Hydrology and Water Quality of the Edwards Aquifer Associated with Barton Springs in the Austin Area, Texas* (Austin: Water Resource Investigation Report 86–4036, U.S. Geological Survey, 1986).

Smith, Brian A., and Brian B. Hunt. *Evaluation of Sustainable Yield of the Barton Springs Segment of the Edwards Aquifer, Hays and Travis County, Central Texas* (Austin: Barton Springs/Edwards Aquifer Conservation District, 2004).

Smithson, Robert. "Frederick Law Olmsted and the Dialectical Landscape," in Jack Flam, ed., *Robert Smithson: The Collected Writings* (Berkeley: University of California Press, 1996), pp. 157–171.

———. "A Sedimentation of the Mind: Earth Projects," in Flam, ed. *Robert Smithson*, pp. 100–113.

Solomon, Daniel. *Global City Blues* (Washington, D.C.: Island Press, 2003).

Speck, Lawrence W. *Technology and Cultural Identity* (New York: Edizioni, 2006).

Spirn, Anne Whiston. *The Language of Landscape* (New Haven: Yale University Press, 1998).

Steelman, Aaron. "Why Cities Grow: Economist Richard Florida Argues that Cities Must Attract Young, Talented Workers—What He Dubs the 'Creative Class'—If They Want to Prosper. Is He Right? And Is there Anything New about this Theory?" *Region Focus* (Fall 2004): 13–16.

Steenbergen, Clemens, and Wouter Reh. *Architecture and Landscape: The Design Experimentation of the Great European Gardens and Landscapes* (Bussum, The Netherlands: Thoth, 1996).

Steiner, Frederick, ed. *The Essential Ian McHarg* (Washington, D.C.: Island Press, 2007).

———. *The Living Landscape* (New York: McGraw-Hill, 2000; paperback edition, Island Press, 2008).

———. "Metropolitan Resilience: The Role of Universities in Facilitating a Sustainable Metropolitan Future," in Arthur C. Nelson, Barbara L. Allen, and David L. Trauger, eds. *Toward a Resilient Metropolis: The Role of State and Land Grant Universities in the 21st Century* (Alexandria: MI Press, Virginia Tech, 2006), pp. 1–15.

———. "Olympic Green," *Landscape Architecture* (Volume 98, Number 3, March 2008): 90, 92–97.

Steiner, Frederick, and Bob Yaro. "A Land and Resources Conservation Agenda for the United States," Innovations for an Urban World, A Global Urban Summit, The Rockefeller Foundation, Bellagio Study and Conference Center, Bellagio, Italy, July 2007.

Steiner, Frederick R., and Robert D. Yaro. "A New National Agenda," *Landscape Architecture* (Volume 99, Number 6, June): 70–77.

Steiner, Frederick, Barbara Faga, James Sipes, and Robert Yaro. "Taking a Longer View: Mapping for Sustainable Resilience," in Birch and Wachter, eds., *Rebuilding Urban Places After Disasters*, pp. 67–77.

Steiner, Fritz, and Talia McCray. "We Knew All Along," *Planning* (Volume 75, Number 7, July 2009): 48.

Strong, Ann L., and George F. Thomas, eds. *The Book of the School: 100 Years* (Philadelphia: Graduate School of Fine Arts, University of Pennsylvania, 1990).

Swearingen Jr., William Scott. *Environmental City: People, Place, Politics, and the Meaning of Modern Austin* (Austin: University of Texas Press, 2010).

Texas State Data Center. *Texas Population Projections Program* (Texas State Data Center and Office of the State Demographer, May 10, 2006).

Texas Transportation Institute. *Urban Mobility Study* (College Station, 2005).

Till, Jeremy. *Architecture Depends* (Cambridge, Mass.: MIT Press, 2009).

TIP Strategies, Inc. *Organizational Recommendations Prepared for The Envision Central Texas Board of Directors* (Austin, July 2008).

———. *Vision Progress Assessment Prepared for Envision Central Texas* (Austin, July 2008).

Tomaso, Bruce. "Dallas Vote Exposes Mistrust of Dallas City Hall," *Dallas Morning News* (November 10, 2007).

Tomaso, Bruce, Dave Levinthal, and Rudolph Bush. "Dallas Voters Endorse Trinity Toll Road," *Dallas Morning News* (November 7, 2007).

Trust for Public Land. *The Travis County Greenprint for Growth* (Austin: Trust for Public Land, 2006).

United Nations Commission on Environment and Development. *Our Common Future* (Oxford, U.K.: Oxford University Press, 1987).

United Nations Development Programme, United Nations Environment Programme, World Bank, and World Resources Institute. *World Resources 2000–2001, People and Ecosystems, The Fraying Web of Life* (Amsterdam: Elsevier, 2000).

United Nations Framework Convention on Climate Change. Fact Sheet: The Need for Adaptation (New York, 2007).

———. Fact Sheet: The Need for Mitigation (New York, 2007).

United States Department of Agriculture Natural Resources Conservation Service. *National Resources Inventory, 1982–1992* (Washington, D.C., 1995).

U.S. National Park Service. *Flight 93 National Memorial, Final General Management Plan/Environmental Impact Statement* (Somerset, Pa.: Flight 93 National Memorial, 2007).

Vale, Lawrence J., and Thomas J. Campanella. "The City Shall Rise Again: Urban Resilience in the Wake of Disaster," *Chronicle of Higher Education* (January 14, 2005): B6–B9

———, eds. *The Resilient City: How Modern Cities Recover from Disaster* (New York: Oxford University Press, 2005).

Verderber, Stephen. *Delirious New Orleans: Manifesto for an Extraordinary American City* (Austin: University of Texas Press, 2009).

Vitruvius. *On Architecture*, Frank Granger, trans. (Cambridge, Mass.: Harvard University Press, 1931).

Vogt, Günter. *Miniature and Panorama, Vogt Landscape Architecture Projects 2000–2006* (Baden: Lars Müller Publishers, 2006).

Vogt Landschaftsarchitekten. *Lupe und Fernglas, Miniatur und Panorama (Magnifying Glass and Binoculars, Miniature and Panorama)* (Berlin: AedesLand, 2007).

Waldheim, Charles, ed. *The Landscape Urbanism Reader* (New York: Princeton Architecture Press, 2006).

Wallace, McHarg, Roberts and Todd. *Amelia Island, Florida, A Report on the Master Planning Process for a Recreational New Community* (Hilton Head Island, S.C.: The Sea Pines Company, 1971).

———. *Lake Austin Growth Management Plan* (Austin: City of Austin, July 1976).

Waltner-Toews, David, James J. Kay, and Nina-Marie E. Lister, eds. *The Ecosystem Approach: Complexity, Uncertainty, and Managing for Sustainability* (New York, Columbia University Press, 2008).

Watterson, Wayt T., and Roberta S. Watterson. *The Politics of New Communities: A Case Study of San Antonio Ranch* (New York: Praeger, 1975).

Wescoat Jr., James L., and Douglas M. Johnston, eds. *Political Economies of Landscape Change: Places of Integrative Power* (Dordrecht, The Netherlands: Springer, 2008).

Wheeler, Stephen M. "The New Regionalism: Key Characteristics of an Emerging Movement," *Journal of the American Planning Association* (Volume 68, Number 3, Summer 2002): 267–278.

———. *Planning for Sustainability* (London: Routledge, 2004).

Wilberding, Seth. "On the Mall, Few Functional Landscapes," *Landscape Architecture* (Volume 98, Number 2, February 2008): 40–49.

Wood, Peter. "37,000 Woodlanders Can't Be Wrong," *Cite* (Volume 31, Winter-Spring, 1994): 17.

Wright, Thomas. "Land Development and Growth Management in the United States: Considerations at the Megaregional Scale," Innovations for an Urban World, A Global Urban Summit, The Rockefeller Foundation, Bellagio Study and Conference Center, Bellagio, Italy, July 2007.

Yu, Kong-Jian, Hai-Long Li, Di-Hua Li, Qing Qiao, and Xue-Song Xi. "National Scale Ecological Security Patterns," *Acta Ecologica Sinica* (Volume 29, Number 10, October): 5163–5175.

Zelinsky, Wilbur. "North America's Vernacular Regions," *Annals of the Association of American Geographers* (Volume 70, 1980): 1–16.

# INDEX

Page numbers in italics refer to figures or tables.

Académie de France à Rome, 175. *See also* French Academy
Acconci, Vito, 102
adaptation, 55, 59, 161, 165, 217, 236
additive structure, 56–57
AECOM, 13, 237
affordable housing, 26, 76, 80–81, 143, 145, 162, 249–250
African American(s), 22, 76, 77, 78, 103–104, 156, 232, 256
Ai Wei Wei, 182
Al Hathloul, Saleh, 118
Alban Hills, 175
Alford, Elizabeth, 25
Allegheny Mountains, 219
Allen, Augustus Chapman, 155
Allen, John Kirby, 155
Allen, Paul, 238
Alley Flat Initiative, 29
Allied Works Architecture, 107
Almy, Dean, 52, 248, *248*
Alter, Kevin, 268n18
Amelia Island, 84, *233, 234*, 235
America 2050, 3, *148*, 164–167
American Academy in Rome, 206
American Academy of Pediatrics, 256
American Institute of Architects (AIA), 36, 89, 93, 94, 97
American Society of Landscape Architects (ASLA), 2, *34*, 39–41, 120, 198, 207
Ammannati, Bartolomeo, 172
Amsterdam, 11, 56, 147, 208
Anderson, Ray, 23
Andersson, Arthur, 227
Ando, Tadao, 157
Andreu, Paul, 181, 182
Andropogon Associates, 35, 119, 198, 224
Ann W. Richards Congress Avenue Bridge, 67, 122
Annette Strauss Artist Square, 111

Apostolic Palace, 171
Appalachian Mountains, 221
Arad, Michael, 102, 105
ArcGIS Online, 55, 153
Archer, Rick, 264n1
Architects Collaborative, 78
Architecture for Humanity, 251
Arctic, 242
Arizona, 15, 31, *32*, 35, 62, *63*, 64, 89, 117, 135, 136, 161
Arizona State University (ASU), 12, 13, 18, 19, 21, 61, 137, 222, 225, 265n4
Arkansas, 10, 37
Arkansas River, 38
Armstrong, Beau, 115
Arnold, Ripley A., 157
Arup, Ove, 251
Ashoor, Omar, 119
AT&T Performing Arts Center, 263n7
Atlanta, 166, 223, 245, 259n10
Austin, TX, 2, 3, 7, 10, 11, 12, 21, 22, 23, *23*, 24, 25, 26, 29, 31, *34*, 39, 40, 56, 65, 67–68, *68*, 70, 71, 72–76, 84, 87, 90, 99, *100*, 105, 115, 121, 122, 125, 127, 128, *128*, 129, *129*, 130, *130*, 131, 132, 133, 135, 136–137, 138, *138*, 140, *141*, 142, 143, 144, 145, 146, 149, *154*, 155, 156–157, *158*, 159, 160, 171, 188, 191, 197, *198*, 219, 221, 223, 224, 225, 227, 239, 242, 247, 253–254, *254*, 255, 257, 260n10, 263n2, 264n1, 265n14, 268n17; leadership, 142; metropolitan region, 2, 75, 125, 130, 132, 133, 136–146
Austin City Council, 72–73, 115, 122, 136, 143, 145
Austin City Hall, 99, 253, 254, *254*
Austin Energy, 22, 67–68, 253
Austin Green Building Program. *See* Austin Energy
Austin–San Antonio corridor, 129, 136, 144
Austin Tomorrow Plan, 72, 136, 146
Australia, *32, 33*, 35, 242; architects and engineers, 182
Austria, 241; architect(s), 241

Babbitt, Bruce, 132, 235
Badanes, Steve, 24
Bagnaia, Italy, 176, *176*, 177
Bailey, Robert, 150
Balcones Canyonlands, 127–128, *129*, 131–132, 254
Balcones Escarpment, 128, 130, 131, 158
Balcones Fault Zone, 130, 158
Balcones National Wildlife Refuge, 254
Balmori Associates, 99
Baltimore, MD, 59, 219
Barcelona, 13, *14*, 64
Bargmann, Julie, 224
Barnett, Jonathan, 161
Baroque, 180
Barra de Guaratiba, 19, *20*
Bartlett School of Architecture. *See* University College London
Barton Springs, 122, 128, *128*, 156; pool, *129*; recharge zone, 115
Bastrop County, TX, 136, 144
Bastrop, TX, 140
Battery Park City, 13, *40*, 250
Batty, Michael, 118, 119
Bauhaus, 69
Beatley, Tim, 56, 132
Beijing, 6, 35, 179–181, *181*, 182, 184, *185*, 186, 187, *187*, 188, *189*, 190, 191, 192, *192*, 193, 194, *194*, 195, 196, 197, 198, 200, 201, *201*, 202, 203, 205, 206, 207, 208–210, *210*, 211, 212, 214, 215, 242, 247, 255, 257, 267n3; administrative structure, 184–185, *185*; Forbidden City, 182, 188, 192–193, *192*, 214; Forestry University, 209; Municipal Commission of Urban Planning, 208; National Centre for the Performing Arts, *181*, 182; Planning Exhibition Hall, 214; Railway Station, 214; Summer Palace, 187. *See also* Yihe Yuan; Yuan Ming Yuan
Beiwu Village, 186, 194, 198
Bell, Bryan, 251
Bellagio, Italy, *5*, 164, *164*, 165, 166, 167, 255, 266n10
Bennett, Edward H., *60*
Benoist, P. Michael, 180
Bercy Chen Studio, 247
Berke, Philip R., 22
Berlin, 238, 239
Berlusconi, Silvio, 171
Bernini, Gianlorenzo, 176
Bertoni, Rita, 241
Berube, Alan, 146
Bian Liang, 204
Bian River, 204
Bigarello, Giampaolo, 240
Biltmore Estate, 14
biophilic design, 19
bioswales(s), *42*, 43
Bird's Nest, 181–182, *182*, 210, 212
Blackland Prairie, 12, 125, 128, 130, 132–133, 139, 156, 158, 160

Blakely, Ed, 166
Blanc, Patrick, 112
Blanton Museum of Art, 3, 99–103, *100*, *103*, 104–105, 254
Blanton Plaza, 101, 102, 104, 105. *See also* Larry and Mary Ann Faulkner Plaza
Blonkvist, Tim, 264n1
BLOOMhouse, *26*, 27, *28*, 29, *30*, 30
Blue Banana, 147, 161
Blumenauer, Earl, 166
Bohl, Charles, 237
Booker T. Washington High School, 107, *113*, 114
Borghese: family, 176; Gallery, 176; Gardens, 172, *173*
Borromini, Francesco, 175
Bos Park, Amsterdam, 208
Bossier, LA, 103, 104
Boston, 13, 17, 60, *60*, 61, 101, 147, 208; Back Bay, 93
Bourbon Trail, 11
Box, Hal, 100
Boyer, Ernest, 10
Brand, Stewart, 19
Brazil, 19, *19*, 20
Brazos River, 231
Brettell, Caroline, 245
Breunig, Bob, 115, 117, 119, 135
Bright, Elise, 149
British School at Rome, 172, 206
Brookings Institution, 146, 166, 265n4
Brooklyn, 13, *53*, 61
Brooklyn Bridge, 56
Broward County, FL, 235
Brown, Lancelot "Capability," 205
Brown, Rachel, 238
Bruder, Will, 15, 35–36, *36*, 64
Brundtland Commission, 21
Brunet, Roger, 147
Brutalist, 101, 118
Bruun, Christian, 241
Bryant, John Neely, 157
Bryant Park, 13
Buffalo Bayou, 156
Bunch, Bill, 115
Bunster-Ossa, Ignacio, 98
Buonarroti, Michelangelo, 172
Burdett, Ricky, 236, 240, 241–242, 248
Burnett, James, 112
Burnette, Wendell, 64
Burnham, Daniel, 14–15, 60, *60*, 162, 206
Bush, George W., 22, 117, 135, 167, 171, 227, 263n1
Bush, Laura, 22, 35
Busquets, Joan, 268n2
Butera, Federico, 215
Butler, Kent, 76, 132
Byrd, Warren, 224, 225, 227

Cadenasso, Mary, 59
Cal Poly Pomona, 22, 43

Calatrava, Santiago, 87, 91, 92, 92, 251
Caldwell, Alfred, 14
Caldwell County, TX, 136, 144
California, 13, 31, 33, 152, 157, 165, 250, 267n6
Callenbach, Ernest, 150, 152
Calthorpe Associates, 137, 138, 140, 141, 142, 239, 267n11
Calthorpe, Peter, 10, 137, 259n13, 267n11, 268n17
Cambridge, MA, 78, 95, 219, 246
Campanella, Thomas, 59
Campidoglio, 204
Campo dei Fiori, 171
Campo Santa Margherita, 241
Canada, 26, 76, 198, 231, 232
Capital Area Metropolitan Planning Organization (CAMPO), 145, 264n5
Caprarola, 177, 204
Carbonell, Armando, 161
Carlozzi, Annette, 101
Carnegie, Andrew, 206
Carnegie Foundation, 10
Carter & Burgess, 112
Cary, John, 251
Casa Sant Andrea, 238
Cascadia Ecolopolis, 152
casino, 171, 176–177
Castelli Romani, 175
Castiglione, F. Giuseppe, 180
Caudill Rowlett Scott (CRS), 79, 118, 118
Caudill, William, 118
Cedar-Riverside, 77
Center for Maximum Potential Building Systems (CMPBS), 24, 25
Center for Sustainable Development (UT-Austin), 2, 21, 22, 25, 26, 41, 253
Centers for Disease Control and Prevention (CDC), 256, 257, 259n10, 268n8
Central Arizona Project, 62
Central Chinese Television (CCTV), 181, 181, 198, 202, 212, 214
Central Park, 13, 56, 58, 207, 210, 212
Cesar Pelli & Associates, 99, 100, 105
CH2M HILL, 97–98
Chan Krieger & Associates, 95, 96, 97, 112, 262n16
Charles W. Moore Center for the Study of Place, 253
Cheatham, Diane, 248–249
Chicago, 14–15, 14, 60, 60, 78, 79, 162, 163–164, 163, 237, 245
Chicago Metropolis 2020, 162–163
Chin, Mel, 102–103
China, 4, 5–6, 5, 9, 34, 35, 119, 165, 169, 179–214, 195, 196, 230, 253, 255, 266n11, 267n3; aesthetic vocabulary, 209; architects and engineers, 182; architecture, 215; cities, 193; design, 189, 207, 209; Grand Canal, China, 204; Great Wall, 184, 184, 188; landscape architects, 208; planning, 5–6; professors, 198; students, 182, 209; tourists, 201; traditions, 212; universities, 183; urban fabric, 183; urban-level planning, 5. See also specific cities

Chinese Landscape Architecture, 207
Chiruchi, Tommaso, 174, 176
Chongqing Institute, 209
Chow, Renee, 250
Church, Tommy, 200
Churchill, Winston, 145
Cibic, Aldo, 242
Cincinnati, 7, 10, 11, 29, 200, 247, 253
City Beautiful, 14–15, 60
City College of New York, 225
city-region(s), 6, 10, 12, 13, 17, 18, 19, 20, 85
Clarke, Fred, 99, 105
Clarke, Michael, 72
Claus, Russell Clive, 81–82
Clay, Grady, 226
Clean Water Act(s), 73, 235
Clément, Gilles, 112
Cleveland, OH, 219, 223, 253
climate change, 42, 45, 124, 145–146, 153, 164–165, 166, 167, 236
Clinton, Bill, 104, 121, 167, 171
Cloepfil, Brad, 107, 114
Clubb, Pat, 101, 102–103, 105
CO$_2$, 165, 215. See also greenhouse gas(es)
coastal areas, 192; communities, 229; erosion, 231; expanses, 87; island, 156; marshes, 51, 55, 59, 229, 231, 242; residents, 59
Coastal Plain, 127, 158, 230. See also Gulf Coastal Plain
College Station, TX, 67, 118
Colorado River, 67, 76, 131, 156, 160, 231
Columbia, MD, 77, 79, 81, 82, 85
community and regional planning, 251, 253. See also University of Texas at Austin: Community and Regional Planning
Community Renewal Project, 103, 104
Community Stewardship Awards Program, 145
commuter rail, 76, 139, 140, 143
Confucianism, 212; Temple, 193–194, 194
Congregation of Holy Cross, 156
Congrès Internationaux d'Architecture Moderne, 75
Congress for the New Urbanism (CNU), 16, 40, 268n17
conservation, 44, 45, 73, 74, 75, 75, 81, 82, 116, 122, 132, 133, 138, 143, 144, 149, 157, 162, 165, 166, 166, 167, 180, 189, 262n15, 266n11; conservationist(s), 14, 189, 255; habitat, 132, 133; water, 2, 32, 43, 47, 49, 135, 210, 266n11
consolidated metropolitan statistical areas (CMSAS), 154, 158, 159
Constantopoulos, Elias, 241
Constantopoulos, Vallia, 241
Coonley House, 15
Corderie dell'Arsenale, 241, 242
Cornell University, 26, 79
Corner, James, 52, 58, 63, 248
Cornfield, The, 248
Cornyn, John, 245

Correa, Felipe, 268n2

Costa, Lúcio, 19, *19*

Count Emo, 203, 205

creative class, 2, 12, 127; urbanism, 248

Cret, Paul Philippe, 1, 2, 3, 65, 68–72, *69, 71, 72, 73, 74,*
    75–76, 99, 100, 247, 261n7, 267n4

cross-ventilation, 27, 198

Crow, Michael, 12, 18

Cruz, Teddy, 250

csc buildings, 99, *100*

Cuan Di Xia Village, 200–201, *201*

Cucinella, Mario, 215

Cultural Axis, 207, *208*

Cunha, Dilip da, 267n6

Curtis, Doug, 111

Cuyahoga River, 165

Cuyahoga Valley National Park, 165

Cynthia Woods Mitchell Pavilion, 81

D.I.R.T., 224

Dagger, Richard, 137, 146

Dallas, 2, 3, 10, 35, 65, 70, 77, 87, 89, 90–98, *90, 91, 92,*
    *94–95, 94, 95, 97, 97,* 102, 107–114, *108, 109,* 117, 149,
    150, 154, *154,* 155, 157, 158, 159, 160, 209, 245, *246,* 248–
    249, *249,* 250, 253, 263n1; Arts District, 3, 107–114, *108;*
    Center for the Performing Arts, 107–114; metropolitan
    area, 157–158; Museum of Art, 107; Nasher Sculpture
    Center, Dallas, 102, 107, *108,* 110, *246;* Rapid Transit
    (DART), 94, 249

Dallas/Fort Worth metroplex, 2, 3, 89, 92, 150, 154, 157, 159,
    245

*Dallas Morning News,* 93, 107, 111, 239

Dallas Plan Organization, 94–95

Dallas Trinity River Corridor Project, 90

*Dallas Trinity River Policy,* 89, 93

Dallas Urban Lab, *248*

Damman, 117, 119

Dangermond, Jack, 13, 256

Dawson, Stuart, 78

daylighting, 27, *46,* 99

Dayton, John W., 111

Dayton, OH, 7, 10, 11, 35, 77–78, *79,* 235

Dayuan (Big Yards), 182–184, 193, 197, 202, 203, 255

dead zone(s), 165, 231, 235, 236

De Stijl, 29

Dee and Charles Wyly Theatre, 109, 110, *110,* 111, 114

Den Haag, 147

Deepwater Horizon explosion, 2010, 229

desert, 15, 18, 31, 118; desertification, 31, 266n11. *See also*
    Sonoran Desert

Desert Botanical Garden, 255

DeShong, Mark, 102

design-build, 24, 25, 29

*design e²,* 25

Design Corps, 251

Desvigne, Michel, 107, 110–111, 112

Detroit, MI, 69, 165, 253

Dewees Island, SC, 82

Dhahran, 117, 119

Dillon, David, 107, 111–112, 114

Diller Scofidio + Renfro, 63

Doll, Larry, 268n18

Dollin, Michael, 64

Dongcheng District, 202

Duany, Andres, 16, 259n13, 268n17

Duany Plater-Zyberk & Company, 237, 259n13

Dubai, 209, 247

Dugger, Rebecca, 92–93, 262n5

Dutch Academy, 206

Dykema, Bibiana, 176

Dykers, Craig, 247

Eames, Charles, 249

Earth, 1, 18, 171, 252, 256, 257, 258

Earth Day, 73

Eastern Scheldt Storm Surge Barrier, *236*

Ebbets Field, 61

École des Beaux-Arts, 65, 68, 70, 75–76, 261n7

Ecological Corridor, 209, *209*

ecology, 1, 3, 15, 17, 21, 41, 53, 59, 73, 76, 78, 79, 80, 81,
    125, 127, 210, 221, 229, 230, 233, 255, 256, 257, 258;
    ecologist(s), 35, 206; human, 3, 73, 137, 258; urban ecol-
    ogy, 4, 5, 15, 17, 42, 51, 59, 192, 193, 206

ecosystem(s), 44, 45, 53, 59, 85, 89, *116,* 150, 184, 209,
    229–230; services, 42, 43, 44, *45, 46*

ecotone, 194, 230

*Ecotopia,* 150, 152

ecozones, *237*

EDAW, 13, 219, 222, 226, 227, 237, 239

Edwards Aquifer, 73, 76, 115, 128, 129–130, *130,* 131, 135;
    Barton Springs Segment(s), 129–130, 131; Northern
    Edwards Segment, 129–130, 131

Edwards Escarpment, 160

Edwards Limestone, 127, 128, 131

Edwards Plateau, 116, 127, 130, 139, 156, 158, 160

Eisenman, Peter, 247

Elaine D. and Charles A. Sammons Park, *110,* 114. *See also*
    Performance Park

Elam, Merrill, 247

Eliot, Charles, 13–14, 60, *60*

Elizondo, Raquel, 222

Elmore, Jim, 18, 61

Emerald Necklace, 13–14, 60, *60,* 93

endangered, *47,* 122, 128, 133, 226, 237; species, 131, 132,
    *132, 133, 162*

energy, 15, 23, 29, 31, 33, 38, 39, 40, *45,* 67, 98, 154, 165, 239,
    249, 253, 256, 257, 258, 262n21; use, 15, 31, 56, 146, 154,
    253. *See also* renewable: energy; solar: energy; and zero-
    net energy

England, 51, 111, 179, 205, 231; countryside, 237; gardens,
    204; landscape, 205; scholars, 161

Environmental Decade (1970s), 2, 68, 73, 122

Environmental Planning and Development Partnership, 78

environmentalism, 35, 84, 133, 137, 237; civic, 133, 137; environmentalists, 116, 122, 137, 237

Envision Central Texas (ECT), 3, 116, 117, 133, 135–146, 154, 162, 253, 268n17; bond election, 143, 145

Envision Utah, 136, 145, 154

ESRI, 13

Este, Ippolito II d', 174

esthetics, 13, 16, 21, 29, 35, 100, 119, 163

Europe, 4, 6, 10, 29, 30, 112, 147, 160, 161, 162, 180, 242, 255; cities, 4, 53; nations, 182; regionalists, 161, 162

European Union, 147, 161, 198

Everglades, 235, 235

Faga, Barbara, 13

Faircloth, Billie, 250

Fanzolo di Vedelago, 203

farmland(s), 31, 32, 33, 47, 51, 52, 78, 132, 133, 147, 152, 153, 160, 204, 257; preservation, 51, 188; protection, 125

Farnese, Alessandro, 177

Faulkner, Larry, 105

FBI, 219, 222, 224, 225

Federal Institute of Technology, Zurich, 238–239

Fellows of the American Academy of Rome, 206

Ferrara, Jackie, 102

Field Operations, 17, 52, 58, 63, 248

Fifth Ring Road, 200, 207, 209, 209

Findlay, Doug, 102, 104

Fink, Jonathan, 19

Fishman, Robert, 167

Fisk, Pliny, 22, 24, 25, 27, 76, 249, 260n10

Flight 93 National Memorial, 219–228, 220, 222, 223, 227, 228, 267n5; competition, 6, 219–228, 220, 221, 222, 225, 226, 227, 267n5; team, 222

flood(s), 32, 34, 45, 55, 59, 81, 89, 98, 90, 128, 131, 153, 164, 188, 191, 229, 230, 235, 236, 237, 239; control(s), 61, 67, 90, 93, 96, 97, 149, 156, 235, 236, 266n11; damage, 80; floodplain(s), 33, 47, 92, 95, 97, 235; management, 14; protection, 96, 97, 236, 262n16; season, 31; water, 89, 210

Florence, Italy, 56, 57, 178, 204, 267n5

Florida, 84, 119, 149, 230, 231, 232–233, 233, 235, 235, 239. See also specific cities

Florida, Richard, 127

Fontana, Giovanni, 175

Ford Foundation, 161, 166

Forman, Richard, 197

Forsyth, Ann, 79, 81, 83

Fort Davis, TX, 30, 30

Fort Sam Houston, 155

Fort Worth, TX, 2, 3, 65, 87, 89, 90, 94, 94, 96, 97, 98, 149, 150, 154, 154, 155, 159, 245, 262n15

Foster, Norman, 107, 109, 110, 111, 112, 114, 215, 241, 247–248, 255

fractal(s), 57, 57

Fragrant Hill, 185, 189, 198

Frampton, Kenneth, 11–12, 15, 242

France, 5, 51, 65, 68, 107, 111, 112, 147, 161, 179, 180, 202, 205, 232, 240, 242; architect(s), 182; geographer(s), 147; landscape architect(s), 107, 111

Franklin, Carol, 119

Franklin, Colin, 198

Franklin, Shirley, 166

Frascati, 175–176, 175

Fregonese Calthorpe Associates, 136, 137, 162, 239, 268n17

Fregonese, John, 137, 138, 268n17

French Academy, 175, 206

Fresh Kills Project, 52, 58, 58

Frick, Henry Clay, 206

Fried, Helene, 219, 222, 223, 267n5

Friends of the High Line, 63

Fulton, Duncan, 107, 111

Fulton, William, 10

Galatas, Roger, 79, 83, 262n21

Galveston, TX, 79, 90, 155, 156, 239

Gambara, Gianfrancesco, 177

Garcia, Gus, 135

Garreau, Joel, 150, 152

Garrison, Michael, 22, 24, 25, 26, 103

Gateway Park Master Plan, 94, 262n15

Gaudí, Antonio, 13, 64

Geddes, Patrick, 204

Gehry, Frank, 163, 247–248, 247

Geographic Information System (GIS) technology, 12, 13, 55–56, 55, 116, 118, 138, 144, 153, 187, 191, 237, 256

Germany, 29–30, 67, 127, 135, 155, 175, 200, 240; architects, 35; scholars, 161; settlers, 67

German Academy, 206

Giardini della Biennale, 238, 240

Giardino all'Italiana, 171

Gideon Toal, 262n15

Gila River, 12

Gilbert, Cass, 70

Gillette, Jane, 120

Gladstone Associates, 80

Global Institute of Sustainability, 18

Global Summit on Innovations for an Urban World, 164

Goddard, Terry, 61

Gomez, Maria, 249

Good Fulton & Farrell, 111, 112

Google, 55, 200, 225; Google Earth, 55, 153, 256

Gottmann, Jean, 147, 265n1

Graves, Michael, 206, 247

Great Lakes, 165, 253

Great Springs of Texas, 115–116, 117, 128, 143

Great Streets Initiative, 67–68, 68

Greater Phoenix 2100, 19

Greece, 10, 38, 65, 79, 174, 241, 262n3, 263n1, 265n1; influence, 204; theater, 204 green building, 3, 22, 26, 35, 36, 39, 40, 43, 115, 215, 249

greenbelts, 207

Greenbuild International Conferences, 39. *See also* U.S.
    Green Building Council

Greene, Herbert, 70

greenhouse gas(es), 31, *33*, *45*; *48*, 165; emissions, *48*; pro-
    duction, 15, 253. *See also* $CO_2$

greenprint(s)(ing), 116, 143–144, *144*, 145, 146

greenway(s), 18, 76, 90

Grey, Spencer de, 109, 111

Gropius, Walter, 69

groundwater, 7, 32, 127, 128, 129, 130, 131, *186*, 191, 207

Grow, Robert, 144

growth management, 75, 127, 146

Guan Zhaoye, 182

Guatemala City, 245

Guggenheim Museum, 15

Gulf Coast, 6, *12*, *55*, 59, 149, 153, 158, 165, 217, 229–233, *231*,
    *232*, 233, 235–237, 239, *240*; region, 229, 232

Gulf Coastal Plain, 155, 158

Gulf of Mexico, 89, 127, 131, 149, 153, 156, 230, 231, 235

Gunderson, Lance, 59

Gunderson, Mark, 245

Gustafson, Kathryn, 163

Gwen, Terry, 164

Haas, Stan, 22–24

Hack, Gary, 10, 214, 247

Hadid, Zaha, 198, 214, 247–248, *247*

Haidian District, 202

Hailong Liu, 179, 196, 206

Halff Associates, 91, 96

Hanley, Joanne, 267n5, 267n6

Hangzhou, 187, 255; West Lake, 187

Hargreaves Associates, 38, 95, 96, 97, 101, *101*, 107, 112,
    262n16

Hargreaves, George, 101

Hartsfield, Robert, 79

Hartzfield, Jim, 23

Harvard University, 10, 65, 69, 75, 78, 219, 221, 268n2; stu-
    dents, 268n2

Hays County, TX, 133, 136, 143, 144

He Rui, 179, 192, 197–198, 204

health, 6, 10, 19, 32, 33, 34, 41, 44, *45*, *48*, 51, 52, 59, 89, 133,
    136, 142, 166, 197, 217, 231, 252, 253, 256, 257, 258

Hebei Province, 9

Hegeler, Robert, 238

Hegemann, Werner, 70

Henderson, Ron, 198

Henry Luce Foundation, 25

Hepburn, Eric, 238

Hersey, George, 19

Herzog & de Meuron, 99, 100, 101, 182, 250

Herzog, Jacques, 263n1

Heymann, David, 22

High Line, 52, *62*, 63, *63*

High Point neighborhood, *42*

high speed rail (HSR), 160

Hilderbrand, Gary, 102

Hill Country Alliance, 116–117

Hill Country Conservancy, 116, 130, 143

Hispanic(s), 76, 82, 127, 135, 156, 264n3

Hite, Jessie, 100, 101

HNTB, 96–97

Hoidn, Barbara, 238–239, 240, 241, 268n18

HOK, 78

Holl, Steven, 181

Hong Kong, 62, 109, 184

Hoover, Larry, 224

Houston, 2, 3, 13, 56, 65, 77, 78, 79, 80, 81, 83, 112, *118*, 137,
    149, 150, 154, *154*, 155–156, 157, 158–159, *159*, 160, 191,
    229, 239, *240*, 253; metropolitan region, 81, 83, 159

Houston, Sam, 67, 155, 245

Hu Jie, 206–207, 208, 209, 210, 212, 214

Huber, Don, 77–78

HUD Title VII Urban Growth and New Community Develop-
    ment Act, 77, 78, 79, 80–81, 82, 262n2

Hunt, Angela, 97

hurricane(s), *12*, *55*, 59, 79, 153, 154, 156, 191, 217, 229, 231,
    *232*, 233, 235, 236, 239, *240*; Andrew, 230, 235; Ike, 156,
    239; Katrina, 6, 59, 96, 191, 217, 229–230, *230*, 233, 236,
    239, 239, 241, 267n1, 267n11; Rita, 191, 192

Hutchison, Kay Bailey, 245

Idaho, 136, 150

Illinois Institute of Technology (IIT), 247

Indiana, 150, 162, 255

Institute of Resource Protection and Tourism, 196

Intergovernmental Panel on Climate Change, 164–165

Intermountain West, 265n4

International Modern Movement, 75

International Style, 9, 68, 75

Internet, 55

interstate highways, 10, 11, 83, 155, 160; I-10, 155; I-35, 76,
    144, 149, 155; I-45, 83, 155; I-55, 203, 255, 256; I-70, 219;
    I-75, 7, 165; I-76, 219

Isozaki, Arata, 182

Istanbul Technical University, 118

Italy, 1, 3, 4, *4*, 5–6, *5*, 9, 53, *54*, *57*, *164*, 169, 171–178, *175*, *176*,
    200, 204–206, 229, 236, 238, 242, 253, 265n14, 267n5;
    architect, 215; architecture, 3, 6; design, 6, 169, 171, 176,
    204; garden(s), 171, 177, 186, *186*, 200, 204–205, 206;
    landscape(s), 204, 205; planning, 4, 169; regions, 5;
    universities, 3

Jackson, Liz, 27

Jackson, Richard Joseph, 257, 259n10

Jacobus, Frank, 238

Janiculum Hill, 171, 206

Japan, 105, 182, 198, 215

Jefferson, Thomas, 164, 167, 182
Jeffersonian grid, 71–72
Jensen, Jens, 14
Jersey Devil, 24
Johnson, Johnson & Roy (JJR), 107, 111, 268n17
Johnson, Lady Bird, 3, 87, 117, 119–120, 121–122, *122*, 124, 125, 135
Johnson, Lyndon Baines (LBJ), 135
Johnson, Philip, 157
Jones, Mary Margaret, 101
Jones Studio, 64
Joy, Rick, 15, 35
Juneja, Narendra, 120
Juscelino Kubitschek de Oliveira mausoleum, *19*

Kahn, Claire, 111
Kahn, Louis, 76, 157, 206, 247
Kallmann McKinnell & Wood, 100, 101, 102
*Kao Gong Ji* (*The Craftsman's Record*), 193
Kapoor, Anish, 163
Karvonen, Andrew, 262n3
Kellert, Stephen, 19
Kennedy, Caroline, 35
Kennedy, Sheila, 250
Kensley, Albert, 69
Kent, William, 205
Kentner, Jason, 219, 221, 222, 223, 224, 225, 226
Kentucky, 10, 152
Kessler, George, 90, 94
Kieran, Stephen, 250
Kieran Timberlake, 249
Kiley, Dan, 206
King Fahd University of Petroleum and Minerals, 117–118, *118*, 119
Kirk, Ron, 90
knowledge capital, 10, 11, 20, 59
Kocurek, Neal, 135–136, 141–142, 143
Kong-Jian Yu, 266n11
Koolhaas, Rem, 36, 107, 109, 181, 242
Krepart, Russell, 29
Kruse, Mike, 144
Kuala Lumpur, 35
Kuehl, Sarah, 102, 104

Lady Bird Johnson Wildflower Center, 2, 3, *34*, 39–41, *40*, 115, 117, 119–120, *120*, 121–122, *121*, *123*, 124, *124*, 135, 157, 200, 253, 255
Lady Bird Lake, 67, 90, 122, 268n17
Lagos, 245
Laguna Veneta, 238
Lake Austin, 2, 69, 72–76
*Lake Austin Growth Management Plan*, 72, 74, 75, 84
Lake Como, *5*, 164, *164*
Lake, David, 247
Lake|Flato, 247, 263n4
Lamar, Mirabeau, 245

Lambert, Nevin, 224, 225
*Landscape Architecture*, 27, 207, 226
landscape architecture, 6, 13, 16, 17, 18, 19, 21, 26, 30, 32, 41, 43, 51, 57, 58, 64, 69, 79, 100, 102, 105, 107, 111, 114, 120, 174, 187, 192, 193, 197, 198, 206, 207, 209, 245, 251, 252, 253, 255; degree, 21, 200, 247; department, 179; faculty, 18, 200; planning, 125, 179, 197, 200; program(s), 6, 169, 185, 200, 208; students, 18, 20, 182, 185, 200, 225, 262n15
Landscape Architecture Foundation, 120, 162, 219
landscape design(s), 2, 10, 16, 27, 84, 85, 87, 91, 93, 101, 102, 105, 111, 112, 113, 135, 177; ecology, 81, 200; planning, 125, 179, 197, 200
Landscape Forms, 165
*landschap*, 51
Lang, Robert, 147, 149, 153, 161, 229, 265n4
Larcan, Laura, 241
Larry and Mary Ann Faulkner Plaza, *103*
Las Vegas, 119, 201
Latino populations, 76, 256
Laurel Highlands, 219
Lazio region, 9
Leadership in Energy and Environmental Design (LEED), 30, 39–40, *40*, 41, 43, 46, 50, 68, 82, 85, *104*, 249, 253
Lebermann, Lowell, 135–136, 143
Lecco (Italy), 255
LEED for Neighborhood Development (LEED ND), 40, 82
Leopold, Aldo, 89, 256
Leppert, Tom, 97
Levittown, 77, 78
Levy, Max, 249
Levy, Mike, 135
Lewis, Karen, *220*, 221, *221*, 222, *222*, 224, 225, *225*, *226*, 227
Lexington, KY, 221, 224, 225
LI, 93
Liang Sicheng, 193, 200, 267n4
Libeskind, Daniel, 247–248
Librach, Austan, 76
light rail, 137, 139, 140
Ligorio, Pirro, 171, 174, 204
Limbaugh, Rush, 11
Lin Huiyin, 267n4
Lin, Maya, 267n4
Lincoln, Abraham, 167
Lincoln Highway, 221
Lincoln Institute, 161, 166
liquid landscape, 230, 267n6
Lister, Nina-Marie, 52
Little Rock, AK, 10, 11, 36, *37*, 38
Lockhart, TX, 140, *142*
London, 236
Long-Term Ecological Research (LTER), 59
Los Angeles, 119, 197, 241, *248*
Louisiana, 10, *11*, *104*, 155, 191, 229, *231*, *231*, 232, 233; citizens, 267n11

Louisville, KY, 10, 11, 38
Lovins, Amory, 39
Lovins, Hunter, 39
Lower Don Lands, Toronto, 17, 52, 52
Lu Han, 198
Lu Lu Shan, 212
Lucca, Italy, 4, 53, 54
Lum, Ken, 223
Lutyens, Edwin, 172
Luxor, Egypt, 117
Luxor, Las Vegas, 119
Lyle, John, 22, 43, 154
Lynch, Kevin, 56–57, 214

Macedonia, 256
MacKay-Lyons, Brian, 35, 263n4
Maderno, Carlo, 175
Madrid, Spain, 29, 149
Mandelbrot set, 57
Manhattan, 40, 63, 245
Mannerist, 176–177
Mao Zedong, 5–6, 184, 192, 193, 194
Marco Polo Airport, 242
Margaret Hunt Hill Bridge, 92
Margot and Bill Winspear Opera House, 109, 109, 110, 111, 114
Marin County Civic Center, 15
Marks, Gerby, 27
Martino, Steve, 64
Marx, Roberto Burle, 19–20, 19
Massachusetts, 78, 231
Massachusetts Institute of Technology (MIT), 59, 81, 214
Mathur, Anuradha, 267n6
Maxman, Susan, 249
Mazria, Ed, 24
McCarter, Mack, 103–104
McDonough, Bill, 249
McHarg, Ian, 1, 2, 16–17, 19, 43, 52, 65, 69–85, 121, 136, 145, 164, 235, 237, 237, 255, 262n2
McKim, Charles, 206
McKim, Mead, and White, 206
McKinnell, Michael, 100, 101, 102
McMichael, Carol, 70, 261n7
McSherry, Laurel, 222, 223, 224
Mecca, 118
Meckfessell, Bob, 249
Medici, 175, 204
Medici, Ferdinando de', 175
Medici, Giulio de', 171
Medina, 118
megacity(ies), 142, 241
megaclimates, 9
megalopolis, 147, 265n1
megapolitan(s), 147, 149, 153, 229
Megaregion Planning Organization, 159

megaregion(s), 3, 125, 147, 148, 149–150, 152–155, 154, 159–161, 165, 169, 229
Meili Snow Mountain National Park, 196, 196, 197
Meinig, Donald, 150, 152, 152
Memory Trail, 222, 226
Memphis, TN, 10, 11, 36–37, 155
MESA, 107
Metropolitan Institute, 147, 153
metropolitan planning organizations (MPOs), 153, 159
Meunier, John, 13, 18, 20, 21
Mexico, 25, 76, 104, 149, 255
Miami, FL, 56, 222, 223
Miami Beach, 219
Miami Valley, 7
Michel Desvigne Paysagistes, 111
Michiana, 150
Michigan, 150, 165
microclimate(s), 9, 32, 113, 172; amelioration, 110
Midwest, 14, 150, 152; prairie landscape, 14
Mies van der Rohe, Ludwig, 9
Miething, Justine, 111
Milan, 56, 147, 204, 241, 255
Milan Polytechnic, 3, 215, 255
Millennium Park, 163–164, 163
Miller, E. Lynn, 200, 219, 220, 221, 221, 222, 222, 223, 224, 225, 226, 226
Miller, Laura, 94–95, 96, 97
Milwaukee, WI, 268n17
Ming Dynasty, 179, 184, 188, 201, 201
Minneapolis, MN, 77
Miralles, Enric, 13
Mississippi, 10, 229, 230, 231, 233
Mississippi Gulf Coast, 237
Mississippi River, 37, 77, 231, 231, 235; floods, 230
Mississippi River Basin, 235
Missouri Pacific (MoPac) Railroad, 155
Mitchell, Deb, 107, 111, 114
Mitchell Energy & Development Corp., 79
Mitchell, George Phydias, 1, 2, 65, 78–85, 262n21
Mitchell, O. Jack, 78
Mitgang, Lee, 10
mitigation, 44, 45, 150, 165, 217, 236, 266n11
Mobile, AL, 149
Modernism, 1, 9, 17, 19, 75–76, 99, 248, 263n4; Modernist(s), 68, 75
Moore, Charles, 247
Moore, Steven, 11, 12, 15, 25
Morgan, J. P., 206
Morgan Stanley, 81
Morial, Marc, 230
Morocco, 117, 263n1
Morris Arboretum, University of Pennsylvania, 41
Morrison Institute, 265n4
Morton H. Meyerson Symphony Center, 107, 110
Moule, Elizabeth, 259n13
Moyers, Bill, 121

Mueller Airport, 27, 29
Mueller, Liz, 25–26
multi-state regions, 149
multidisciplinary, 2, 14, 21, 132, 162
Mumbai, 245
Mumford, Lewis, 10, 75, 253
Murase, Robert, 101, 102
Murcutt, Glenn, 24, 33, 35
Murdoch Architects, 225, 226, 227, 228, 267n6
Murdoch, Milena, 224, 227
Murdoch, Paul, 224, 227
Murphy, Henry, 182, 189
Musée du quai Branly, 112, 112
Museo Nazionale Etrusco, 172
Museum of Northern Arizona, 117
Mussolini, Benito, 4, 200

Napa Valley, 152
Nasher, Ray, 245
Nashville, TN, 10, 11
National Environmental Policy Act (1969), 73, 77
National Framework for Conservation and Development, 166
National Landscape Conservation System, 167
National Landscape Survey, 166, 167
National Mall, 2, 22, 24, 25, 26, 27
National Recreation and Parks Association, 41
National Science Foundation, 59
National Wildlife Federation, 254
Native Americans, 7, 127, 156, 264n3
Natural Resources Defense Council (NRDC), 39, 40
Nature Conservancy, 41, 196
Nelson, Chris, 153
Netherlands, 17, 35, 51, 52, 147, 148, 236, 236, 241, 248, 255
new community, 78, 79, 80, 80, 81, 83, 85; law, 77, plan, 65; planners, 83; planning, 77–85
New Community Development Act, 77
New England, 150
New Haven, Connecticut, 105
New Jersey, 116
New Mexico, 24
New Orleans, 6, 11, 77, 96, 166, 191, 229, 230, 230, 232, 232, 233, 237, 239, 239, 241, 262n2, 267n1, 268n17
New Suburban, 84
new town(s), 77, 79, 82, 85, 131, 139–140, 262n2
New York City, 13, 17, 52, 53, 56, 58, 58, 61, 62, 63, 63, 77, 102, 119, 120, 137, 155, 161, 162, 208, 212, 225, 237, 245, 247, 250, 263n1
New York State, 77
Newark, NJ, 219, 221, 222
Newfields, 78
Niemeyer, Oscar, 19, 19
Nile River, 117
Nixon, Richard, 73, 122
Norman Foster + Partners, 111, 112
Norquist, John, 268n17

North America, 29, 30, 52, 59, 67, 112, 122, 147, 150, 152, 191, 200, 209, 231
North Central Texas Council of Governments, 94, 97
North Texas Tollway Authority, 262n5
Nouvel, Jean, 247, 250
Nova Scotia, 35, 232, 263n4

Obama, Barack, 90, 167
Obata, Gyo, 78
Office for Metropolitan Architecture (OMA), 36, 107, 109–110, 111, 112, 114, 181–182, 212
Ohio, 10, 11, 31, 35, 77, 78, 165, 235, 255
Ohio River, 7, 11
Ohio State University, 222
Oklahoma, 89
Old National Road, 255
Old Summer Palace. See Yuan Ming Yuan
Olin, Laurie, 169, 179, 197, 198, 206, 224, 226, 228
Olivieri, Orazio, 175
Olmsted Sr., Frederick Law, 13–15, 16, 60, 60, 61, 67, 93, 210, 212
Olympic Forest Park, 6, 182, 206–210, 208, 209, 210, 211, 212, 212, 213, 255
Olympic Green, 207, 208, 208, 212
Olympic Village, 209, 210, 214
Olympics, 13, 214; 2008 Olympics, 6, 35, 181, 182, 192, 193, 194, 206–210, 211, 212, 215, 255, 267n3
Omnibus Public Land Management Act of 2009, 166, 167
Omniplan, 78
Oregon, 153
Orr, David, 1
Oslo, 247
Ostia Antica, 204
Ottoman Empire, 263n1
Oudolf, Piet, 163
Ouroussoff, Nicolai, 242, 250
Ove Arup & Partners, 182
Overland Partners, 122, 135, 263n4, 264n1

Pachauri, Rajendra, 164–165
Pacific Northwest, 102, 150, 152
Page Southerland Page, 236n2
Palazzo Grassi, 238
Palladian, 205, 240
Palladio, Andrea, 31, 33, 203
Palleroni, Sergio, 25
Pan American Union, 68, 69
Pantheon, 171, 172
Parc André-Citroën, 112, 112
Parc Diagonal Mar, 13, 14
Paris, 11, 68, 111, 112, 112, 206, 237
parking lot(s), 32, 34, 41, 41, 62–63, 163, 224
Pearl River, 231
Peets, Elbert, 70
Pei, I. M., 107

Peking University, 179, 188, 189, *190*, 198, 266n11

Pelli, Rafael, 249, 250

Pennsylvania, 6, 162, 219, *220*, *223*, 226

Pennsylvania State University, 30, 150, 200

Performance Park, 111, 112, 114. *See also* Elaine D. and
    Charles A. Sammons Park

Perot Jr., Ross, 248

Persian Gulf, 34

Peter Walker and Partners, 101, 102–103, 104–105, 107, 120

Philadelphia, 35, 56, 65, 68, 69, 70, 136, 166, 224, 253

Philosophical Society of Texas, 245

Phoenix, AZ, 12, 18, *18*, 19, 31, 35–36, 39, 53, *54*, 55, 59, 61,
    *61*, 62, *62*, 64, 136, 137, 188, 255; Arts Commission, 61;
    Central Library, 36, *36*

physical, 18, 114, 119, 253, 256; design, 16; environment,
    147; planning, 6, *161*; regions, 10, 50, 151, *151*; systems,
    *237*; well-being, 45

physiographic features, 150; regions, 74, *74*, 150

Piano, Renzo, 107

Piazza Navona, 171, *177*

Piazzale Roma, 238

Pichelmann, Gustav, 241

Pickett, Steward, 59

Pieprz, Dennis, 207

Pinchot, Gifford, 14, 21

Pincian Hill (Collina del Pincio), 175

Pine Barrens, 116

Pittsburgh, PA, 56, 78, 219, 224

place-making, 11, 18, 58, 214

*Places*, 236–237

Plan for Chicago, 1909, 60, *60*

Plaquemines Parish, LA, *231*

Plater-Zyberk, Elizabeth, 83, 237, *237*, 259n13

Pocantico Hills, 161, 162

Polshek, James, 37–38

Polyzoides, Stefanos, 259n13

Pontchartrain, 77, 262n2

Ponte dell'Accademia, 241

Popik, Barry, 155

popular regions, 150, *152*

Porta, Giacomo della, 175

Porterfield, Neil, 78

Portland Metro, 137, 153, 268n17

Portland, OR, 87, 107, 153, 268n17

Postmodernism, 1–2, 9, 17

Powers, Bill, 105

Prairie Crossing, IL, 79, 82, 162, *162*

Prairie House, 15

Prairie Style, 14

Predock, Antoine, 135

Prince-Ramus, Joshua, 109, 111

Pritzker Laureate, 24

Pritzker Prize, 247

Promethean Project, 89

Prospect Park, 13, *53*, 208

Provost, Alain, 112

PTW Architects, 182

Public Architecture, 251

Public Art Program, 62

Puerto Rico, 26

Pulitzer Prizes, 247

Putnam, Robert, 10, 146

Pyramid Arena, 36–37

Qianmen, 214

Qin Dynasty, 184

Qing Dynasty, 179, 180, 182, 186, 188, 189, 201, *201*

*Qing Ming Shang He Tu*, 203–204, *204*

Quale, John D., 24

Quality Growth Toolbox, 145

Quantrill, Malcolm, 263n4

Que Zhenqing, 192, 193, 198, *199*

Queen Creek, AZ, 63

Rachofsky, Howard, 111, 114, 245

rain gardens, *46*, *49*, 50

Rainey, Reuben, 228

rainwater, 47, 193, 210; collection, 22, 23, *34*, *40*, *123*

Randall, Samantha, 25, 26, 29

Randstad Holland, 147

Ranney, George, 162, 163

Ranney, Victoria, 162

Raphael, 171, *172*, 204

Rather, Robin, 135, 191

Rawls, Alec, 267n6

RECLUS, 147

Red River, 104

Red Sea, 117

Reed, Chris, 52

Reed, Doug, 102

Reed Hilderbrand, 101, 102, 219

regenerative design, 22, 32, 43, 44, 113, 154, 217

Regional Plan Association (RPA), 3, 63, 147, 159, 165–167,
    237, 239

regionalism, 1, 3, 7, 9, 10, 11, 12, 125–167, 177, 204, 230,
    257; Critical, 11–12, 15; new regionalism, 1, 2, 7, 125–161,
    161–167

regionalist(s), 161, 162, 257; new regionalist, 257

Reh, Wouter, 177–178

Reiter, Wellington "Duke," 225, *226*, 227

Renaissance, 171, 172, 174, 176, 177, 178, 204, 205, 206,
    261n7

renewable, 33; energy, 23; products, 45–46, *45*; sources, 33,
    34, *48*

Repton, Humphry, 205

resilience, 6, 59, 153–154, 217, 229, 230, 233, 236

resilient, 7, 53, 59, 191, 217, 229

*resilire*, 229

Reston, VA, 77, *78*

Rhode Island School of Design, 198

Richard Browne Associates, 80

Rieff, Susan, 120, 121
Rio de Janeiro, 19, 56
Rio Grande River, 231
Rio Salado, 18, *18*, 61, 62
River Walk, 90, 155
Riverside, IL, *15*, 79
Robert Wood Johnson Foundation, 104, 257
Roberts, Bill, 235
Robertson, Donna, 247
Robie House, 15
Rockefeller Center, 120–121, 184
Rockefeller Foundation, 3, 26, 166; Bellagio Center, Italy, *5*, 164, *164*, 266n8
Rockefeller, John D., 161, 206
Rockefeller, Laurance, 121
Rocky Mountain Institute, 39
Rodriguez, Robert, 156
Rohrbach, Gerwin, 78
Roma, *56*
Rome, 10, 6, 53, 56, 114, 118, 171–178, *173*, *186*, 204, 205, 206, 237, 242; gardens and villas, 171–178; urban landscape, 178
Rome Prize(s), 35, 206
Roosevelt, Franklin, 167
Roosevelt, Theodore, 164, 167
Rose, Deedie, 107, 109, 111, 114, 245
Rotterdam, 147
Rouse Corporation, 81
Rouse, James, 79, 83
Rowlett, John, *118*
Rybczynski, Witold, 31

Sabine Hills, 174, 175
Safe Drinking Water Act, 129–130
Sahara Desert, 117
Salt Lake City, UT, 120
Salt River, 12, 18, 61
San Antonio, TX, 3, 77, 87, 90, 127, 128, 129, 130, 131, 135, 149, 150, 154, *154*, 155, 157, 158, 159, 160, 247, 253; Alamo, 155; metropolitan regions, 133
San Francisco, 56, 60, 150, 200, 219, 222, 224
Sardinia, 256
Sasaki Associates, 207–208, 209
Sasaki, Hideo, 78, 105, 107
satellite(s), 256; imagery, 13, 153, 256
*Saudi Gazette*, 118
Save Our Springs (SOS), 115, 130, 146
Scarpa, Carlo, 240
scenario(s), 137–142, *139*, *140*, *143*, 146, 163, 165; preferred, 142, *143*
Scheer, Brenda, 247
Scheeren, Ole, 181
Schmidt, Robert, 264n1
Scotland, 65, 69
Scott Brown, Denise, 247
Scott, Wallie, *118*

Scottsdale, AZ, *32*
Searle, Colgate, 198
Seattle, 35–36, *37*, *42*, *46*, 56
Secret Service, 119–120
September 11, 2001, 22, 24, 58, 59, 83, 119, 162, 217, 219, 222, 226, 227
Severe Acute Respiratory Syndrome (SARS), 197
Shanghai, 197, 198
Shanksville, PA, 219
Shelley, Mary, 262n3
Shipley, Dan, 249
Shreveport, LA, 103, 104, *104*
Sichuan Province earthquake, 2008, 35, 59, 230
Sicily, 204
Sidwell Friends School, *49*, *50*, *251*, 252
Silas, Beverly, 136
Simmonds, Roger, 10
Simonds, John, 78
Simonds, Philip, 78
Sinclair, Cameron, 251
Sino-Italian Energy Efficient Building, 214–215
site planning, 59, 80, 110, 111, 209
Sitio Burle Marx, *20*
Sixth Banchan, *186*
Sloan, Kevin, 93, 111–112, 114, 249, *249*, 250
Smets, Bas, 111
Smith, Gary, 119–120, 124
Smith, Lamar, 25
Smith, Madison, 264n1
Smithson, Robert, 253
SNAP House (Super Nifty Action Package), 25, *25*
Snøhetta, 247
Snyder, Vince, 249
Soares, Valeska, 102
Solaire, The, 250
Solar Decathlon, 2, 21–30, *25*, *27*, *28–29*, *30*, 260n10; Solar Decathlon Europe, 29
solar, 26, 29, 34, 203; collectors, 26; energy, 29, 30, 34; heated, 27; heating, 22; houses, 26, 29; lighting, 22; orientation, *23*, *33*, *172*; panels, 103; power(ed), 2, *25*, 27; technology, 27; tracking, *36*; village, 24, 27
Soleri, Paolo, 15, 35, 198
Solomon, Dan, 259n13
SOM, 107
Somerset County, PA, 219
Somerset, PA, 223, 224, 226
Sonora (Mexico), 25
Sonoran Desert, 31, 64
Sorin, Edward, 156
South America, 231
Southern Hemisphere, 164
Southern Methodist University (SMU), 245
Southwest Airlines, 89, 157
Soviet, 182, 198; influences, 182
Sowell, Jason, 241, 268n18

Spain, 26, 29, 87, 127, 149, 172, 231, 240, 241, 263n1; colo-
nists, 232; explorers, 131, 155; missions, 155
Speck, Jeff, 259n13
Speck, Larry, 99, 100, 112, 263n2, 263n4, 268n17
sprawl(ing), 6, 16, 31, 76, 77, 81, 135, 137, 146, 162, 172, 179,
206, 236, 256, 257, 258
St. Edward's University, 156, 253, *254*
St. John Community Center, 22–23, *23*
St. Louis, MO, 78, 155, 253
St. Peter's Basilica, 204
Stanford University, 13, 15
Stanolind Oil and Gas Company (Amoco), 79
star architects, 3, 112, 181, 236, 246–247, *247*
Stastny, Don, 223, 224–225, 267n5
Staten Island, 58
State Highway (SH) 130 Summit, 144–145
Steenbergen, Clemens, 177–178
Steiner, Bill, 267n5
Steiner, Halina, 163–164, 225, 227
Steiner, John, 219, 224
Steiner, Sandy, 224
storm surge(s), 45, 55, 217, 229, 235, 237, 239, *240*
stormwater, *41, 46, 47, 49*, 81; management, 266n11
StossLU, 17, 52
Stratus Properties, 115
strip mine, 6, 220, 221, 222, 224, 227, *227*
Su Di Causeway, 187
Sullivan, Louis, 14
Sun Corridor, 161
sustainability, 1, 6, 7, 9, 13, 14, 15, 16, 18, 19, 21, 22, 23, 25,
32, 34, 39, 41, *42*, 43, 44, *47, 48*, 49, 67, 99, 131, 135, 146,
154, 217, 249; analysis, 13; criteria, 13; education, 21, *48*;
metric, 39; principles, 41; programs, 18; projects, 18;
standards, *42*, 43; summit, 39; theorist, 11
sustainable, 6, 13, 43, 44, 157, 160, 217; architecture, 122;
design(s), 2, 6, 21, 22, 25, 30, 35, 44, 84, 135, 172, 250,
253; development, 13, 21–22, 23; planning, 253; materials, 39; site(s), 40, 41, 42, 43, 46; site design, 122; technologies, 22
Sustainable Development Council, 120
Sustainable Sites Initiative, 2, 3, 39–50, *42, 47–48*, 82
Suzhou, China, 5, 255; Garden of Cultivation, 5
SWA, 107
Swiss architects, 35, 87, 99, 238–239; (architecture) firm(s),
3, 100, 101, 182

Taiwan, 184
Taliesin West, 15
Tan Zhe Temple, 200–202
Tannehill, John, 200
Tashkent, Uzbekistan, 185
Taylor 28, *46*
TeamHaas Architects, 22–24
Technische Universität Darmstadt, *28–29*, 29
Tehachapi Hills, *33*

Tempe, AZ, 18, 61
Temple of Azure Clouds, 185–186, *185*
Temple of Heaven, 207
Ten Eyck, Christy, 64
*territorio*, 51
*terroir*, 51
terrorism, 6, 22, 24, 31, 58, 162, 219, 222, 227, 267n6
Texas, 2, 3, 6, 7, 10, 11, *12*, 26, 29, 31, 55, 65, 67, 70, 77, 78, 82,
85, 87–124, 125–167, *152, 159*, 160, 230, 231, 232–233, 245,
249, 253, 260n10, 263n4, 263n1, 265n14; architect(s),
109, 118; architecture, 2; Central Texas, 3, 10, 67, 116,
*116*, 119, 125, 127, 128, 129, 135–146, 150, 155, 156; cities,
171; city planning, 2; coast, *55*, 191, 239, *240*; growth,
160; highways, 157; landscape, 144, 245, limestone, 70;
region(s), 12, 102, 131–137, 150; urbanism, 1. *See also
specific cities and counties*
Texas A&M University, 27, 65, 79, 101, *118*, 149, 260n10,
262n15, 263n4
Texas Department of Transportation, 90, 97, 262n5
Texas Hill Country, 12, *116*, 117, 125, 127, *128*, 129, 130–131,
*130*, 188
Texas-Mexico border, 104, 149
Texas Society of Architects, 245
Texas State Legislature, 115, 136, 146, 157
Texas State University, 136, 264n3
Texas Triangle, 3, 125, 147, 149–150, 154–160, *154, 158, 159*, 161
Thomas, Gail, 96
Thoreau, Henry David, 258
Three Hills and Five Gardens, 179, *180*, 184, *185*, 186, 187,
188, 189, 191, 194, 196, 198, 214
Tiananmen Square, 192
Tiber River, 177
Tibet, 186, 196
Tibur, 174
Till, Jeremy, 19, 253
Timberlake, James, 250
Tivoli, Italy, 172, *173*, 174, *174*, 175, 176
Tod Williams Billie Tsien, 249
Tohono O'odham, 31
tollway(s), 92, 93–94, 96, 97, 98
Toronto, 17, 52, *52*; waterfront, 69, *69*
Town Lake. *See* Lady Bird Lake
transportation planning, 95, 142, 146, 159, 160
transect(s), 10, 11, 187, 203, 236–237, *237*
transit-oriented development (TOD), 143
Travis County, TX, 73, 132, 133, 136, 143–144, *144*
Trinity parkway, 87, 90
Trinity River, 87, 89–98, *90*, 92, 95, 97, 157, 160, 231, 262n15;
floodplain, 97
Trinity Uptown Project, 96, 97
Trust for Public Land, 116, 143–144
Trustee Hall, 253, *254*
Tschumi, Bernard, 250
Tsien, Billie, 247
Tsinghua, China, 200, 202; Big Yard, 182–184, 193, 197–198,
202–204, 255; campus, *183*, 184, *199*, 203, 209, 214;

Department of Landscape Architecture, 6, 169, 179,
180, 186, 200, 208; officials, 215; School of Architecture,
187, 193, 194, 198, 200, 203, 214; Science Park, 184, 207;
University, 6, 169, 179, 182–184, 183, 189, 197, 198, 199,
200, 202–204, 203, 206, 208, 209, 214, 215, 242; Urban
Planning and Design Institute, 197, 208
Turin, Italy, 241, 267n5
Turquoise Necklace, 62, 62
Turtle Creek Boulevard, 94
27th Avenue Solid Waste Management Facility, 61, 61
Twin Cities Metropolitan Region of Minnesota, 69
Typhoon Damrey, 192, 196, 197

Udall, Stewart, 121
Ulrich, Sven, 238
United Airlines Flight 93, 6, 219, 221, 222, 224–225, 224, 227
United Arab Emirates, 118, 247
United Nations (UN), 18, 21, 164–165, 229, 233
United States, 151, 166. See also specific government bodies;
regions; states
University College London, 118, 242
University of California, Los Angeles (UCLA), 257, 259n10
University of Cincinnati, 29, 101, 101, 200
University of Colorado, 24, 26
University of Illinois, Urbana-Champaign, 162, 208
University of Kentucky, 221
University of New Orleans, 239
University of Michigan, 26, 166, 167
University of North Carolina, Chapel Hill, 59
University of Pennsylvania, PA, 22, 41, 65, 68, 69, 79, 147,
149, 161, 164, 166, 214, 221, 224, 247, 255, 267n4, 267n6
University of Texas at Austin, 2, 3, 11, 30, 30, 36, 41, 65, 68,
70–72, 70, 71, 72, 73, 87, 99–103, 100, 101, 121, 143, 156,
200, 241, 263n1, 264n1, 265n14; alumni, 20, 22, 24, 99,
117, 135, 171, 200, 247, 255, 264n1; Board of Regents,
65, 70, 87, 99, 100, 121, 263n1; campus, 2, 3, 21, 25, 36,
65, 67, 70, 71, 72, 72, 73, 73, 76, 99, 101, 102, 104–105,
254; campus plan, 65, 68, 69, 70–72, 71, 72, 99; College
of Engineering, 26–27, 30; College of Natural Sciences,
121; Community and Regional Planning, 25–26, 132,
145, 252; East Mall, 104, 105, 105; Friends of Architecture, 171, 175; Jester Hall, 101; Law School, 97, 105; LBJ
School of Public Affairs, 102; School of Architecture, 2,
6, 21, 22, 29, 72, 99, 115, 116, 117, 121, 138, 171, 236, 252,
264n1, 265n14; stadium expansion controversy, 72, 73
University of Toronto, 223
University of Utah, 247
University of Virginia, 24, 56, 224; Dell, 46; Lawn, 182
University of Washington, 24
Updike, John, 35
urban, 19, 20, 37, 85, 160, 197, 236, 258
urbanism: Celebrity Urbanism, 247–248, 247; Landscape
Urbanism, 2, 17, 51–64, 248, 248, 268n2; New Urbanism, 9, 16, 17, 40, 51, 52, 83–84, 137, 154, 236–237, 242,
247, 267n11, 268n2, 268n17; pragmatic urbanism, 248,
248

Urban Land Green, 120–121
Urban Land Institute (ULI), 120–121
Urban Reserve (Dallas), 248–249, 249, 250
U.S. Army Corps of Engineers, 79, 96, 97, 98, 262n5
U.S. Botanic Garden, 2, 40–41
U.S. Bureau of Land Management, 167
U.S. Census (also city census, census, Census Bureau, and
2000 Census), 81, 82, 149, 153, 155, 158, 159
U.S. Congress, 24, 77, 122
U.S. Department of Agriculture (USDA), 149, 152–153
U.S. Department of Energy, 2, 24, 26, 29
U.S. Department of Housing and Urban Development
(HUD), 77, 80, 82, 83, 262n2
U.S. Environmental Protection Agency (EPA), 41, 149–150,
157–158, 159
U.S. Fish and Wildlife Service, 132
U.S. Geological Survey, 158, 159
U.S. Green Building Council (USGBC), 2, 38, 39–41, 40, 46,
68, 82. See also Greenbuild International Conferences
U.S. National Park Service (NPS), 24, 165, 166, 166, 219,
220, 222, 223, 226, 227, 267n5, 267n6
U.S. Pavilion, 240, 241, 242
U.S. State Department, 256
USGBC Greenbuild International Conferences, 39
Utrecht, 147

Vale, Lawrence, 59
Vanderbilt, George W., 14
Vanderbilt, William, 206
Vasari, Giorgio, 172
Vatican City, 171
Vatican Gardens, 171, 172
Vaux, Calvert, 210, 212
Veneto, Italy, 205
Venice, 56, 236, 237, 238, 239, 241, 242; Grand Canal, 238,
241; Murano, 238; University of Venice, 238
Venice Biennale, 6, 236–242, 241
Venturi, Robert, 206, 247
Verde River, 12
Victory Park, 248, 249
Vienna, 53
Vietnam, 197, 221
Vignola, Giacomo Barozzi da, 172, 176–177, 203, 204
Villa Adriana, 114, 172, 173, 174, 176, 204
Villa Aldobrandini, 175–176, 175
Villa Aurelia, 206
Villa d'Este, 174, 174, 175, 176, 204
Villa Emo, 203
Villa Falconieri, 175
Villa Farnese, 177, 204
Villa Giulia, 172
Villa Lante, 176–177, 176
Villa Madama, 171–172, 172, 175, 204
Villa Medici, 175
Vireo Nature Preserve, 129

Visionaire, The, *40*
Viterbo, Italy, *176*
Vitruvius Pollio, Marcus, 10, 16, 20, 33, 62–63
Vogt, Günter, 51, 114

Wageningen, the Netherlands, 255
Wagner, Roswitha, 171
Waldheim, Charles, 52
Walker, Peter, 3, 102–103, *104–105*, 107, 120
Wallace Roberts & Todd (WRT), 97–98, 145, 239
Wallace, McHarg, Roberts and Todd (WMRT), 65, 69, 72,
    73–75, 76, 80, 84, 262n2
Waller, Edwin, 156
Walpole, Horace, 205
Wang, Wilfried, 241–242, 255, 268n18
Ward, Alan, 207, 208, 212
Warsaw, 203
Washington, D.C., 2, 22, 24, *25, 26, 27, 29, 34, 49, 50,* 60,
    67, 68, 69, 82, 136, 147, 166, 206, 219, 221, 222, *251, 252,*
    260n10
Washington State University, 267n5
water quality, 14, *47,* 73, 92, 131, *132,* 144, 153, *162,* 165, 207,
    210, 253
watershed(s), 9, *45,* 73, 128, 130, 149, 150, 158, 184, 191
Watson, Kirk, 135
Watson, Robert, 39
Weese, Ben, 78
Weese, Harry, 78
Weisman, Alan, 6
West Causeway, Xi Di, 187
West 8, 17, 52, 248
WET Design, 111
Wheeler, Stephen, 161
White House Conference on Natural Beauty, 121–122
White Pagoda, 214
White, Stanford, 206
Wiedemann, Nichole, 268n18
Wilberding, Seth, 27
Wildland Urban Interface, *132*
William J. Clinton Presidential Library and Museum, 11,
    36–38, *37*
William Pereira Associates, 80
Williams, Terry Tempest, 120
Williamson County, TX, 136

wind distribution, *12;* generators, 33; industry, 33; power, *33,*
    34; turbines, *33,* 97, 98
Wisconsin, 162; glaciations, 7; glaciers, 31, 255
Woodlands, The, 2, 65, 69, 77–85, *80, 82, 84, 85,* 262n2,
    262n21; Development Corporation (also The Woodlands
    Corporation), 80, 81, 83; Religious Community Incorpo-
    rated (also Interfaith), 83
World's Columbian Exhibition of 1893, 14, *14,* 206
World Heritage Site, 187
World Trade Center, 58
World Trade Center Memorial, 102, 105
World War I, 65, 68, 155
World War II, 4–5, 65, 69, 79, 99, 118, 155, 156, 175, 236,
    268n17
World Wide Web, 13, 46, 136, 141, 145, 150, 222, 225
Worth, William Jenkins, 157
Wright, Frank Lloyd, 14, 15, 33, 246; organic architecture, 15
Wright, Thomas, 166
Wu Liangyong, 200, 214
Wu Yixia, 210, 212
Wuhan, China, *4*
Wynn, Will, 25, 143, 144, 145

Xiangshan Park, 185

Yang Rui, 179, 184, 185, 186, 193, 196–197, 198, 200, 203,
    214
Yangtze River, *4*
Yaro, Bob, 161, 165–166, 167, 266n11
Yeang, Ken, 35, 251
Yellow Mountain Plan, 196–197
Yihe Yuan, 187–188, *187,* 188, 189, *190,* 194, 198. *See also*
    Beijing: Summer Palace; Yuan Ming Yuan
Yuan Dynasty, 185, 193
Yuan Ming Yuan, 179–181, *181,* 182, 188, *189;* Xiyanglou, 180

Zangrilli, Christie, 27
Zelinsky, Wilbur, 150, *152*
zero-net energy, 20, 103
Zhang, Ming, 198, 200, 214–215, 255
Zhang Zeduan, 203–204
Zhao Monastery, 186
Zhu Wenyi, 198
Zhuang Youbo, 182, 196

St. Louis Community College
at Meramec
LIBRARY